FORRESTAL AND THE NAVY

Forrestal and the Navy

BY ROBERT GREENHALGH ALBION

AND ROBERT HOWE CONNERY

With the collaboration of Jennie Barnes Pope

Foreword by William T. R. Fox

COLUMBIA UNIVERSITY PRESS

New York and London 1962

Foreword

NO SUBJECT in contemporary American political science has had a more vigorous development in the past decade than the study of national security policy and the processes by which it is made. Similarly, no aspect of the history of our times in the United States has commanded more serious scholarly attention than the history of military policy. In this study of James Forrestal and the United States Department of the Navy, we have a book which is important both as political science and as history and important to each discipline in an area in which it is being most rapidly developed. It is wholly appropriate that a study with this dual importance should be the joint product of a maritime historian and a student of American national government, each of whom were participant-observers in the Department of the Navy during Secretary Forrestal's period of service in the Department. Professor Albion was Historian of Naval Administration and in that capacity brought Professor Connery into the Navy Department to serve as the historian assigned to Forrestal's office during the war; they have worked with primary source materials in this study, but they have been able to bring to their analysis of the primary sources the special understanding that can only have come from being in the Department when many of the events described were occurring.

It might have been possible to write a biography of Forrestal in World War II and after with the main theme being the good fortune of the United States in having an unusually well-qualified person holding important jobs at a critical juncture in American history. It is true, of course, that each national crisis demonstrates how many men of extraordinary talent and high dedication can be drawn away from their private concerns and enlisted in the nation's service. James Forrestal belongs in that twentieth-century line of public servants who have first achieved great success in the New York world of law or finance and then moved on to serve with distinction in one of the military departments of the national government, and to do so in a very unpartisan way. This tradition also includes men like Elihu Root, Henry Stimson, and Robert Lovett.

It is a far cry from the time of the Spanish-American War when the Army and the Navy each went their separate ways, when there was hardly any such thing as military policy or naval policy, when the two Departments coordinated very little with each other and hardly at all with the Department of State, and when military policies, such as they were, were only most distantly and imperfectly coordinated with industrial mobilization policies. In the 1960s there is purposeful formulation of military policy in each service, there is interservice coordination through the Joint Chiefs of Staff, there is coordination of military policy with foreign policy and industrial mobilization policy in the National Security Council, and there is coordination of national policy with that of our NATO allies through the instrumentalities of NATO. The most critical phases in the evolution of contemporary institutions for making and implementing national security policy occurred in the period in which Forrestal was playing an increasingly important role. Whether one is interested in transformations in the organization of the Navy Department and the Navy, in the evolution of military and especially naval and naval aviation technology, in problems of interservice coordination and unified theater commands, or in processes by which the United States adjusts its defense posture to the changing threats of the postwar world or in shaping the pattern of armed services unification, there are important things in this book to read.

In the contemporary period, civilian control of the military requires a great deal more than simply "preventing the high brass from taking over." Civilian control demands competent civilians. Furthermore, national security must rest on an integration of military and civilian skills which can only be supplied by a civilian organizer. In this study of James Forrestal, we see the principle of civilian control applied under modern conditions. Above all, we see the major contribution which civilian organizational skills have been able to make to more rational decisions about problems of national security.

Columbia University   WILLIAM T. R. FOX
Professor of International Relations and
Director of the Institute of War
and Peace Studies

Preface

THIS IS an account of Forrestal during his years in the Navy Department. While it does not pretend to be a comprehensive history of naval administration in World War II, nor a biography of his life, it does, however, have much to say on both those subjects in the broad areas where they overlapped in such significant fashion. It emphasizes civilian-military relationships as a case study of an extraordinarily able civilian executive in a military department.

The authors believe that they have been in a unique position to contribute to such an account. For a dozen years, off and on, they observed naval administration and policy-making in many places and at many levels. They have known personally many of the civilians and officers most intimately concerned, including Forrestal himself. During the war and for a while afterwards, Albion served as Historian of Naval Administration in the Navy Department, with Connery, a reserve commander, as his deputy for part of that time. Forrestal himself later had Connery gathering and organizing material for his projected book on his Navy experience. Since then, both authors have made the most of opportunities to discuss the various facets of Forrestal's career with those who knew him best. Connery served on the staff of the Armed Services Task Force of the first Hoover Commission in 1948; and Albion was one of those selected to present the Navy's administrative experience before that group. Later, Connery served as consultant to the Secretary of Defense, returning in 1953 to the Navy Department for a brief period in the Secretary's office. Over a span of twenty years, Albion has lectured before various naval groups, including the Naval Finance and Supply School, the Naval Academy, and the National

War College. In 1946, he accompanied Assistant Secretary Hensel to England to study the workings of the Admiralty in connection with Forrestal's interest in that subject.

Aside from those personal contacts, the authors have made use of the Navy Department files, Forrestal's extensive personal files now at Princeton University, and his "diaries," likewise at Princeton. Those diaries, from which Walter Millis and Eugene S. Duffield selected and edited pertinent passages for publication, cover only the last three of his seven years in the Navy Department. Some of the topics in this study may be found in great detail in Connery's *The Navy and the Industrial Mobilization in World War II* (Princeton University Press, 1951) and in Albion's manuscript studies in naval administration, 1798–1947.

The authors would like to thank all those who have helped; frequently they gave many hours of their time, often at considerable inconvenience to themselves. Their names are indicated in the rear of this volume, except in a few cases where the information came from persons who desired to remain anonymous.

This volume carries the story to that day in 1947 when Forrestal moved from the Navy Department to the Pentagon as first Secretary of Defense. The tragic account of his last twenty months has been left for another time. That is a different story, and would be a less pleasant one to write, involving as it does the forces and persons who fought and finally overwhelmed him.

Harvard University   ROBERT G. ALBION
Duke University   ROBERT H. CONNERY

Contents

Illustrations

FORRESTAL AND THE NAVY

I

The Road to the Cabinet

———

JAMES FORRESTAL was sworn in on August 22, 1940 as the first Under Secretary of the Navy, a post created two months earlier. On September 17, 1947, he became the first incumbent of another new office, Secretary of Defense. Almost midway between those two dates, he was made the 47th and final full Secretary of the Navy with Cabinet rank. All three oaths were administered in the spacious Secretary's office in "Main Navy" on Constitution Avenue, where he was to do his most significant work.

At the time Forrestal entered government service, he was virtually unknown outside Wall Street financial circles, where he had been the head of the aggressively successful investment house of Dillon, Read & Company. Not once was his name in *The New York Times Index* for 1939. That would have been, to be sure, a matter of scant concern to him, for he was a man who did not seek or want publicity for himself. He did not even bother to fill out information for *Who's Who in America*. By 1944, when he became Secretary, his picture had appeared so often that a good segment of the public would recognize that taut, keen, thoughtful face. Although it was only four years since he came to the Navy Department, he was generally recognized as the man best fitted to be Secretary.

Such appreciation of his work with the Navy must have been a gratifying recompense for the intense strain and severe responsibilities of a naval executive in wartime. It was obviously a far more taxing job than Wall Street, not to mention a salary shrunk to the official stipend. But he gave no indication that the loss of his reputed salary of $190,000 deterred him, nor on the other hand that considerations of power made the Navy post more attractive.

His appointment to the Navy Department, along with that of his close associates, is a striking case study of the way political executives are recruited for the federal service. It indicates the part that politics, chance, administrative experience, and personality play in the selection for such high posts in the American system. The candidates, moreover, frequently have their doubts and hesitations about entering public life, as did Forrestal. He showed a definite reluctance when an actual offer materialized, although the general idea had stimulated his interest.

Apparently several men deserve a share of the credit for bringing him to Washington. A major element seems to have been the movement that led to the Securities Act of 1933 and the Securities Exchange Act of 1934. In this connection, both Forrestal—then vice president of Dillon, Read & Company—and Robert A. Lovett —a partner in the private banking house of Brown Brothers, Harriman and Company, who later held high posts in the War, State, and Defense Departments—attracted the attention of two lawyers actively directing this reform movement. William O. Douglas was first head of a bureau of the Securities Exchange Commission studying reorganizations and bankruptcies, later a member of the Commission, and finally its chairman before becoming an associate justice of the United States Supreme Court. The other, Thomas G. Corcoran, who had been associated with the law firm that served as counsel to Dillon, Read, was special assistant to the Attorney General of the United States and was aiding the Congressional committees in drafting the Securities Exchange bill. Many financial houses in Wall Street and elsewhere resented this measure which brought the federal government, under the guidance of President Franklin D. Roosevelt, into the regulation of Stock Exchange practices. Although their own companies were naturally affected, Forrestal and Lovett cooperated in generous, though unpublicized, fashion with the reform efforts.

Because of that 1933–34 contact, Douglas and Corcoran both thought of Forrestal in 1940, when men were needed to strengthen the government in the crisis of impending war. Justice Douglas later wrote:

I met Forrestal at the SEC and he was quite helpful to me behind the scenes in the work I did in reorganizing the New York Stock Exchange.

He was interested in coming to Washington. I encouraged him in the project and recommended him to Roosevelt. What others may have done at that time I do not know.[1]

Corcoran, meanwhile, had been exercising his influence, which was not inconsiderable; by 1940, the ebullient "Tommy the Cork," as Roosevelt called him, was a power at the White House. According to him, Forrestal was

a part of the movement to reform the New York Stock Exchange and the investment banking business in which I participated for the Government. . . . I suggested to President Roosevelt that the Administration needed liberals who were effective administrators. I then negotiated between the President and Mr. Forrestal in his own entrance into the White House organization as an Administrative Assistant to the President.[2]

Forrestal, who became a consummate salesman of ideas, had undergone his apprenticeship in the hard competition of the investment market. He received his basic training in salesmanship from William A. Phillips, sales manager of the Dillon, Read firm. Phillips, later a dominant partner, along with his Harvard classmate, Clarence Dillon, deeply influenced the young Forrestal. According to Dean Mathey, another partner, who was three years ahead of Forrestal at Princeton and who had been responsible for bringing him into that office shortly after he left college, he always continued to feel a great affection and respect for Phillips. From this initiation, Forrestal became a past master of the art of persuasion, not only in selling investment securities but also in inducing others to help work out his ideas. After 1937, as president of the firm, he demonstrated this latter ability in finding the right men to staff concerns being financed by the company. He became an excellent, though not infallible, judge of men; constantly stored up information as to where to turn for those best fitted for a particular niche; and then was able to talk even normally hard-to-get individuals into working with him.

A memorandum to Roosevelt, apparently drawn up by Corcoran, indicates much of this:

Following up your suggestion that you might want to take Forrestal as one of your administrative assistants to help find the men with "big names" and organizing ability to handle the problem of industrial production of war materials. . . .

He has been the acknowledged leader of your crowd in Wall Street.

From the point of view of what you said you needed now, Forrestal has three outstanding qualifications:

(1) His specialty is industrial personnel—he has been rounding up management material for Dillon's companies for a long time.

(2) He has enormous courage to do things that have never been done. He has pioneered financing jobs that everyone else in the Street was afraid to touch—like this new common stock utility financing.

(3) He has followed the German situation closely for many years because of Dillon's post-war German financing—he understands the situation thoroughly and bitterly and he has followed you eagerly in your perception in the need to get the nation ready. . . .

The appointment *together* of Forrestal (as administrative assistant) and of Sumner Pike to the Republican vacancy on S.E.C. would head off all the pressures Henry Luce is engineering to force you to "recognize" Willkie.[3]

Both the President and Forrestal consulted Bernard Baruch, the New York financier, who had been chairman of the War Industries Board of World War I and, thereafter, was to be in constant demand for his sage counseling in national policies. He later wrote:

President Roosevelt asked me to give him my opinion of Forrestal, telling me that he wanted him there at the White House as one of his anonymities. I spoke of Mr. Forrestal in the highest terms. I do not know who suggested him to the President. . . . after receiving the request from the President . . . I asked Mr. Forrestal to come to my house . . . and told him the President's request and advised him that if he got the call to go.[4]

A handwritten note sent to Corcoran at this point by Forrestal is perhaps more characteristic than almost any of the thousands of other Forrestal letters:

Dear Tom:

Just to clarify our talk of yesterday:

I have some misgiving whether I can be effective in the role you outlined and I think there are better men available. Bob Lovett is one who comes to my mind. But this is no time for prima donna tactics and I don't want to be in that light. The whole picture is too serious for that. So I'm giving you my proxy—and I shall be happy either way it works out. I want neither publicity nor glory—the price of both is too high.

As ever

JVF [5]

Forrestal spoke of his worry about making the change to an old friend, Arthur Krock, while in Washington for his appointment with Roosevelt: "I'd give anything to get out of this." The dean of Washington journalists, at the moment out of favor at the White House, retorted, "Just tell him that you're going to stay with me down here—that ought to fix it." [6] But Roosevelt was himself a prime persuader; and on June 23, Forrestal was sworn in as the fourth of the newly created Administrative Assistants to the President.

That post, which he held for only two months, was one of a group established by statute in 1939 in the Executive Office of the President. The program, drawn up by the distinguished political scientists Charles E. Merriam, Louis Brownlow, and Luther Gulick, stated that these appointees ought to have a "passion for anonymity." [7] This phrase evoked considerable comment; Krock called one of his columns "The Six Anonymous Eremites." The term had first been used somewhat humorously by one of Lloyd George's secretaries in describing the longtime secretary of the British Cabinet, Sir Maurice Hankey. [8]

Forrestal was not happy with the job. No one, apparently, had thought out just what he was to do. He was supposed to handle certain Latin American affairs, with which he had had some, but not intimate, experience. The Havana Conference provided him with a little business for a while, as did a project to get ore from Brazil. [9] One day, a friend found him sitting behind a desk, quite clear of papers, obviously restless. In a national crisis, this was not the sort of job he had expected.

But it so happened that within three weeks of the time he began these duties, his transfer to the Navy Department was already under consideration. This was not as radical or as surprising a change as his initial coming down from New York; the new post, however, would give him a decisive role in the war years ahead.

For months, the House Naval Affairs Committee had been holding hearings aimed at a major reorganization of the Navy Department, a time-honored and generally futile occupation. [10] Finally, Roosevelt put his foot down; he would approve only two relatively moderate changes—the merger of two bureaus [11] and the creation of a new post, Under Secretary. Congress complied in the so-called Naval Reorganization Act. [12]

These were weeks of strain and near-war activity at Washington, as the unchecked westward sweep of German forces triggered new developments, thick and fast. Roosevelt, on June 14, signed the "Third Vinson" bill, authorizing an 11 percent increase of naval strength [13] though he objected to the much more drastic "Two Ocean Navy" bill that Carl Vinson, veteran chairman of House Naval Affairs Committee, insisted upon introducing that same day. On June 20, Roosevelt signed the afore-mentioned Naval Reorganization bill; and also angered the Republican National Convention by appointing two Republican interventionists as Secretaries of War and Navy. Two days later France signed an armistice. Roosevelt was nominated for a third term to run against Wendell Willkie on July 18. The next day he signed Vinson's "Two Ocean Navy" bill, giving the green light for a 70 percent expansion in construction.[14] Altogether the combined impact of all this produced a turning point in the Navy Department rivaled only by the later hectic weeks after Pearl Harbor. It came to date its war period from mid-1940, with July 1 normally taken as the starting point for statistics.

The choice of the 1936 Republican candidate for Vice-President, Frank Knox, as Secretary of the Navy, probably appealed to Roosevelt because it brought to his Cabinet a sincere and extremely vocal supporter of his interventionist war policy, and it toned down an equally vocal and often bitter critic of his internal New Deal administration in an election year. Knox had refused his first offer the preceding December of the Navy post, which had been vacant since the death of Secretary Claude Swanson several months earlier.[15] Charles Edison, son of the inventor and Assistant Secretary since 1937, was then made full Secretary on what was to be rather precarious tenure. He soon resigned to run for the New Jersey governorship. In the spring, within a week of the German invasion of the Low Countries, Knox lunched at the White House and told Roosevelt he was at his service on condition that he have a Republican companion in the Cabinet. A distinguished "opposite number" for War Secretary was found in Henry L. Stimson, a New York lawyer, who had already served in that post under Taft and also as Secretary of State under Hoover.[16] Both men, already read out of their party, received rough treatment as avowed interventionists from the respective Senate Committees before being confirmed by divided votes. Knox was sworn in on July 11.

He was a bluff extrovert of rugged physique, with bighearted and generous impulses. And, unlike Forrestal, he loved to talk. He was generally referred to as "colonel"—as a college boy he had been in Theodore Roosevelt's Rough Riders in the Spanish-American War and had commanded an ammunition train in France in World War I. He always remained under the spell of Theodore Roosevelt, whom he followed in the Strenuous Life, the Big Stick, Progressivism, Manifest Destiny, and much else. His life was spent in a combination of newspaper work and politics. After deciding not to return to college, he began as a $10-a-week reporter and rose to the top of the newspaper field. Soon he and a partner were able to buy a Michigan newspaper, and in 1912 they shifted operations to Manchester, New Hampshire. His chief influence, however, came from his controlling interest in the distinguished Chicago *Daily News*.

Roosevelt is said to have promised Knox that he could pick his own deputies or at least veto any outside suggestions.[17] Edison, in becoming full Secretary, however, had secured the promotion to his former post for Lewis Compton, whom he had brought down from New Jersey as his special assistant. Consequently, Compton was now Acting Secretary and as such signed the annual report in the interim between Edison's resignation on June 24 and Knox's installation on July 11. In such a situation, the way was not clear for a Knox appointment in the Assistant Secretaryship until February 1941, when Edison placed Compton in his state government.

The new Under Secretaryship, however, went to Forrestal within six weeks. Knox seems to have first offered it to Colonel William J. Donovan, later head of the Office of Strategical Services, who declined it; and then to another Republican friend, Ralph A. Bard, Chicago investment banker. Bard also refused; then reconsidered too late as the post by then had gone to Forrestal.

In the circumstances that led to Forrestal's shift from the White House to the Navy Department, Justice Douglas again played an important part. So, too, did Corcoran. Secretary of the Interior Harold L. Ickes states flatly in his diary: "I think it was Tom who was largely influential in bringing Forrestal here . . . and then, at Tom's suggestion, I told Frank Knox that I thought he would make a good Under Secretary of the Navy." [18] That was apparently around the second week in July, for Knox was barely in office when he conferred with the President twice that week and then took the opportunity to look over the prospective deputy.[19] On Sunday, July 14, three days after he was sworn in as Secretary, Knox wrote his wife, then in New Hampshire:

All offices close at noon Saturdays so when I got back from the White House Bill Donovan, John Sullivan, Jack Bergin of N.Y., Jim Forrestal of White House staff and I went aboard the *Sequoia*, the Sec. of Navy's yacht, had lunch aboard and cruised down the Potomac until about 6 o'clock. Then Bill and I got into dinner clothes and went to dine with the British ambassador Lord Lothian at 8 p.m.

This morning I played golf at Burning Tree Club with Forrestal, Capt. Deyo (my aide) and a friend of Deyo's just arrived from Shanghai —then at 2 o'clock we boarded the *Sequoia* where John Sullivan and a friend and wife were awaiting us, including Jim Forrestal's wife, and had dinner aboard and cruised the afternoon and evening, getting back about 9 o'clock.[20]

Sullivan, incidentally, was a long-standing family friend from Manchester; he would ultimately succeed Forrestal in the Navy Secretaryship, when Forrestal became the first Secretary of Defense.

In this second hour of decision, Forrestal again turned to Baruch, who was later to write: "He was very anxious to talk to me about what he would find in the Navy . . . I continually urged him and brought to his attention the lack of preparedness in the Navy, going into many details." [21] The Navy, to be sure, was not a complete mystery to Forrestal. Though he had seen no action in World War I, he had trained as a naval aviator and then had been assigned a minor job in the Department at Washington.

Knox's impression having been definitely favorable, Forrestal was nominated as Under Secretary on August 5, and on August 22 formally began his seven-year tour of duty in the Department. A week later, Knox was writing his wife, "Jim Forrestal is going to be a great relief to me and will make my job much easier." [22]

When Compton left the Assistant Secretaryship, Knox turned again to his friend, Bard. Although ranking below the new Under Secretaryship, it was historically one of the most distinguished of the "little cabinet" posts. Its first incumbent, Gustavus V. Fox (1861–66), a former regular naval officer, brought luster to the position through his valuable work during the Civil War. Two future presidents, Theodore Roosevelt (1897–98) and Franklin D. Roosevelt (1913–20), served as Assistant Secretary earlier in their careers. In fact, the Roosevelt family claims upon this position did not end there: it was held between the wars by Theodore Roosevelt, Jr. (1921–24); Henry Latrobe Roosevelt (1933–36); and by Theodore Douglas Robinson (1924–29), whose mother was "T.R.'s" sister. In later days, the cognizance of the Assistant Secretary had centered particularly in the navy yards and other parts of the Shore Establishment; this led into the wartime speciality of civilian personnel.

Bard was one of the hardest working members of a very hard working group. The son of a founder of the Republic Steel Company, he was a graduate of Princeton, where he was long remembered as a versatile athlete and exceedingly popular member of the class of 1906. In fact, he was remembered around the university with more affection than Forrestal, who left an impression of being a "young man on the make." Bard eventually developed his own investment house, specializing in the financing of moderate-sized concerns. He was not one to be rushed into precipitate action even in the quickened tempo of wartime Washington; his initial response to new proposals was inclined to be "No." One of his most significant acts climaxed his four years in the Department when he alone, of the over-all committee on atomic policy, firmly opposed the dropping of the bomb on the Japanese without warning.[23]

A later appointment revived the dormant post of Assistant Secretary of Aeronautics, now called "Air," which had been established in 1924, along with its counterpart in the War Department.[24] "Army Air" had grown increasingly autonomous in the intervening years, but the Navy post had been allowed to lapse altogether in 1933.

One summer morning in 1941, after spending the night down the Potomac on the *Sequoia*, Knox announced to his special assistant Adlai Stevenson, a future Democratic presidential candidate, as they were climbing the long steps from the river up to Fort Washington, "Oh, by the way, Ad, I have a good man Jim Forrestal picked for me for the air job. Don't remember his name, but he was quite a flier and is a big New York bank president." [25] Around that time, Knox wrote his wife:

Also I secured F.D.R.'s approval of the appointment of Artemus Gates as assistant secretary of the Navy for air—the one vacancy on my major staff, and one for which the President wanted me at one time to appoint Tom Corcoran, and to whom I strenuously objected because of the political implications.[26]

According to Corcoran's understanding with Roosevelt, he was to become Under Secretary. But Knox, when appointed, asked him "as a personal favor" to let that new post go to one of his friends, saying that the dormant Assistant Secretaryship for Air was to be reactivated and would be "much better suited" to his "energy and abilities." Corcoran consulted Roosevelt and went along with this. Knox delayed for over a year; there were complications of various sorts. In view of personal business reasons and the political aspects, Corcoran "decided not to create problems by taking the job." [27] He was doubtless supported for it by Forrestal, who was known to have a high opinion of Corcoran's "ability and courage and initiative" and "seemed disposed to do what he could to keep Tom in Washington." [28] The personal friendship of both Gates and Corcoran with the War Department Secretarial group was apparently a factor in their favor; such a consideration always counted strongly with Forrestal.

Artemus L. Gates, a famous Yale tackle, was noted for his daring exploits in World War I as a naval aviator in the crack Yale unit, which had included his opposite number, Lovett, at the War Department. Gates, long associated with his father-in-law, Henry P. Davison, in the latter's New York Trust Company, became its president in 1929. More than once, he wrote Knox asking just what he was supposed to do, for the duties of the new post were rather hazy and were blanketed by the naval air setup. When the General Board was consulted, the answer was still rather vague.[29] Gates's most valuable work came in the field of personal liaison; his first-name basis with the War Secretaries sometimes saved negotiations when the rival groups of aviators were at loggerheads. As Forrestal wrote Roosevelt, Gates "stands very well with Congress, and, as you know, is a close friend of Jack McCloy, Bob Patterson and Ed Stettinius, and is therefore very effective in relationships with the other Government Departments." [30]

The relations between Knox and Forrestal remained on a very warm basis. Together, they restored Secretarial influence in the Department; it would be difficult to determine exactly how much each one contributed toward that end. Knox's personal achievements were particularly noticeable in the field of public relations and in support of the President's war policies. No matter how conspicuous Forrestal became as Under Secretary, Knox never showed the slightest jealousy. He continued to give his deputy a free hand and stood ready always to back him up if necessary. A smaller man than Knox might have fouled things badly, by resenting and curbing his junior's strenuous activities. A note to Mrs. Knox the day before the Colonel died indicates Forrestal's appreciation: "I have never been associated with any man with whom I felt a closer relationship." [31] And to a friend, he declared "Frank Knox never had a devious thought." [32] One of Knox's valuable contributions to the war effort came from the fact that he served as a sort of emotional buffer between his two immediate brilliant subordinates, Forrestal and Admiral Ernest J. King, and so a headlong clash was postponed until they had developed a kind of frosty mutual respect.

In late April 1944, Knox's death came suddenly. He had been to the funeral of his old newspaper associate in New Hampshire, and returned to Washington unexpectedly very ill. He was only able to sign a few letters at the Department before he had to go home. "I blame myself a little for not having forced him to modify the tempo and vigor of his existence," Forrestal wrote Mrs. Knox that day. "We all made the attempt but he is not easily put under restraint, as you probably know better than any of us." [33] He was buried in Arlington Cemetery with an impressive service as "Major" Frank Knox; likewise, five years later "Lieutenant" James Forrestal was buried there with similar honors, which in neither case would have been given a civilian Secretary, as such.[34]

Forrestal was Acting Secretary for the next twelve days only. In the speculation about Knox's successor, Forrestal's excellent performance as Under Secretary made him the first choice of most of the commentators. Knox's own paper, the Chicago *Daily News*, however, brought up one of the geographical technicalities that have so often entered into the building of a cabinet. No matter how "logical from the standpoint of smooth continued administration," the choice might cause party repercussions because there were already three New Yorkers in the Cabinet as well as two Philadelphians.[35] That it was again an election year as it had been when Knox was selected gave added prominence to the situation. The newspaper lists included Wendell Willkie, who had just been defeated in important midwest primaries and was not likely to repeat his 1940 role as Republican presidential candidate; Admiral Leahy, chief of staff to President Roosevelt; Harold Stassen, at the moment a lieutenant commander in the Pacific; Carl Vinson, chairman of the House Naval Affairs Committee; Andrew Jackson Higgins, colorful New Orleans boatbuilder; and even General Douglas MacArthur.[36]

Three of Forrestal's friends have given accounts of some circumstances surrounding his being chosen. Bernard Baruch tells that "When Secretary Knox died, Mr. Roosevelt was at my place in South Carolina, and there a discussion took place at the table between various people. Mr. Roosevelt announced that he was going to advance Forrestal to the post." [37] Justice William O. Douglas of the Supreme Court tells that he personally strongly urged the President to appoint Forrestal.[38] A Wall Street friend of Forrestal's, who desires to remain anonymous, brings out another significant angle:

Forrestal was reluctant to push himself on the death of Knox. I convinced him it would be a serious reflection on him if he did not succeed to the job of Secretary and convinced him that he should promptly tell President Roosevelt that he would have to have the job or retire from the government. I knew that Roosevelt was considering other people and I knew that he did not want to lose Forrestal as it would reflect upon him and I was sure that Forrestal was in a position to force his hand—it worked that way.[39]

The evidence from the White House files, from the Forrestal personal papers, and from the person best in a position to know, seem to show that Forrestal did nothing to bring pressure upon the President, either by letter or in person; his only contact with the White House was a brief conference the day before his name went to the Senate.[40] Although a good many seem to have taken the Willkie possibility seriously, the President made no formal approach to him. In any case, there are good grounds for believing Willkie would not have associated himself with that Administration.[41]

Whatever may have been Roosevelt's motives in Knox's case, politics were conspicuously lacking from the other naval Secretarial appointments until the last weeks of the war. Not one of them received his post "for party services rendered"; not one was a New Dealer. Forrestal was the only Democrat; his father had been in politics in a small way in Roosevelt's home county in New York, but he himself had not been active politically. Bard was a personal friend of Knox, and Gates of Forrestal. Election year though it was, it was also a crucial period in the war. There was every reason for preventing loss of momentum, with the Navy in high gear about to undertake its tremendous drives in Normandy and the Marianas. Forrestal, moreover, was better equipped for the Secretaryship by his four strenuous years in the No. 2 position than any other man available. Consequently, Roosevelt discounted that traditional geographical prejudice that Henry Stimson, Henry Morgenthau, and Frances Perkins were cabinet members from New York State.

The decision for Forrestal was a popular one; certainly none of his predecessors had come to the position better qualified by experience. The Senate confirmation was unanimous by a rising vote. As his friend, Arthur Krock of the New York *Times*, wrote: "The fortunate situation developed that the best thing for the Navy, for the war, and for the country was also the best thing politically." [42] It was said, however, that when someone remarked to Roosevelt, "The appointment will please everyone," his reply was "No, everyone but one. . . . Ernie King." [43]

Late on the afternoon of May 9, while Forrestal was as usual working overtime, his confidential secretary, Katherine Foley, answered her telephone. It was Leslie Biffle, secretary of the Senate, with news of the President's message to the Hill nominating Forrestal. "Kate, tell him he's in." She stepped into his adjacent big office: "You're Secretary of the Navy." For several minutes he sat and grinned at her like a small boy. It was the only time in their nine years together in government service, she said later, that anything broke through the mask that habitually hid his emotions.[44]

2

Executive in Action

THE MIXTURE of the intellectual and the astute businessman in Forrestal presented a pattern that was unusual in executives. Referring to this dualism, the editor of his diaries wrote: "What makes Forrestal a unique figure in the high levels of war and post-war government was his restless sense that answers were needed, and his constant efforts, while carrying tremendous burdens of intensely practical administrative work, to reach closer to them." [1] He was a much more effective executive than many of those who held that post, and his experience gives a pretty good picture of how an efficient Secretary operates, the kind of people he sees, the questions that come to him for decision, the quality of the staff he has, and, in general, the environment in which he works. Forrestal's success in establishing civilian administration was not entirely a matter of organizational innovations,[2] but depended in part upon the techniques which he used in handling problems as they arose. Most executives, of course, must be judged by those two standards, which might be called the opposite sides of the same coin; but in Forrestal's case some of his special techniques reflected both the operator and the thinker.

Characteristic was the remark he once made that some people could simply sit at their desks and drift with the tide of whoever or whatever happened to come along, then go home, feeling they had put in a full and busy day.[3] He himself resented any wasted minutes. His day began well before the big black limousine delivered him at "Main Navy," usually not long after the opening hour. And he generally stayed on for at least two hours after most of the offices had emptied in the 4:30 P.M. rush. Several times a week, however, some physical exercise was wedged into his afternoon.

At the breakfast table, either in the house which he first rented near the Shoreham or at the larger home which he bought in Georgetown, were six newspapers—the *Times*, the *Herald Tribune*, and two tabloids from New York; and the local *Washington Post* and *Times-Herald*. A similar group of papers was in his car, so that he could continue his reading on the way down town, and a third identical collection awaited him at the office. These were supplemented during the day by various later editions of the Washington papers.

A few items from the memoranda of the day's immediate business, which he found on his desk, indicate the typical grist during his Under Secretary period:

Notify Colonel Knox to hold up press release regarding Navy taking only volunteers.

Question of information being made public in Congressional hearings—notice Admiral Towers declined to give confidential information regarding planes and bases and said he would be glad to submit a confidential memorandum or give the information at executive session of the House committee.

You asked Admiral Yarnell to find out about aerial mines developing.

Data on the Arma Engineering Company is being assembled and sent to Mr. Knudsen.

Ask Admiral Holmes to come in [for you] to take a look at him.

Check on whether inspectors at various plants have been told to report possible blocks where OPM may be of assistance.

Tell Bureau chiefs that Nelson will be over to the 10 o'clock meeting tomorrow, Friday.

Question of using Admiral Bowen as plant organizer.

Regarding Kennedy midshipman appointment, you promised Lyndon Johnson to see Secretary Knox and then let him know.[4]

And so on day after day. Once he became full Secretary, the scope of such memoranda would naturally broaden.

Where a telephone call or letter would not suffice, the more time-consuming office interview was, of course, necessary. Some of these interviews resulted from a direct summons by Forrestal himself. Others were held with men who had a sort of ex officio access to him—Secretarial colleagues, bureau chiefs, procurement executives, and the like. Then, there were the outsiders who were able to persuade some one of the inner circle that they rated a few minutes of Forrestal's carefully cherished time—minutes which seldom came under the head of pleasure for many. Even those fairly close to him were apt to find them formidable. About the only informal note was the ubiquitous pipe clenched in his teeth. With those few who combined a bluff heartiness with a thorough grasp of the subject, the contacts might be mutually enjoyable. But some of their colleagues, for whose ability Forrestal might have equal respect, annoyed him by taking up too many details. By and large, it would seem that the standard tactics for a Forrestal conference called for speaking one's piece as concisely as possible, being ready to answer his questions with brevity, and then getting out. Even in full council meetings, he would lose patience and be very curt with anyone, of whatever status, who seemed vague, elusive, or obviously not prepared. Like Knox, he had a blacklist of problem characters who were not to be admitted under any circumstances. On one occasion at least, he is said to have brusquely refused the suggestion that he personally thank a group of experts who were finishing their temporary service in the Department— "They were paid, weren't they?" he snapped.

That rather fearsome manner from behind his office desk stood in sharp contrast to the charm that permeated his correspondence files. Instead of the perfunctory, wooden uniformity of many official letters, his gave very much of a tailor-made impression. Now and then, of course, he worked up a form letter, when a whole swarm of letters called for answers on the same subject. Thus, when the draft boards in 1941 were breathing down the necks of a large part of the male population, a great many suggested to Forrestal their readiness to serve ashore with reserve commissions. He drew up a polite brushoff:

Thank you for your letter of March 11 outlining your experience and qualifications.

It is difficult to find places which will fully utilize men of your intelligence and experience where you would feel that you were really doing constructive work in the national defense.

I shall keep your letter on file, and if the opportunity presents itself where I feel you can be of real help, I shall let you know.[5]

At times, a more individualized letter would politely but firmly advise a friend to keep hands off:

I don't agree with your view about the Navy giving you and Mr.
—— the run around as you say in your letter.

In any case, my experience in this incident leads me to conclude
that any interference with the grinding of the official mills is probably
unwise—winds up in everybody getting mad.[6]

Like many another executive with a keen sense of public relations, he maintained a "tickler file" to remember birthdays and
anniversaries. Frequently, appointments to office also brought con-
gratulatory letters. When Senator Walter F. George of Georgia
became chairman of the Finance Committee, Forrestal wrote: ". . .
in these critical times, it is important that such posts be held by
somebody in whose fundamental patriotism the country believes
and I can assure you that this is the case with yourself." [7] He wound
up a note to the new chairman of Foreign Relations, Senator Tom
Connally of Texas: "Large words these but I believe the country
shares my feelings." [8]

He freely followed the current use of first names and nicknames,
but he systematized it. An office notebook gave the form he wanted
used for correspondents, such as "Jimmie" Byrnes, "Ed" Stettinius,
"Bernie" Baruch, "Don" Nelson, "Bill" Knudsen, "Harold" Ickes,
and "Sonny" Whitney. A few admirals were on the same basis,
though in return, they tended to be very correct, addressing him
as "Mr. Secretary." While abbreviating others' names, he also ex-
perimented with his own, which seemed to irk him. When he
entered Princeton, on transfer from a freshman year at Dartmouth,
he signed three different blanks in three different ways: "James
Forrestal," "Vincent Forrestal," and "J. V. Forrestal." [9] By the
time he reached Washington, the middle name and even its initial
were pretty well discarded—he is said to have remarked jokingly
that he was giving up the "V" for victory. Often he signed the
single word "Forrestal" in the best British state-paper style, but he
usually used "James," too.

He was not what one could call an orderly administrator. Frequently, when needing certain information in a hurry, he would
send two or three assistants on the same quest. Eventually, they
learned to avoid duplication by quietly clearing with each other
beforehand. He was always impatient for results, but then when
the information came in he had sometimes forgotten all about it.

Once, two research assistants asked the naval aide for some indication of priority among thirty different "rush" items; Forrestal found only eight that he still wanted at once.[10] One able officer, who had mastered successfully the art of operating at King's right hand, was brought into close contact with Forrestal in the reorganization negotiations toward the end of the war. He wrote that those with whom Forrestal dealt

. . . on a day-in-and-day-out basis were at the end of a squawk box, and I used to get sent for anywhere from one to six times a day, as did the others. As is well known, Mr. Forrestal didn't pay much attention to the clock when he was working, and that made things pretty tough on those who were working with him, particularly his staff.

One day I went bird shooting in Virginia, and while I was gone he wanted me for something. Frantic efforts were made to get me on the telephone but of course I was where I couldn't be reached, and the next morning everybody jumped on me, more or less breathlessly, because I had gone to a place where he couldn't get me the day before. When I went in to find out what he wanted, he said, "Oh, yes, now I remember. You told a story a couple of days ago and I wanted to be sure I got the punch line correct!"[11]

A crop of yarns developed from his habit of occasionally wandering—sometimes without warning—around the Department. Dropping in one morning on the weekly technical conference of the Bureau of Ordnance, to which he had a standing invitation, Forrestal heard a tedious report on the difficulties in trying to weld two kinds of metal together without results—"we tried this, we tried that." He asked with a deadpan face, "Captain, did you try glue?"; the captain soberly relayed the question "Lieutenant, did we try glue?"[12] Then, there was the firsthand story of a young reserve ensign ordered to report at an office on the "second deck" of the Department. Appalled by the constant procession of admirals and captains in the hall, he was relieved to spot a civilian leaning over a drinking fountain. Tapping him on the back, he demanded, "Say, bud, where's the Office of Naval History?" "Down the next corridor to the left" came the reply as the civilian straightened up. The boy recognized the Secretary of the Navy. "Thank you, *sir*"*!*, he stammered. "O.K. bud," replied Forrestal with a smile.

Few cabinet officers worked as hard to keep in good physical trim, but even in this he seemed to drive himself at top speed. To his associates, his golf looked as if it were more medicine than sport.

How much fun he found in it remains a moot question that only he could have answered, but, of course, it was his way to attack everything with the same serious drive. Nevertheless, it was fairly respectable golf, averaging around 85, and he played nine holes about three times a week. His impatience was so obvious while others were driving off that he was usually allowed to play through. To and from the country club, Chevy Chase or Burning Tree, however, he kept on with his perusal of newspapers or documents.

During critical situations, at the Department in particular, Forrestal was apt to prefer tennis; it took less time, and he found the more strenuous exercise more relaxing.[13] In bad weather, he turned to badminton. At both, his game was intense and smashing, although not expert. His opponents often happened to be better players, and that bothered him for fear they might ease up a bit to let him score. His close friend, John McCloy, Assistant Secretary of War, who was in a class to have played with Tilden, was a case in point. There is no doubt that this sports program did keep him unusually fit physically. As one friend remarked, most men over forty have to slow down because their bodies play out; Forrestal's never did.

Most cabinet officers have enjoyed the social prerogatives of their position; Forrestal made them a means of fact gathering. Naval officers, industrialists, educators, labor leaders, newspaper editors, and ambassadors or ministers were his constant guests. Even at breakfast and constantly at lunch, he was seldom free from business. His dinner companions were inclined to be less "in line of duty." Representative John V. Anderson of California recalled an early morning breakfast discussion of matters coming before House Naval Affairs.[14] At least once, Forrestal had two breakfast sessions; one with Winthrop Aldrich at home, and then, a second elsewhere with Senator Tom Connally and Frank Folsom.[15] Luncheon, after he was Secretary, was ordinarily served in his dining room, next to his office, by Filipino mess boys; the Secretarial china, decorated with the blue four-star flag, was used. He preferred small groups, with whom he found his purposes were best achieved either in persuading others or in "pumping" them. Sometimes he had larger gatherings, such as a full Congressional committee, and on one occasion in 1944, ten were invited for a discussion of naval history.[16] One unusually full lunch hour, while he was Under Secretary, is said to have included four business conferences, beginning with soup with Secretary Knox, the main course with his own guests, dessert at the White House, and winding up with coffee at the Metropolitan Club.[17]

At dinner, he sometimes had guests at home, but far more often, after he became Secretary, aboard the official yacht. The *Sequoia* was berthed at the Washington Navy Yard alongside the President's *Williamsburg* and Admiral King's *Dauntless*. He did not live aboard her as Knox had done for a considerable period, but he found her a good place to entertain. Incidentally, many of those invited found the naval atmosphere of the old Navy Yard with its Marine guards and dinner aboard ship a colorful experience. To Forrestal, the main value of the *Sequoia* lay in having a quiet place to talk, safe from interruptions. A close admiral friend described the general pattern of such evenings:

We used to go for short evening trips on his yacht. He would invite about four or five of us. After dinner on board, we would sit on deck and talk while we cruised up and down the Potomac. When we had returned to the dock at the Navy Yard he would go to the gangway, turn about and say good night and then leave—no ceremony—the affair was over so let's go home.[18]

But Forrestal begrudged, as a waste of time, the cocktail hour, which loomed so large in the Washington way of life. According to one account: "If he went to a cocktail party, it was 'hello,' one Martini, and 'good-bye.' Once a friend clocked him at one; he was in and out in eight minutes flat." [19]

Occasionally, toward the end of an afternoon, when he saw a chance for a free evening with personal friends, he would have his secretary see what she could do about getting a few together at short notice. She had a special list of "people whom he liked," which she also used for filling in when he entertained formally. He kept his non-intimate, "purely social" engagements to an irreducible minimum; but at that, his regular social calendar is firsthand evidence of the pressures to which a top civil servant is exposed (see Appendix D). To executives already driving to their limit, this curtailment of their brief leisure time and the consequent lack of rest or relaxation adds to the toll taken by their jobs.

Even that pressure of work in Washington did not keep Forrestal from getting out to the field. Admiral Edwards, Deputy Commander-in-Chief, U.S. Fleet, lamented he had not been able to get "west of Georgetown during the war," but Forrestal made many flying trips near and far. Even in wartime, such travel was apt to be somewhat suspect, with the phrase "Is this trip necessary?" often heard. No one who went on one of Forrestal's inspection trips would ever have called it a junket. Even his young Marine aide found them man-killing. There was an endless round of conferences, long days of work, short nights of rest, and prodigious distances covered. In commenting on Secretarial trips, Knox told a press conference in 1942:

. . . you can do a much better job if you get out into the field and see actual conditions, and as you know probably, I have been doing a lot of that myself and so has Mr. Forrestal, and Bard and Gates. . . . Mr. Forrestal has just taken a good look at the whole Pacific layout, and I propose to take a good look at everything south of here along the Atlantic. . . . It not only informs me and informs my associates to do this, but it is a source of inspiration to the men in the field. If . . . nobody comes down to see how they are getting along, they feel neglected; and certainly it is a definite aid to morale. So those here in Washington who are in charge . . . go over the things they want in the future, estimate their value and come back and act far more intelligently. . . .[20]

Forrestal did not take a real vacation during his time at the Department, but at least twice he stated that a short absence would combine business with pleasure. In the spring of 1945, he wrote President Truman:

With your permission I shall expect to be away from Washington from either next Wednesday or Thursday afternoon to the following Tuesday.

It will be seventy-five percent holiday—so that if for any reason you think I should be here I shall esteem it a favor if you will so advise me.[21]

Later in the year, he wrote to the President's naval aide:

Please advise the President that subject to his approval I shall be away from Washington from Sunday December 23rd to Sunday December 30th or possibly January 2nd. I shall be in Florida on the *Sequoia* and propose to inspect our post-war lay-up facilities at Green Cove Springs, St. Johns River and also to make inspection trips to Panama and Roosevelt Roads, Puerto Rico.

That memorandum returned to the Department with the scrawled endorsement "O.K. Have a good time. Wish I could go, too. H.S.T." [22]

In addition to frequent trips around the United States to speak or to inspect installations, he went seven times beyond the seas. He was in London in 1941 to confer on Lend Lease and in 1945 at the Potsdam Conference. In the late summer of 1942, he inspected naval installations from Pearl Harbor to Noumea in the South Pacific; and returned determined to try to relieve the desperate shortages found down there.[23] Early in 1944, he was present at the taking of Roi and Kwajalein in the Marshalls, the first time a Navy Secretary had been at an actual fighting front. Again that summer, he observed landings at close range—this time in Southern France. Early in 1945, he went ashore in the beginning of the terrific fighting on Iwo Jima. His longest trip took him around the world between June 25 and July 25, 1946. The immediate occasion was the original Navy-directed atomic tests at Bikini atoll in mid-Pacific. From there, he continued on to the Far East, where he conferred with various military, naval, and diplomatic leaders. He returned by way of Rome and Berlin, eventually reaching London, where he had luncheon with the King and Queen, and dined with the Admiralty.[24]

The public gradually became accustomed to pictures of Forrestal out at the edge of the fighting. In the informal khaki without insignia, usually worn by the civilian observer, he was often not recognized; a boatswain's mate once shouted, "Hey, buddy, where's your hat?"[25] Though he discounted the danger, he was actually under fire more than once; in the Marshalls' landing a Japanese shell struck within fifteen feet from him. When he once said of his landing at Iwo Jima "it was as safe there as it is right here in this room," a naval captain was heard to murmur: "Yes, it was safe there. Twenty-three men were killed on that section of the beach that morning."[26]

He intensely disliked the personal publicity, which he could not avoid. In connection with the landings in Southern France, he wrote to Chairman Vinson of House Naval Affairs:

I am enclosing a diary of my visit with Admiral Hewitt's Fleet which I made primarily with a view to getting for him the credit which it seems to me he deserved. The news out of the Mediterranean area so far as the Navy is concerned has been rather slight, but I think there will now be some improvement. My mission I think was fairly successful on this score, with the qualification that I got a little too much publicity myself. . . . it is my view that the Secretary of the Navy can be of only slight use in augmenting Navy publicity.[27]

Likewise, it took considerable persuading before he made a radio broadcast from Guam to the United States on his way back from Iwo Jima. He spoke of his "tremendous admiration and reverence for the guy who walks up beaches and takes enemy positions with a rifle and grenades or his bare hands." [28]

His ever-inquiring mind drove Forrestal fast and far. With his tireless determination, he insisted that all the cold facts about immediate problems be lined up to use as the basic tools of his administrative functioning. But his urge to know went farther afield than that; he wanted to find out about those political, economic, military, diplomatic, and philosophical questions that might bring him a better comprehension of the direction toward which the nation was heading.

The relationship of that intellectual curiosity to his college education presents something of a puzzle. Certainly his three years at Princeton indicated little particular thirst for knowledge, seldom yielding grades above the "gentleman's third group." The less said the better of his scholastic record in his Freshman year at Dartmouth—academically it was almost a total loss.[29] It did not furnish enough credits for him to be eligible in three years for his Princeton degree; and apparently, not bothering to do anything to make up those missing credits, he left before commencement day. Yet, there seems to have been an important residue from those Princeton courses, however mediocre their grades. He developed a lifelong admiration for the works of Bagehot, Bryce, and Mill, in particular, and his wartime reading seems to have included much solid material as well as some relaxing "whodunits."

His passion for information appears to have stemmed from his Wall Street days. Shortly after he went to work for Dillon, Read, knowing almost nothing of the world of finance, he began studying with vim. Night after night following dinner, he left the two men with whom he shared rooms to turn in early with that day's *Wall Street Journal*. Before many months of studying it from first page to last, he was said to have had at his fingertips an uncanny knowledge of the history, distinctive features, and the likely prospects of just about every stock and bond issue on the market.[30] Such exact "intelligence," of course, had been essential for successful financiers since the days of the Fuggers and the Rothschilds; and as he

climbed the financial ladder, Forrestal never slackened in this ferreting out of facts.

Going into the strange world of the Navy, he naturally felt
even more urgently that driving need to learn. His personal files
bristle with constant requests for information, not all of it purely
naval in nature. In that quest and the wide range of his interests,
he resembled Winston Churchill. He retained his curiosity about
things financial and economic, partly from his concern as to how
far the nation could stand the ever-mounting costs of military
outlays. His own aides bore the brunt of this ceaseless pursuit,
but he also turned to the top experts of the Navy and other departments, to research groups such as the Office of Naval History, and
to outside specialized research talent.

The following are sample notes jotted down for his aides:

Please furnish me daily with a brief (one page) report on the activities of the Truman and Vinson committees and their counsel with
reference to their investigations of the Navy Department and any
matters of particular interest to the Navy.[31]

I would like to have put in my brown folder the leading financial
statistics about the Navy—current authorizations, appropriations and
expenditures; similar data for the last four years and then a summary
of Navy spending for the last war; and total expenditures, compared
with the present outlay, in the last 40 or 50 years. I think you got this
figured up for me some time ago. It may be that I have in mind what
the Navy spent since its foundation.[32]

I would like a digest of the July 1st changes of the WMC's [War
Manpower Commission's] procedure.

I should also like a statement of what is to be considered at the
Bretton Woods Conference; what are some of the proposals for the
World Bank, and has anyone yet stated how international investment
is to be supervised? Is stock in the World Bank to be owned by all
the governments or only by the British, Russians and ourselves?

Who are the people in town that are giving thought to the handling
of our own debt after the war—is Hansen a leading thinker, or are
there others? How good is Harry White? [33]

I would like to have a brief memorandum each week outlining the
principal points of discussion at the weekly WPB meetings. Could you
let me have it the day after the meeting? I would rather not wait for
the formal minutes.[34]

There was one memorandum in the files that probably did not
bring the answer sought. Dated February 1942 and addressed to
the Commander-in-Chief, U.S. Fleet, it read "Since the 7th of

December, numerous meetings of committees and planning bodies have been held to determine broad plans for the prosecution of the war. I should like to have one page of specific plans that have been evolved and the manner in which they are being prosecuted." [35] It might have been fun to have seen what went on in Fleet Headquarters when that arrived. Neither then nor later was Admiral King disposed to tell the civilian executives anything specific about operational planning; and this came from merely an Under Secretary.

Sometimes a broad synthesis was desired, and almost invariably, even for this type of report involving more extensive work, he expected—and got—speed and brevity as a matter of course. In one such instance, a request came to Naval History one afternoon for an account of exactly how the Navy Department had been organized when he came in, and what changes had taken place since; it was to be not over twelve pages and to be ready the following forenoon for him to take along on a flight to the west.[36] A more extended study of similar efforts for the past quarter century was assigned toward the end of the war, while Forrestal was preparing his thoroughgoing reorganization. The result, a stout processed volume, included pertinent correspondence, Congressional hearings, and brilliant brief summaries for each period.[37]

At times that multiplicity of interests generated confusion for all concerned, from his own aides to the top experts, not excluding himself. It seemed to some as if he were perhaps attempting to master too much too quickly in areas that required comprehensive background knowledge. His requests were not always clear, and it did not prove easy to find out just what he did want answered. According to an outstanding Navy authority on politico-military affairs, a future commander-in-chief, it was difficult and sometimes impossible to determine in consultations with him "exactly what basic question was in his mind. I have seen many examples of this. He might have asked, 'What about the Kurile Islands?' and then one was left wondering just what aspect of the 'Kurile Islands problem' he was really interested in." [38]

A case in point concerned the type of research for which in mid-1945 he called in an expert in economics from Smith College, probably the first economist to serve on a Navy Secretary's staff. Forrestal gave Edward F. Willett, an old friend of his with past business experience at Dillon, Read, the choice of doing general research "in any of a wide variety of matters in which he might be interested or . . . in international matters. . . ." Although Willett chose the latter assignment, he found himself immersed in the former. The problems of the armed services occupied him along with others for his first months. Then, his remaining time to May 1946 was spent on fifty-four research reports (see Appendix G) in response to a variegated list of Forrestal inquiries. These spread far afield from the Navy job itself, but were significant, as well as indicative of Forrestal's thinking at the time.[39]

Forrestal's predilection for one-page reports was by no means a monopoly of his. President Roosevelt had told Corcoran to "give me Forrestal on one page" when his name was proposed, and Admiral King had the same preference. Forrestal's refusal to read a longer memorandum, "if he could help it" resulted in one officer's getting necessary information to him by "writing him memoranda on the same subject so that he would have a series of one-page documents." [40] As for those working under him, they used the numerous typewriters that appeared around the Department equipped with pretty fine minion type; with that and very narrow margins quite an essay could be squeezed onto a single page.

Along with making himself better oriented in that crucial period, Forrestal was utilizing various means to influence the thinking of others. There was much that he felt the public should realize about the problems facing the Navy and the nation. He wrote Arthur Krock at a later date:

When I came down here, I remarked, and I think it may have been to you, that anyone serving in Government had really two functions: (1) he had to do a good job, and (2) he had to convince the public that a good job was being done. In business there is the same need but not to the same degree because, after all the income account is the criterion of the corporation executive's success or failure.[41]

Whether or not he had the personality to appeal to the public at large—and there was considerable doubt on that point—he made scant effort to do so. His arguments were directed rather toward what might be called the more thoughtful minority. With that selected group—a generous share probably of those who read such commentators as Hanson Baldwin, Walter Millis, Arthur Krock,

Walter Lippmann, James Reston, and the Alsops—he seemed to have won some warm supporters for what he was trying to achieve.

He used speeches for his chief medium. To one of his innate shyness, this was far from easy. On one occasion, he wrote the president of the Naval War College, "With the exception of the ordeal of public speech, which is never anything but pain, I could not have enjoyed myself more." [42] His first efforts at speaking were anything but successful; the same was true of his early testimony in Congressional hearings.[43] Part of the trouble was that his first three speeches had been handed him ready-made by the Public Relations staff in the Department, which was accustomed to grinding out speeches by the dozen for delivery by the officials and officers too busy to write their own. Knox, Bard, King, and Horne were among those who drew heavily upon their services. But, after hearing the way Forrestal droned through these "canned" talks, his aides urged that even if he would not be able to accept as many speaking invitations, he would have to write his own if he expected to have any effect.[44]

This placed him in a dilemma. As he explained it later, "It was not modesty that prevented me from accepting speaking invitations, but my strong feeling that I couldn't be thinking about the happy bromide and felicitous cliché at the same time that I was trying to learn a new and complex business." [45] But before long, as he became more accustomed to the techniques of speech-writing, he turned down fewer requests, in spite of the care with which he rationed his time. He appeared before all kinds of groups all over the country; between October 1941 and June 1, 1946, he delivered 110 speeches, exclusive of the times when he spoke extempore. In 1944, for example, he spoke on fourteen occasions in the East, three in Chicago, once each in Minneapolis and Los Angeles, and by broadcast from Guam (see Appendix E).[46]

Although it was literally true in his case that he wrote the draft of a speech himself, his staff, particularly his public relations assistant, had plenty to do with it. One difficult chore was running down the quotations Forrestal often inserted from memory, and his recollections were just about 90 percent accurate for pertinent quotations. That missing 10 percent, however, was apt to entail a needle-in-the-haystack search for something that he might have read months or years before; and with a voracious reader of his sort, this meant hunting over a wide area in periodicals as well as books. To cite a sample of his preparations, there was the speech he delivered at a Jackson Day dinner at New Orleans in 1946. Its six drafts ran from an original three double-spaced typed pages to fourteen, with the final revision twelve and a half pages. Some points received strong criticism from those assisting him, a not uncommon occurrence; if he liked an idea or phrase, he was inclined to be stubborn about changing it. This time, his sentence, "Mr. Shaw, you may remember, in *Androcles and the Lion* underlined with gentle irony the smugness of one of the early saints who boasted of his humility" was criticized in a marginal note, "Good, but query appropriateness for New Orleans." Obviously the note-writer had in mind the politicians at the dinner. But Forrestal curtly scribbled "Leave in." Another remark brought forth protests: "Jackson, who has been called a political radical, it seems to me actually was, like many radicals come to power, a conservative in action." It was pointed out to Forrestal that in view of recent writing on Jackson, he could never be called a conservative. Again Forrestal liked the idea and wanted to keep it, but eventually modified it to read, ". . . actually became, like many radicals come to power, *more* conservative in action." [47]

He would not speak unless he was sure of his footing. He replied to his friend Justice Douglas, regarding a Jefferson Day talk:

Before acting on the suggestion that I speak at Charlottesville I tried to set down what I might possibly have to say.

It doesn't look very hot to me—it isn't sharply enough defined nor does it have much punch.

Also, I haven't done enough reading about Jefferson. Most of what I have said is derived from Claude Bowers' book on Jefferson and Hamilton. [48]

Another time, he canceled a speech, already distributed to the press, for delivery to the Navy Industrial Association, because it "hit Russia," and so he "ad libbed" on a less controversial subject. [49]

The colleges were another area where he sought to arouse interest in the nation's growing world primacy. In 1943, he proposed to "pass the hat" among his friends for lectures in naval history at Princeton until he found that this might jeopardize a projected full-time professorship.[50] He shifted instead to the idea of regular college courses in the subject, writing Knox in 1944:

If the opportunity should present itself at your dinner of the University Presidents on Tuesday, I would appreciate it if you would raise the question of the introduction of a course on Naval Warfare and Strategy in the universities.

I have been working on this a little with Harold Dodds of Princeton and haven't gotten very far. My general thought was to have a regular course based on sound scholarship . . . supplemented by lectures from the Services. Roughly, this will include discussion of strategic geography, logistics, foreign policy, etc.

I have talked a good deal with Walter Lippmann who is very keen on it. . . .[51]

As Navy Secretary, he was to have the power to go ahead on his own with his next project—the addition to the college and university naval "V-12" officer training units of a course in politico-military fundamentals. Called "Foundations of National Power," the course was tried out, for shakedown purposes, in six universities, including Princeton—where the civilian teachers who would give it were later brought together for indoctrination, when it was extended to all fifty-two "V-12" units.[52] After the wartime program ended, the course was taken over by the Naval Reserve Officers Training Corps units.

To tap a broader and immediately more influential audience, he called a meeting at the Department in 1945 for a discussion of the new national status with leaders from Congress, the press, the colleges, Foreign Policy Association, State Department, Navy, and other groups. To widen knowledge of the Navy during the unification struggle, he had the Department get out a small book about its distinctive past and its present aspects, which was distributed on a fairly wide basis.[53] On occasion, he was ready to foot the cost himself to spread ideas he felt were vital, as in the case cited by Secretary of the Interior Ickes in the 1940 campaign: "Under Secretary Forrestal of the Navy called me. He was worried about the campaign! He wanted one minute every hour for a repetitious statement to go out to the farmers of the country. He was willing to pay for that time." [54]

Of these various attempts of his to arouse concern over the dangers ahead, the Navy Industrial Association had lasting results.

This new project, in which the educational element figured strongly, had a far broader purpose than the program of awarding the "Navy E" to manufacturers for industrial work well done, which was only symbolic recognition. The Association was composed mainly of the officials of big industrial establishments engaged in supplying Navy material. Its purposes, as announced in August 1944, outlined a two-way channel for the exchange of ideas and "know-how" between it and the Navy. One point mentioned was to "provide, and give direction to, scientific research in all fields, which affect the maintenance and growth of the Navy." [55] The Association got underway with a dinner in New York where some 1,600 heard Forrestal speak vehemently on the naval side of the war. A year later, he and Ferdinand Eberstadt,[56] spoke with equal vigor against the Army's merger plans. Courses were arranged at Columbia to give industrialists an over-all picture of the Naval Establishment.

Perhaps the most popular aspect of the program was the utilization of the Navy's old "boat-ride" technique. The industrialists proved no more immune than Congressmen to the allurement of short trips in naval craft; as a public relations device they have had few equals. A general, glumly watching a cruiser sail away one day with a load of Congressmen, was heard to say plaintively—or so a story goes—"And all we can do is take them for a walk!" A dozen years later, that practice was continuing in the semi-annual Joint Orientation Conferences in which the Navy still furnished the "boat rides," but the Association's name, reflecting Forrestal's broader cognizance, was now the Armed Forces Industrial Association.[57] Eventually, it became the National Security Industrial Association.

An integral and significant aspect of Forrestal's working habits was his close utilization of his immediate staff, both as Under Secretary and Secretary. Secretaries had, quite commonly, had one assistant and an aide or simply an aide, but it was a new development to have, as he did, a coordinated trio always close at hand, each with his particular sphere of activity. His use of the administrative possibilities of a naval aide was clearly an innovation and so, too, was his choice always of a lawyer as one civilian assistant and an experienced public relations man as the other.

Few outsiders realized their importance. They functioned in a similar way to staff officers, who are said "to have no name"; but his assistants were trusted to do a good deal in Forrestal's name. Not the least of their power lay in the control of his signature. Many of the routine letters that bore his name were never seen by him as the signature on them was machine-written. Over the years a few of the assistants knew the chief well enough to say "Jim, that's a lousy idea"—and have him listen. One civilian assistant and one prospective naval aide withdrew quickly, unable or unwilling to work under the high pressured tension of that far-from-smooth-running office. But the rest appeared to find more than adequate compensation in all that was accomplished in such a stimulating atmosphere. Yet there was a strange anomaly in all that haste. On occasion, the facts, the background, and the interrelations of some question assembled at top speed on Forrestal's order would be rushed to him; and that was the end of it for a long time. His slowness probably came from his invariable habit of studying both sides and his constant anxiety to be sure he understood the point of view of the other person or group. There was, however, disagreement among some who knew him well as to whether it was rather that it was "difficult for him to make a decision." That very caution, of course, may have had a good deal to it with making him a good executive.

Another angle on this may perhaps be found in his attitude toward those with whom he worked and the problems that they had to face together. He was anxious to keep their good will and, to a large degree, he succeeded. He always kept in mind that he would have to continue to work with those with whom he disagreed on some specific question. He did make many tough decisions and made them stick, but these he made carefully and usually with the full support of his organization. Believing that a "decision that leaves scars" should be avoided if humanly possible, he tried to lead people to what he felt was a sound decision by presenting the facts and discussing alternatives. He preferred to leave a means of retreat for those who took a hard position, rather than overcome their opposition by blunt orders.

Such tenets helped make him a master at handling conferences. He generally had one of his immediate staff present to give the facts in a given matter and recommend the course of action. His conference technique, in fact, made it essential that some member of his entourage be on hand and ready for a good argument. In case one did materialize, Forrestal's system was to adjourn the meeting, while keeping out of the disagreement by not expressing his own opinion. After a cooling-off period, he tended to consult individually with the principal spokesmen at the conference. He believed that a restatement of the facts in personal negotiation, as one reasonable person to another, often resulted in a decision that all parties might accept with good grace. He was persistent, however, in continuing negotiations, and came back to them time and again until a decision was reached.[58]

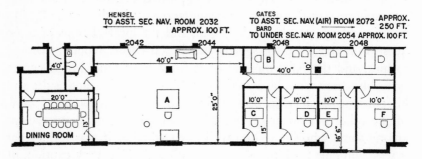

Office of the Secretary of the Navy (1946), Second Floor, "Main Navy" building, Constitution Avenue at 18th Street N.W.

A Hon. James V. Forrestal; *B* Lt. Edward Elder USMC; *C* Miss Katherine Foley; *D* Eugene S. Duffield (Public Relations); *E* Capt. Edmund Taylor (Naval Aide); *F* Major Mathias Correa USMC (Legal Aide); *G* Reception Area

Highly effective was his arrangement of the impressive Secretarial quarters. These were on the same second "deck" of Main Navy as his fairly similar offices as Under Secretary. A long reception room ran parallel to the corridor and to Constitution Avenue; a Marine officer, as guardian of the portal, had his desk here. Opening from it was the Secretary's office, a dignified room large enough for the weekly meetings of the bureau chiefs or press conferences with their dozens of newspapermen. Before the windows stood the massive desk. Over the fireplace, the calm, handsome face of Benjamin Stoddert, the first Secretary, looked down. Beyond that office, was a good-sized private dining room, with another old painting, the portrait of Benjamin W. Crowninshield, Salem shipowner and onetime shipmaster, who had asserted his authority over the "brass" in 1815. The unique part of the arrangement was that his immediate assistants had their desks in cubicles closely cramped on a gangway between the rear of the reception room and the Constitution Avenue windows. This made it possible for them to come and go to Forrestal's office completely out of view from the reception room or the main corridor.

The nearest cubicle was that of Forrestal's personal secretary, Katherine Starr Foley, universally known as Kate. Sister of the then Under Secretary of the Treasury, she held the post throughout Forrestal's nine years in Navy and Defense; previously, she had been in various government departments and agencies. Her knowledge and judgment made her practically indispensable in helping his work proceed more smoothly. She did much to lessen his onerous burden by taking over the management of those innumerable factors, both large and small, that could have plagued him endlessly.

The three staff posts had a succession of occupants, but most of them were overshadowed by the initial trio who carried the bulk of the wartime load. They were at Forrestal's side during most of his four Under Secretary years, and stayed on briefly into the Secretarial period: John E. Gingrich (August 1940–July 1944); Charles F. Detmar, Jr. (August–October 1940, September 1941–October 1944); and Eugene S. Duffield (November 1942–July 1946).

Commander Gingrich's post as naval aide to the first Under Secretary might have meant almost anything, judging from the past. Too often the captains or commanders, who wore the four-stranded aiguillettes, or "fishguts," the symbol of their status, had a semi-social sinecure. An aide had long been assigned to the Secretary and to each of his deputies; their duties were not specific and at the minimum had involved little more than personal or social duties in Washington or on Secretarial trips. If a Secretary encouraged it, the aide could do much in matters pertaining to "military" advice and naval personnel. A tactful aide might be able to modify impulsive or unwise Secretarial actions. But the post had obvious hazards, for there always tends to be jealousy of "palace favorites," and in the case of civilian-military friction, the zealous support of one's Secretary might not help a future naval career.

It so happened that almost every Secretarial aide during the war went on to a good sea command, and eventually became at least a rear admiral.

Gingrich had just come in from an aide's job with the Fleet and was serving as secretary of the General Board. Admiral John H. Towers, the veteran naval aviator, is said to have recommended him to Captain Morton L. Deyo, Knox's naval aide. Deyo asked Gingrich how he would like the post. "What's he like?" asked Gingrich. "He's a tough so-and-so," was the reply. "Will he get things done?" "He certainly will." "Then I'll take it." When Gingrich reported to Forrestal, who had just been sworn in, he was met with "Take off your coat and get to work." "Don't you want to check up on my qualifications?" "No." [59]

Gingrich's first major job was to wangle adequate quarters for the new Under Secretary—this meant ousting Naval Operations from the suite next to the Secretary's office. More and more Forrestal came to depend upon him in military matters. Admiral King, then in his top dual role, suspected Gingrich was behind certain steps taken in Forrestal's name. Time and again, passing the aide in the hallway, he would bow low from the waist with a sarcastic "Good morning, Commander." [60] Gingrich returned to sea in 1944 in command of the new cruiser *Pittsburgh;* his seamanship met a crucial test when a typhoon snapped off 104 feet of her bow, and he managed to swing her around to safety.[61] He returned later to the Department, handling among other responsible matters the postwar reserve program. Retiring as a four-star admiral, he went on to an important business post. Forrestal gave him high praise, "He was invaluable to me, being far above the ordinary officer in his understanding of the Navy's relations with the public and with civilians." [62]

Like Knox, who had Adlai Stevenson and then R. Keith Kane, Forrestal realized that he needed a personal legal adviser. It was natural for him to turn to the New York law firm which was counsel for Dillon, Read. Originally Cotton and Franklin, it had become Wright, Gordon, Zachary, Parlin, and Cahill. Several of its lawyers were to come to Forrestal's office. Detmar had been for some time on a "Jim" and "Charlie" basis. A graduate of Columbia College and Law School, he was thirty-five with a puckish smile and had a mind like a steel trap. When Forrestal asked to see him, he wanted to know how many shirts to bring down—those being the days before "drip-dry." "Oh, two ought to be enough" was Forrestal's poor guess; it was three months before Detmar got back home, so great was the avalanche of contracts facing him in Washington. During the coming year, James D. Wise and then William M. Dulles from the same firm followed him at the Department. In October 1941, he resigned from the firm to be special assistant for legal affairs, which in his case was to mean that he was "in on everything." Probably no one was closer to Forrestal for the next three years.

During the early Under Secretaryship, Gingrich and Detmar sat side-by-side just outside Forrestal's own office, and screened everything that came in. Only important top policy went straight through to Forrestal. Normally, Gingrich took the military matters and Detmar, the legal and business, but often it was catch as catch can with mutual consultation.

A preliminary step toward having a third man to relieve the increasing work load was made early in 1941 with the appointment of Ferol D. Overfelt, top man in his Annapolis class and later a banker. He ultimately directed, as a reserve captain, a division of the Office of Production and Material.[63] He was partially responsible for bringing Duffield into this "inner circle"; the latter had been a local reporter for Washington newspapers for most of the time after his graduation from the University of Wisconsin.[64] For a year, he had been an assistant to the Secretary of the Treasury, and was now chief of the Washington Bureau of the *Wall Street Journal*. After leaving the Department, he joined the editorial staff of the New York publishers, McGraw-Hill, and later was managing editor of the Cincinnati *Enquirer*, and joint editor of Forrestal's diaries.

Duffield's work in the Department might be called public relations in the broadest sense. His functions were numerous: much editing of speeches, scanning of press releases, having charge of the already accelerating fact-finding demands, and much else. He wanted people to bring in new ideas and left his door open in that expectation. He himself thought that his principal service was to translate such ideas of others into action either through regular bureau channels and offices or special arrangements.[65] Few realized that he was a reserve officer, ultimately becoming a captain—Forrestal decided that he might function better out of uniform. Unaware of this military status, an irate admiral, whose proposed directive had been edited by Duffield, was heard to vow: "If I could only have that young so-and-so under discipline for half an hour!" [66]

That triple pattern of special assistants for that general division of tasks was maintained by Forrestal during the rest of his time in the Department. As those first assistants went on to other things, successors were appointed to each post. The turnover was so rapid, however, that the total time in office of the later appointees was scarcely equal to that of the original incumbents (see Appendix C).

Once Forrestal had demonstrated the value of such an integrated "inner circle" of staff assistants, the practice was to develop further. In 1954, the Navy Secretary, no longer of cabinet rank, had "a Naval Aide (Captain, USN), an Administrative Aide (Captain, USN), a Marine Corps Aide (Lt. Colonel, USMC), an Assistant for Legal Matters, an Assistant for Research, and an Assistant for Administration." [67]

In addition to his immediate assistants, Forrestal kept a large number of other so-called special assistants very busy during the war years in what might be called a staff "outer circle." This group was indicative of his recognition of a Navy Secretary's need of men with many different kinds of skills—ranging as they did from research scholars to lawyers and businessmen. The vague but important sounding title of special assistant was convenient when one was in a quandary as to what to call an appointee. Its extreme flexibility might be used to cover almost any sort of project. Also, a special assistant, even for a major place in a Secretary's immediate staff, might be put to work at once with a minimum of red tape—particularly as to duties and stipend—that complicated all civil service appointments. The work normally involved "staff" members rather than routine administrative duties, and was generally fairly close to someone at the top. Altogether, these factors helped attract excellent talent, with a mutual freedom from binding commitments. Forrestal did not invent this status, but it had hitherto been rare. Franklin D. Roosevelt, Assistant Secretary in World War I, had leaned heavily on Louis D. Howe, the man who shortly afterward decided to make him President. Charles Edison, when

Assistant Secretary in the late thirties, had brought Lewis Compton down with him from New Jersey.

But it was Forrestal who made the special assistant a numerous and important category in the Department. Some forty men, although not more than ten at any one time, served under that title during his tenure. They were attached to the office of one or another of the four Secretaries; this total was exclusive of the numerous lawyers in his Procurement Legal Division.[68] Not only their background and experience varied widely but also their status. Some were reserve officers, and others were civilians either on contract at so much a day or in temporary civil service, but that difference between reserve officer and civilian was a negligible factor. It was their qualifications and ability for the job at hand that were significant.

But these administrative techniques and the broad terms by which he interpreted the scope of the Secretarial posts were only the first stages toward the far-reaching organization he was creating.

3

Traditions and Precedents

AT FIRST glance, one may well wonder what possible connection there might be, except in name, between the tiny Naval Establishment inaugurated, in 1798, by Benjamin Stoddert, its first Secretary, and the mighty power administered by Forrestal. Actually, the whole tapestry of the Navy's history from those early days was significant in the Navy of the 1940s, because initial precedents and ingrained habits wielded a lasting influence.

In its first hundred years, the Navy, like the nation, might have been called a force, but never a power. Most of the time, the active Fleet was simply two or three dozen wooden cruisers, showing the flag from the Mediterranean around to China. Except in 1812, its opponents had been of a size it could handle—the fringes of the French fleet, pirates in various seas, and Mexicans. Even the tough little Confederate Navy was no match for it. With the end of its first century, Dewey's victory at Manila Bay opened, almost overnight, a new era of world power for the nation and the Navy.

The Fleet might be said to *be* the Navy; without it, there would have been no reason for a Secretary of the Navy, the Department with its bureaus, the Shore Establishment with its navy yards and stations, or the Congressional committees on naval affairs. At the same time, the Fleet has not been an end in itself; rather, along with the other armed forces, it has been simply one instrument of national policy. The Secretary before 1947 was the channel through which policies, as determined by Congress, by the President, and by the State Department, were transmitted to the rest of the Navy. Reduced to the simplest terms, naval administration has consisted of distributing three functions—military, civil, and policy-making

—among the three top level categories of "line" officers, staff corps officers, and civilian executives in the three major spheres of Fleet, Shore Establishment, and Department. These triple aspects have created problems not confronting purely civilian business of the government but inherent in the administration of armed forces in a democracy, particularly in the blending of civilian authority with professional experience. The problems involved have made efforts toward naval reorganization a chronic pastime with not a single decade between 1798 and 1947 free from some move in that direction. Command at sea has been an obvious responsibility of line officers and policy-making of the Secretary; otherwise, the duties ashore have shifted between the three groups.

The American system was so complicated and overlapping because in 1798 the Navy went halfway but only halfway in copying the administrative practices of Britain's Royal Navy, then riding the flood tide of victory over the French, Dutch, and Spanish. Shipboard organization, the most basic and clear-cut element in naval administration, was copied virtually intact. So, too, were the ranks, ratings, and general status of officers and men, along with regulations and protocol. In the Shore Establishment, the adoptions went part way with some duplications. At the top level, on the other hand, the United States steered her own erratic course, which resulted in more than a century of floundering.

No one, starting afresh, would ever have designed anything like the Navy Department. Its organization rested on a century and a half of push, pull, and adjustment.[1] It lacked the clear-cut symmetrical pattern which the War Department received with its General Staff in 1903 and streamlined still further in 1942, but efforts to emulate that met resistance in the Navy Department.[2] And however illogical the departmental organization might be, the Navy certainly did as good a job of administration during the war as did the Army. "It's a queer system," remarked the wartime Vice Chief of Naval Operations, "but somehow we make it work." [3]

This evolutionary development makes the Department's past phases essential parts of the later Forrestal problems. The Department was inevitably his primary concern. He was in it and of it for seven years, and it was there, in the "home office," as some of the businessmen called it, that he had to make his basic decisions effective. In recording its own history, the Navy, unlike both the Army and Britain's Navy, has shown scant interest in anything except the "shooting" part of the story. Consequently, there is relatively little available in print to which the reader may be referred for an understanding of what Forrestal found in 1940.[4]

It was apparently not a matter of national pride that the British pattern was not followed at naval headquarters, as there had been no hesitation in copying everything afloat. The Royal Navy at the time was working out a fairly successful blend of over-all civilian executive authority with the "know-how" of the professional sailors that was by no means perfect, but was better than anything realized at Washington until well into the twentieth century. A single top group, the Lords of Admiralty, was headed by a civilian First Lord, with an admiral in second place, ultimately called the First Sea Lord. The British had similar boards for financial and commercial matters. In the framing of the American Constitution, preference was shown for the French pattern of single-headed executive departments. Alexander Hamilton, who strongly sponsored that view, argued against the use of administrative boards because "their decisions are slower, their energy less, their responsibility more diffused." [5] That may have been all right so far as non-naval branches of the government, such as his own Treasury Department, were concerned, but the fact remained that the absence of an effective civilian-professional liaison would leave American naval administration far less effective than the British.

The initial American setup provided only a Secretary of the Navy with a few clerks. Tradition, vested interest, and a distrust of military control managed to perpetuate an unbalanced system which more or less "just happened." It was not too effective in peace and was quite inadequate in war. Not until after Pearl Harbor would something resembling an appropriate balance be achieved between civilian and military.

Forrestal's particular sphere of action, the Secretary's Office, was older and had become even more heterogeneous than the rest of the Department. During Knox's Secretaryship, the office was divided formally into the Secretary's Office proper (SO) and the Executive Office of the Secretary (EXOS). The former, SO, included the immediate entourage of the Secretary and his deputies.

Secretary of the Navy Forrestal (right center) tells newsmen at conference that unification of armed forces was a "most decisive step" in military policy

Forrestal's base of operations from 1940 to 1947. The Navy Department on Constitution Avenue, Washington, D.C.

The mongrel remainder, EXOS, lacked any other common denominator than not belonging to a bureau or to Naval Operations. Its diverse 16 units in 1940 grew to 60 by 1946.[6] In many cases, Secretarial control was pretty tenuous. A few units had prestige and influence, especially the distinguished General Board, which felt that its relegation to EXOS was an affront to its dignity, but many of the others did not. The oldest, the Chief Clerk, dated from 1798 and for some time thereafter the title carried considerable weight virtually equivalent to that of Assistant Secretary later. A remarkable individual, Charles W. Goldsborough, as Chief Clerk, Secretary of the Navy Board, and first chief of Provisions and Clothing, was pretty much factotum of the Department most of the time from 1798 to 1843. An intelligent if not brilliant repository of tradition and "know how," he was very important in view of the frequent comings and goings of inexperienced Secretaries. With most higher Department posts held by officers, the ambitious civilian saw no future as Chief Clerk, and with the decline in the caliber of the incumbents, the office became reduced to routine matters. Under Forrestal pressure, it ceased to exist in 1942, leaving a vacuum for a new development of his.

One element in the Secretarial sphere, the Office of the Judge Advocate General, "JAG," was legally recognized as having virtual bureau status. It would be the focal point of one of Forrestal's first major innovations. The original post had been a temporary one with a civilian appointed in 1865 as Judge Advocate General and Solicitor, the latter title suggesting the handling of the Navy's business transactions. When it was revived in 1880, an officer was "JAG" and the two functions were merged. The separate post of Solicitor was restored in 1906, when the current Secretary sought competent legal advice on contractual matters, but in 1925 it was abolished again. The Judge Advocate General's Office was staffed, except for a few civilians, by regular line officers with some legal training, who alternated between it and sea duty. Navy Regulations stated that the "JAG's" duties included "all matters of law arising in the Navy Department," but they primarily concerned courts-martial.

The nominal role of the most dignified unit of all, the General Board, composed largely of line admirals, was to advise the Secretary. Established in 1900 "to ensure efficient preparation of the fleet in case of war and for the naval defense of the coast," it had been for many years a name to conjure with, but eventually Naval Operations had taken over its planning functions, leaving it little to discuss beyond ship characteristics. Both before and during the war, the Board's membership was a particularly distinguished one, but occasionally the complaint was heard, "They don't give us questions any more."

Since all units of EXOS, along with certain general matters, were allocated to the specific control of the Secretary or one of his deputies, Forrestal as Under Secretary was given a number of heterogeneous boards and functions. Upon becoming Secretary, his cognizance shifted to a more important assortment. In 1940, he was charged with responsibility for "Liaison with Departments and Industrial Agencies other than Budget, Army, Material and Labor; Legal Matters (routine legislation); Judge Advocate General; Contracts; Tax Questions; Compensation Board; Naval Examining Board; Naval Retiring Board; and Board of Medical Examiners." [7] After Knox's death, his cognizance included: "The Budget; the Joint Board; The General Board; Naval Petroleum Reserves; Public Relations; Aeronautical Board; Joint Economy Board; Office of War Savings Bonds; Training Liaison and Coordination Division; Lend Lease Liaison Office; Interior Control Board; Coordinator of Research and Development; and Board of Decorations and Medals." [8]

The bureaus were the second major element of the Department. Most of the early Secretaries had been shipping men, familiar with the fairly simple problems of the days of wooden sailing vessels, but by the end of the War of 1812, even they were asking assistance. In 1815, Congress created a Board of Commissioners of the Navy, or Navy Board, with three outstanding frigate captains given the collective responsibility for material and logistical functions. Such an arrangement made it difficult to fix responsibility. Consequently, in 1842, Congress copied the example set by Secretary of War John C. Calhoun and substituted five bureaus. This was a sufficiently elastic system to permit the addition of new ones or the abolition or merger of some as circumstances warranted; there were seven in the Forrestal period.

The system's distinctive feature was embodied in the mystic word "cognizance." This implied responsibility for, and authority in, a particular sphere of technical performance necessary to successful operation of the Fleet. It made possible a workmanlike mastery of a particular problem but at the same time, it meant a compartmentation of naval administration. This had been a major problem for decades before Forrestal's turn to wrestle with it.

The bureaus' personnel fell into two major groups, staff and line. The line—the "fighting" officers in the line of command— prided themselves on their versatility, and all wore the same gold star. In contrast, the Army line wore the separate symbols of infantry, cavalry, artillery, and so on. In the early days, with only three or four officers aboard small warships, that versatility was indispensable; the risk of specialization would have been too great, should death or disability strike the quarterdeck. And in that comfortable static age of sail, what one learned as a midshipman still held good when one became a commodore. But even then the doctrine of line versatility stopped short of the surgeon and the purser or paymaster. The story goes that the line officers recognized that the former's duties were beyond them and considered the latter's beneath them, nor did they challenge the specialties of the naval constructors and civil engineers ashore, who originally were civilians.

With the advent of steam around 1840, however, the line officers did not try to master the mysteries of engines and boilers, and an Engineer Corps developed, with its members operating at sea as well as ashore. After decades of friction, the engineers were "amalgamated" into the line in 1899. This line engineering eventually worked out aboard ship, but the need for technical knowledge of engine designing led to the anomalous category of line officers for "Engineering Duty Only" (EDO), set up in 1916. They were, to all intents and purposes, staff specialists and, though wearing the line star, were barred from command at sea.[9]

Aviation and the submarine obviously necessitated radical modification of line versatility. The aviators contemplated a separate corps, but gave it up to remain in the line along with the submariners. Each had a monopoly of their specialities, in the air and below the surface of the sea.

Despite those exceptions, the doctrine of line versatility still held, and became a factor definitely to be reckoned with in naval administration. Aboard ship, it continued to work fairly well, the average officer having had some training in various spheres since

Annapolis days. The trouble came with the shore billets, where versatile omniscience was too often taken for granted without preliminary preparation. Another complication was an old naval doctrine: "Tell them what, when, and where, but never insult them by telling them how."

That matter of versatility and specialization was an integral part of the bureau system, which combined staff and line, and of Naval Operations, which was a line monopoly. Until Forrestal opened up a new three-star, vice-admiral's post in the material field, a staff corps officer could look no higher than a temporary "spot" promotion to rear admiral as a bureau chief, along with heading his corps. On the other hand, in the Spanish-American War, the Navy leaders—Dewey, Sampson, and Schley—and in World War II, the first five-star admirals—Leahy, King, and Nimitz—had all been line bureau chiefs.

Forrestal learned that much depended upon the qualities of the chief and the assistant chief, likewise automatically a temporary rear admiral after 1940. More or less by accident, the Navy hit upon a principle widely held in management that an admirably matched pair came from one of these being a general executive and the other a technician.

The bureaus translated their jealously guarded "cognizance" into "hands off" to all outsiders. By 1864, their spheres of cognizance were being written into the annual appropriation acts; then, and for years afterward, Yards and Docks included the Navy's oxen and shade trees under its cognizance.[10] Much of this spirit had persisted, but Forrestal limited his efforts toward coordinating bureau work to business matters rather than technical spheres.

His particular concern with the bureaus was the "hardware" for the new vessels in Ships, the new aircraft in Aeronautics, and the guns, torpedoes, ammunition, armor, and the like in Ordnance. His relative connection with the bureaus as a whole is indicated in the following table of their wartime expenditures, in billions of dollars, from July 1, 1940, to August 31, 1945.

Ships	30.6	Naval Personnel	1.0
Supplies and Accounts	21.1	Medicine and Surgery	0.3
Aeronautics	15.7	Marine Corps	2.3
Ordnance	13.8	Coast Guard	1.5
Yards and Docks	7.0		

Source: Secretary of the Navy, *Annual Report, 1945*, Table A-8.

The heavy Supplies and Accounts total is misleading in this connection, as much of it went for the pay, food, clothing, and other expenses of Navy personnel.

Tradition, type of personnel, and way of doing things tended to give each bureau its particular atmosphere. Ships (BuShips), established along with the Under Secretary post in the Naval Reorganization Act of 1940, was both the newest and in part one of the oldest bureaus, being a merger of Construction and Repair of the original 1842 quintet and of Engineering, originally Steam Engineering of 1862.[11] The former had been staffed by the Construction Corps, an elite group selected eventually from the top Annapolis graduates for postgraduate work in naval architecture, and the latter, since the 1899 amalgamation, partly with general line but mainly with Engineering Duty Only officers.[12] The Act stipulated that in the new Bureau of Ships if its chief came from one group, the assistant chief must come from the other. At one time, two other bureaus, Equipment and Ordnance, also shared in what went into a vessel. Equipment was abolished in 1914, but Ordnance still kept cognizance over armor. This multiple cognizance had long plagued naval shipbuilding, but matters had come to a head in the late 1930s. A new class of destroyers was found topheavy, because there had been no over-all control in their planning, and consequently, too much had been compressed into the slender little vessels.[13]

The resulting merger came from the efforts of Assistant Secretary Charles Edison, in one of the rare cases of effective Secretarial leadership between the World Wars. Between September 1939 and June 1940, Construction and Repair and Engineering went through a period of preparation for merger under Rear Admiral Samuel M. Robinson, the first chief of Ships. Then full Secretary, Edison tried to bring Ordnance's cognizance over armor also into the merger, but was blocked by a triple play on the part of the Chief of Ordnance, Chairman Vinson of Naval Affairs, and the President.

With the new construction program getting underway, Ships faced major problems in its three chief functions—design, shipbuilding, and maintenance. Despite changes in priorities, material shortages, and disputes with the Maritime Commission as to which had the better right to the limited supply of turbines, BuShips turned out an unprecedented volume of tonnage.[14] Forrestal was particularly troubled about the Bureau's estimates of its monthly needs of steel and other essentials, a matter seriously complicated by the frequent changes in the relative priority of different types of vessel, as determined by higher authority.[15] One particular midnight meeting, for example, meant that BuShips had to "drop everything" in other fields to concentrate on landing craft. It even had to order a partly completed battleship be floated out of drydock at Norfolk Navy Yard to make way for the landing craft construction.[16]

Ordnance (BuOrd), another of the 1842 group, was by and large known as one of the most conservative and "stuffy" bureaus. It was staffed by regular line officers, who could boast "We come in from the sea and we shall go back to sea." As one Assistant Chief declared: "Our ships are designed by men who do not go to sea; and our planes by men who do not fly; but by godfrey, our guns are made by the men who'll fire them." [17] Outside the bureau, some were known to murmur, "That's just the trouble!" That ship-and-shore pattern dated back to Rear Admiral John A. Dahlgren of Civil War days, who designed the big guns that bore his name. Despite disgruntled grumblings that he was a shore-based staff specialist, he was given command of the fleet that used the guns against Charleston. Officers of the "Gun Club" often gained the highest posts; Leahy, Stark, and Richardson all came from Ordnance. It is small wonder that young Annapolis graduates were advised: "Get behind the big guns and stay there." BuOrd's big 16-inch guns and most of its ordnance performed well, but its Newport torpedoes were tragically ineffective. Also inadequate at the outset were its antiaircraft guns; foreign Bofors and Oerlikon guns had to be used to meet the situation. Late in the war, with the cooperation of civilian scientists, the proximity fuse shells in BuOrd's quick-firing 5-inch guns finally gave adequate antiaircraft protection.[18]

Aeronautics (BuAer) 1921, another line bureau, loomed large in Forrestal's material procurement program for, unlike Ships and Ordnance, it did no manufacturing. All its 75,000 planes during 1940–45 had to be purchased. Also, unlike Ships and Ordnance, its "Material Branch" was only a major part, not its entire concern. Some of its other units, particularly its "Flight Division," verged on the operational. BuAer insisted on doing its own training, though that was supposedly under Navigation (Naval Personnel), and also in sharing supply functions with Supplies and Accounts. Thus, it was a sort of little autonomous empire within the naval organization, unencumbered with the well-encrusted practices and prejudices of many older bureaus; and with its branch of the service expanding at an unprecedented rate in size and scope, it was perhaps more open-minded toward innovations in meeting its problems. Since it was for the most part staffed by aviation line officers, its personnel turnover was rapid, for not only were they in high demand at sea, but they wanted their share of that service.[19] Ultimately in 1959, Ordnance and Aeronautics would be merged in the Bureau of Naval Weapons (BuWeps).

From the first, Forrestal's associations with the old Yards and Docks (1842) were similar. Normally the smallest bureau, it presented yet another variation in pattern. It started out as a line bureau, charged with the building, maintenance, and control of the Shore Establishment, but early in this century it was transferred to the small Civil Engineer Corps and henceforth was a staff bureau with "public works," its main job. In the war, it was faced with a tremendous program for facilities in the far Pacific and elsewhere overseas as well as at home.[20]

Supplies and Accounts (1842), a staff bureau, was named Provisions and Clothing until after fiscal functions were added. Manned by officers of the Supply Corps (Pay Corps), S&A still fed and clothed the Navy, furnishing during the war a billion barrels of oil and gasoline and a billion cups of coffee, as well as handling the payment of personnel and of accounts.[21] Its traditional purchasing functions brought it into conflict with the Forrestal procurement program, although it simply processed orders prepared by other bureaus.[22]

Some of the personnel problems of Naval Personnel (BuPers), a "line" bureau, until 1942 the Bureau of Navigation (1862), were of lively interest and concern to Forrestal as Secretary. Started as a scientific bureau in 1862, it gradually acquired cognizance of officer and then enlisted personnel and also of the Naval Reserve.[23] From the 1880s until the creation of the Chief of Naval Operations in 1915, its Chief had enjoyed a powerful position in the operational controls of the Navy. Even after that, the position still carried considerable influence and prestige. Both the Chief and the Assistant Chief often went on to higher things, as in the case of Chester W. Nimitz, Chief in mid-1940, who became Commander-in-Chief of the Pacific Fleet and then Chief of Naval Operations. It meant much, obviously, to be able to decide the next tour of duty of the officers. Since the Bureau had the responsibility of training officers and men, its task became gigantic with almost four million men entering the Navy in World War II.

Since 1842, Medicine and Surgery (BuMed) staffed as it was by the Medical Corps and the less venerable Dental Corps, lived in an atmosphere of splendid isolation, having little to do with the rest of the Department; its performance was generally regarded as excellent.

Reckoned as an element of the Department was the Headquarters of the famous Marine Corps. Its Commandant, despite his title, exercised administrative rather than actual command functions; those rested with the Fleet Marine Force under direct naval authority, and under the commanding officers of shore units where the Marines served as guards. A similar relationship existed with the Coast Guard, which in wartime was shifted from the Treasury Department to the Navy.

The units of the Office of Naval Operations (Op-Nav) contrasted in two respects with the heterogeneous autonomy of the bureaus. They were under a single head, the Chief of Naval Operations (CNO), and were manned exclusively by the seagoing "line," to the exclusion of staff specialists.

Naval Operations was the closest the Navy had come to the neat pattern of line control embodied in the Army's reorganization of 1903 when all of its activities were placed under a general staff. This was headed by a Chief of Staff who insulated the civilian Secretary of War from day to day control.[24] The Navy "line," as the fighting element, had long sought some such arrangement. Something of the sort was needed for there was no one, except the often inexperienced civilian Secretary, to coordinate the bureau efforts or direct the movements of ships. Some line integration, to be sure, had been achieved temporarily by the Chiefs of Navigation and by the system of "aides" established in 1909 by Secretary George von L. Meyer, but was allowed to languish by his successor, Josephus Daniels.

The line officers secured a notable gain in 1915, when Congress created a Chief of Naval Operations.[25] The original bill gave this

CNO authority over the Fleet, similar to the powers of the Army Chief of Staff. Secretary Daniels whittled that down, however, so that the CNO did not have full control over either the Fleet or the bureaus. Even at that, the new office contributed much to the Navy's efficiency by providing a professional coordination and operational direction that had previously been lacking.

With those reduced functions, the prime purpose of Naval Operations on the eve of war might be summed up in the word "readiness." And the Navy in 1940 was not ready. The scope of Naval Operations itself then covered War Plans, Intelligence, Communications, Inspection, Fleet Training, Fleet Maintenance, Ships Movements, Naval Districts, Naval Reserve, and the Central Division, which included State Department relations. The quite inadequate Material Procurement Section under Fleet Maintenance was Forrestal's immediate concern.[26] He was also involved with line control to some degree as Under Secretary, and to a much greater degree as Secretary, when Naval Operations tried to control everything.[27]

Like other good Secretaries, Forrestal normally left the operation of the Fleet to the professional high command. But since its strengthening was the ultimate goal of his post, he had to seek an understanding of its operation in order to achieve effective leadership to that end.

Through World War I, much of the Navy's strength was in the Atlantic Fleet, but in 1919, with the Panama Canal completed and the German battle fleet scuttled, half the ships were sent to the West Coast.[28] With the increased Japanese threat between the wars, this Pacific Fleet grew steadily in size while the Atlantic force dwindled to a mere squadron. The Asiatic, a third Fleet and one in name only, divided its time between the Philippines and the China coast. The proximity to Japan made it unwise to leave more than a modest force there, but it had a full four-star admiral for dealing with other nations on the proper command level. The outbreak of World War II, the establishing of a Neutrality Patrol, and the fall of France quickly resulted in more ships for the Atlantic, and early in 1941 the command was restored to Fleet status.

In 1940, there were many, even in high place, who "could not see beyond the splash of a sixteen-inch shell," and still expected a future decisive encounter of battleships, such as those British and German giants that had duelled to a stalemate at Jutland in 1916.[29] The dozen superdreadnoughts in service were much older than usual, because battleship construction had been suspended in accordance with the stipulations of the Washington Naval Conference of 1922. They ranged in age from the *Oklahoma* and *Nevada*, launched in 1914, to the *Colorado* and *West Virginia*, launched in 1921.[30]

With the breakdown in disarmament agreements in 1935–36, the battleship proponents immediately had plans drawn up for a new class with armament more or less unchanged but faster, larger, and far more expensive. The last of the old ships at 31,000 tons had cost $27 million. The *Washington* and *North Carolina*, launched in June 1940, ran to some 35,000 tons and $70 million. The battleship urge did not end there; later that month, the keel was laid of the *Iowa*, the first of a quartet, at 45,000 tons and 33 knots at a cost of some $100 million.[31] Ironically, in the greatest battle of naval history at Leyte Gulf in 1944, that costly extra speed was used to carry those great ships *away* from where they were needed.[32]

The battleship conservatives were already being challenged by some other officers, who foresaw that even the immediate future lay with the aircraft carriers, of which there were only four in the Pacific in mid-1940. Tacticians were already experimenting with the idea of a fast carrier task force, which could extend its hitting power far beyond the range of any 16-inch gun.

The immediate center of authority over those distant forces lay aboard the old *Pennsylvania,* perennial flagship since 1916. The Commander-in-Chief, United States Fleet (abbreviated CincUS until changed after Pearl Harbor to Cominch) had nominal overall command of all forces afloat, but was primarily concerned with the Pacific Fleet. Theoretically, he was junior to, if not subordinate to, the Chief of Naval Operations but this command relationship was decidedly hazy until after Pearl Harbor.

Forrestal would learn of the concern of the CincUS, Admiral J. O. Richardson in 1940 over the basing of his ships at Pearl Harbor. He had taken them out from the West Coast to Hawaiian waters for the annual maneuvers, expecting to return shortly to San Pedro and San Diego. Instead, he was ordered to remain until further notice, because, so it was explained, this should serve as a "deterrent" to the Japanese. Richardson, knowing that more men and munitions were required to put the ships in fighting shape, went twice to Washington to urge the fleet's return to the West Coast. But instead of removing the fleet, Roosevelt removed the admiral, whose successor, Husband I. Kimmel, would become indelibly associated with that Pearl Harbor base.

Before the war, the command of the Navy's vessels was still largely in the hands of regular line officers, mostly Naval Academy graduates; only about 1,800 reserve officers were on active duty, as against 10,800 regulars.[33] The war completely reversed that ratio; even the larger ships then had only a few regulars in their complement, while the reserves rose to the command of many smaller vessels.

From the first, Forrestal's procurement activities brought him into contact with the Shore Establishment, as they came within its industrial orbit. Its administration at the civilian level, on the other hand, was the sphere of the Assistant Secretary, not the Under Secretary. The shore stations have had dual roles since their establishment in about 1800. They engaged in the production, maintenance, or storage of equipment required by the Fleet, while as bases, they constituted focal points for servicing ships and, later, aircraft. At this time, the navy yards stretched from the East Coast, with the original six—Kittery-Portsmouth, Boston, New York, Philadelphia, Washington, Norfolk—and the later Charleston, South Carolina, to the West Coast's Mare Island and Puget Sound-Bremerton, and overseas to Pearl Harbor and Cavite.[34] The early yards not only built and repaired most of the vessels, including some manufacturing, but also began to meet other needs of returning vessels with ordnance depots, general stores, hospitals, and receiving ships to train new recruits. This duality of function was recognized at the end of World War II when the yards were rechristened "naval bases" with their industrial portions renamed "naval shipyards."

The non-industrial shore stations concerned Forrestal only slightly, however important they were in the general picture. Some of them represented the all-round base function that the old navy yards had exercised so long. At Hampton Roads was a huge Naval Operating Base, with lesser ones elsewhere; on a more modest scale, various "Naval Stations" carried on similar services to the Fleet. There were 41 Naval Air Stations and other air activities, some engaged in training and many more in actual operations. This group, whose total would rise to 171 during the war, would be the responsibility of the Assistant Secretary for Air, so far as civilian cognizance went. More specialized were the numerous hospitals and supply activities, Marine Corps stations, and, in the field of naval personnel, the Naval Academy at Annapolis, the Naval War College at Newport, the Naval Prisons at Portsmouth and Mare Island, and several Naval Training Schools. Aside from all these "shore stations" proper, representing physical plants, there were hundreds of other shore activities, particularly in connection with recruiting and inspection, which were conducted on a more modest scale.[35]

While existing for the service of the Fleet, the Shore Establishment during the Navy's so-called "Dark Ages" starved the Fleet into insignificance by draining off much of the Navy's money for its own uses. In that sorry period between 1869 and 1881, Secretarial control was very weak and line influence strong in the person of Admiral David D. Porter. Other nations were steadily forging ahead with improvements in steam, iron or steel, and ordnance, while the United States was showing the flag on distant stations with a handful of obsolete wooden cruisers, armed with old-fashioned smoothbores and operating chiefly under sail. Her ships were too slow to run away and too weak to stand a chance in a fight. In 1875 a British service journal wrote: "There never was such a hapless, broken-down, tattered, forlorn apology for a navy as that possessed by the United States." [36]

That low condition was customarily blamed on the niggardliness of Congress, which reflected the post-bellum shift in interest from the sea to the interior. Actually, there was money enough; from 1871 to 1875, the Navy spent more than double the amount it had spent in 1851–60, when it was almost equally strong. Yet Britain, in 1871–75, was maintaining the most powerful navy afloat and keeping up with the latest developments on just double the amount of American expenditure.[37]

In an effort to keep the navy yards busy after the Civil War, there had been a wasteful leakage of funds in the patching of old wooden ships. The fastest vessels were laid up and the rest were

often repaired at more than their original cost. The only real bene-
ficiaries of this policy were the civilian workers, often political
henchmen. "Don't give up the ship!" became a navy yard slogan
as the workers did their best to stretch out each repair job.[38] Congress stopped the tinkering on wornout hulls of worthless vessels
in 1882.[39]

Some Navy money was also syphoned off to bolster the income
of beached line officers. The Department to some extent shared the
blame with the Shore Establishment in seeing that there were jobs
enough to keep the many surplus officers, not needed at sea, on full
pay ashore. Before the Civil War, the Navy had followed the
British "half pay" example of placing most surplus senior officers
on "furlough" at very sharply reduced pay. By 1869, there were
few shipboard billets for the long lists of senior officers.

Unfortunately, a general order dictated by Admiral Porter decreed that in every line career periods of shore duty should alternate
with sea duty.[40] With new jobs created in the shore stations, on
special boards, and in the Department, a much higher proportion of
officers was able to stay on full pay than a similar proportion of
officers in the Royal Navy.[41] Many of these land-based jobs were
sinecures that involved little more than occasionally signing "Captain, U. S. Navy" to papers prepared by subordinates. Real tasks
ashore called for the specialized talents of the naval constructors,
civil engineers, surgeons, and paymasters. The best quarters at any
station, however, generally went to the line officers. They developed
a mystique about the need for line supervision—if all other arguments failed, they could always fall back on "But how could a
constructor or a paymaster set up a court martial?" The practice
of shore sinecures did not die out completely even after World
War II. Most notorious was the Naval Home at Philadelphia, a
moderate-sized institution for aged pensioners, yet three- or four-
star admirals have scrambled for the post of superintendent in
order to stay on full pay after retirement and have a free car and
driver as well.

By Forrestal's advent, the Shore Establishment had become one
of the nation's most extensive industrial organizations, with its 248
stations estimated as representing an initial cost of some $743 mil-
lion, more than a quarter of the $2,522 million cost of the 383
combatant vessels of the Fleet. The annual upkeep came to $129

million, as compared with $217 million for the Fleet. New York Navy Yard, the largest of the shore stations, represented a cost of $67 million as compared with $44 million for the *Lexington*, the most expensive of the warships at that time. Those costs mushroomed rapidly along with the Shore Establishment and everything else.[42]

The industrial side of the Shore Establishment presents the constant policy question of how much should be produced by the Navy itself and how much procured from private industry. So long as wooden hulls were in vogue, nearly all vessels were built in the navy yards, but most ordnance was purchased. A sudden reversal came in the 1880s with the technological demands of the "New Navy." Most warships thereafter came from private yards, but the Navy began to manufacture its own big guns and some other ordnance items. As for planes, the Navy relied completely upon private producers; the Naval Aircraft Factory at Philadelphia was used only for experimentation.

The main problem centered around shipbuilding, the pros and cons of which had been debated by the British long before there was a United States Navy. Aside from quality and cost, two basic considerations always affected the decision; the need in peacetime to give enough business to private yards to enable them to keep a nucleus of skilled workers and to have enough such yards available in wartime so that at least part of the navy yards would be free for emergency repairs.[43] The mysteries involved in fashioning steel hulls for the "New Navy" were another cogent reason favoring private facilities; from 1895 through 1910 only one major warship was built in a navy yard. Then, constant political pressure from local interests to keep navy yards busy gradually resulted in the development of facilities for building major ships at the New York Navy Yard, then at Philadelphia and Norfolk (see Appendix H). The Navy consequently utilized these yards extensively in World War II, when they accounted for nearly 30 percent of the major ship tonnage in contrast to only 7 percent in World War I (see Appendix H).[44]

Next to shipbuilding, the manufacture of ordnance was the biggest industrial job of the Shore Establishment. For more than half a century, the Naval Gun Factory at Washington Navy Yard had turned out most of the Navy's big guns, up to the maximum

16-inch battleship weapons. Much of the peacetime powder supply was produced by the Naval Powder Factory at Indianhead, Maryland. Numerous ammunition depots and two naval mine depots loaded as well as stored shells or mines.

In two other major ordnance activities, armor and torpedoes, the situation was less clear-cut. One important "New Navy" decision had been that the United States should produce its own armor plate instead of purchasing it from Britain. Bethlehem, Carnegie, and other steel companies were encouraged to undertake its manufacture. Under political pressure, a naval armor plate plant was established near Charleston, West Virginia, during World War I, but the Navy continued, probably quite wisely, to look to the private steel industry for most of the great plates. The Naval Torpedo Station at Newport during World War II drew such damning criticism upon itself that it was closed shortly after the war, despite its potent political support.[45]

The bulk of the industrial Shore Establishment work was carried on by civilians. In mid-1940, the Navy's 113,000 civilians were almost as numerous as its 144,000 enlisted men afloat and ashore. Of those civilians, 4,300 in the Navy Department and 15,300 in the Shore Establishment were "white collar" civil service employees receiving salaries fixed, and often frozen, by statute; many of them were women stenographers and typists.[46] The remaining 100,000, however, were a quite different sort. Instead of receiving fixed salaries, these "blue collar" industrial workers were paid wages on a weekly or hourly basis, adjusted to the scale in private industry nearby. Many devoted their whole careers to such government employment. In one major respect, the Navy's civilian workers differed from those working in private establishments on defense contracts. The latter were free to strike, while the former were not. Forrestal would consequently have one vigorous old admiral take over several strike-bound private plants in the name of the Navy in order to keep work going on naval contracts.[47]

The industrial workers were under the Assistant Secretary, who had a special Shore Establishments Division, later changed to Industrial Relations Section. Forrestal's concern, on the other hand, was not with the workers but rather with the products of the Shore Establishment or outside facilities. Actually, conditions were quite similar at Philadelphia Navy Yard and at "New York Ship" across the river in Camden, except at the upper levels where the Navy used officers instead of civilians, but even then, it attached numerous officers to the private yard to supervise shipbuilding.[48]

All told, the industrial Shore Establishment was already an impressive organization in mid-1940 and would become still more so in the war years ahead. As Forrestal stated in his annual report in 1945:

Before the war, the then existing establishment was valued at about $750,000,000. Today the Navy's shore establishment represents an investment of about $12,000,000,000. In other words, the Navy has a plant account 25% larger than the combined plant accounts of General Motors, United States Steel and American Telephone and Telegraph. The Bureau of Ships alone has an investment account almost as large as United States Steel, and the Bureau of Aeronautics has one substantially larger than that of General Motors.[49]

The principle of civilian supremacy, still another part of the heritage from England's past, was probably the most important of all these traditions. There is no evidence that Forrestal, any more than most people not personally involved, had given much thought to this, but he was to learn that the civilian-military relationship was one of the most complicated and difficult problems facing him. The continuing insistence upon civilian authority in the military field in England had doubtless stemmed in part from the decade of bald dictatorship under Oliver Cromwell, just at the time when the colonies were taking form.

In the United States, since the first days of the nation, civilian supremacy has been a major concern, but its emphasis has changed since the eighteenth century. As Huntington, an expert in the field, puts it, the framers of the Constitution

were more afraid of military power in the hands of political officials than they were in the hands of military officers. Unable to visualize a distinct military class, the framers could not fear such a class. But there was need to fear the concentration of authority over the military in any single governmental institution.[50]

Consequently, they divided the power over the military between the national government with its standing army and navy and the states with their militia; between the President and Congress by the separation of powers theory; and, within the Executive Branch, between the President and the departmental Secretaries. The Constitution, moreover, made the President's role that of Commander-in-Chief and gave to Congress control over the military purse.[51]

As time went on, there developed a more cohesive professional military group. Some presidents were to find popular professional officers useful in rallying Congressional support for their proposals for increased military appropriations when they were larger than Congress favored. On the other hand, Congress, becoming gravely concerned over the effect on the national economy of the steadily rising costs of armament, began to insist upon making its own independent review of military roles and force levels. It asserted its right to the same professional military advice which was available to the President. Thus on any really important issue of national policy, the high ranking military officers tended to be drawn into the legislative-executive struggle on one side or another. As a result, the separation of powers presented a major problem in determining military policies and, at the same time, in maintaining civilian control. Forrestal was more successful than most Navy Secretaries in bridging this gap between Congress and the President.[52]

One acute observer in speaking of the military departments noted:

Generally speaking, secretaries fall into three categories: those who are merely figureheads, furnishing a facade of civilian authority but being devoid of effective control or even of major influence; those who function efficiently as ambassadors of the military command in the civil councils of government, but lack controlling power in a reciprocal direction; and finally the rare and great secretary who, while ably representing his department in the government at large, is able at the same time to give it strong leadership in terms of both policy and organization.[53]

Forrestal, in the minds of many people, belonged in the last category. But he also came to realize that few of the larger problems confronting the Navy were strictly military or strictly civilian. Sound answers to them required a blending of knowledge, which was a task for the top civilian leadership, and one for which he himself was particularly well-fitted.[54]

Much, of course, has depended upon the individuals who occupy the Presidency, the Secretaryships, and high military commands. But the Commander-in-Chief clause and the separation of powers have been stumbling blocks to real control by the Secretary of the Navy. No wonder Forrestal occasionally looked with envy upon the British cabinet system which seemed to provide better solutions to these problems. His struggles to be master in his own Department, to balance the influence of White House and the Hill, and to find organizational solutions in civil-military relationship are a major theme of the pages that follow.

This, then, from bureaus and shore stations to Secretarial relationships, was the Navy with which Forrestal was associating himself in mid-1940. The complex Naval Establishment was partly, but only partly, ready for the great burdens which lay just ahead. Nevertheless, from being tied for first place with Britain's embattled Royal Navy in 1940, its remarkable expansion in the next five years was to make it stronger than all the other navies of the world combined (see Appendix A). Operating above, upon, and beneath the waves, it became the mightiest sea force known to man.

4

Getting Under Way

FORRESTAL TOOK office as Under Secretary just as the armed services were beginning their expansion, and preliminary steps were underway to mobilize industrially to meet their heavy demands. His work with the Navy's material program and with national industrial mobilization ranks as his outstanding achievement as Under Secretary. It was this experience that gave him his pertinent ideas about Navy organization in general and civilian-military relations in particular. He might have reached some of his conclusions in peacetime, but this war experience certainly sharpened his perspective and made his ideas more definite.[1]

Anyone entering the Department in mid-1940 as Forrestal did would have found that the Navy's accumulation of traditions and precedents was not limited to organization charts but was embodied in the attitudes of the officers with whom he had to work. At first glance, the overwhelming preponderance of military personnel in positions of importance was not apparent, for until Pearl Harbor uniforms were not worn at the Department. That was a matter of policy, as some Congressmen felt that officers belonged at sea. Actually, civilians in places of authority could almost be counted on one's fingers; the vast majority in the top posts were admirals, captains, commanders, and lesser ranks in business suits (see Appendix B).

At the head of this officer hierarchy stood genial Admiral Harold R. Stark, Chief of Naval Operations, with headquarters, for the moment, near Forrestal's. His career had assumed something of a "headquarters pattern"; he had been on Admiral William S. Sims's staff in London during World War I and was later Secretary

Charles Francis Adams's aide. There had been some surprise, however, when he succeeded Admiral William D. Leahy, as CNO in March 1939. It was a particular disappointment to a hard-bitten three-star admiral—Ernest J. King—who felt that his last chance had gone for that coveted post.[2] Like Leahy, Stark was a member in good standing of the "Gun Club," having been assistant chief of Ordnance. But above all both shared President Roosevelt's recollections of close contacts back in his Assistant Secretary days, Leahy having been skipper of the Secretarial yacht and Stark's destroyer having cruised Maine waters with Roosevelt aboard. The President still joked about the time he had suggested taking over its command, only to meet the lieutenant's firm refusal that it was contrary to regulations.[3]

Stark was at his best in the broader phases of strategic planning; his "Memorandum on National Policy" of November 12, 1940 became a landmark in the determination of the nation's war role.[4] His record as an over-all administrator, however, left much to be desired. Time and again he became swamped in details. Secretary Edison recalled saying to him, using the nickname that had clung to him since Annapolis days, "For God's sake, Betty, forget that damned sewer down at Dahlgren—Ben Moreell will attend to that, and you have more important things to think about." [5] Forrestal later voiced a similar view in one of the major points of his 1944 review of the Pearl Harbor blame: "4. Submersion of CNO in details of material to the extent that he became insensitive to the significance of events." [6]

Forrestal had fewer direct contacts with Stark than with some of the bureau chiefs. One of these with whom he worked most closely was Samuel M. Robinson, just appointed first chief of the new Bureau of Ships. He had been Chief of Engineering and had presided ably over its nine-month preparation for its merger with Construction and Repair to form the Bureau of Ships. Wise, shrewd, and technically competent, Robinson possessed qualities which would lead Forrestal to select him early in 1942 as first head of his over-all procurement agency. Later that year, when Robinson's successor proved unable to hold in check the disruptive forces and ambitions within BuShips and it was drifting into ineffectiveness, Forrestal was largely responsible for the appointments of Edward L. Cochrane and Earle W. Mills as chief and assistant chief. These two young planners in the bureau had requested assignment elsewhere, dismayed at the situation. Cochrane, a naval constructor with brilliant imagination and administrative skill, was, among other things, the designer of the Destroyer Escort (DE) and the Landing Ship Tank (LST); he later headed the procurement office. Mills, a one-time destroyer commander and later an engineering specialist, was brought into close and pleasant contact with Forrestal through handling contracts for the bureau; he was to succeed Cochrane as chief.

Ben Moreell, Chief of Yards and Docks, became another close Forrestal associate. In 1937, Roosevelt had overridden the bureau recommendations for chief and selected Moreell, a University of Utah graduate, whom he had happened to run across in the Azores during World War I. Moreell used methods as successful as they were unconventional in meeting the unprecedented demand for new facilities both stateside and later in the newly won Pacific regions. He considered time a much more vital wartime factor than cost, and without too much regard for red tape, he achieved virtual miracles. For the facilities at home, the bureau could utilize private contractors, but for the Pacific bases he originated the unique Construction Battalions—the "Seabees"—which developed an unusual degree of capacity and morale.[7]

William R. Furlong was Chief of Ordnance, and was followed by William H. P. Blandy early in 1941. Blandy worked well with Forrestal and did an excellent job as bureau chief. When, later in the war, he returned to sea in the best tradition of the "Gun Club," Forrestal had a hand in the choice of his able successor, George F. Hussey, Jr. John H. Towers, the Navy's senior aviator, was Chief of Aeronautics in 1940. When he left, he was followed in rapid succession by a number of other prominent aviators. Altogether, Forrestal's contacts with those material bureaus were close, and he developed satisfactory working relations with their chiefs. He had relatively little contact with Medicine and Surgery or, at the outset, with Navigation (Naval Personnel).[8]

With the Bureau of Supplies and Accounts, however, he encountered stubborn obstructionism. Ray Spear, its chief in 1940, and even more his successor, William Brent Young, proved to be blind and hostile to Forrestal's efforts to reorganize the supply system. Spear insisted on business as usual, and in late 1941 was still maintaining that the bureau had too many clerks and the Supply Corps too many officers. Those Paymasters General were in sharp contrast to Samuel H. McGowan, an ebullient South Carolinian who had much to do with Supplies and Accounts' splendid World War I record. Had a man of his caliber headed the bureau in this war, it probably would have moved into an important procurement opening. The Judge Advocate General, Walter B. Woodson, was likewise negative toward the Forrestal reforms.

Such admirals, along with those in Naval Operations, would represent the largest proportional increase in the rapid Navy Department personnel expansion during Forrestal's seven years. In mid-1940, there were only 30; in mid-1944, when he became Secretary, with the war in full swing, there would be 80; and, in mid-1947, when he left the Department, with relatively few billets afloat and with the creation of new positions in Naval Operations and the bureaus, there would be 91—more than a third of all the admirals in the Navy. They had not shared in the postwar diminution which all the other categories experienced in the Department:

	Total	Civilian	Officer	Enlisted
September 1940	4,786	3,787	722	277
June 1944	46,109	18,839	10,913	16,357
June 1947	20,679	13,612	3,515	3,552

Source: Navy Department Files.

Since the duties of the new post of Under Secretary had not yet been defined, it was largely by accident that Forrestal became involved in the material side of the Navy. As Knox later explained to a House Appropriations Committee:

Here we were confronted with a situation in which you gentlemen were pouring into my lap billions of dollars, and I personally was responsible for their expenditure; and the reason that Jim Forrestal is holding the position that he is today is that I recognized in him a shrewd, competent businessman who would aid me in discharging that responsibility . . . the first thing I said when I found this job confronting me was, "Jim, this is yours; it is too big a job for a man to undertake in my position with all the other responsibilities I have." So that job was given over to the man who has handled it. . . . with superb satisfaction and to my great gratification. I do not know any man in the picture who has done a better job than Jim Forrestal—a job which has to do with this procurement program, which involved before the war an annual expenditure of a couple of millions, or whatever it was, and which has grown to 20 billions. You have to have a different machinery to handle such a job.[9]

The day after Forrestal was sworn in, he was assigned contracts, tax and legal matters, and liaison with other government agencies except the Army, Budget Bureau, and labor agencies.[10] There was little to indicate that his office was to develop as the material coordinating agency. It was an evolutionary process. Signing contracts opened his eyes to the need of reforming legal procedures; the lack of industrial plants to fulfill the contracts involved him with the national industrial mobilization agencies; and the necessity to avoid competition for scarce supplies led to his close working relations with his opposite number in the Army, Under Secretary Robert Patterson.

His first major problem lay in the flood of contracts resulting from the newly authorized ship, aircraft, and base construction programs.[11] To compound the confusion, the money would not be appropriated before September,[12] and the Navy had to resort in many cases to a temporary device called a letter of intent. Only morally binding, it served to get construction started before a formal contract could be completed.

Fortunately, Forrestal happened to have just the sort of knowledge and many of the particular attributes demanded by this assignment. His understanding of business organization and practices and his wide acquaintance with industrial leaders, gained in his investment banking, were of special value. His knowledge was that of a "generalist," a favorite term of his, rather than that of a specialist in industrial mobilization. Forrestal knew the broad principles and how and from whom to obtain specialized information. His combination of wide intellectual curiosity with an intensely practical realization of "the possible" in any given situation was of immeasurable help to him. His inquiring mind led him on many occasions to anticipate problems before they were noticed by others. He was, moreover, willing to take the initiative in working out solutions and had the courage to act. He had, too, that awareness, invaluable in an administrator, of proper timing in taking action.

Each morning, messenger boys pushed carts stacked high with contracts and letters of intent into his office for his signature. But the usual request "Sign here, Mr. Secretary" was not long met by

Forrestal, who wanted to know what he was signing and why. Shortly after taking office, he was confronted with a contract leasing the yacht of an acquaintance of his for what seemed an exorbitant sum. Learning that all contracts were prepared in the Judge Advocate General's office, he asked Rear Admiral Woodson, to confer with him. The "JAG" arrived, immaculate in summer white uniform, with pince-nez glasses hanging from a black ribbon. Forrestal asked, "What is your opinion of this contract, Admiral?" Woodson deliberately polished his glasses and carefully read the contract. "This is a perfectly legal document, Mr. Secretary." Forrestal replied, "I assume that it is legal, but does it represent a good business deal for the Navy?" "That is something about which I have no knowledge," responded Woodson. Forrestal inquired how contracts were prepared and who did determine whether the Navy was getting its money's worth. The admiral hemmed and hawed—apparently they were drafted in various ways after calling for bids. In the main, they consisted of standard forms which could be filled in by clerks in the various bureaus. As Judge Advocate General, his only concern was their legality and not their financial soundness.[13]

Forrestal found that some contracts for ships, facilities, and supplies were sent him to sign, while many others were signed by the bureau chiefs. Some contracts contained a clause authorizing a bureau chief to amend as circumstances might require—thus, a one-ship contract might be expanded to build fifty ships. Neither did Forrestal like the "letter of intent" though recognizing it as a useful temporary measure. By the early spring of 1941, there were some four billion dollars' worth of these "letters" outstanding.

All this seemed a most unsatisfactory way of doing business; especially his own part as Under Secretary often seemed meaningless. At this point, he wrote to several of his legal friends for suggestions for an expert to make a survey of the contract situation. One name came back on every list—H. Struve Hensel, member of a leading New York law firm. Some time before, when faced with a bottleneck in getting tax amortization certificates approved, Forrestal had persuaded Hensel to undertake a study of that matter—a task that he completed quickly. Now Forrestal asked him to examine this other legal problem.

Hensel found that Navy purchasing, in the sense of determining the particular items to be procured, was decentralized among the technical bureaus; and such overlapping as occurred was not serious. The preparing and signing of contracts, on the other hand, was partly centralized and partly decentralized for reasons that seemed largely traditional. The Bureau of Supplies and Accounts, for example, theoretically prepared and signed all Navy contracts, but there were major exceptions, which actually in dollar value were generally more important than those which S&A did draw up. Contracts for guns, heavy armor, and projectiles were not only prepared but also signed by Ordnance. Likewise, contracts for Shore Establishment construction were prepared and signed by Yards and Docks. But contracts for complete ships were prepared by the Bureau of Ships and signed by the Under Secretary. Aeronautics had the least satisfactory arrangement as it prepared only the technical portions of its contracts; then, the requisitions were sent to Supplies and Accounts, which drafted the contracts. Each subsequent amendment was handled in the same way. This cumbersome system added nothing to the quality of the contracts.

The extent to which standard form contracts were used was another of Hensel's major criticisms. Full of outworn legal phrases, they often required procedures much too slow for a war mobilization. Contracts were generally awarded, moreover, on the competitive bid system, which depended upon having a substantial number of bidders. But contractors naturally hesitated to submit a firm bid for bases in Alaska or the Pacific islands, for instance, without including exorbitant amounts to cover possible uncertainties. Furthermore, in the matter of scientific equipment, many items were so new that a contractor had no basis for determining their probable cost. A "negotiated contract" tailored to meet the needs of each situation seemed the answer; and soon the majority of contracts took this form with across-the-table negotiations replacing the competitive bidding.

This was another situation calling for legal skill. The Judge Advocate General did not see contracts for approval until they were in their final form. Hensel argued that an attorney could not possibly make intelligent comments on a contract, which he had had no part in negotiating.[14] He drew a distinction between the two parts of the purchasing process—the determination of technical specifications, including the time of delivery and other such details, and the preparation of the contract itself. He considered that specialists were needed for both: the technical bureaus with their engineers, ordnance experts, and scientists and, also, lawyers specially skilled in commercial and industrial legal practices. He concluded that bad as the contract procedures were, part of the difficulty lay in the lack of lawyers with that training.

Consequently, he recommended that a new legal unit be established in Forrestal's office. He specified that it should be headed by a civilian lawyer with extensive commercial experience and that associate counsel with similar background should be placed in each bureau.[15]

This proposal of a competing civilian organization that would withdraw work from the Judge Advocate General's office struck at a very sensitive nerve, indicating as it did that that office was not doing the kind of job the Navy needed at this juncture. The JAG's office already employed some civilian lawyers but a Congressional ceiling of $5,000 a year on their pay made it difficult to obtain and keep good ones. Consequently, some promising regular Naval officers were sent each year to law school and, thereafter, were rotated between regular line billets afloat and legal duties ashore. While these officers were competent to handle courts-martial, they did not have commercial or industrial experience.

Admiral Woodson, the Judge Advocate General, charged that the proposal "was from an organizational standpoint fundamentally unsound . . . contrary to statute . . . would not be conducive to efficiency and expedition of the Department's legal work" and that "the present organization is running smoothly." He did not agree that a new office was necessary, and insisted that Congressional approval was required to establish it.[16] Hensel maintained that a statute was not essential,[17] but Forrestal decided to request a provision in the pending deficiency appropriation bill for fifteen additional employees for the Department at salaries in excess of $5,000 a year. Considerable opposition to the request developed in the House Naval Affairs Committee. Navy Department liaison with that committee was in the hands of the hostile JAG's office. When Forrestal appeared before the committee, Carl Vinson the chairman, wanted to know just why additional lawyers were needed, whether they would not duplicate the work already done by the

JAG, and whether he could not get lawyers from the Naval Reserve.[18] When another committee member, a former regular naval officer, pointed out that the JAG had "a good many high grade lawyers," Forrestal was careful to avoid saying that they lacked the ability to do the job and instead emphasized the importance of working experience. "I could read parliamentary law but I know I would not do very much in a debate on the floor of the House of Representatives because I have not had the background of daily contact." [19] Vinson was pleased at this diplomatic remark, but the committee reported out the bill for only one special attorney, instead of fifteen, in the Under Secretary's office, and in that form it was passed on June 25, 1941.[20] The project also ran into jeopardy at the hands of President Roosevelt, who was, with difficulty, persuaded not to cancel it because of its intrusion on the JAG's functions.[21]

Forrestal selected Hensel as that sole attorney on a temporary per diem basis. Later in the summer, he made him head of the new Procurement Legal Division, which he established as part of his office. He managed to obtain a staff of attorneys for Hensel for assignment to the bureaus because he had the power to appoint "special assistants" on the temporary per diem status, with its flexible salary range.

Hensel's quick and penetrating mind made him one of Forrestal's most valued lieutenants. Indefatigable and aggressive, he was ever ready to fight for his principles. He moved on from the Procurement Division to become General Counsel of the Navy for much of the war; and in 1945–46 was Assistant Secretary. His later government service was not continuous, as he returned more than once to his lucrative New York law practice. He did not feel that he could afford to stay in Washington constantly except in wartime. His last service there was in 1954 as General Counsel and Assistant Secretary in the Department of Defense.

The Procurement Legal Division was of major importance. Through it, technical bureaus now had to submit to the Under Secretary their requests to negotiate any contracts. This put the division on notice that a contract was in the making while it was still in its formative stage. Now with men directly responsible to the Under Secretary placed in each bureau, one of the Secretarial hierarchy had for the first time succeeded in having his agents at the working level, and thus was able to exercise his authority more intelligently.

Forrestal soon found that his assignment to supervise contracts was leading into other questions in industrial mobilization. One chronic problem concerned how far the Navy should utilize its own industrial Shore Establishment instead of turning to private industry. Whereas private plants were used exclusively for aircraft, shipbuilding and ordnance were divided between the two (see Appendix H). Forrestal had plenty of trouble on occasion in holding private plants to contract specifications and production schedules. Nor were the Navy's own plants less a headache.

The Navy in fact probably had more trouble with torpedoes than with any other major item. Submarines—the only major element of the Fleet in condition for immediate action after Pearl Harbor—suddenly, out in the Pacific, found many of their torpedoes faulty. One submarine crew after another, getting into position at great risk for telling blows against Japanese warships or merchantmen, saw their torpedoes either miss the mark or fail to explode. One irate skipper summed up the bitter reaction: "It's a helluva thing to go all the way to the China Sea to find your damned torpedoes won't work." [22]

The fault lay partly with the Bureau of Ordnance, itself, but more particularly with its Naval Torpedo Station at Newport. "There was no direct line between the Station and the Fleet, and only tenuous liaison was maintained by line officers, skilled in torpedo engineering . . . the ultimate consumer was allowed no say in the matter." [23] Yet even those specialists who rotated between sea duty and this highly desirable shore billet were apparently unaware of the inadequacy of their output. A particular complication was the extreme secrecy maintained by the bureau over its magnetic-influence exploder; so that most of those out in submarines were ignorant of its functioning. Prewar economy was a further cause of trouble; instead of using live warheads that would actually explode in the trials, the aim was to recover the torpedoes to use again. It was assumed that if they passed under the target, they would accomplish their purpose. "It is humiliating to think," writes Morison, "that poor 'have-not' Japan liberally expended live torpedoes and hulls in realistic tests, which 'rich' America could not afford." [24]

Finally, there was a very sour combination of labor unionism and local politics among the civilian workers at the Station. For more than ten years, they blocked the bureau's efforts to reopen the World War I torpedo station at Alexandria, near Washington. So far as politics went, the Newport situation was "one of the worst, in more ways than one." [25]

Vice Admiral Charles A. Lockwood, commander of submarines in the Pacific Fleet hastened to Washington to demand "If the Bureau of Ordnance can't provide us with torpedoes that will hit and explode, or with a gun larger than a peashooter, then for God's sake let the Bureau of Ships design a boat hook with which we can rip the plates off the target's sides!" [26]

Eventually, the torpedoes began to improve, and Lockwood was warm in his praise of Forrestal's efforts. In addition to reopening the Alexandria factory finally, the Navy contracted with the American Can Company to build and operate, as an agent, a large torpedo plant at Forest Park, Illinois, and later to convert another plant being built at St. Louis. Similar arrangements were made with Westinghouse and with Pontiac Motor-International Harvester.[27] These private plants, with their up-to-date machinery and industrial "know-how," produced better results than the old Torpedo Station at Newport, where the employees were less in touch with the latest methods. Because of that experience, Newport was closed down after the war.

Before the end of 1940, Forrestal found the procurement program in a very precarious position because of the lack of adequate government controls over the nation's economy. Civilians were buying more because defense contracts meant more jobs and higher wages. Moreover, both the Army and the Navy wanted more guns, more planes, more barracks, and more training stations. This produced inflationary pressures which had to be controlled if the nation's defense program was to be carried through. Forrestal, to his amazement, found that the government was unprepared to provide these controls so necessary for a quick industrial mobilization. This experience made such a lasting impression on him that he would make industrial mobilization planning a major part of his postwar reorganization plan.

The Navy's whole experience with defense planning shows how

a past war influences the next one. After World War I, Admiral Sims had been very critical in his testimony before Congressional committees of the lack of operational war plans. As a result, the professional naval leaders centered their attention on Fleet plans. Actually they were quite successful in forecasting what a war with Japan would be like. They foretold the Japanese invasion of the Philippines even to the beach where troops would land. They planned the retreat to Bataan and Corregidor where the Army would hold out until the Fleet arrived. What those naval strategists did not foresee was Pearl Harbor.

But industrial mobilization planning was another matter, for in this, the Navy had had far less experience than the Army. In World War I, the Army had to equip land forces that numbered millions of men, while the Navy's role had not given it a similar rehearsal. When Congress, after the war, reviewed procurement problems, it was natural that the Army received all the attention. The National Defense Act of 1920, consequently, made the War Department, and its Assistant Secretary in particular, responsible for industrial mobilization planning in the future.[28]

As a consequence of that Act, the Assistant Secretary of War had set up a planning division. In 1922 an attempt was made to draw the Navy into this sphere by the creation of the Army and Navy Munitions Board,[29] consisting of the two Assistant Secretaries, to coordinate plans for acquiring munitions and supplies. It went for years between the wars without even a meeting. Eventually, the Navy assigned a few officers to the Board's planning staff, but otherwise showed scant interest. The War Department's planning division, however, drew three successive Industrial Mobilization Plans in 1931, 1936, and 1939; the last was the most realistic, as it made provision for a prewar defense period that might require mobilization. This version stated: "When war becomes imminent, and without waiting for serious economic problems to develop, the coordination and utilization of our national resources should be initiated immediately." [30]

Unfortunately that last plan was not ready in 1938, at the time of the Munich crisis, when Roosevelt asked what plans were available. He was shown the 1936 version, which did not suit him because it provided for no action before a declaration of war. Not knowing that that provision was being included in the plan still in preparation, he directed his legal staff to search for legislation already on the statute books, which might be the basis of an industrial mobilization agency. They came up with a 1916 statute authorizing the President to appoint a Council of National Defense, which was simply six cabinet members, and a seven-member Advisory Commission. By the time the 1939 plan was ready for presentation, Europe was at war. Roosevelt decided then that all such plans would be impracticable, as well as politically dangerous, when strong national currents were running in favor of neutrality and keeping out of war at all costs.[31] As a result, that carefully made 1939 plan was never used and a series of makeshift substitutes were set up one after another.

The first of these was for a Council of National Defense—that relic from 1916. It appealed especially to Roosevelt because as a statute already on the books it did not require Congressional approval; its significance could be played down; and its accompanying Advisory Commission gave an opportunity for various contending pressure groups in the country to be represented.[32] But as it turned out, the Council itself never met and the Advisory Commission, which Roosevelt appointed three weeks before Forrestal came to Washington, was the real operating body. Each of its seven members had a vague area in which to "advise." Those most important for the Navy were William L. Knudsen for industrial production; Sidney Hillman, labor; and Leon Henderson, price stabilization (see Appendix F). There were no rules of operation, no definition of relationship to the armed services, and no agreement as to whether it might act on its own. Though Roosevelt talked about its advisory function, he delegated operating duties to it. A major omission was a chairman with power. When Knudsen asked "Who's boss?", Roosevelt announced "I am." [33] Forrestal had to operate with this group on a host of matters.

Previous to this Presidential creation, an attempt to set up a civilian "War Resources Board" to advise on military industrial planning came from within the service departments. Early in August 1939, having received Roosevelt's authorization, Charles Edison, Acting Secretary of the Navy, and Louis Johnson, Assistant Secretary of War, worked out an impressive list for membership on such a board (see Appendix F). This was the same Johnson, who would succeed Forrestal as Secretary of Defense and whose bungling weakened the armed forces on the eve of the Korean conflict. He read that list to Roosevelt, who approved all the names but that of Bernard Baruch, probably the most experienced from his service as head of industrial mobilization in World War I.[34] The Board went to work at once, but New Deal opposition soon expressed itself against a group two-thirds business executives and mainly Republican.

It quickly ended a complete fiasco. Roosevelt met with them once and, in an obviously critical frame of mind, questioned their status, disapproved two memoranda, and requested one on their functions.[35] In October he called Edison to the White House and told him to have the Board draw up some kind of report and then send the members home. Edison protested but Roosevelt was adamant, murmuring some excuse about politics and finding a place for Sidney Hillman, his favored adviser on labor matters.[36] The Board's reports, never made public, strongly favored that 1939 War Department plan, just out that month, and recognized the possibility of a "temporary abandonment of some peacetime objectives," thus confirming New Deal apprehensions.[37]

How Roosevelt came to approve the appointment of such a group in the first place is an unanswered question. Congress was again debating the Neutrality Act. The isolationists were charging the President intended to lead the country into war while he was promising that no American boy would be sent to die in foreign fields. The public discussion of industrial mobilization seemed to support the isolationists' contention. Even the name War Resources Board was bad politically. Moreover, a book entitled *Adjusting Your Business to War*, for which Assistant Secretary Johnson had written the preface, was being given wide publicity. With isolationists, labor leaders, and New Dealers all up in arms, the reasons for the Board's abrupt dismissal were politically understandable.

The first problem that brought Forrestal into contact with the Advisory Commission was the expansion of plant facilities. He found these particularly lacking in the production of the all-essential armor plate for vessels; there were only four privately owned plants in the entire country with a total output far below Navy needs. With the President's announced goal of 50,000 planes a year, the aviation industry was in even worse straits. The whole industry —and it was government policy to purchase all aircraft—was producing only about 1,200 planes a year. The building of new facilities when necessary had been authorized in the Naval Expansion ("Third Vinson") Act of June 11, 1940; but there was a catch in this. The amount of money appropriated was so small that only a beginning could be made. Through Harry Hopkins's aid, the Reconstruction Finance Corporation was induced to establish a subsidiary agency, the Defense Plant Corporation, to build plants and lease them to private operators with war contracts.[38]

The Advisory Commission, coming on the scene, thought that vast amounts of additional funds could be raised for this purpose if the period permitted for amortizing the cost of such new facilities under income tax statutes was reduced from twenty to five years.[39] A bill for this had already been introduced in Congress, but the commission opposed it as not fully protecting the government's interests.

It advocated, and Congress adopted in October, a complicated plan which required the manufacturer who wanted to take advantage of the five-year provision to obtain three types of certificates to be issued by the War or Navy Secretary and approved by the commission. To make the tangle of red tape worse, the commission failed to agree on any standard for its approval, and so it had passed only ten Navy certificates by the end of 1940. Thus, even in a crisis, it was unable to decide how its own plan was to operate. In the long run, over the whole war period, about $1.5 billion of new construction was brought about by this method, but it was of little help in 1940–41.

Presumably, Roosevelt planned to establish some controls on the awarding of defense contracts, but whether he intended the commission to examine contracts merely to obtain information upon which to draft broad policies or to approve each individual contract was never made clear. Roosevelt informed the armed services that they must obtain Knudsen's approval on all important contracts; soon afterward, he named Donald Nelson, vice-president of Sears, Roebuck Company, as Coordinator of National Defense Purchases and gave him similar power regarding contracts. It was never decided where his authority began and the commission's ended.[40] Knudsen's fellow commissioners wanted their say too, about how he and Nelson exercised their authority. It was eventually decided that both of them must "clear" all military contracts with the commission, but that Knudsen should act only with the unanimous approval of the commission. Even then, the commissioners wasted much time in fruitless arguments about what should be required; some were concerned primarily with "good business deals," others with labor's rights or with maintaining social gains. By the end of 1940, despite the confusion, contracts totaling billions of dollars had been signed; but very little progress had been made in filling them. Industrial facilities in certain key industries were still far from sufficient, and funds for government-financed expansion were not available in the amounts required. The commission's pet project had not brought the flow of private capital anticipated, because of the administrative difficulties.

As Donald Nelson later said of the commission, it "began to stagger in the late summer and early autumn of 1940. In November it was punch-drunk." [41] Stimson, Knox, Patterson, and Forrestal, on December 17, agreeing that "seven advisers cannot make decisions," went in a body to the President to urge that Knudsen be made the one responsible director of war production. All they could get was another inadequate, short-lived agency, the Office of Production Management (OPM), again with no single head. It replaced the Advisory Commission, January 7, 1941, and lasted only a year. It had two "co-pilots," Knudsen and Hillman, but Roosevelt kept the over-all authority. The War and Navy Secretaries completed the board. Having won a third term, Roosevelt was at last willing to pay some attention to the stagnant industrial mobilization, but he still refused to put in a single director, declaring "you cannot, under the Constitution, set up a second President." [42] Originally, Churchill had also opposed a "czar" for British production.

Within eight months, OPM was also encountering heavy going and increasing public criticism. A new competitive factor—the Lend-Lease program—was making its claims felt on American production. The immediate problem was the balancing of the needs of the British and Russians against those of the nation's own forces. On August 28, Roosevelt created an additional agency, the Supply, Priorities, and Allocations Board, to fix the amount of materials to be allocated to military needs, Lend-Lease, economic warfare, and the civilian economy (see Appendix F). Both the Army and the Navy were, in general, opposed to releasing supplies to foreign governments when they were needed for the nation's own defense programs. Knox, in particular, fought hard against the granting to Russia, for purposes she refused to specify, of products that were critically short for Navy needs, such as machine tools for shipbuilding and a vast amount of aluminum for aircraft. The Board approved them nevertheless, since the White House felt the Soviet Union should be encouraged in its resistance to the invading Germans.

The failure of the Office of Production Management did not come from lack of effort by its members; Knudsen, for instance, worked himself almost to a physical breaking point. Instead, it failed because the Office was not properly organized to direct a full industrial mobilization and the nation was not yet ready to accept the restrictions and discomforts that would come with it. As one official warned, "1941 will go down in history as the year we almost lost the war before we got into it." [43] The nation was neither in the war nor out of it. Roosevelt, master at gauging the political climate, had originally thought it possible to impose the defense program upon the civilian economy without disturbing it to any appreciable extent. Most of the initial government expenditures had gone into plant expansion, tool manufacturing, and "soft" military equipment, which did not require any radical changes in civilian economy. Defense spending, however, slowly began to increase the already substantial demand for automobiles and various household appliances.

Forrestal, disturbed by this general ineffectiveness, was most concerned, of course, with its relationship to the Navy's needs. He canvassed each bureau chief for his opinion on the proper role of an agency like OPM. The replies varied. Robinson, then in BuShips, thought that such a civilian agency should only intervene in those matters that no single government department could handle; it ought to consider defense housing, civilian supplies, allocation of new facilities, and priorities through a board that included a Navy representative. Furlong of Ordnance wanted OPM to assist in obtaining raw materials, machine tools, and new industrial facilities, and to coordinate procurement where more than one agency purchased the same material. Towers, whose Aeronautics program was the most handicapped by the facilities shortage, felt that it was absolutely essential to coordinate Army Air Force and Navy Air needs with the capacity of the aviation industry. This would mean allocation of orders through some over-all coordinating agency. Only Spear, of Supplies and Accounts, argued that "any authority superimposed over the purchasing authority now vested by law in the Secretary of the Navy will impede rather than speed up our national defense effort"; and that priorities should be left to a Navy priorities board.[44]

Forrestal's experience in this situation led him years later to urge that industrial mobilization planning be made a continuous function of a high level organization in the Executive Office of the President. Then, if a crisis came again, the country would be spared this indecision and lack of direction. Furthermore, he realized that the Navy itself could not mobilize the material resources it needed without the help of some sort of over-all industrial agency, to which it should be able to state exactly what it needed, in what amounts, and when. This called for knowledge of the whole industrial process along with statistical skill of a high order. But he found little support or appreciation of those needs in the Navy itself.

In regard to Forrestal's personal relationship and work in this national end of industrial mobilization, Herbert Emmerich, secretary to OPM, recalled: "I always had the feeling that he was influential in the OPM days, but it is also my recollection that he was apt to be silent at meetings." [45] His name is rarely to be found in the stenographic minutes. When conflict of interest took place between various agencies, he appears to have followed his characteristic habit at meetings of being primarily an observer.[46] Obviously, his negotiating was, as usual, done privately and informally, believing as he did that heat aroused by controversy made compromise settlements more difficult. His "opposite number" and close friend, Under Secretary of War Patterson was more impetuous and very active in committee debates. Undoubtedly, they shared a strong mutual dissatisfaction with the state of mobilization, though one was outspoken and the other reticent. Serious as the situation might be, they were not above ribbing each other when a good occasion offered itself. One day at Patterson's office, Forrestal and his staff found him looking out intently on Constitution Avenue. Swinging around, he exclaimed "Look at those Coca Cola trucks out there. That's what I mean—thousands of tons of sugar going to the civilians when it should be used in the war effort." Forrestal's aide whispered in his ear, and Forrestal said with a grin "Mr. Secretary, I'm sorry to disappoint you, but I'm informed that those trucks are on their way to the Naval Air Station from which the Coca Cola is to be sent by air to our forces in the Pacific." Patterson scowled fiercely for a minute, and then said, "Clausewitz, you always have the answer." [47]

The two were brought into even closer relationship when they replaced the Assistant Secretaries as the representatives on the Army and Navy Munitions Board in June 1941. Forrestal saw at once that the Board was accomplishing little. Diminishing machine tool production was constituting a specially dangerous threat to the whole industrial program—the dies, presses, and machines to make machines being the first step in mass production.

In this potentially most serious of shortages, Forrestal quickly turned to a New York investment banker, Ferdinand Eberstadt, because during the thirties he had handled, along with his banking activities, the successful reorganization of several machine tool companies. The two had known each other since their undergraduate days at Princeton, where Eberstadt and Forrestal had both served as editor of the college newspaper. Their friendship had continued, when they found themselves together in Dillon, Read after World War I. Later Eberstadt established his own investment banking firm, while Forrestal stayed on to become president of Dillon, Read. Of all the many men whom Forrestal would bring into the procurement picture at Washington, Eberstadt and Hensel would rank as two of the most valuable. Patterson, too, shared Forrestal's confidence in this appointment. Able, aggressive, intelligent, and hard-working, Eberstadt, like Forrestal himself, had a broad understanding of organization and operations of American industry as a whole. Much of that knowledge came from his banking experience, but his own abilities made him an excellent judge of men and their capacities.

Within two weeks, Eberstadt formulated two steps preventing a bottleneck that would have had bad consequences. The companies with munition contracts had not bothered to order their machine tools ahead, expecting that military priorities would get them without delays. To remedy this cause of the diminishing production of such tools, Eberstadt recommended that those contractors who failed to order in advance of needs be refused special last-minute preference. Next, he urged the military departments to place orders themselves immediately for common types of machine tools; and then, later assign them as needed to contractors. Thus, the tool industry was assured of being kept operating at a high level.

No sooner had Eberstadt solved that machine tool block than Forrestal and Patterson recruited him to help make a more effective organ of the Army and Navy Munitions Board. Eberstadt, as a result of his survey, found that the Board was not filling the role for which it was intended, either within the armed services or in industrial mobilization generally. He thought it a sad commentary "that a group which had given years of careful thought and study to the many intricate questions of industrial mobilization . . . should not be called upon for more substantial contributions." [48] After the war, Donald Nelson recorded the same conclusion. Eberstadt thought that the Board ought to estimate Army and Navy requirements and convert them into terms of raw materials and productive equipment as well as assist civilian agencies to meet these requirements. He visualized the Board as standing between the military services and the civilian agencies and aiding the work of both. The absence of working relations at the operating levels between those who knew more than anyone else what was needed by the services and those who knew the productive capacity of industry was in his view a definite factor in the slow mobilization. Admittedly, neither side knew as much as they needed to know, but closer liaison at the operating level and more vigorous leadership at the top might help.

His recommendations were for a reorganization of the Board, a full-time civilian chairman, and much closer liaison with the Office of Production Management and other war agencies down through the operating levels. Submitting his report ten days before Pearl Harbor, he was at once asked to take the chairmanship of the Board by Forrestal and Patterson. He declined; but the Japanese attack changed his mind about entering government service, and he accepted.

In his day-to-day contacts, Forrestal saw more clearly that centralized direction of every stage of the material program was essential if the Navy were to obtain what it needed. Some bureau chiefs refused to admit that their material programs needed coordination, but to Forrestal this was of greater concern than the internal operation of the bureaus. He found that no existing unit was "ready, willing, and able" to undertake the task of coordination in this field.

There was no question about the willingness of the two obvious candidates, the Office of the Chief of Naval Operations and the Bureau of Supplies and Accounts, but plenty of questions about their readiness and ability. Naval Operations' own record was against it, but it had strong support as the proper agency for the purpose. Material planning was already one of its functions, assigned it after World War I, and given division standing. Eventually, it had been reduced to a mere section—along with many odds and ends—in the Fleet Maintenance Division, and it was not returned to division status until just before Pearl Harbor. According to its directive at that time, it was to be the liaison agency between the Navy and outside civilian procurement bodies as well as the coordinator of the Department's material programs. Even then, its staff numbered only 150, whereas its counterpart in the War Department had 1,250. Furthermore, only one officer was assigned to the expanding of production facilities, while 24 were added to the Board of Economic Warfare—apparently its title seemed to imply fighting.[49] Operations was a dismal failure as this coordinating body. It faced great difficulties, to be sure, particularly in the lack of personnel with industrial experience. Only junior grades were available for reserve officer commissions. Perhaps its biggest handicap was the fact that the CNO, Admiral Stark, and the officers closest to him did not appreciate the scope and vital importance of this field or the Navy's part in it.

Under any circumstances, it would not have been easy to dislodge so august a body. In addition to having been officially assigned material planning long before, it was also so designated in those prewar plans of the Army and Navy Munitions Board. They proposed that in wartime the CNO would represent the Navy as a whole on material matters. This may have come about because Naval Operations had furnished the officers of the Navy's portion of the working staff, and because most of them had taken the course at the Army's Industrial School. Other proponents were many of those who supported the "General Staff theory" that the authority of the CNO should be strengthened. As they considered material procurement merely a part of logistics, they thought it naturally belonged in Operations.

On the other hand, Supplies and Accounts (S&A) had its vocal supporters who pointed to its very successful record in World War I, when procurement activities were centralized in it. It was urged, too, that the bureaus anyway were better for the purpose than Naval Operations, manned as it was by line officers, for the bureaus offered both continuity and specialization in procurement matters. This group proposed centralization in S&A, with a degree of decentralization among the technical bureaus for special types of equipment. S&A had repeatedly challenged those provisions in the war plans that favored Naval Operations, jealously seeking to protect its own rights as the principal material bureau.

These claims for S&A might have succeeded had it not been for the bureau's "head in the sand" attitude during 1940–41, when Naval Operations was showing little interest in material activities. As late as April 1941, S&A's chief, Ray Spear, argued that the Navy's expansion "would require only increased orders from its normal source of supply," overlooking the fact that some of those sources might not be available.[50] The bureau was firmly committed to competitive bidding, although in wartime there would be few voluntary bidders in many areas of great urgency. Even despite criticism from other material bureaus, notably Aeronautics, it opposed any changes in contract procedures. When Spear was asked if he could use women in uniform, he emphatically stated his preference for civilian clerks and typists, ignoring their scarcity in wartime. When urged to train additional supply officers, he claimed there were already too many, and he planned to reduce the number under him. The bureau, moreover, was bitterly opposed to the introduction of civilian lawyers and was unimpressed with the need for civilian negotiators from the business world. Spear saw no need for any over-all industrial mobilization agencies at all—just leave the Army and the Navy supply agencies well alone and the industrial mobilization would be successful. Obviously his frankly voiced scorn of all efforts to hurry matters did not make for cordial relationships with those who feared war was close.

In the meantime, Forrestal had decided that, with the industrial machinery still crawling at a turtle's pace but without even its steady progress, the only answer was a new organization. This he planned to have in his own office, similar to the planning unit in Patterson's. In a sense it was probably many instances—small in themselves but, taken together, building up to a possibly disastrous situation—that caused him to overhaul and not just tinker with the coordinating machinery. The success of his Procurement Legal Division undoubtedly encouraged him. He was, moreover, under increasing pressure from OPM to supply accurate statistical information about the Navy's program. His questions at the bureau chiefs' meetings in the fall of 1941 indicated his vain attempts to obtain this information and his growing concern with the inadequacies of the material staff. When he asked whether one hundred thousand extra cots were needed for the shore bases or if there were enough on hand, one chief felt there were plenty, and another insisted a huge number were required instantly. It was not known whether Navy contractors were working five, six, or seven days a week. But, more alarming still, no one seemed to know even how to get such information quickly.

Forrestal pondered the pros and cons; it was such new territory for him that it took him a while to get the full picture, without which he never took action. Probably the deciding factor was the attitude of the Navy units entrusted with procurement. Neither Stark nor Spear seemed to appreciate the urgency of the situation, nor did their organizations offer the kind of working environment where specialized talent from private industry might have a free rein to operate effectively. Professional officers lacked the experience of such civilians in planning production in the broadest sense —compiling follow-up statistics, ferreting out scarce materials, and negotiating contracts realistically. Production planning was one of the areas, where a civilian Secretary could contribute directly to the efficient operation of the Navy.

In the meantime, as war loomed closer, Forrestal felt increasing urgency in the Navy's unreadiness; all in all, no control point existed in the Department for the growing number of production and procurement problems. It had no sound system of relating its material requirements with military and strategic needs. In peacetime, cost, expressed in dollars, was the important thing, not needs in terms of tons of raw material. And no one knew better than he that the strong line being taken in the Far East and the Atlantic by the

White House and State Department was accelerating a crisis. He was aware from Admiral Kimmel's memoranda to the Department that the fleet, based precariously at Pearl Harbor, was far from ready for war, and also that Admiral King's forces, in the Atlantic, had great deficiencies.

The public was constantly being given an overly optimistic view of both the military realities abroad and the progress of rearmament at home. The latter was hampered by more than the Washington muddle over industrial mobilization. There were strikes, demands for higher wages, and union reorganization on the one hand, and on the other, the hesitation of management to convert to war production and to undertake plant expansion, while Roosevelt still talked of "all measures short of war" and of "the defense program." Such were the difficulties of a partial mobilization in a democracy, with the people ready to accept strict measures of control over its industrial system only when war is actually a reality.

On the credit side of the ledger for the Navy—with in a way much the same problem as the nation's—was the fortunate fifteen months in which Knox and Forrestal took the measure of its weakness before the shooting started. They had an opportunity to build up their team of administrators, who were to provide real civilian leadership during the years ahead. Hensel was well established in the Procurement Legal Division. Eberstadt's study for the reorganization of the Army and Navy Munitions Board was completed. Detmar had begun his work as special assistant, and the group from finance and industry, who proved so invaluable to Forrestal, were being recruited. Such were the tangible credits of the months before the storm broke.

5

The Impact of Pearl Harbor

FORRESTAL SPENT the weekend of December 7, 1941 in Princeton, his old college town. Flying back Sunday morning, he landed shortly after noon at the Naval Air Station near the Washington Navy Yard, at just about the moment the news of the Japanese sneak attack was stunning the Navy Department. He heard it on his car radio as he was driven across the city to his office.

That morning he had doubtless already seen the headlines of the Sunday papers. "Navy is inferior to none, says Knox," his annual report picturing it on a full war footing.[1] Elsewhere in the papers, though, were hints of trouble: a heavy concentration of Japanese troops and shipping were said to be heading toward the Straits Settlements; Roosevelt was urging Emperor Hirohito not to move against Thailand, the strategic gateway to the Malay Peninsula and India; the Japanese press was being charged with "rattling the sword"; and in Washington a Japanese peace delegation was continuing negotiations. One paper, to be sure, carried a letter from a former Assistant Secretary of State, resident in Hawaii, arguing that talk of war with Japan was ridiculous.[2] Only the New York Times's military expert, Hanson W. Baldwin, warned that current negotiations "were perhaps a less important index to the seriousness of the Pacific situation than the actual military forces" being mobilized "in the theatre of the potential struggle."[3]

Incidentally, that same paper carried a feature story on Forrestal and his opposite number in the War Department, Robert P. Patterson. "No two men in the Administration are closer to ultimate responsibility for spending billions on billions of dollars, yet one of the few parallels that unite them is the fact that no pair of men appear to be less hurried, less worried, than themselves—in fact, they are the two most approachable men in the capital." They were called "longtime acquaintances, who were not phrasemakers but doers, and who were fortunate choices to head the material programs of their respective departments." Forrestal was called a man who "looks Navy and is Navy"; and though his broken nose might lead Hollywood to cast him in a tough role, he would never live up to it. His aversion to the limelight was stressed with that old story of his refusal to give facts about himself to *Who's Who in America*, because "the Under Secretary doesn't believe in that sort of thing." [4]

Secretary Knox had been in Washington all weekend. Saturday evening, while at dinner at his hotel, an officer messenger delivered thirteen decoded portions of an intercepted fourteen-part message to the Japanese delegates. Copies also went to the President's and Admiral Stark's naval aides.

Early Sunday morning, when Lieutenant Commander Alvin Kramer, the Naval Intelligence officer in charge of decoding, read the finally decoded fourteenth part, he became suspicious of its emphasis on time. It instructed the envoys to present their message to the Secretary of State exactly at one o'clock that afternoon. Copies were rushed to Stark's office, the White House, and the State Department, where Knox was just arriving for a ten o'clock meeting of the State-War-Navy Secretaries. [5]

Several opportunities to warn Pearl Harbor were missed that fatal day by the narrowest of margins, both in Hawaii and at Washington. At Stark's office, for example, just a few steps from Forrestal's, a group of intelligence officers figured out from a time chart on the wall that 1.00 P.M. in Washington, the hour emphasized by the Japanese, was 7:30 A.M. in Hawaii. Captain Wilkinson, the Director of Naval Intelligence, proposed that Admiral Kimmel be warned immediately at Pearl Harbor. The Navy's excellent communications could have delivered the message two hours before the attack, but service protocol intervened. Stark declined on the ground that the Army was responsible for the safety of Pearl, so Marshall should do the notifying. Unfortunately, the general was not located until 11:30, but even then there was some leeway before the attack. The Navy offered to transmit the warning, but the Army decided to do its own communicating. Its channels were clogged, so it used Western Union—the warning was delivered hours after the Japanese had struck.[6]

At the Japanese Embassy, meanwhile, where security reasons forbade the use of its regular typists, the only officer who could type at all was frantically struggling to pound out a clean copy of that just-decoded dispatch. With the Ambassador standing at his shoulder, he made so many mistakes that he had to keep recopying —contrary to plan, the bombs were already falling on Pearl Harbor, when the dispatch was delivered to Hull.[7]

Shortly after one, Knox was back at the Navy Department and talking in his outer office with Stark when a naval communications officer rushed in with the historic message from Pearl Harbor: "All ships and stations: We are under enemy attack. This is no drill." Knox burst out, "My God, this can't be true. This must mean the Philippines." Stark, picking up the message, replied, "No sir, this is Pearl." [8]

Unlike Knox, Stark, and certain other top officials, Forrestal's name was never mentioned in the post-mortems on the blame for that disaster—the duties of the Under Secretary did not include the larger aspects of foreign policy. He was not even on the distribution list for that decoded message. All he had known was that Navy Communications had broken the Japanese code. Morison, reviewing the Pearl Harbor responsibility twenty years later, wrote: "It was the setup at Washington and at Pearl, not individual stupidity, which confused what was going on. No one person knew the whole intelligence picture; no one person was responsible for the defense of Pearl Harbor. Too many people assumed that others were taking precautions that they failed to take." [9]

Forrestal's first concern, upon reaching his office, was the Panama Canal. Naval stations and ships around the world as well as naval installations at home had already been alerted. He summoned Stark and Assistant Secretary Gates, and was soon joined by Robert A. Lovett, Assistant Secretary of War for Air. They thoroughly canvassed the situation at the Canal. Air attack or sabotage might close it for months. Forrestal also queried Stark about West Coast naval bases that were vulnerable to sneak attack. Stark could offer little to reassure him. The bases were in no better defensive position than

Pearl Harbor; all depended upon the Army for defense against air attack. At Forrestal's insistence, they were ordered to look to their own defenses.

Details of the Pearl disaster were slow in arriving. Not until toward late afternoon when telephone communication was established with Admiral Claude C. Bloch, commandant of the Navy Yard there, was it even known whether the enemy had made landings. Knox went immediately to the White House with Bloch's preliminary estimate of casualties and damage; Forrestal stayed all night at the Department.[10]

The Navy had made war plans, naturally, but those for the Third Naval District were at the New York Headquarters in a safe with its lock set for Monday morning. Fortunately, the District War Plans Officer remembered their details so well that more than 90 percent of them were already in operation when the safe was opened.[11]

Though free from responsibility for the Pearl Harbor debacle, Forrestal had had plenty to do with that great progress made under the naval expansion acts of mid-1940. By the fourth quarter of 1941, 100 destroyers and a few larger ships had been commissioned in a total of some 1,300 vessels, which included small craft and auxiliaries. The rate of delivery of ordnance and aircraft was rapidly rising. Naval personnel on active duty had almost trebled to 350,000. Yet, from San Diego to Puget Sound, the Navy had only a handful of overage ships and a few modern planes, and even less in the Atlantic. Wherever Forrestal turned in the days after Pearl Harbor the phrase "too little and too late" was too appropriate.

Blame for this unpreparedness has frequently been laid at Stark's door, since he was, at least, most directly charged with the "readiness" of the Navy, but in retrospect, no small part would seem to have been misdirected. Congress, the President, and public opinion had their share in the failure; nor may earlier Chiefs of Naval Operations, including Stark's predecessor, Leahy, be held blameless. The hard truth was that with the funds available between the World Wars, the admirals had to choose among the many essential needs —and often their selection was unwise.

Deficiencies were marked in antisubmarine and antiaircraft defenses. Many of the larger ships lacked modern sound gear and had no real protection against submarines unless accompanied by destroyers. The Navy still had no program for small vessels for convoy duty.[12] There were not nearly enough aircraft carriers or planes to protect the Fleet from air attack. Not only was antiaircraft ordnance lacking but the quantity needed had been gravely underestimated. Even when the American submarines got into action, many of their torpedoes were faulty.[13] In its radar research, however, the Navy was fortunate; a Congressional Appropriations Committee had insisted upon granting funds for it, even when the Navy itself had been ready to ignore the need.[14]

The first year of fighting would have been far more crucial than it was—and 1942 was bad enough—had it not been for the strenuous eighteen months of preparation before Pearl Harbor. At the same time, this had been handicapped by political considerations with the national attitude divided between intervention and isolation.

In an episode in the fall of 1939 involving the President, Congress, and the Navy, the former told Stark, then CNO, that he wanted some seaplane bases built along the South Atlantic coast for the protection of coastwise shipping against submarine attack. Stark informed the bureau chiefs of this. Rear Admiral Ben Moreell, Chief of Yards and Docks, who would have the main task of building new bases, asked:

What are we going to use for money? All new naval shore construction must, under the law, be specifically authorized by act of Congress and specifically appropriated for. All of the construction funds which we now have available in the Department are allocated to specific projects and cannot be diverted to other projects without violating the law.

The other bureau chiefs stated that they had no funds to equip such stations. Moreell suggested that in the light of the "limited National emergency" declared by the President, the Secretary of the Navy would be justified in directing the bureau chiefs to proceed with the work, making the charges to a dummy account which would later be eliminated by a deficiency appropriation to be voted by the Congress provided, however, that the President would sign a memorandum authorizing the Navy Department to follow this procedure. Stark took that proposal to the White House. Returning within the hour, he told the bureau chiefs, "I have never seen the President so angry. He pounded the table and asked 'Who wants something on a piece of paper?'" Stark said he called it "just the general feeling." "Well, you go back and find out which one of those bureau chiefs wants something on a piece of paper and I will give him something on a piece of paper, but it will not be what he expects." Moreell suggested that if the Secretary wanted to accept personal responsibility for proceeding contrary to law, the bureau chiefs would have to accept his order. Stark replied that he himself was Acting Secretary, as both the Secretary and the Assistant Secretary were away. In that capacity, he thereupon gave orders to the bureau chiefs to proceed with the construction, an action which they appreciated as both courageous and generous. Subsequently, an appropriations bill covering these projects was strongly attacked in the House Appropriations Committee, but the measure was passed.[15]

The shock of Pearl Harbor initiated the Navy's fourth, and one of its most thoroughgoing, major reorganization. These had occurred at two pair of dates, a century apart—1815 and 1842, 1915 and now 1942. Forrestal would be affected closely by these 1942 changes, both in the command and the procurement fields, because of their effect on the delicate balance of civilian-military relations.

In the first of the command changes, eleven days after Pearl Harbor, the post of Commander-in-Chief of the United States Fleet was separated from the Pacific command and transferred from a distant flagship to the Navy Department Building in Washington.[16] Admiral Ernest J. King, commanding the Atlantic Fleet, was promoted to the new command, which was created primarily so that the Pacific and Atlantic operations could both be directed from a central position. The change would be completed three months later, March 12, 1942, with the merging of the post of Commander-in-Chief of the United States Fleet (now Cominch) with the senior post of Chief of Naval Operations (CNO). By this move, King, with the double-barreled title of "Cominch-CNO," supplanted Stark.[17]

The Executive Order combining those functions was drafted overnight by Admiral J. O. Richardson, member of the General Board and former Commander-in-Chief of the Fleet. In the description of the authority of the Chief of Naval Operations, King was "charged, under the direction of the Secretary of the Navy, with the preparation, readiness and logistic support of the operating forces . . . and the coordination *and direction* of effort to this end of the bureaus and offices of the Navy Department except such offices (other than bureaus) as the Secretary of the Navy might specifically exempt." [18] That phrase "and direction" was only penciled in at the last minute, but it gave King a degree of authority within the Department that had been lacking since 1915 when Secretary Daniels had whittled down the original specifications for the Chief of Naval Operations. It was still a much looser relationship than the Chief of Staff of the Army had gained a few days earlier in the War Department reorganization.[19] Another phrase of the Richardson order had even wider implications. As Chief of Naval Operations, King was to be "the principal naval adviser to the President on the conduct of the war, and the principal naval adviser and executive to the Secretary of the Navy on the conduct of the activities of the Naval Establishment." On the other hand, as the Commander-in-Chief's authority was spelled out, the Secretary of the Navy was pretty much left at one side, with the line of authority running directly from the Commander-in-Chief to the President. The Commander-in-Chief, according to the wording of the order, was "directly responsible, under the *general direction* of the Secretary of the Navy, to the President of the United States." That phrase "general direction" would prove to be very general. A similar provision had been in the text of the Army's reorganization; in sending his approval of this measure to Secretary Stimson, Roosevelt "directed, however, that part of the order be rephrased to make very clear that the President, as Commander-in-Chief, could exercise his command function in strategy, tactics and operations directly through the Chief of Staff." [20] Consequently, both King and Marshall would deal directly with the White House on operational matters.

This solution was very gratifying to all three parties concerned; but it left the Secretaries of War and Navy decidedly out of the strictly military running of the war.[21] Forrestal accepted this as proper in war,[22] but had, however, very definite ideas against it in peace.[23]

King rarely exercised his authority as CNO, delegating most of the functions, which were chiefly logistical, to Vice Admiral Frederick J. Horne, the Vice Chief of Naval Operations. The traditional seniority of the title CNO was its primary importance to King. On one occasion, noticing a letter headed "Office of the Vice Chief of Naval Operations," he issued a curt memorandum that no such office existed—there was only that of the Chief of Naval Operations.[24] As Commander-in-Chief, King also worked through a deputy—Vice Admiral Russell Willson and then Vice Admiral Richard S. Edwards as chief of staff; the latter ultimately became "Deputy Cominch-CNO." [25] King made it clear that while his Cominch headquarters were on the "third deck" of the Navy Department Building, they were definitely not a part of the Department but belonged to the Fleet and might theoretically put to sea at any time. "Keep out" signs were not actually posted to prevent Secretarial intrusion from the "deck" below, but that attitude was constantly conveyed in many ways.

King branched into another area that would take even more of his time. When Churchill rushed to Washington directly after Pearl Harbor to make sure that the United States did not shift its main efforts from the Atlantic to the Pacific, he brought his chiefs of staff—the heads of the three branches of the armed services. They met with their American opposite numbers to form a group, soon officially established as the Combined Chiefs of Staff. At about this same time, the American members of this new Anglo-American body started to meet by themselves as the United States Joint Chiefs of Staff (JCS). Then, very informally, they took general inter-service direction into their own hands, and without formal legit-imization, developed steadily in influence. At first, Admirals Stark and King both sat for the Navy until King was given his dual posts; Generals Marshall and Arnold represented respectively the Army and the virtually autonomous Air Forces. By the summer of 1942, Admiral Leahy, in a new position as Chief of Staff to the President, was added to the Joint Chiefs as its senior member.[26]

They took over not only the Joint Board's old role, in which the Army and Navy had worked together in planning for nearly forty years, but also direction of operations. Their decisions were subject only to Presidential review. Thus, they were not exclusively an advisory body but the apex of the complex Joint Staff that in-cluded a large group of officers to do the preliminary screening of facts, evaluation of data, and working out of details.

King came to these manifold duties from the command of the Atlantic Fleet during the uncertainties of 1941, when he had kept his ships "one speech ahead of the President." Few naval careers could match his unusual breadth of pertinent experience with so many branches of the many-sided naval service—with submarines, with aviation, with a wartime fleet staff, and with the Navy Department as a bureau chief and a member of the General Board. He had, besides, reorganized the Postgraduate School, attended the Naval War College, written articles on naval organization in the Naval Institute *Proceedings*, and had advanced plans of his own while on the General Board.[27] From his graduation, fourth in his class, from Annapolis in 1901, his was considered one of the best minds in the Navy. But he lacked the art of getting on easily with people, at which the less intellectually inclined Leahy was adept. King was well known as a rigid disciplinarian. Yet even among the many who murmured against him, there appeared to exist a widespread feeling in the Navy that probably no one else could have handled the job as well as he—and that has been said about relatively few CNOs.

King estimated that his duties with the Joint Chiefs took about two-thirds of his time. It was the consensus of opinion that his Commander-in-Chief task received most of the balance, with his functions as Chief of Naval Operations consuming barely 2 percent. That allocation of time fitted fairly closely King's capabilities. He was at his very best in his brilliant strategic analysis; some felt that he was by far the most brilliant of the Joint Chiefs, and that his insistence in that group and in the Combined Chiefs, saved the Pacific theater from complete neglect. He was also an excellent Commander-in-Chief, though his choice of men was not infallible. More to the point here, his work within the Navy Department was regarded by some as falling well behind his usual high quality level.

With his wide experience, he was a strong supporter of versatility and seemed to feel himself competent to handle anything in the whole complicated Navy. That, coupled with his efforts to control everything, likely lay behind much of his friction with the civilian executives. Forrestal expressed deep respect for King as a brilliant strategist, but he did not consider him a good administrator. That view was shared by most of Forrestal's lieutenants, one of whom wrote, much later,

the top military leader in the War Department—General of the Army Marshall—happened to be an outstanding general executive. It is not safe, however, to *count on* general administrators coming to the military top. It did not happen in the Navy Department.[28]

There were, of course, other views. One officer, who probably did more than anyone else to assist King in his work on reorganization, wrote: "It was almost a disease with him to be working on reorganization . . . and the truth of the matter is that his efforts and persistence had more to do with the existing law of the land on the subject than any of the others." [29]

An emotional element in the King-Forrestal relationship should not be overlooked. Forrestal, according to many, always spoke of King with deep respect and gave no hint of animus.[30] King had developed friction with many people, including the British, during the course of the war.[31] Yet in his postwar semi-autobiography, Forrestal was the only one who remained unforgiven—as several fairly bitter passages attest.[32] Not only did King have some specific grievances, but the account charged: "At times Mr. Forrestal seemed bent on harassing King in some ways, to which King's response was to tell the exact truth as he saw it." [33] One explanation of King's resentment might have been that even with the greatest concentration of power ever bestowed upon an American naval officer, he still had to defer to his civilian superiors. Although apparently always coldly correct when with Knox or Forrestal, his irritation at any reminder of their authority was at times obvious, as several oral accounts have verified. One admiral quotes King as declaring, after a meeting in which Knox called him down for caustic comments on another admiral, "I've never been so treated in my life, and I don't propose to start now." [34] The very fact of being summoned to Forrestal's office would seem to have irked him by the way he was apt to pace up and down in the anteroom if he had to wait. On one such day, a story goes, when Forrestal was held up by a long distance phone call, the Marine orderly slipped into the inner office to murmur anxiously, "Sir, the admiral is behaving something terrible out there." [35]

More fundamental doubtless was the interraction from their very different personalities and their opposite approach to problems. Forrestal's temperament seemed to have been more annoying to King than the admiral's mannerisms were to Forrestal. The patterns of their thinking were not at all alike. Forrestal's approach was more intellectual and less direct. Interested in ideas for their own value, he liked to speculate and discuss at length. One of his favorite expressions was "That seems like a good idea, what do you think of it?" [36] All this was apparently intensely irritating to King, who was entirely down-to-earth and practical in dealing with a situation. Blunt almost to the point of rudeness, he wanted to waste no time on nonsense, but to get on with the war. Firm in his convictions— and generally conservative in outlook—he either accepted or rejected a proposition and for him that ended the matter. He apparently did not appreciate that Forrestal's method was a definite means of getting at the heart of a problem by sorting out the issues, and not just idle conversation.

One might speculate whether Forrestal would have developed the strong Secretary's Office if he had had the "open door" relationship with King that Stimson had with General Marshall. Their offices were side by side, and, it is said, they were "always walking back and forth to each other." [37] Perhaps as a result of those shared confidences, the Secretary's Office did not develop in the War Department as did Forrestal's.

During those same early weeks of 1942, another reorganization was taking place in the national industrial mobilization which affected Forrestal closely. A month after Pearl Harbor, President Roosevelt had replaced the Office of Production Management with the War Production Board.[38] Quite unlike its predecessors, its chairman, Donald Nelson, was given full authority to run the industrial mobilization. His decisions were final, whether or not he had his board's consent. The function of its members was purely advisory. As in the previous agencies, these included both military and civilian representatives: the War and Navy Secretaries; Jesse H. Jones, Federal Loan Administrator; Vice President Henry Wallace, Chairman of the Board of Economic Warfare; William A. Knudsen, now a lieutenant general in charge of War Department procurement; Sidney Hillman, Director of the Labor Division; Leon Henderson, Administrator of the Office of Price Administration; and Harry Hopkins, Special Assistant to the President in charge of Defense Aid.

Almost immediately, Nelson had to decide whether to take over military procurement. Certain Congressmen and some newspapers were loudly advocating "a ministry of supply" for the armed forces. This would be a civilian agency and would take over all Army and Navy material procurement. Some of the enthusiasm for it came from the mistaken notion that Churchill had adopted such a plan in the British Ministry of Supply, but actually that was simply the Army's procurement agency. In fact, Churchill regarded such a concentration of power as a real ministry of supply would entail with great suspicion. In the United States, this demand arose from the widespread criticism of the way the Army and Navy were awarding war contracts. On the whole, these were not going to small businessmen, many of whom were finding it difficult to obtain raw materials for their normal peacetime production. Moreover, civilians in the former Office of Production Management were charging that the military did not know what they wanted, nor when, nor how much.

Forrestal was generally credited with a share of the responsibility for the defeat of a ministry of supply. At any rate, warned by Bernard Baruch of the pitfalls involved and persuaded by Forrestal, Nelson did not go along with it.[39] He accepted the alternative Forrestal suggested and placed his own men inside the Army and Navy procurement organizations. This continued the decentralization of operations while keeping the control of policy in Nelson's hands. Frank M. Folsom, later president of the Radio Corporation of America, was assigned by Nelson to Forrestal's office.

Frequently representing Knox on the War Production Board, as on its predecessors, Forrestal had from the first been concerned about the Navy bridge to that powerful agency. There is little doubt that that serious drive for a centralized supply agency made him more conscious of the necessity to allay some of the criticism by changing the Navy's own system. In his opinion, both Naval Operations and Supplies and Accounts lacked understanding of what had to be done and the kind of trained staff needed to do it.

Liaison between the regular Navy procurement bureaus and the War Production Board, he decided, could best be maintained through his own office. He worked out the details with the help of his intimate associates—Eberstadt, Detmar, Hensel, and Booz—all of whom had had experience with the Navy's inadequacies in this area. Knox put the new plan into effect on January 30, 1942, by issuing General Order No. 166. This established the Office of Procurement and Material in Forrestal's Office. Its abbreviation OP&M is not to be confused with OPM—the earlier Office of Production Management.

The task of OP&M was to secure from the Chief of Naval Operations and the material bureaus detailed programs sufficiently in advance to make planning more intelligent. It watched the awarding of contracts; prepared Navy estimates of the total amount of raw materials, facilities, and components required; and supervised production schedules closely enough to discover potential bottlenecks before they had a chance to develop. Rear Admiral Samuel M. Robinson (widely known as "Mike"), the first chief of the Bureau of Ships, became head of OP&M with the rank of vice admiral. Most of the staff were civilians or recently commissioned reserve officers. Despite the word "procurement" in its name, this was not a purchasing agency. It did not buy anything; its job was to coordinate the activities of the material bureaus. Hensel's Procurement Legal Division was not included as originally proposed, because he objected that "OP&M will establish Navy channels that are devastating to individual thought." [40] Consequently, it remained a separate entity in the Under Secretary's Office.

Rapidly, OP&M took shape in four branches. Planning and Statistics analyzed production and procurement requirements of raw and industrial materials. Procurement coordinated the whole process of negotiating and awarding contracts. Production was the troubleshooter for production problems. Resources referred to the Navy's part of the Army and Navy Munitions Board. A fifth branch, Inspection Administration, was added several months later, to coordinate the work of Navy inspectors of material. This was the brainchild of Lewis L. Strauss, New York financier, reserve officer, and postwar head of the Atomic Energy Commission. He pointed out to Forrestal that the rapidly growing force of inspectors, then under bureau control, would lead to duplication without some coordinating machinery. His prediction was proved correct; before the war ended there were over 28,000 inspectors.

Testifying before the Naval Subcommittee of the House Appropriations Committee, Forrestal said his OP&M had three functions:

One is internal program coordination. The Navy's battle plans for six months or a year hence must be translated into material and facilities. Production of weapons must be scheduled and supervised as a united whole, planes must be on hand when aircraft carriers are commissioned, bases must be ready when men report for training.

The second problem is coordination with other agencies, particularly with the Office of War Mobilization and with the War Production Board which controls the raw materials and facilities required by the Navy program. The Navy needs a single spokesman to arrange priorities, obtain allocations, arrange for new or converted facilities, report progress and especially to represent it on the scores of interagency committees which gear the Navy into the general industrial mobilization.

The third coordinating function . . . is one of supervising contract letting. The Navy needs a central coordinating office to standardize the use by its various bureaus of negotiated contracts, to eliminate overlapping procurement and to exercise the contract clearance functions which have been delegated to the Navy by the War Production Board.[41]

The creation of this office proved a master stroke—some have gone so far as to claim that without it the Navy could not have carried through its wartime program. To compete with the Army, Merchant Marine, Foreign Aid, and civilians for scarce material, an accurate, documented statement of Navy needs was essential. Also, within the Navy some agency had to synchronize and follow through, if ships, guns, trained men, supply depots, and all the other intricate machinery needed to put a fighting ship into action were to be ready at the same time. Without OP&M, this would have been impossible. As the major liaison between the Navy and the War Production Board, the prestige of the office gradually increased, although the material bureaus were never enthusiastic about it.

A few months after its birth, OP&M became the bone of contention in a bitter civilian-military dispute, which threatened to nullify if not to destroy it. Under King's leadership, Naval Operations suddenly initiated desperate efforts to regain control of material procurement, which it had long before neglected. Possibly, King would have opposed the formation of OP&M at its start, had he then been CNO. Now he included its control in his plans for reorganizing the Department.

Forrestal, characteristically, did not seek the fight, but he was determined to keep his coordinating setup out of the hands of the military command. In the ensuing contest, Roosevelt and Knox "carried the ball," but Forrestal saw to it that both his superiors were fully informed of the issues at stake.

Helpful to King's purpose was the drastic administrative overhaul, just undergone by the War Department. In this, the Army's counterpart of material organization was shifted from civilian oversight to concentrated military control under the Chief of Staff, in the new Service Forces. According to Secretary Stimson, "The increasing centralization which it ensured somewhat shifted the functions of the Secretary of War, who retained direct control only over the Bureau of Public Relations and his own office." [42]

It so happened that Roosevelt approved this without a murmur; yet he persistently resisted King's efforts to curtail civilian authority in the same manner in the Navy Department. Consequently, the impact of Pearl Harbor diminished the sphere of the War Secretary but had the opposite influence on his civilian counterpart in the Navy.

Even before he was sworn in as CNO, the first of King's many reorganization attempts began. In this, the language of the midnight order combining Cominch and CNO which permitted him to "direct" the efforts of the bureaus became important. He interpreted it to mean reorganizing the Department to make him the administrative as well as the operational chief. In a memorandum, March 17, 1942, he wrote, apparently to some of his immediate subordinates:

The President has ordered that the organization of the Navy Department be "streamlined" at the earliest practicable date.
It is apparent that I have to undertake this work personally—and I must have help and advice. . . .
To date, my ideas are to assemble appropriate activities in four grand divisions, namely, Material, Personnel, Readiness, Operations.
The four grand divisions are now in being, even though they are not now adequately correlated and colligated. [43]

He further explained that Personnel was under Rear Admiral Jacobs (everywhere regarded as King's "man"); Readiness under Vice Admiral Horne, as Vice CNO; and Operations under his own Fleet headquarters. That obviously left Material—OP&M—under Vice Admiral Robinson and Forrestal as the major projected change.

By May 22, King's ideas had crystallized further, according to a memorandum to eight prominent officers, entitled "Reorganization of the Navy Department" and including a chart:

The constant effort shall be to centralize the formulation of guiding policies and plans but to decentralize the execution of such policies and plans to the utmost; and to effect whole-hearted and loyal cooperation throughout the entire organization.

His proposed inroads upon civilian authority were specific:

Naval Materials under CNO will take over from the Assistant Secretary of the Navy the general administrative control of the material activities of all the shore establishments.

Naval Material under CNO will take over from the Under Secretary of the Navy the administration of the Office of Procurement and Material except that the Under Secretary will continue to maintain general supervision and administer such components dealing with outside agencies as are essential and appropriate.[44]

King's proposals drew fire from the White House within three days. Roosevelt had expressed himself on the subject of cutting down civilian authority in the Navy in 1920, while Assistant Secretary, and had reiterated those views in 1934, during his first term as President, when reorganization was being discussed.[45] Eight years more had not appreciably changed his attitude as indicated by his memorandum to Knox:

I have just read the proposed reorganization of the Navy Department.
1. It is true that I think the Department should be streamlined by two methods: (a) Reducing the length of the "chain of command." (b) Change top personnel until you can get people who will operate with each other.
2. I do not mean by this that the whole administrative structure should be changed in the middle of the war. This proposal is a reorganization and not a streamlining. . . .
4. If this organization chart were set up it would take the Navy Department at least one year to learn just what is meant by it. . . .
6. I do not think there is any useful purpose to be gained by sending this out for comment or criticism to anybody in the service. . . .
Incidentally, we ought not to have all the administrative problems of personnel and material, shore establishments, production, etc., go up through the Chief of Naval Operations. When you come down to it, the real function of the Chief of Naval Operations is primarily Naval Operations—no human being can take on all the other responsibilities of getting the Navy ready to fight. He should know all about the state of that readiness and direct the efforts of ships and men when they are ready to fight. If they are not ready to fight or are slow in getting ready, it is his function to raise hell about it. Details of getting ready to fight ought not to bother him.

Let us try again to get something out along the lines I have indicated —instead of the present chart—remembering always that we are in the middle of a war and that we are learning lessons from it every day.[46]

Five days later, Knox heard from King, to whom Roosevelt had sent a copy of this memorandum. The gist of his note was "I do not get the point of most of the comment." [47]

Meanwhile, Forrestal also had expressed his views to Knox:

There are three main divisions of the activities of the Navy: procurement, supply, and operations—the only reason for the existence of the first two being the third. I believe the operational side of the Navy should control the material side to the extent of determining what kinds of ships, ordnance, aircraft, etc., it wants to use. The procurement of this program should then be left to the procurement side with a minimum of interference in the way it is done. Operations has obviously all it can do in its own field.[48]

King's plan, Forrestal felt, would return the Department to its former method of no coordination of certain functions common to all parts of the Navy, such as the purchase of machine tools, insurance, and contractual and legal policies; no "overall picture of raw materials, etc.," and no control of inventories in terms of materials. In addition, any attempt to evaluate the Navy's program as a whole, such as in scheduling its completion dates and its major deficiencies in accomplishment, would be left to a very inadequate section of the Office of the Chief of Naval Operations.[49]

The real excitement began when King took matters into his own hands. Despite Roosevelt's clearly expressed views, he issued a directive on May 28 to the Bureaus and Offices of the Navy Department:

1. There are hereby established in the Office of the Chief of Naval Operations agencies to deal with all appropriate and duly assigned matters relating to personnel and material. These agencies shall be under the immediate direction of an Assistant Chief of Naval Operations (Personnel) and an Assistant Chief of Naval Operations (Material) respectively, who shall be responsible directly to the Vice Chief of Naval Operations.

2. The duties of the Assistant Chief of Naval Operations (Personnel) shall be performed by the Chief of Naval Personnel and the duties of the Assistant Chief of Naval Operations (Material) by the Chief of the Office of Procurement and Material, and shall be in addition to their present duties. . . .[50]

Thus Robinson was to be brought definitely under King's control. A similar directive on May 15 had given the Chief of Aeronautics additional duty as Assistant Chief of Naval Operations (Air).[51]

Horne, taking the new arrangement as an accomplished fact, transferred to Jacobs as Assistant CNO (Personnel), which was the latter's new title, "all personnel functions now performed by other bureaus and offices. . . ." [52] This gave Jacobs what he had wanted, for Personnel had resented the fact that certain of their functions had been "usurped" by the "Seabees" of Yards and Docks and the aviation training of Aeronautics.

That directive let the cat out of the bag. An officer from the Secretary's Office, visiting another office, happened to see a copy. Forrestal, then Knox, and then Roosevelt "got the word." The President was annoyed; he learned of it, while shaving, from his naval aide, Captain John McCrea. "Why didn't he tell me?" he exclaimed, "How does he know I'd approve? I don't care if the whole Navy approved it." [53] On a copy of the May 28 directive, Roosevelt underscored the word "duties" in two places, drew lines to the bottom of the sheet, and wrote "What are the duties? What is the authority given? F.D.R." [54] On June 9, he summoned Knox and King to the White House. The next day, Knox wrote the admiral: "Don't you think in the light of our talk with the President yesterday that you should suspend or cancel the attached orders at least until the President makes that chart of organization he told us he was going to work on over the week-end?" [55] King returned that note the next day with the informal endorsement, "I judge the [new] Ass't CNO's will be all right. I have already had Horne's ltr. cancelled." [56]

King was given oral instructions by the President to cancel his directive and call off his reorganization plans on June 12. Roosevelt is also said to have handed King a curt note after that interview to the effect that any reorganizing in the Department would be done by himself and Knox, and suggesting that King devote his attentions to sinking submarines, then uncomfortably active off the coast. That same day, Roosevelt wrote Knox:

I am more and more disturbed by the two Operations' orders which went out to the Bureaus. There may be more of them which neither you nor I have seen. Therefore will you please do the following:

(a) Direct Operations to cancel the two orders which we have seen and tell them to let you and me have copies of the cancellation.

(b) Please ask Operations for all orders in any way affecting departmental organization or procedure, for thirty days back. You and I can then see if anything else needs to be cancelled.

The more I think of the two orders which you and I saw, the more outrageous I think it is that Operations went ahead to do, without your approval or mine, what I had already disapproved when I turned down the general plan of reorganization. I am very much inclined to send for the Officers down the line and give them a good dressing down. They are old enough to know better—and old enough to know that you are the Secretary of the Navy and that I am Commander-in-Chief of the Navy.[57]

The next day, King formally canceled the two directives, reporting to Knox that he had had suspended "all activities connected with the President's oral directives." [58] But that rebuff did not prevent him from returning to the attack. As he said in discussing the matter a year later: "The need for it was so obvious that I simply directed that it be put into effect. But I stumbled on one little pebble—I neglected to consult the President and the Secretary first." [59]

The next time, however, May 1943, King notified both Roosevelt and Knox of his proposed changes. His latest plan promoted the proposed "Assistant Chiefs of Naval Operations" of his rejected draft to "Deputy Chiefs," and again there were to be four—Operations, Material, Personnel, and Aviation. Eventually, that title received formal recognition, though with only a fraction of the powers now suggested. According to the draft of a proposed General Order to implement the scheme, their duties were to be "supervisory and policy-making in character," while "the bureaus and offices allocated under their control shall function primarily as executive technical agencies." At the same time, "administrative supervision" of all matters relating to Material, Personnel, and Aviation were placed under "the general cognizance of" the Under Secretary, Assistant Secretary, and Assistant Secretary for Air respectively.[60] Altogether, this program proposed a much tighter Operations control over the bureaus than had ever existed before.

That the functions of Forrestal's Office of Procurement and Material would be absorbed in the new setup was indicated by the duties assigned to the new Deputy CNO (Material):

. . . coordination of all the material procurement activities of the Navy Department, the supervision of programs for the procurement of ships and materials of every character, and with the correlation of appropriate and necessary policies for the effectuation thereof. He shall be the principal naval adviser to the Under Secretary.[61]

The King memoirs assert that the draft "met with practically unanimous approval from everyone except the bureau chiefs." [62] That may have been true of King's "Cominch-CNO" henchmen, but the civilian executives seem to have felt otherwise. One of those closest to Knox at the time is certain that the Secretary did not favor the plan, as was stated in the memoirs, and no records show any trace of such approval. Bard definitely voiced his disapproval. Noting that only "general cognizance" over various activities was allotted to the civilian Secretaries, he said, "I would call the word cognizance somewhat of a weasel word. I don't think it carried any authority." He further pointed out that a chart in the proposals indicated a direct line of command from King to the bureaus, while there were merely dotted lines, signifying advisory authority only, running from the Secretary to the bureaus.[63]

The bureau chiefs themselves had plenty to say against the plan. Rear Admiral W. H. P. Blandy, the vigorous Chief of Ordnance, also put his finger on the policy-making aspects involved in connection with the relationship to civilian authority. King, according to Blandy,

. . . must have and now does have . . . military control over the bureaus . . . I conceive that this military control involves issuing directives regarding *what* is wanted, *when* and *where*. . . . The "*how*" including all business and industrial matters, is left to the bureaus, under the direct supervision of the Secretary, the Under Secretary and the Assistant Secretaries. This bureau subordinates itself to both of these types of directives, and as far as the Chief of Bureau can ascertain, they are being carried out satisfactorily. . . .

The proposed reorganization, in assigning military and administrative jurisdiction over the bureaus to the deputy CNO's would also deprive the Secretary, the Under Secretary and the Assistant Secretary for Air of their direct administrative contact with the bureaus. . . .

Each bureau, he continued, "would still have to do the greater part of its own internal policy-making and planning" and there would simply be extra delay in "passing papers over another row of desks." [64]

The President did not like the plan either, calling it "complex and difficult to understand," and disapproved it.[65] The one tangible result was the establishing that summer of a Deputy Chief of Naval

Operations (Air), primarily to take over part of the functions of the Bureau of Aeronautics.

Later that summer, King resumed his reorganization efforts, with particular emphasis on changes from the traditional navy yard organization. There were definite merits in these proposals which did not affect civilian authority and would be adopted with modifications at the close of the war. At the moment, however, Roosevelt was dead set against any of them. He scrawled a little penciled note to Secretary Knox: "F.K. Tell Ernie *once more:* No reorganizing of the Navy Dept. set-up during the war. Let's win it first.

F.D.R." [66]

In the meantime, Forrestal had been facing new and difficult problems on the national level in the procurement field, that were beyond the control of his Office of Procurement and Material. Until its last quarter, 1942 was a year of bad news from the war fronts, of an almost frantic rush for faster mobilization of the national resources, and of general uncertainty about much that was being attempted. It looked at times as if the world's greatest industrial nation was losing a war for the first time in its history—and for the unnecessary reason that it was not going to be equipped in time.

For months after its appointment, the new War Production Board (WPB) had not even thought out its program, let alone made any decisions about what should be done or how to do it. Nelson, as he said himself, had greater powers than those ever bestowed upon any individual in the nation below the President; yet he gave no indication of exercising them. Forrestal was also in doubt now about Nelson's attitude toward the Army and Navy, though their personal relations had been friendly. This whole uncertain picture was not one that men like Forrestal and Patterson would be apt to let alone.

Determined that interservice competition for material must be avoided, they pressed forward with the reorganization of the Army and Navy Munitions Board,[67] to provide a civilian chairman. Eberstadt had recommended this, but refused the post for himself. On Pearl Harbor day, however, he telephoned Forrestal that he was at the country's disposal in whatever assignment he could be best used; that settled the chairmanship. Although the Board's reorganization was not approved by the President until weeks after the WPB and the Navy's OP&M, Eberstadt went to work at once. A strong administrator and successful negotiator, his Board already organized with Forrestal and Patterson as military representatives, Eberstadt was ready to move ahead of WPB and OP&M. Under such a triumvirate, it was almost inevitable that this Board would present a far more consistent approach to war production as a whole than did Nelson. In fact, it went far beyond its original task of coordinating military programs and settling interservice disputes.

The most valuable work of the Army and Navy Munitions Board was that it focused attention on the need for dynamic production early in 1942. And by spring, it took the initiative by urging the rapid conversion of industry to war purposes, when Nelson was proving reluctant to use his great powers. It strengthened his position in many instances against pressure groups advocating a more gradual transition to war economy, but he continued to procrastinate. Whereas in British naval history the phrase "Nelson touch" had implied consummate, skillful daring, those words now connoted quite the reverse to an impatient Army and Navy.

The Munitions Board's stand was not popular, nor was it easy to achieve, particularly when it began to make recommendations that specific industries convert to military production. In a series of letters to Nelson, the Board urged that plants making refrigeration machinery, radios, and office equipment could most readily be converted to military products. A group in the War Production Board heartily endorsed that position; but Nelson did not hurry to act. He seemed fond of saying that his agency was traveling untrodden paths; [68] if so, it trod them slowly despite the vital needs of the battle fronts. Eventually, in late January 1942, the manufacture of gaming machines was stopped, then metal office equipment, but that of automobiles for civilian use was continued until April 1, and refrigerators, until April 30.

The Munitions Board, stressing the necessity for conserving goods already in civilian hands, also prodded Nelson to ration gasoline and tires, [69] since that dual control would help save scarce rubber. Defense plant employees had to use cars for transportation, but pleasure driving could be curtailed. The petroleum industry and agricultural interests, which were advocating instead the manufacture of synthetic rubber from alcohol made from agricultural products, lobbied hard against rationing. While the Board's counter-arguments to the President were of no little value in strengthening Nelson's hand, still he did not act.

As a result, the authority that Nelson originally held began to pass to others. Finally, the rubber shortage became so acute that Roosevelt appointed a committee headed by Bernard Baruch, which urged a director for rubber with complete authority subject only to Nelson. In time other "czars" were appointed for similar reasons.

Unnecessary rail travel also came under fire from the Munitions group as rail equipment was vital to war. Passenger schedules for normal travel were not attacked, but, as Eberstadt reminded Nelson, the transportation of large crowds to football games or racing meets when industrial traffic loads were at their peak seemed "somewhat remote" from the war effort. This applied particularly to the 328 railroad passenger cars, including a number of private cars, for the Kentucky Derby.[70]

The Board's opposition to Harry Hopkins's shipments of machine tools, raw materials, and other critically needed goods to other countries under Lend-Lease agreements was not as successful. Eberstadt stated that his Board felt "that a good deal of foreign demands are being granted without careful preliminary screening as to their necessity and use."[71] A particular instance concerned a Soviet Union order for automatic screw machines, critically needed in this country. The Russians even refused to state how they intended to use them; they received them nevertheless.

In August 1942, at the time of the Marines landing on Guadalcanal, Forrestal was making a quick trip to the Pacific to "see for himself" how well his production program was adjusting to battle needs. At Pearl Harbor he saw Nimitz, then he flew southward to the headquarters of Ghormly, the South Pacific commander, at Nouméa in the French New Hebrides. He had just arrived when the burned survivors of Savo Island were being brought in to improvised hospitals; four cruisers had been sunk in a matter of minutes by the Japanese. The Army had moved out as many of its own sick and wounded as possible; and doctors were working around the clock. Forrestal stopped to talk to the men here and there in the hospitals, but refused to make a speech: "What could I say in the face of such heroism and such suffering except to bow my head."[72] Stripped of cruisers and supplies very short, the desperate condition of the American forces was obvious, even though the

Marines were still holding their lines at Guadalcanal. There were 76 freighters at Nouméa and at Espiritu Santo, but only some 300 tons a day were reaching shore because docking facilities and long-shoremen were lacking and the vessels had not been combat-loaded. An attack in force on those supply bases might bring disaster to the whole South Pacific.

At Pearl, on his way home, Forrestal urged immediate reinforce-ments, but Nimitz pointed out that his three available battleships were "oil hogs" and he did not have enough tankers to keep them at sea.[73] On the West Coast, Forrestal arranged for additional tankers. Back in Washington, he urged—in reporting to the President, Knox, and the Cabinet as a whole—that all branches of the services rush assistance, particularly stevedore battalions. Stimson, much con-cerned over other battle fronts, had little use for this kind of talk. He said, smiling, "Jim, you've got a bad case of localitis." Forrestal retorted, "Mr. Secretary, if the Marines on Guadalcanal were wiped out, the reaction in the country will give you a bad case of localitis in the seat of your pants." [74] Forrestal's firsthand report did help in expediting men and materials to the Pacific. It aided, in particular, the rapid formation of the valuable construction units, the "Sea-bees."

At home the Munitions Board had been keeping up its struggle to have all new production reserved for the military programs, while the civilian economy "lived on its fat." By the late summer of 1942, however, its energetic, intelligent, and above all fearless leadership was less needed, for the War Production Board had at last completed its organization and set its major policies. Eberstadt, moreover, moved to the latter Board as its vice chairman at Nel-son's invitation and with Forrestal's and Patterson's approval.

His particular role there was the administering of his Controlled Materials Plan, which linked priorities for critical materials with actual quantities available. It proved to be one of the most effective weapons for winning the battle of production. The term "priority" as used during the prewar "defense" period simply meant giving military orders preference over civilian ones. This was not suffi-cient after Pearl Harbor, because many manufacturers were then using all their facilities for military production. Thus the priority system had to be changed from an order of production to a means of obtaining material, and this was done by the Controlled Material Plan. The earlier system had given a manufacturer with a top priority rating a "hunting license" to search for scarce materials he needed. As such ratings were given freely, he could not be sure of succeeding. This system broke down when there were no longer enough raw materials and components to go around.

In the meantime, the War Production Board had been elaborating on a "warrant system," sponsored by the Navy, which would put allocation of materials on a coupon basis, similar to the new civilian rationing for food and clothing. Eberstadt felt that this system did not go far enough; he believed the government should first determine the amount of raw materials and components available over a given period, and then decide how it should be distributed. He insisted on a simple plan, limited to a small number of critical items, arguing that there was no point in rationing those in plentiful supply.[75] Studies in his office and in Forrestal's procurement office resulted in the Controlled Material Plan, a completely new rationing system. Henceforth, the Requirements Committee of WPB under Eberstadt took over the balancing of the nation's supplies against the demands of the armed forces and the home front.[76]

Some writers have succumbed to the temptation to picture those early years of industrial mobilization as a struggle between civilians and the military. This theme offered simplicity and dramatic appeal with its triumphant hero and defeated villain. Generally the story would run something like this. Long before the war, the Army and Navy had worked together secretly on a plan by which, in war, they could seize all production for military purposes. Fortunately the civilian economy was saved in 1940, when Roosevelt, too discerning to accept this plan, called civilians to his aid and organized the Defense Advisory Commission, the Office of Production Management, and the War Production Board. The military, thus foiled, turned to the Munitions Board as a means of continued opposition to the War Production Board, which emerged victorious after a bitter struggle. Then came another major battle, when the military under Eberstadt tried to infiltrate WPB itself.[77]

This tale should be questioned both on fact and interpretation. Actually that prewar plan and its revisions, though drafted by Army and Navy officers, clearly provided for civilian control in wartime. It was prepared, moreover, with the advice of a number of thoughtful civilians, Bernard Baruch, John Hancock, and others with World War I experience in industrial mobilization. In 1940, to be sure, there emerged many differences of opinion regarding an effective policy and some struggles to control administrative machinery, but these were not essentially between civilians and the military. Actually, in the complicated situation, there was neither a united military nor a united civilian front. Alliances were formed on a particular issue and reformed with other allies a month or so later. The striving for power, usual in such a situation, was undoubtedly intensified by the tempo of the period and the pressure for speed. Everyone wanted to "get on with the war" quickly, but each in his own way. Civilians within the defense agencies attacked other civilians as "impractical planners," as "politicians," or as "businessmen intent on resisting conversion." Army and Navy officers disagreed among themselves. Airmen talked about "battleship admirals" and "land-bound" generals. But the struggles were usually between civilians, even though many of them were in uniform as reserve officers. Administration abhors a vacuum, and with such ineffective machinery at hand at first, some group was almost certain to take the lead. It might well have been disastrous to the war effort had the Munitions Board held back at that juncture.

Actually it was in the military departments themselves that civilian control was in question, and not between the armed services and outside civilian agencies. In the War Department, the professional military pretty much had their own way. In the Navy, thanks to Knox and Forrestal, there was a division of tasks based more on skill and a larger degree of civilian leadership throughout.

6

Midpassage

THE THREAT of defeat that had lain heavy upon the Allies was
beginning to lift in the late autumn of 1942. The British stopped the
Germans in North Africa, and the Russians checked them at Stalin-
grad. The Americans in the Solomons beat back what was to be the
last major Japanese offensive. A year and a half later, soon after
Forrestal became full Secretary, the Allies launched their own
mighty offensives in Normandy and in the Marianas. And doing
its part in making possible these overwhelming attacks was Forrestal's procurement organization, then moving in high gear into
what might be called its third stage. Whereas his first problems had
centered on organization and contracts, and his second on the early
hectic rush for production, his role was now shifting to the broader
one of the delicate adjustment of military needs to a wartime civilian economy.

Paradoxically, the Navy was finding that speedy delivery had
exchanged places with cost as its primary concern. A Navy that had
been starved for funds was now allowed, indeed almost encouraged,
to spend like a drunken sailor. Wartime appropriations, far sur-
passing peacetime bills, went through Congress with much less discussion. On a May afternoon in 1943, with only seven Democratic
Representatives and some twenty Republicans on hand, the House
granted the Navy thirty billion in the appropriation bill for "Fiscal
1944" in twenty minutes. Representative Hoffman of Michigan
asked sarcastically, should there not be "at least one member on the
floor for each billion dollars?" [1]

Forrestal continued to be primarily concerned with procurement
in 1943 and 1944. Hensel's legal work was expanded and new groups

of contract negotiators and production trouble shooters were added. But more significant, in a period when there were not enough raw materials, factories, or labor to meet the demands of the military services, the civilian economy, and the Allies, was his vigorous presentation of the Navy's needs before the War Production Board. He realized that he would have short shrift with that Board if the Navy's system permitted waste or was careless in determining its requirements and fixing its priorities. Consequently, he devoted these months to developing a contract which would be an incentive to contractors to put forth their best efforts; to curbing unnecessary military construction; to desperate battles over price controls; and to efforts to obtain scarce items like valves and small motors.

In expanding the activities of his legal staff in 1942, Hensel met opposition from some of the bureau chiefs, notably Rear Admiral Brent Young—now Chief of Supplies and Accounts. They opposed Hensel's endeavor to place commercially experienced lawyers from Forrestal's office in their bureaus. Young joined forces with Rear Admiral Woodson, the Judge Advocate General and Hensel's earlier opponent. They protested to the Chief of Naval Operations, Vice Admiral Horne, at this "interference in bureau affairs." He called in the other bureau chiefs, and they descended together upon Forrestal, who immediately summoned Hensel. The latter knew that some bureaus, especially Aeronautics, were dissatisfied with S&A's handling of contracts. Although Aeronautics determined what it wanted to buy and often negotiated with a contractor, it still had to send a requisition through S&A before a contract could formally be awarded. This process led to tedious delays, which held up vital supplies.[2] After patiently listening to the chiefs' case for bureau cognizance, Hensel turned the attack by asking the Aeronautics chief if his procurement was being satisfactorily handled. The latter launched a deluge of bitter complaints, in which the other bureau chiefs joined. Listening in amazement, Horne realized the complexities of the contracting program and the consequent need for decentralizing it.[3]

As a result of this conference, Forrestal issued the important directive of December 13, 1942, which let each bureau decide whether to use Supplies and Accounts or to negotiate, prepare, and award its own contracts. Most of the bureaus took advantage of this escape clause to set up their own contracting systems. Congress was suspicious, however, of this decentralized system, since reformers had been preaching for years the doctrine of centralized purchasing as the means of economy. What was not so generally known was that big business had found that beyond a certain point consolidation tended to lead to inefficiency, and thus to greater cost—and the Navy's experience was to bear this out. Forrestal, familiar as he was with current business practice, was confident that decentralization was the better way in this procurement situation.

Next, an Office of Counsel was set up in each bureau under a Hensel appointee who reported back to the bureau chief and also directly to the Under Secretary. To aid the bureaus in using negotiated contracts—authorized under the First War Powers Act—in place of competitive bids, a Negotiation Division was created in the Office of Procurement and Material, with a small central staff and a branch in each bureau. Its head, W. Browne Baker of Houston, Texas, had a broad business background, and so did the men he recruited.[4] The actual negotiating of each contract thus lay with a team of one or more technical men from the bureau, lawyers from the Procurement Legal Division, and businessmen from this new unit. Such a combination of specialists, according to Forrestal, was the key to successful contracting. Each team was furnished a mass of statistical and accounting data collected by the Navy cost inspectors from S&A, by material inspectors from Inspection Administration, and by other government agencies including the Army and Maritime Commission.

Forrestal also established a "contract clearance system" in OP&M itself to insure that the factors ordinarily considered in private business were taken into account in the Navy's contracts. Frank Folsom, whom he borrowed from Donald Nelson, had to certify that contracts met Forrestal's specifications before they could be signed.[5] Since Nelson soon accepted Folsom's clearance as indicating that Navy contracts also met WPB standards, the Navy was able to make extensive use of these negotiated contracts.

Forrestal thought that contractors who did a good job should be allowed larger profits, but the fixed price contract and the cost-plusa-fixed-fee contracts ordinarily used had no such incentive arrangements. The old notorious cost-plus-a-percentage contract of World War I, with a bonus for increasing costs, was fortunately no longer used. Forrestal succeeded in having a real incentive contract developed, in which the Navy estimated the probable costs and fixed a base price that included a reasonable profit. If a contractor's expenses ran above that base figure, the Navy guaranteed his loss up to a specific amount; beyond that point, his profits would diminish as his costs rose. But if he pushed his expenses below the base price, he could gain a substantial part of such savings in addition to his normal profit—and therein lay the incentive for economy on his part.[6] As Forrestal said:

This kind of contract gives the company a definite incentive to cut its cost. In fact, the heart of the contract is the conviction that American business can perform miracles at low cost production if it is given a profit incentive for doing so. The Navy Department by giving business this incentive stands to save millions of dollars through lower costs on munitions. You will perceive, however, that the sine qua non for an incentive contract is a contract price which is based on actual cost experience and which is very close to the current cost line. Without a firm closed contract price the incentive contract would be open to abuses. The contractor would achieve a saving by merely squeezing the water out of an inflated contract price.[7]

The reverse of the incentive program was price control. Not only did inflation threaten to send Navy costs up but there was the widespread public suspicion of war profiteering. Investigations and legislation during the thirties had cast lurid reflections on the so-called "merchants of death" and had led to demands to "take the profits out of war." Price controls, however, presented the armed forces with a dilemma. Well-intentioned laws and regulations, that might keep prices and profits down, might at the same time discourage manufacturers from undertaking the burdens and risks of military production.

As Forrestal testified before the House Naval Affairs Committee early in 1942:

There is no one panacea for the problem that is created by the vast procurement program upon which the Government is now launched . . . it is my opinion that we must limit earnings or recapture profits up to that point beyond which further penalty would destroy the incentive for efficient operation of industry. And we must remember that the efficient and economical and prosperous management is the one that usually, when all is said and done, will produce the weapons that we need, with the greatest speed.[8]

Altogether, in view of the difficulties involved, the results were highly satisfactory. The success of the price control program as a whole made it possible for Knox to boast in the spring of 1944 that the Navy between July 1, 1940 and December 31, 1943 had saved $17 billion that would otherwise have been spent had the price of war materials risen as they did in World War I. Although average wage rates and prices increased, few soared. In World War I, the cost of a Navy blanket, at $4.40 in 1916, had risen 78 percent by 1918 to $7.84; this time, the price in 1942 of $6.60 went up only 6 percent or 40 cents by the end of the war.[9]

The astronomical figures of the major implements for warfare itself actually went down. In January 1945, the Navy was paying approximately a million dollars less per destroyer than it had paid at the beginning of 1942. The cost of one type of fighter plane had been reduced from $66,000 to $32,000 per plane. Generally speaking, the Navy by 1945 was obtaining "about 25% more war supplies for each dollar expended." [10] Such figures as are available indicate that between January 1942 and January 1945 the Navy price index declined by nearly 30 percent, contrasted with a general rise of nearly 7 percent in wholesale prices. But there were some qualifying angles to this extraordinary record.

In the beginning, Forrestal and Patterson had fought hard to place military contracts in a special category, subject only to military controls. They had feared Henderson's Office of Price Administration would slow down production by arbitrarily fixing prices. They not only failed in this but it was one of the few times their judgment seemed to be wrong. Henderson insisted that there be no exceptions to his authority; and the Emergency Price Control Bill, introduced into Congress a few days after Pearl Harbor, covered military as well as civilian items. Much disturbed, Forrestal and Patterson wrote the chairman of the Senate Banking and Currency Committee, Robert F. Wagner of New York, requesting that their departments be allowed to "make their own price determinations" in defense procurement.[11] Wagner consulted Henderson, who would only agree to except military end-products, such as tanks, submarines, and bombers, as properly under military departments. The Senate Committee concurred.

Next, the two Under Secretaries appealed to Roosevelt:

We are fully conscious of the need for price stability, and we will be very sparing in negotiations above the ceiling prices, without the advice of the Price Administrator. When we deem it essential, however, we should be empowered to go forward, without even the slightest delay . . . without seeking his consent.[12]

The President also supported Henderson: "The Army and Navy must conform as well as everybody else."[13] He only conceded that a dispute between them and Henderson could be referred to him. The Price Control Act became law January 30, 1942 and contained no exemptions for war materials.[14]

Forrestal and Patterson were back in the fight when Henderson soon extended price ceilings to diesel and gas engines, even though he exempted ships, planes, tanks, guns, and ammunition. Vainly they argued that war goods did not constitute a threat to the cost of living.[15] He retorted that they seemed "to minimize the indirect effect of inflation in the military goods area." He questioned the ability of the armed services to recapture excessive profits completely, and declared that he did not believe that they were "equipped to undertake, or should undertake, the job of fighting inflation." Nevertheless, he agreed to refrain from extending military price controls for the present if the services would do all they could to control prices and profits.[16] Later that fall Henderson finally agreed to place no further ceilings on combat military items beyond the first stage of production and to give the services advance notice of any contemplated action that might effect them.[17] The Navy on its part agreed to do more about controlling prices in the later stages of production. This became one of Forrestal's more important duties. Cost breakdowns became a normal part of contract making. In time, elaborate price indexes were developed against which these itemized statements of the contractors' expenses could be evaluated. Although this procedure did not always reveal excess profits, it made it harder to hide preposterous costs. No longer did the contractors have "all the information on their side of the deal," as one Navy negotiator had put it earlier in the war. It frequently happened, moreover, that with mass production the Navy paid less than ceiling prices.

Contrary to the forebodings of Forrestal and Patterson, the Price Control Act was generally operated in such a way that the armed services derived much benefit and encountered a minimum of interference. The few delays in contract negotiations did not actually hold up production. Yet had they not made an issue of the matter, OPA might have been less cooperative, while poor administration by cutting initiative might well have meant intolerable obstacles to procurement.

Even in planning for the wartime expansion of the Fleet, which seemed definitely the function of the naval professionals, Forrestal soon realized the need for civilian oversight, since those needs had to be adjusted to the nation's industrial capacity. His attitude grew increasingly critical as he saw the results of that planning in the destroyer escort and other programs. Part of the trouble came from the rigid secrecy in which military policy makers naturally had to work. Better liaison between them and the procurement group, however, would have facilitated faster filling of orders when strategy changes occurred. After the war, Ferdinand Eberstadt criticized this "remote relationship between the Joint Chiefs of Staff and the agencies charged with responsibility for procurement and logistics. . . . Communication between them was carried on principally by exchange of letters and memoranda, frequently extending over many months with respect to single subjects." [18]

The determination of naval "requirements" rested primarily with the Chief of Naval Operations and his immediate subordinates, usually acting after consultation with the "elder statesmen" of the General Board: only then were the bureaus told to go ahead. With the coming of war, these requirement problems became a major worry in various fields—aircraft, facilities, personnel, and much else —but the complex demands and frequent shifts of emphasis from one type of vessel to another made shipbuilding the most complicated problem.

There was a whole series of wartime shipbuilding programs. [19] With most of the battleships of the Pacific Fleet sunk or damaged at Pearl Harbor, repairs were the first case of top urgency. Fortunately, the ships lay in shallow water next to a well-equipped navy yard, so salvage and repair were possible for most of them. Close upon this came the frantic call for adequate escort vessels for the Atlantic, where German submarines were savagely attacking even in coastal waters. Those same months were emphasizing the fast-growing importance of large carriers, which were dangerously scarce. To make way for them, plans for five super-battleships were indefinitely postponed. Forrestal found on his 1942 trip to the South Pacific that cruisers, too, must be another "crash program," because of losses in the Solomons. The biggest emergency, however, came from the need for landing craft, which like escort vessels should have been provided long before the war started. With the coasts of Europe and much of the Far Pacific in enemy hands, obviously troops would have to force their way ashore, often on shallow beaches. These small vessels remained high on priority lists from the spring of 1942 in preparation for the North African landings until near the end of the war. Eventually, auxiliaries of various sort rose to the top of those lists, while battleships, so over-emphasized before the war, slid steadily downward.

These changes in emphasis were one of the severest strains on the whole procurement system. The building of a major warship, for example, required a myriad of different parts from hundreds, if not thousands, of contractors and subcontractors, and all had to be scheduled to reach the shipyard at the exact time to be fitted into construction. Such items loomed large in the estimate of materials and facilities which Forrestal was trying to make more systematic; but all such planning went out the window when battleships, for instance, were sidetracked for small landing craft.

Some of these upheavals were unavoidable in the changing fortunes of war, but others came from the lack of foresight of the professional naval experts. Part of the trouble may have stemmed from the still potent belief in battleships and a conservative attitude toward three novel types: destroyer escorts, escort carriers, and landing craft. But part may be blamed on penury and perfectionism, resulting from the lean 1930s, when the Navy had to count costs and insist upon getting the very best possible for its money. Then there was time enough to achieve perfection, but the attitude lingered on to some extent even after Pearl Harbor in Naval Operations, at Fleet headquarters, and in the General Board. From the industrial angle, even relatively simple construction problems became grievously complicated in these last-minute scrambles.

Forrestal's faith in the infallibility of those top military planners was particularly shaken by their successive wrong guesses and the ensuing delays in the destroyer escort program that left shipping needlessly exposed to U-boats for more than a year. In 1940, for example, the Navy had only 225 destroyers and no destroyer escorts (DEs); by the end of the war, they stood at 373 and 385 respectively. The delay in DEs was inexcusable for the need for this type should have been obvious from the submarine experiences of World War I. By mid-1940, Britain's desperate need for escort vessels should have brought some action.

To the uninitiated, this new type looked little different from a destroyer proper. The vital reasons for the DE were that it made less of a demand upon critical materials and precious man-hours; could be built faster; and with its lesser speed was far cheaper, costing about five and a half million, than the wartime destroyer at about eight million. Yet the DE was nearly as big, and its 20-knot speed in contrast to the destroyer's 35-knots was sufficient for chasing submarines away from the slow convoys of 10-knot merchantmen. Also, being of near-destroyer size, it could stand the grueling work of the North Atlantic, for which the old 110-foot subchaser and the newer 175-foot patrol craft were too small.[20]

From the top military rank itself in the person of Admiral King, who had had to suffer the consequences of the early bad guesses, came some of the most scathing criticism of the DE muddle. His memoirs charge that Naval Operations and the General Board "began bickering about details of displacement, speed, and armament, and behaved as if time were of no consequence." As the years passed, he "regretted even more bitterly the perfectionism" that had caused the delay.[21]

The question of DEs was first posed when Admiral Stark asked the General Board in 1940 to "establish characteristics for an ideal escort vessel adequate to the purpose but capable of rapid and not too expensive construction in large numbers." They talked over a vessel similar to the eventual DE, for some seven months; then decided the relatively small saving in cost did not justify a new type. Apparently they completely overlooked the key fact that such a vessel could be built much faster. In February 1941, Stark consequently decided to concentrate on destroyers proper.

At just about that time, Captain Edward L. Cochrane and Commander Earle W. Mills of the Design Division of the new Bureau of Ships returned from four months in England where they had been studying the impact of modern weapons upon men-of-war. They had absorbed the British naval belief that the future escort vessel would have to be primarily an antisubmarine rather than an anti-aircraft vessel. By early 1941, Cochrane had designed what came to be known as the destroyer escort. Tremendously impressed with the almost unlimited demand for convoy craft, he induced Stark to create an informal board to study all types of small craft. This board recommended that vessels of the DE design be built because of their potential value in protecting convoys.

Once more, the General Board opposed the project. In April 1941, they reported that they "did not believe the resulting vessel, because of its weakness against air attack, is a proper vessel to escort convoys or that its military value is commensurate with the excessive cost." Stark a month later concurred in that cost-conscious judgment of the General Board, noting: "It is believed further that destroyers perform the duties of escort more satisfactorily and are of more all round use to the Naval Service." Consequently, he again recommended that no DEs be constructed. Knox agreed to this on May 19, 1941.[22]

Since the British naturally had a more immediate appreciation of the need for such vessels in view of the terrific toll from the U-boat wolf packs, Cochrane turned to them to apply pressure. Admiral Dorling, the British Admiralty Supply representative, transmitted the news to London with recommendations. On June 14, he received from the Admiralty a cablegram, which read in part:

Extended activity of enemy submarines has increased the necessity for vessels for convoy protection. . . . We understand that the United States have designed such a vessel. . . . If there is a reasonable prospect of early production of such vessels, some of them would contribute much to solving our escort program.[23]

On June 27, 1941, the British Supply Council formally requested one hundred DEs.

By that time, American shipyards were fully committed. The Bureau of Ships reported that the British request could be met only by constructing new yards, temporarily delaying some destroyer construction, or preferably by delaying battleship construction. Stark, on recommendation of the General Board, still believers in battleships, decided to have new facilities built.

As a result, the Pearl Harbor attack found the nation with only one hundred new destroyers and no DEs, except those British ones, even planned. The Navy had practically nothing available to protect the tankers and freighters that were being sunk in sight of American shores. Many of the little patrol craft on hand were slower and more weakly armed than the submarines they were hunting. A tale made the rounds of one such subchaser, too slow to get out of the way of her own depth charges; her commander reported "Sighted sub, sank self."

Forrestal now took a hand in the emergency. In a memorandum to Stark he urged DEs and pointed out the need for speedy acquisition of new facilities.[24] The submarine menace was so threatening that DEs were at last accepted, with 250 the immediate goal. Even so, Naval Operations put them in sixth place on the priority list behind everything else except submarines. Later that spring, the landing craft program was suddenly given top priority.[25]

The rest of the story concerns the difficulties of carrying the program through in the midst of the scarcities of an industrial mobilization. A year earlier, it would have been much simpler. The chief trouble lay in the lack of raw materials and component parts, particularly a shortage of valves of all types, needed for landing craft, merchant shipbuilding, synthetic rubber plants, and the atomic energy program.

By autumn 1942, the situation was so serious that Knox urged Roosevelt to cut back merchant shipbuilding, arguing that it was useless to build Liberty ships which the U-boats would sink if there were not enough DEs. The Americans and British together needed 1,400.[26] Admiral Robinson, analyzing the problem from the procurement standpoint, stated that not more than 300 could be completed in the next fifteen months. Even that, he said, would be possible only if DEs had top priority for materials above other naval shipbuilding; if skilled labor in shipyards and other crucial component plants were exempted from the draft; if DE engines were given priority by machine tool builders; and if 13 battleships, carriers, and cruisers on the ways were delayed three to twelve months. Instructing Nelson to expedite DE materials, Roosevelt said "All plans for offensive operations are hampered and limited because of the critical shortage of escort vessels." Month after month, the DE program was dogged by bottlenecks and shortages arising from competition with other programs.[27]

The first DE, one of that initial British group, was not completed until February 1943. By the end of that year, only half the 500 planned for the period had actually been built. Valuable as they proved themselves when finally at sea in quantity, they would have been infinitely more useful in the desperate days and nights of 1942.

The whole question of how military "requirements" were determined had begun to be questioned by Forrestal before the DE situation developed. Fairly early in his procurement program, he wanted to know whether the mechanics used in deciding the number of ships, aircraft, and trained men required were accurate, efficient, and unpadded. Yet years later what the military meant by requirements was still being thrashed out. Not until 1945, when materials and manpower in some areas were in particularly short supply and strategic plans were increasing their demands on industry did Forrestal as Secretary establish with King's consent the Requirements Review Board for better correlation. Hensel, then General Counsel, was its senior member, with Admiral Horne as Vice Chief of Naval Operations, and Admiral Robinson, as procurement head. Its purpose, according to Forrestal's instructions, was "to assure that balance is maintained within and between Navy material and personnel procurement programs and to keep procurement consistent with actual needs."

It did not satisfy Forrestal to be told that "airplane requirements" were determined by the number of carriers in service at the time, although twice as many could be used. "But in the case of submarines," he pursued his point, "it is truly a requirement, isn't it, because you could build more if you wanted them? How then did you determine the number?" The answer that requirements were related to crew training facilities did not seem realistic to him since, if more were actually "required," they could be built at the expense of other vessels. Horne and Robinson agreed that in this instance "estimates" with its implication of some "guessing" might be a better word. Hensel suggested "target" as closer to reality, citing rockets as an example, since certainly the war would go on whether or not a certain number of them were obtained. But the others present claimed that in other categories such as in outfitting ships and supplying advance bases only the term "requirements" was accurate. Actually the figure set as "required" depended on available manufacturing facilities, since the Navy wanted all it could get.[28]

Another real difficulty was control of military or command construction over which neither the Army and Navy Munitions Board nor the War Production Board had any say. Even at the end of 1942, when the most urgent military installations were well underway and steel, copper, and other building materials were in short supply, requests multiplied for all sorts of less essential military construction. As Nelson wrote to Knox:

As things now stand, facilities and construction, including many projects not related to the war effort . . . will absorb between 1/5 and 1/4 of the total war production. . . . Military construction should be reviewed. . . .[29]

The latter reacted in characteristic fashion with a brusque order to the bureau chiefs:

Facilities ashore designed for the convenience and comfort of personnel must be sacrificed before curtailing combatant facilities . . . work will be stopped immediately. . . . On quarters for married officers and men, chapels, auditoriums, and theatres . . . greenhouses, swimming pools, hostess houses, solariums. . . . the quality of facilities to be provided will be reduced to a scale now being provided for advance bases in the Pacific.[30]

Rear Admiral Moreell, Chief of Yards and Docks, voiced the general resentment to the Secretary:

All bureaus and officers are making a conscientious effort to comply with the Secretary's directive. In many instances there is an opportunity for exercising judgment with resultant differences of opinion . . . the Secretary's directive substitutes arbitrary dicta for considered judgment. This will result in confusion and false economy.[31]

Knox withdrew his directive after the bureaus had agreed to re-examine their construction projects.

The success of this self-policing by the bureaus was open to question. Both Forrestal and Robinson, on occasion, would disapprove an "industrial facility," only to find it being built anyway because it had been reclassified as a "command facility," and, as such, had been approved by the Chief of Naval Operations. This convinced Forrestal that rigid regulation of command facilities belonged only with the civilian Secretary since otherwise they posed a threat to any material program.

One of Forrestal's lieutenants in discussing in 1960 the lasting impact of his innovations in procurement, stated:

Forrestal believed in planning ahead and introduced the programming of requirements, the preparation of a catalog, inventory control, the matching of procurement against requirements, and efforts intelligently to deal with the overseas and combat stocks and their replacement. This concept has continued to flourish with vigor in the Navy. . . . The major reforms I think Forrestal introduced were to center responsibility for purchases in the designing and buying bureau and to combine technical, business and legal services at the negotiating table. . . . The concept of a civilian legal department has spread to all of the services and to the Office of the Secretary of Defense. It was a good idea and has been accepted, whereas I feared it would fade away.[32]

Included under Forrestal's cognizance, as Under Secretary, of the Judge Advocate General's Office were naval disciplinary procedures and the administration of Navy prisons. He acted for the Secretary in confirming sentences for courts-martial. For the first few months he followed the prescribed routine, signing on the dotted line without question. One day in 1942, however, he stopped to read the record of a young enlisted man sentenced to "confinement at hard labor for two years and a bad conduct discharge" for larceny, disobeying a lawful order of a superior, and resisting arrest.[33] Once the legal verbiage was stripped away, Forrestal found that it was a case of breaking into a ship's service store on a naval station and stealing two bottles of beer; he refused to confirm the sentence. He kept on examining all cases until there were too many for his crowded schedule. Forrestal also learned that he was not sufficiently familiar with Navy procedure to judge adequately and so turned the cases over to his aide, Commander John E. Gingrich. This did not mean any arbitrary setting aside of the Judge Advocate General's decision; in most cases it was confirmed. Forrestal's questioning continued, however, and extended to courts-martial procedure in general and to the prisons.

With the vast increase in personnel and the consequent rise in disciplinary actions, long delays resulted. There were three types of courts-martial: one-man deck courts for minor offenses, three-man summary courts for the intermediate category, and general courts convened on the Secretary's order for the most serious cases. The first step toward speeding that slow peacetime procedure was the recall, with Forrestal's approval, of some retired senior officers to establish permanent general courts in the naval districts.

But the backlog of cases steadily grew after Pearl Harbor. When

Forrestal and Gingrich passed through San Francisco on returning from the South Pacific in the fall of 1942, they were shocked to find the brigs full of men awaiting trial, some for many months. Added to Forrestal's original desire to see impartial justice was his concern over the waste of manpower. A letter to Rear Admiral Denfeld, Assistant Chief of Naval Personnel, suggested greater use of summary courts and the transfer of men with shorter sentences to outlying stations in place of confinement. BuPers did not consider, however, that 1,200 cases awaiting trial and 675 serving sentences were "excessive" out of 1.1 million men; it pointed out that these were fewer than "in World War I for a Navy of less than half this number." [34]

Forrestal grew impatient by the following June, when the numbers had increased to 3,346 awaiting trial and 1,177 in prison.[35] He was not finding it easy to explain to inquiring Congressmen why their constituents in trouble were being held so long before trial. He suggested to Knox that Arthur A. Ballantine, a distinguished member of the New York bar, be asked to investigate the situation. With the help of Noel T. Dowling of Columbia Law School, Ballentine recommended the authority to convene general courts-martial be delegated to commandants of naval districts without awaiting departmental approval. Forrestal put this into effect on July 24, with the further instructions that the commandants use the permanent courts-martial, already established in their districts; apply standard punishments for common offenses; and use certain disciplinary barracks for men sentenced to nine months or less, instead of the prisons at Portsmouth, New Hampshire, and Mare Island, California.[36] Forrestal was following precedent in this; Franklin D. Roosevelt, as acting Secretary, had signed a similar directive on April 10, 1918.[37]

Within weeks, Forrestal created the Naval Clemency and Prison Inspection Board under Vice Admiral Joseph K. Taussig, with wide powers to correct inequalities, reward good prisoner behavior, and generally supervise brigs and prisons. Forrestal also abolished the publication of the names of officers convicted in general courts-martial. At the same time, he was never one to coddle the petty criminal or the malingerer. In reassuring Mrs. Franklin D. Roosevelt, for example, that Portsmouth Naval Prison, about which one of her socially-conscious friends was complaining, was operating satisfactorily, he added that, although he did not approve of brutalities in any prison: "I must say that when I consider the hardships which thousands of young Americans are facing in the front lines, I do not have much sympathy for men, who, through their own fault are serving sentences in the relatively comfortable and safe conditions of a prison." [38]

Forrestal's continuing concern over material problems led him again to the question of departmental reorganization. Whereas King and he had seen eye-to-eye on the DE delays, they were far apart on correlating the Navy's program and industrial mobilization. Both Knox and Forrestal considered it essential that the Navy's material program be synchronized with the military plans of the Joint Chiefs of Staff and the material situation under the War Production Board; King was not impressed with the importance of this. Back in 1942, in Europe, for instance, he admired the bluish-gray uniforms of some Allied forces so much that, upon his return, he abruptly issued a directive replacing khaki with gray for all officers' summer uniforms. Within a few hours, Folsom, descending upon Forrestal, protested on behalf of the War Production Board that this color change required hundreds of thousands of yards of new material, which could only be manufactured at the expense of other urgent clothing needs.[39] King was stubborn, and gray uniforms were already being worn when Forrestal canceled the directive. It has often been asked what real difference it would have made if King had succeeded in controlling material procurement; perhaps herein lies an answer.

Shortly after that attempt in 1942 by King to reorganize the top structure of the Navy with the Forrestal procurement organization the obvious target, there was a counterattack to split his new dual role by detaching him from the Chief of Naval Operations post. This move may have been generated by the general impatience at his persistent efforts at reorganization; and it was his authority as CNO, and not that as Commander-in-Chief of the United States Fleet, that he had been utilizing for reorganization. There was a feeling, too, in civilian executive circles, that he had originally wanted the Naval Operations post mainly because it was traditionally senior to the Fleet command. Whether or not this was so, he had left virtually all the logistical duties of that office to his Vice Chief, Admiral Horne.

King, according to his semi-autobiography, blamed Forrestal as the initiator of those counter proposals claiming that Forrestal had sought to convince Knox, the bureau chiefs, and others of the need for separating the two posts. At the first Quebec Conference in August 1943, the King account continues, Knox suggested to King that he take personal command of the Fleet for the forthcoming Pacific offensive and leave Horne to be Chief of Naval Operations. King countered "on the ground that Nimitz . . . was carrying out his duties admirably. . . . and his own personal presence was entirely unnecessary." Moreover, his double post had been created "because it was necessary to have one man, and one only, responsible for the military part of the Navy." When King sent for Horne in Washington, the latter "denied having had any hand" in the matter, "the Secretary had asked him about it" and he had replied that "the present organization seemed to him satisfactory." [40]

The movement gradually gained momentum. On September 23, 1943, Leahy was surprised to hear from Harry Hopkins that Roosevelt was considering the step, and recorded that he himself had always thought the two jobs separate.[41] As a matter of fact, each senior admiral disapproved of the other's wartime role.

Forrestal directed Horne to draw up a recommendation for the step, which by mid-January was embodied in a proposed Executive Order canceling those of December 18, 1941 and March 12, 1942, that had given King his double top position.[42] By this draft, he would keep his proposed five stars with a new title, "Admiral of the Navy and Commander, United States Fleet." Horne, with four stars would be in a post independent of King, as the "Chief of Naval Logistics and Material." [43] Those specific titles were so worded for very particular reasons. There was Roosevelt's resentment of the use of "Commander-in-Chief" by anyone but himself, as Knox mentioned in writing King.[44] "Chief of Naval Operations" was discarded because it had developed so many connotations over the past twenty-nine years that it seemed best to make a clean break with tradition and use more pertinent wording. The draft provided that the Chief of Naval Logistics and Material:

under the direction of the Secretary of the Navy . . . shall (1) be responsible for the preparation, readiness and logistic support of the United States Navy, (2) be responsible for the procurement of all ships, aircraft, personnel, material, and supplies required by the Commander, the United States Fleet, and (3) direct and coördinate the activities of the several Bureaus and Offices of the Navy Department, the United States Marine Corps and the United States Coast Guard which relate to the responsibilities of the Chief of Naval Logistics and Material.[45]

On January 15, 1944, Forrestal discussed the proposal at lunch with Leahy, Bard, and Vice Admiral Emory S. Land, head of the Maritime Commission. Leahy repeated that he personally thought that the two jobs should be separated; then, later, wrote in his memoirs: "the question could have been settled quickly by a strong Secretary of the Navy but it was a festering controversy for a long time and was finally placed in the hands of the President." [46] Roosevelt and Knox agreed on the desirability of separating the offices. There are indications that they later discussed the change with Carl Vinson, chairman of House Naval Affairs, who also approved it.[47]

In that last connection, the King memoirs give a contrary account. Vinson, according to them, appeared one day in King's office and asked several times if there was anything the latter wished done. Several days later, Vinson called on Knox and apparently got him to assemble his principal civilian and military subordinates. Thereupon Vinson asked King if there were any changes that he wanted made in the Department, since Vinson "would be glad to have them dealt with in Congress at once." King replied that things seemed to be going well, but he would like to find out any changes which Knox desired, whereupon the meeting ended. Some weeks later, the account continues, King suddenly realized that this might have had something to do with the Cominch-CNO separation.[48]

During the middle weeks of January, one officer and official after another took a hand in composing alternative drafts on the subject. Those emanating from King and his immediate subordinates sought to retain the *status quo* in the double-barreled title. Some drafts added the previously rejected Deputy Chiefs of Naval Operations as well as new features. Knox voiced his reactions in a long memorandum to King, which said in part:

After reading them all I am oppressed by the fact that evidently I cannot get across to anyone what I want and what the President and I have agreed should be done. First, this is not to be any reorganization of the Navy Department. It is, first of all, an elevation in rank for yourself and, second, a division of the duties of the Office of Com-

Under Secretary Forrestal aboard the battleship *USS New Jersey*

At one of the many dinners on his active schedule, Secretary Forrestal (right) chats with Admiral Ernest J. King (center), Chief of Naval Operations, and Admiral William D. Leahy (left), Chief of Staff to the Commander-in-Chief

mander in Chief, U.S. Fleet and that of the Chief of Naval Operations. The change is designed to relieve you of that portion of your duties which relate to logistics and to confine your efforts to the actual conduct and operation of the fleet. It will enlarge the Office of the Chief of Naval Logistics so that he will assume entire responsibility for the supplying of the fleet after you, as Admiral of the Navy, have determined what, where and when the supplies consist of. The Office of Naval Logistics is not subordinate to you; it is independent of you. In fact, the express purpose of this change is to relieve you of this responsibility. In so far as it may be necessary for the proper supply of the fleet for the Chief of Naval Logistics to direct and coordinate the other Bureaus and Offices of the Navy Department, that shall be done. But it is not contemplated that either you or the Chief of Naval Logistics will take over entire management and control of the Navy Department. That will remain as hitherto, just where it is now—in the hands of the Secretary of the Navy.[49]

Knox died just three months later; and the solution would lie in Forrestal's hands.

7

The White House and the Hill

IN NAVAL matters only occasionally did a President actively exercise his latent authority; but the power of Congress was always in evidence. Coming in as Under Secretary, Forrestal had little to do with the White House and not much more with the Hill, but such contacts steadily increased in frequency and importance, reaching a climax in his last two years as Secretary.

A Secretary's ability to achieve the proper liaison with the President and Congress influenced the degree of his control within the Navy. Sometimes the military by-passed a Secretary to deal directly with the White House and the Hill. Such a break in the chain of authority made real civilian control difficult because the President lacked the time and, usually, sufficient information to exercise close and continuous direction of naval affairs; and the same was true of most members of Congress. Forrestal early recognized the vital importance of this relationship.

His contacts with the White House seem to have fallen into five periods. From June to August 1940, as Administrative Assistant to Roosevelt, his relationship was far less intimate than his title implied. Next, as Under Secretary until May 1944, he was seldom in direct communication with Roosevelt. But, thereafter, as a Cabinet member, he was in close contact with the White House: with Roosevelt until his death in April 1945, and continuing as Navy Secretary under Truman until September 1947, when he became the latter's Defense Secretary. The differences between those periods emphasize the highly subjective relationships with both Presidents and with the chairmen of Congressional committees. It is not enough to say in textbook fashion: "The President does so-and-so; the Chairman does this and that; and the Secretary does the following." Such generalities have scant validity when dealing with such men as Franklin D. Roosevelt, Carl Vinson, and James Forrestal, each of whom was an individual in his own right.

As far as the Roosevelt situation went, the actual amount of communication with Forrestal was less significant than the President's persistent close interest in naval matters. His predilections, prejudices, and practices in relation to the Navy had a deep significance in any analysis of civilian authority during all his twelve years in office, 1933–1945.

Since its beginning, the Navy had been just another branch of the government to most of the Presidents. The Adams and Roosevelt families were the exception. The tendency of each of the latter to be "his own Secretary of the Navy" suggests a shipboard analogy. Whereas the control of shiphandling movements ("conn") is in the hands of a succession of officers of the deck, the basic responsibility, of course, is the captain's, wherever he may happen to be. Normally, he does not participate in that routine, but under certain circumstances, such as entering port or engaging in battle, he may announce to the watch officer that he is taking over the "conn" himself, thus assuming direct control over actions for which he would be ultimately responsible anyway. A President who may decide to "act as his own Secretary" in a department is exercising a similar legal prerogative, though he rarely announces his intention. Too often, moreover, a President has neglected the further shipboard procedure of formally turning back the "conn" to indicate that, with the emergency over, the Secretary is on his own again.

Forrestal shared the general belief that it was proper for a President to take personal control in any department at a time when its operations were of national importance. Lincoln, as a war President, even interfered with the Army's strategy. It was unique, however, for a President to be constantly concerned, even in peacetime, about service minutiae as Roosevelt was with the Navy's. He had too many other things to do to attempt to be a full-time Secretary, but as a part-time one, his interest was unflagging. He had had, of course, eight years in the Navy Department as Assistant Secretary under President Wilson. Certainly, on the whole, the Navy profited greatly, especially in the matter of large appropriations from this flattering attitude, although it aroused some jealousy in other departments.

But that Presidential interest had its price, however, and naval officers were sometimes heard to murmur, "I wish to God he'd get absorbed in the Army for a change." The war, moreover, revealed some serious Navy shortcomings that might have been avoided had not Roosevelt kept an ailing Secretary, Claude Swanson, in office for the first six years of his Presidency, at a time when vigilance was essential. This gave Roosevelt the chance to act as his own Secretary. He developed a habit—that he thoroughly enjoyed—of dealing directly with the Chief of Naval Operations, Standley, Leahy, and Stark in turn. Admiral W. H. Standley reports that during much of his term as CNO, 1932–36, he was also Acting Secretary of the Navy:

> The President had an inflated opinion of his own knowledge of naval stategy and tactics and he much preferred to be his own Secretary of the Navy. With no Assistant Secretary of the Navy and Swanson so ill, F.D.R. could run the Navy pretty much as he pleased. . . .
> Until my retirement, I sat as a full fledged member of the New Deal Cabinet. The President and I developed a very successful working arrangement because we both wanted the same thing—an effective sea going Navy, fully manned and built up to full treaty strength.[1]

With the President's left-handed attention at best occasional and with no civilian leadership within the Department itself, civilian control became spasmodic.

At the same time, Roosevelt knew that the Navy could resist domination, as he once told the head of the Federal Reserve Bank:

> . . . the Treasury and the State Department put together are nothing compared with the Na-a-vy. The admirals are really something to cope with and I should know. To change anything in the Na-a-vy is like punching a feather bed. You punch it with your right and you punch it with your left until you are finally exhausted, and then you find the damn bed just as it was before you started punching.[2]

The Roosevelt influence, or interference as some called it, continued in all kind of things with his later Secretaries. His caprice led him into some very minor details, more or less on a par with his interest in stamp collecting. A paper in the old records shows how even as Assistant Secretary he once spent a delightful half hour deciding whether a new minesweeper should be named *Snipe* or *Plover*. Because of a whimsical moment in his later days, a big carrier had to suffer the name of *Shangri-La*. His naming of vessels, however, went beyond playful moods. It was a tradition that every deceased Chief of Naval Operations rated having a destroyer named for him, but there was no *Coontz* until 1961. Assistant Secretary Roosevelt had not approved of the second CNO, and so, President Roosevelt had accordingly scratched out his name, whenever it was suggested.

Altogether the Roosevelt hand probably fell most heavily on personnel questions. It was said he kept a well-worn copy of the *Navy Register* at hand, and would sometimes run through the lists of admirals and captains, making pungent comments upon name after name. These usually reflected his reactions back in his Assistant Secretary days. Some like Leahy and Stark were remembered favorably, a few others were not. Admiral Joseph K. Taussig felt the repercussions of a run-in with the Assistant Secretary a whole quarter century later. Also unfortunate were some who had not crossed his path; in 1938, he scratched out the name of the nominee for the Fleet battleship command—"Why, I do not even know Admiral X." [3]

His participation even extended to matters of hospital design. While a new National Naval Medical Center was under discussion, Roosevelt on a trip was intrigued by the state capitol's tall, thin tower in Lincoln, Nebraska; later, the skyscraper "Cathedral of Learning" at the University of Pittsburgh caught his eye. Thereupon, he sketched a high, slender tower as the dominating feature for the new Medical Center. In vain did the Surgeon General, Rear Admiral Ross T. McIntyre, his personal physician, backed by the Assistant Chief, urge that this ran counter to all trends in hospital design and meant enormous extra overhead with the need for full ward equipment for each small tower floor.[4] They succeeded only in getting a somewhat wider tower.

A corollary of that Roosevelt naval interest was his jealous insistence upon being kept informed of everything that went on at the Department. His naval aides, who served as his "eyes and ears" there, regularly brought up copies of most of the interesting documents. Forrestal as Secretary established the Commendation Ribbon as a new decoration without consulting the President. Many had been awarded before Roosevelt heard of it; it is said that only with difficulty was he restrained from ordering its abolition.[5]

Perhaps no other President took quite as seriously as Roosevelt the constitutional title, "Commander-in-Chief of the Army and Navy," even resenting that each fleet, following British tradition, had a commander-in-chief. As Knox once expressed it: "The President feels that there is only one "Commander-in-Chief and that is himself." [6] Just before the war, he issued a unique "Military Order" under which Forrestal would have to live. This first extension of White House operational control—others followed during the war —had brought the joint Army and Navy boards "under the direction and supervision of the President as Commander-in-Chief." [7]

Another development of like nature was the establishment of the novel role of "Chief of Staff to the President as Commander-in-Chief" for Admiral William D. Leahy, former CNO and more recently Ambassador to France. It was through him that Roosevelt learned of the deliberations of the Joint Chiefs of Staff and the Combined Chiefs of Staff; he was by seniority chairman of both.[8]

The "map room" in the White House basement was another manifestation of the President as Commander-in-Chief. Churchill, during his visit after Pearl Harbor, had had one set up for himself; and Roosevelt was much intrigued. The British had long had their Admiralty Map Room, a highly secret, closely guarded hideaway, where maps and charts might safely be kept up-to-date to give instantly a comprehensive picture of current operational developments. Churchill's traveling outfit was a pretty sketchy counterpart of this, consisting of a few collapsible easels and some rolled-up charts. Roosevelt wanted something of the sort for himself. All he had available were a "few charts lying on a table in the old Cabinet Room, a pair of parallel rulers, and a set of dividers, and a Navy Chief Quartermaster to help out"; he was keeping his most secret dispatches in a desk drawer. His naval aide, Captain John L. McCrea, with the help of Lieutenant (j.g.) Robert Montgomery, the movie star, who had had duty at the Admiralty Map Room, set up the one in the White House. Later, McCrea also had the services of Lieutenant William C. Mott from Naval Intelligence in deciding what information should be entered on the maps. Army and Army Air soon participated, but the naval aide remained in charge. There were watch officers around the clock. Roosevelt turned over those secret dispatches of his to McCrea, saying he was assured that here they would not find their way into any columnist's hands. He usually visited it twice a day, and Harry Hopkins was the only other civilian regularly admitted. According to Admiral Leahy, more information was concentrated here than in any other office in Washington. McCrea does not recall Knox or Forrestal ever visiting it, but one day in the fall of 1942, the President remarked to McCrea "about as follows: 'Our Secretary of War, Harry Stimson, needs a lesson in geography and Papa is just the fellow to give it to him.'" When Stimson arrived, they went around the Map Room discussing operations in various parts of the world. "When we came to the Pacific," McCrea continues, "the President talked at length about the naval operations." He kept repeating: "Remember, Harry, the Pacific Ocean is not like the Atlantic: the Pacific is an ocean of vast distances." [9]

Although Forrestal never questioned that high policy was the province of the President and the admirals, he did expect to be informed—as was the Secretary of War—about their decisions in order to bring the Navy's organization into conformity. He realized that most military decisions involved political questions in the sense of public policy. The North African invasion, for example, not only required endless decisions about manpower and material but also involved the attitude of the allied forces toward the French government in Algiers, which was a politico-military problem. It was in such larger questions of policy, the relation of military force and foreign relations in the areas that concerned the everyday administration of the Navy that Forrestal, once he became Secretary, insisted upon being the liaison with the White House.

Roosevelt's tendencies to shift the Navy's control to his own level were doubtless fortified by his constant communication with Churchill, who did not hesitate to ride roughshod over admirals and subordinate officials. He had been First Lord of the Admiralty from 1911 to 1915 and again in 1939–40 before becoming Prime Minister. The two made many major strategic decisions at their conferences, to which they took their military advisers but rarely any of the Armed Services Secretaries. Though both men considered themselves prime authorities on all things naval, Roosevelt was not inclined to interfere with his admirals in operational details of the

Fleet, any more than with his generals.[10] Churchill, however, drew forth bitter professional naval criticism for not limiting himself to grand strategy.[11] Roosevelt's exclusion of civilian Secretaries from strategic and operational matters lasted throughout his Presidency. He was not able, however, to keep his hand in internal naval administration as much in the wartime rush, but otherwise he did not change his course.

Forrestal's personal relations with him seem to have been cordial, but not intimate or particularly frequent. During his weeks as Administrative Assistant, he rarely saw the President, but other White House connections he gained then were useful later. While Under Secretary, for instance, needing to resort to indirect channels to get a message through to Roosevelt, he knew Stephen Early of the "palace guard" well enough to write "Dear Steve: Can you get the gist of this message to the Boss, or should I do it through some other channel? I should appreciate your advice." [12]

Now and then, while Under Secretary, Forrestal "sat in" on Cabinet meetings in Knox's absence. Aside from that, he apparently saw the President most frequently early in 1941, before and after his trip to London on Lend-Lease business. He was at the White House six times between February 13 and March 12, and dined there once.[13] Some of those conferences seem to have been very technical, judging from this memorandum:

> Other questions discussed last Friday:
> 1. Flying by easy stages via Newfoundland, Greenland and Iceland does not seem practicable owing to bad weather conditions and impossible landing field conditions at Greenland.
> 2. Transfer of small planes by carriers to Takoradi or Lagos is practicable if carriers have adequate protection of cruisers or destroyers.
> 3. There is another question that you asked—that is with reference to the use of 70 and 77 foot sea sleds with pompon and Y-gun. The answer of this is not yet available but Admiral Ingersoll is working on it.[14]

Very different was the grist of administrative matters being discussed after Forrestal became Secretary. On January 2, 1945, he sent to Roosevelt the following agenda, which "I would like to talk with you about":

> 1. Carl Vinson wants us to ask for appropriations to use up the 750,000 tons unused authorizations. His argument is that we may suffer drastic losses as we move into the infighting stage in Japan.

2. I would like to suggest the termination of Admiral Stark's tour of duty in London as of March 1. Ghormley or Hewitt would be available to succeed him.

3. I want to discuss with you the replacement of Admiral Young as head of S&A.

4. Certain promotions in various staff corps.

5. The possibility of giving the Assistant Secretary for Air seniority over the Assistant Secretary by Executive Order. The reason: Di Gates has been here three years and Hensel, of course, is a newcomer. This only has significance, of course, in the event of the absence of both myself and the Under Secretary.

6. Legislation on the Joint Chiefs of Staff. Carl Vinson proposed this last summer and wanted us to draft a bill. I told him that we could not do this without a discussion with you. He proposes giving statutory permanence to the JCS.

7. Awards to civilians working for the Navy. This latter I am rather anxious about because it is the only way by which we can give substantial recognition to civilians who have done exceptional work directly serving the Navy.

8. When Arthur Sulzberger returned from the Pacific he expressed the view very strongly that the interest of the public in the Pacific war would be greatly enhanced by permitting publishers to make the same trip he did—he came back greatly impressed with the scale and scope of our operations. I wonder if you would be willing to review your original decision. I do not believe that we would have an avalanche of applicants.

9. I would like to get your wishes on the Under Secretaryship.

10. Review of Naval history.

11. Revision of Navy Regulations.

Respectfully,
James Forrestal [15]

Once he was full Secretary, Cabinet meetings usually brought Forrestal to the White House every Friday afternoon. His various diary entries indicated that their rather desultory and ineffectual character disturbed him as it did most of his fellow members. The meetings were convenient occasions beforehand and afterward for discussions; but the meetings proper left much to be desired. Eventually, he recommended a secretariat; this was put into effect under President Eisenhower in 1954.[16]

Another White House contact was Harry Hopkins, Roosevelt's very influential adviser, with whom Forrestal's name had been linked from the outset. He lived in Lincoln's old study on the "family floor" of the White House from May 1940 until the fall of 1943, but had been a close Roosevelt associate from the early 1920s. The public at large thought of him as the "Chief Apostle of the New Deal," the freehanded spender of some nine billion dollars. But in the words of his biographer he became "the second most important individual in the United States Government during the most critical period of the world's greatest war"; although he had "no legitimate official position." [17]

Forrestal has been credited with making Hopkins an ardent interventionist. According to this account, Forrestal disagreed with the New Dealers'

reservations about committing the Government to combat the world crisis, and told them that the practical way to put the New Deal program across was to sell it as Preparedness, not as Reform. . . . The main convert . . . Harry Hopkins . . . with characteristic zealousness, jumped . . . to the opposite extreme.[18]

Forrestal and Hopkins were brought together often when the President put the latter in charge of Lend-Lease. Both had unusual analytical ability, and they developed a mutual regard. Forrestal suggested that Hopkins be added to the group in the reorganized meetings of the State-War-Navy Secretaries. Stimson, King, and Marshall were likewise impressed by this "new" Hopkins, whatever the danger implicit in the highly subjective and informal role of such a "President's familiar."

With the death of Roosevelt on April 12, 1945 and Truman's accession to the Presidency, the pattern of Forrestal's White House relations were radically altered. In contrast to the Rooseveltian olympian air of omniscience, there was a brief, albeit very brief, humility in Truman. Likewise new to grand strategy and in a lesser but still considerable degree to international relations were Edward R. Stettinius, Secretary of State, and his successor in July, James F. Byrnes. At this time, too, Churchill fell from power. Also, Harry Hopkins, long ill, could no longer work. With this disappearance of the Roosevelt-Churchill-Hopkins triumvirate, Forrestal became the senior of the State-War-Navy Secretaries in September when Stimson turned over the War Department to Robert P. Patterson (see Appendix B).[19]

Even more significant in enhancing his relative importance and influence, in the politico-military field especially, was that he had early appreciated the major implications of the new American world leadership. And now he realized that he not only had the knowledge to speak out as a leader but was in a position where he could take the initiative in meeting the coming problems. There were, moreover, none more experienced in that field than he left in the Cabinet to overshadow him. Consequently, he undertook the "education" of Truman in vital matters. Scarcely anyone had been bold enough to engage in the impious *lèse majesté* of indoctrinating Roosevelt, and humble as Truman had first seemed, this was a hazardous occupation. Years later, Truman wrote that he had dismissed Byrnes for trying to do too much on his own, and Secretary of the Interior Ickes because he had "grown too big for his breeches." [20]

Forrestal persisted, however, for Truman, though acquainted with the material side of the military-naval picture from his Senatorial investigating, was a neophyte in much else. Actually, Forrestal had begun this process while Truman was a Senator. The first entry of the Forrestal diary, July 4, 1944, tells of lunching with Truman: "We endeavored to persuade him of the unwisdom of the resumption of civilian production." The entry ended: "When he left I had the impression that we had not made great headway with our argument." [21]

Now and then in the diary Forrestal made personal comments about Truman. Writing about bringing up unification with him at Potsdam, Forrestal added: "It is clear that most of his thinking was predicated upon his experience in the Army during the last war and in the National Guard since then. . . . My impression is that he is not close-minded nor will he hold rigidly to his own views." [22] Four months later, the diary indicated a somewhat different view; in regard to Truman's strong pro-Army stand, Forrestal records telling the President that he had not yet considered "the real merits of the case." [23]

Forrestal was to see far more of Truman than he had of Roosevelt, but appears to have been no more intimate with him. Their more frequent meetings seem to have remained on the formal side. Truman instituted Cabinet luncheons in addition to its weekly meetings. But beyond those routine affairs, many other occasions brought Forrestal—often accompanied by civilian deputies, admirals, or Naval Affairs chairmen—to the White House. Sometimes he had been summoned, but generally he took the intiative himself.

A Forrestal master stroke, in the best naval "boat ride" technique, was getting Truman to sea aboard the big carrier *Franklin D. Roosevelt*, in April 1946. He suggested it to Captain Clark Clifford, then naval aide: "What are the chances of the President's being aboard Mitscher's flagship for a couple of days in the forthcoming maneuvers?"[24] The Navy made the most of its opportunity to "demonstrate the distinctive mysteries of sea power" during those days of what was also doubtless persistent persuasiveness on Forrestal's part.[25] This was probably his closest continual contact with either President during his years in the Department.

Under Truman, Forrestal also succeeded fairly well in making himself master in his own house. In departmental administration he was at last able to enjoy full authority. Truman, being a former commander of a National Guard battery in France, had no possessive feelings about the Navy. Forrestal in dramatic fashion showed that he intended no longer to be excluded from the major policy conferences by "crashing" the Potsdam-Berlin Conference in July 1945. He was likewise victorious in a strenuous encounter with King over the relationship of the postwar Chief of Naval Operations to the President and to the Secretary.[26]

"Forrestal is the best Secretary of the Navy I've ever had," once declared Carl Vinson, perennial chairman of the House Naval Affairs Committee.[27] That superlative "best" is less significant than the proprietary tone of the "I've ever had." If the President had said this, it would have been less surprising, but coming from Vinson it spanned the wide gap between Legislative and Executive established by the Founding Fathers in 1787 when they wrote the principles of separation of powers into the Constitution.

Forrestal himself was always interested in narrowing the Executive-Legislative chasm—symbolized by the mile separating the White House from the Capitol. He saw certain advantages in the British system, under which the Cabinet ministers exercised authority only as long as their party retained the confidence of the House of Commons. One of his more academic proposals, which never got off the ground, was to adopt that part of the House of Commons practice whereby the First Lord of the Admiralty and every other Cabinet member had to have a seat in the House of Commons or the House of Lords. What particularly interested Forrestal was the custom of the "question hour," when the First Lord or one of his deputies could be subjected in Parliament to formal questioning on the state of the Navy. He not only failed to appreciate the difficulties of grafting this procedure onto the American government, but, in time, he came to feel that hearings before Congressional committees were much more effective than formal questions in the Commons.[28]

Perhaps his most fruitful efforts came from his wide acquaintanceship in Congress. Its surprising extent, even early in the war, came to light when Knox asked Forrestal, Bard, Gates, and Adlai Stevenson —a special assistant of his—to list the members of Congress whom they knew fairly well. Knox had decided that it would be advisable for the civilian executives to consolidate their efforts toward improving relations with the Hill. In the replies, Forrestal reported seventy names, the others only fifteen or twenty each.[29] Of these, only Lyndon Johnson of Texas appeared on all four lists, but he was, to be sure, on the House Naval Affairs Committee and was also a reserve lieutenant commander whom Forrestal had ordered, two days after Pearl Harbor, to report to his office for special duty.

By the time that Forrestal became full Secretary, he knew "at least fairly well" many more than that initial seventy. His personal files and the records of his telephone calls indicate that this was not just by chance but quite deliberate. He had made good use with Senators and Congressmen of his techniques of tailor-made correspondence; luncheon, dinner, and even breakfast invitations; and boat rides,[30] even though with some of the less popular members, he would write Knox in this vein: "I think it will be wise to have Senator —— up for lunch if you can stand him." These contacts, too, were potent instruments in Forrestal's incessant quest for opinions and equally persistent efforts to plant ideas. Again and again he appeared before some of these same acquaintances collectively in the necessary and frequent hearings before one Congressional committee or another. Altogether, the influence he achieved through association and by reputation for astuteness would later stand the Navy in good stead on the Hill (see Appendix J).

Congress has always had wide powers over what the Navy should *be* in contrast to the Executive's over what it should *do*. Most important are the twin hurdles of authorization and appropriation which expenditures for personnel and material have to pass. Commissions, promotions, and top civilian posts normally require Senate confirmation. In Forrestal's case his three nominations went through the Senate virtually by voice vote. Some isolationist opposition, on the other hand, kept Knox from unanimous confirmation, while some other civilian executives found it rough going.[31] There is also the potent function of investigation to which Congress frequently resorts. Finally, through general legislation, it exercises oversight of naval administration. A unique feature has been the extent to which Congress virtually delegates a great deal of this authority to permanent "standing" committees. Originally set up to sift out facts and make recommendations, Congress has come more and more to rely on their judgment in legislation affecting the armed services, as well as in foreign affairs, commerce, and the other functional areas.

Those committees pertinent to the Navy might be said to have exercised over it, down through the years, the most constant and perhaps the most potent form of civilian control. Certainly, it has been the most obvious. Several times each year the Department's top officials, military and civilian, journey to the Hill to be questioned about new proposals, to "justify" appropriations, or to face an investigation. Closest to the Navy were the Naval Affairs Committees—the Senate's in existence since 1816 and the House group six years younger. While a wide variety of naval matters, great and small, came under them, the authorization of expenditures has probably been their most important function, since the size and composition of the Navy was in the first instance dependent upon the authorization acts.[32]

But the days of those two committees were already numbered when Forrestal became Secretary. Congress in 1946 as part of its own major reorganization decreed that in both Senate and House, the venerable Naval and Military Affairs Committees be merged into the new Armed Services Committees. Thus, Congress anticipated in its own organization the unification of the armed services.[33]

The formal role of the various committees was modified strongly by the personalities of their chairmen. The custom of Congressional seniority involved an almost appalling element of chance, with the chairmanship going to that member of the dominant political party with the longest continuous service on that particular committee. The Navy, generally fortunate in the men who had headed Senate and House Naval Affairs through the years, was never more so than in Carl Vinson of Georgia, one of the great American naval legislators. That shrewd veteran of the House had achieved seniority by starting young. A country lawyer admitted to the bar at the age of eighteen, he was elected to Congress in 1914 at thirty-one. Three years later found him on House Naval Affairs, and there he stayed indefinitely, becoming chairman in 1931. The personality and astute mastery of legislative strategy and tactics of "The Admiral," "The Swamp Fox," or "Uncle Carl," as he was nicknamed, made him a power in the whole House.

Under him, the Committee was remarkable for its nonpartisan harmony and cooperation. When, in 1944, a gracious ceremony marked his completion of 30 years in the House, three Republican members of the Committee led in conducting the affair. At the close of hostilities the following year, Forrestal wrote to Vinson "I hold the belief that the cooperation of the Naval Affairs Committees in both House and Senate constitutes one of the finest examples of teamwork between the executive and legislative departments of the Government in our history." [34] In 1946, at the last meeting of the Committee, Forrestal added his public tribute to Vinson's nonpartisanship:

You have maintained the responsibility of the party in power, but you have, it seems to me, always been scrupulously careful to give your colleagues on the Republican side of the House a complete and equal chance to express their views, and that, it seems to me, is an affirmation of the fact that this is an important function of a democracy and shows that democracy is functioning at a time when it has serious problems ahead of it.

In your conduct of the committee you have proved that the two-party system can work.[35]

Likewise, Vinson was repeatedly expressing warm and continuing admiration for Forrestal. Although the latter's confirmation as Secretary of the Navy was naturally a Senate, not a House, matter, that did not keep Vinson silent. He wrote Forrestal that he had "learned with the utmost satisfaction" of the decision, and enclosed a formal resolution by House Naval Affairs: "No one has a more thorough knowledge of the Navy and no one is more eminently qualified to lead it through the remainder of this greatest of all wars to final victory. He knows the Navy and the Navy knows him." [36]

Much later in the dark days of the spring of 1949, when everything seemed to be tumbling into ruins for Forrestal, Vinson again went out of his way to honor him. On March 29, the day after he resigned as Secretary of Defense, he was invited by Vinson to attend a special meeting of the House Armed Services Committee "to take official notice" of his retirement. After an impressive review of Forrestal's official achievements, Vinson said:

Mr. Secretary, in the years I have been a member of the Committee on Naval Affairs and, more recently, this committee, a number of great and distinguished Americans have held the office of Secretary of the Navy. . . .

It is, in fact, a fair statement, Mr. Secretary, that you have assumed and performed with distinction duties far transcending in responsibility any heretofore undertaken by any previous Navy Secretary in the history of our great nation.

That you filled the office in such critical and momentous days would be honor enough for any man.

That you filled the office with such outstanding success entitles you to distinction and recognition far beyond that attainable by more than a few men in our history.[37]

The Hill was with Forrestal to the end. At his tragic death, two months afterward, many other members of Congress paid further glowing tribute to him as a great public servant.[38] A more conspicuous evidence of the feelings of the House Naval Affairs-Armed Services Committee came later. One of Forrestal's old friends on that Committee, Jack V. Anderson of California, determined that the great new supercarrier that was being planned be called the *Forrestal*. Defense Secretary Louis Johnson opposed both the ship and the name.[39] House Armed Services, on Anderson's motion, inserted in an authorization measure that Forrestal's name should be given to the vessel, which when she was launched, would be the mightiest warship afloat.[40]

Not only did Congress look to Vinson as the Navy's authoritative spokesman, because of his remarkable grasp of naval affairs, but the Navy itself was always ready to ask his advice. Whether or not he actually referred to "my Navy," his attitude was paternalistic if not possessive. Like Roosevelt, his desire to know everything that was going on made it routine to consult him on almost every new development, even when not within his immediate cognizance. He was jealous of any encroachment on the powers of

Congress in general and Naval Affairs in particular. Although the First War Powers Act permitted naval reorganization by executive action, Vinson called Forrestal's attention to the desirability of Congressional legitimization in some such matters. During the war years, Vinson and Forrestal were drawn together more closely by the former's special investigating function than by regular Naval Affairs matters.

In comparison, Forrestal's relationship with the last chairman of Senate Naval Affairs was a pale and casual affair. David I. Walsh was elected in 1918 as Massachusetts' first Democratic senator since the pre-Civil War era.[41] Defeated in 1924, he returned in 1926, to remain until defeated again in 1946. He was nine years older than Vinson, but twelve years junior in continuous Congressional service. Originally an isolationist, Walsh supported the war when it came. He took a brief but fairly important part with Forrestal in early unification proceedings at the close of his chairmanship, but did not give such single-minded concentration to naval matters as Vinson, of whom he became decidedly jealous around 1940.[42] He did not enjoy the same relative primacy within his own committee. Also, he was inclined to be more partisan than Vinson in many matters, and the Republican minority in his committee felt the difference.[43]

With the merger in January 1947 into the Armed Services Committees, nine months before Forrestal moved to the Pentagon, both chairmanships ended. Walsh was no longer in the Senate, now with its Republican majority. Vinson, however, continued on the new House committee, but only as ranking minority member. The new Republican chairmen, Senator Chan Gurney of South Dakota and Representative Walter G. Andrews from upstate New York, were both experienced on the old military committees. Two years later, Vinson succeeded Andrews as chairman of the House Armed Services Committee, with the Democrats again in control.

While these committees authorized naval projects, the necessary funds had to be voted by the appropriation committees. This had not always been so. Between the mid-1880s and early 1920s, the Naval Affairs committees had been in the happy situation of granting the funds for projects they had, themselves, authorized. Thereafter, the naval subcommittee of House Appropriations—subcommittees did the bulk of the appropriation work—quickly became a power to be reckoned with in the naval system. Its probing hearings called for "justification" of every detailed item, and its members developed a thorough grasp of naval matters in the process. The Senate subcommittee generally seemed inclined to take a less exacting revisionary stand. The fear of possibly "getting in wrong" with those potent groups continually hung over the Department—officers wearing ribbons for bravery against the Germans or Japanese could pale at that thought.

Representative Henry R. Shepard of California, who succeeded to the chairmanship of the House naval subcommittee in 1943 when James G. Scrugham of Nevada became Senator, worked hard at his appropriations duties. Shepard came to Congress in 1937 having retired from business at the age of forty-nine. He had had a varied career that ranged from the study of law, activity with the Brotherhood of Railroad Trainmen, a copper business in Alaska to a "beverage and laboratories" corporation. Republican control in 1947 brought Representative Charles A. Plumley of Vermont, former president of a bank and of Norwich University, to the chairmanship. But for once, it was the chairman of the full House Appropriations Committee, John Taber of New York, who figured in the foreground of the naval appropriations picture in some strenuous tussles with Forrestal.

The Senate Appropriations subcommittee devoted much less time to naval matters, partly because of the traditional House initiative in fiscal matters and partly because its members had so many other committee demands. The chairman most prominent and helpful in the Forrestal picture was Leverett Saltonstall, the shrewd "proper Bostonian," who also came to the post in the 1947 Republican taking-over. He was a tower of strength to Forrestal, both there and on Senate Armed Services.

Investigations of naval matters assumed a rather irregular pattern during and after the war when they were a major Congressional activity. The Senate's "Special Committee Investigating the National Defense Program," better known by the name of its first chairman, Harry S. Truman, covered both Army and Navy matters, but the latter received only a minor part of its time. The scope of the House investigations was much the same, but instead of one special committee, the House delegated its investigating function to its two standing committees, which meant in the Navy's case, its Naval Affairs Committee. Thus, for six years—April 1941 to January 1947—"Vinson's Committee," under his chairmanship, "wore two hats," with this additional duty superimposed upon its regular work. Forrestal had much to do with those investigating committees, for during the war they tended to concentrate on procurement and other material aspects. Forrestal's relationship was particularly close with the House committee, while Robert E. Kline, Jr., formerly with the Navy's Procurement Legal Division, served as the committee's general counsel. In fact, he was even invited to Forrestal's weekly council meetings.[44]

Forrestal, although known as a past master in man-to-man contacts before he came to Washington, had to develop a technique for his appearances before these committees and others less intimately associated with the Navy. His early efforts seemed to have left much to be desired. With his natural shyness, the rough-and-tumble give and take of a Congressional hearing was, if anything, less pleasant for him than for some other Secretaries, but he forced himself to face up to it. Some of his predecessors had withdrawn in disgust to leave the testifying to the officers.

His ultimate success in developing an easy manner for dealing with hearings was achieved despite two handicaps beyond his control. It was something of an anomaly that, while the Secretary was expected to be the primary liaison between the Department and Congress, many committee members preferred to deal directly with the naval officers, rather than another civilian, perhaps less experienced than themselves in naval matters. Rear Admiral Bradley A. Fiske, brilliant stormy petrel of thirty years before, never an enthusiast about civilian authority, wrote that in those days when he inquired of Congressmen why they got their ideas "filtered through the mind of a Secretary, who might transmit certain inaccuracies in the process of filtering," their answers "amounted to saying 'The military must be subordinate to the civil authority.' "[45] Even Vinson and some of Forrestal's other eventually warmest supporters had that general predilection for getting their information "straight from the sea dog's mouth."

Forrestal's other handicap applied only to his own situation; the Judge Advocate General, whose opposition to his Procurement Legal Division was so bitter, was the normal liaison between the Navy and the Naval Affairs committees. Plenty of stories exist of the in-fighting arising from that coincidence, but the JAG's men did not seem to make much headway in turning the minds of Congressmen against Forrestal.

Candor, self-control, and competence—or at least the appearance of them—might be said to be requisite for a successful witness. As was customary, Forrestal usually started off with a prepared statement that might run into several hundred words; for this, there was, of course, the chance to think it out and get critical advice or other assistance back at the Department. The real test for all Congressional witnesses came in the later stages of the ordeal when they had to handle any sort of question that might be fired at them; in that, Forrestal eventually became adept.

He showed a convincing frankness in discussing embarrassing charges, as in the following dialogue before the Truman Committee:

> Senator Brewster: Both Mr. Nelson and Mr. Ickes have indicated that there had been hoarding in some phases of the program. Would you care to comment on that?
>
> Mr. Forrestal: I have heard that, Mr. Senator, but I don't like to make statements that aren't visually supportable.
>
> Senator Brewster: Have you taken pains to avoid hoarding within the Navy Department?
>
> Mr. Forrestal: We have taken pains to avoid it, but I wouldn't agree it hasn't occurred. It might be too embarrassing to discuss.
>
> The Chairman [Truman]: I am glad you don't guarantee it, because it does happen.
>
> Mr. Forrestal: There is no question about it. Sometimes we are lucky that it did.
>
> The Chairman: I'll agree with that, too.[46]

Forrestal had no difficulty in conforming to that doctrine of "Hill tactics" that a witness never flared back even though the question might verge on the insulting or repeat what had just been fully answered. His emotions were ever in tight control. He would not have committed the tactical error attributed to one post-Forrestal Secretary of the Air Force before the potent Appropriations subcommittee. Called to account on some matter, he is said to have snapped back "Well, what's so important about this committee, anyway?"[47]

In the third requisite, competence, Forrestal was likewise particularly strong. He revealed a surprisingly intimate mastery of one subject after another in both broad and detailed aspects, only occasionally having to fall back on the experts: "But if you get down to the minute valves involved, you run as high as 24 hundred, which range in size from an eighth of an inch to 6 inches in diameter; and in weight, Admiral Mills, what should I say?" [48] This stood in marked contrast to the confession of Secretary John D. Long forty-five years earlier:

Went with Captain O'Neil, Chief of the Bureau of Ordnance this morning before the Senate Committee on Naval Affairs, in regard to armor plate. Of course I know nothing about it, and go through the perfunctory business of saying so, and referring the Committee to Captain O'Neil . . . I make [it] a point not to trouble myself overmuch to acquire a thorough knowledge of the details pertaining to any branch of this service.[49]

Many of the other amiable "stuffed shirts" who served as Secretary doubtless acted similarly—that may help explain the Congressional preference for officers.

Hill tactics, however, occasionally gave even the conscientious Forrestal a bad quarter hour. As Under Secretary he was called to account for backing a stadium as essential for the war effort. In mid-March 1944, the naval subcommittee of House Appropriations began to examine recommendations for several hundred items of public works construction. In the absence of Knox, this list went to Forrestal. Suddenly, one forenoon, the subcommittee requested his immediate appearance along with King and Horne. Neither admiral was free to attend, so Forrestal went alone, without the usual briefing. "It seems to some of us, Mr. Forrestal," said Plumley, the future chairman, then senior Republican member, "that the public has some reason for feeling that the Navy is trying to take advantage of the emergency to get while the getting is good, to establish itself for postwar during the war." The dialogue grew increasingly embarrassing:

Mr. Shepard: At this time, to sum it up and be bluntly frank about it, you have no recommendations to make to this committee which the committee could follow through and make reductions which, in your opinion, would not be hazardous to the projected programs that are under consideration.

Secretary Forrestal: That is true, yes. I am frank to say, though, that this does not represent a close examination on my part of each one of these items; but I do know, in more or less general terms, what they are based on.

Mr. Plumley: I do not think the Secretary wants to let that answer stand, because he knows there are items in here he would not take to justify himself. . . .

Mr. Thomas: . . . What consideration do you give these projects, Mr. Forrestal?

Secretary Forrestal: They only reach me in the absence of the Secretary . . . I question some; send them back.

Mr. Plumley: Did you see the item which involved an appropriation of something like $7,000,000 for a stadium down at Annapolis?

Secretary Forrestal: I saw it today. That was the reason I was somewhat embarrassed in answering some of Mr. Shepard's questions.

Mr. Plumley: That is the reason I called your attention to it.

Secretary Forrestal: I can assure you it will never be built.

Mr. Plumley: Well, it will never be appropriated for, if I know this committee. . . .

Mr. Thomas: I think you have done an awfully good job, and any questions I have asked have not been in a spirit of destructive criticism.

Secretary Forrestal: We do not regard it as criticism. They are healthy questions, and it is a good thing to have them asked than to have them simmer in the minds of the public and never get any attention.[50]

The affair was still rankling a year later. "I don't want to have what happened last year," he told the Organization Policy Group. "We were hit on a Monday morning without any advance notice, causing us to go down there and look quite silly; at least, I think I did." [51] Still later, he wrote Arthur Krock: "The bad administration only shows up when you are made an ass of by some committee in Congress." [52] At that, it was perhaps less embarrassing than the story about another Secretary. To smooth ruffled local feelings, he went to some length to explain why economy reasons were forcing the Navy to close down a great air base. Then, an officer from Naval Operations came on the stand and explained that apparently the Secretary hadn't gotten the word that the Navy was not going to close down the base after all.[53]

The various subjects that involved Congress shifted sharply in their comparative importance. During the war years, Forrestal's chief concern was with the investigating committees, particularly in industrialization mobilization matters. Unlike the Civil War Congressional investigating committee, both of these kept away from command and strategy aspects. Truman, who had studied that earlier experience, blamed meddling by the Committee on the Conduct of the War for some of the Union defeats, and felt that Congress should concentrate upon seeing that the armed forces had the material they needed.[54] The Navy emerged from these inquiries with a relatively clean bill of health.

Only five of the Truman Committee's cases involved the Navy alone, although it was one of several interested parties in thirty-six others. In the potentially most serious of these strictly Navy cases, the Committee in 1942 strongly castigated the Bureau of Ships for clinging to its own inadequate "tank lighter" landing craft design when a private builder had turned out a much better one. Forrestal's replacement of the Chief and Assistant Chief by Edward L. Cochrane and Earle Mills that autumn stemmed in part from that situation, and did much to prevent its repetition.[55]

Out of the thousands of regulars, reserves, and civilians engaged in the $100 billion procurement program, the Truman Committee turned up only one black sheep. A Naval Academy graduate who had soon left the Navy eventually became a partner in a management engineering concern. He retained half interest in that concern after returning as a wartime reserve officer. Heading the production management unit of the Bureau of Ordance, he was charged with coercing contractors to use his firm's services. Truman snapped out in the committee "I think it is the most flagrant violation of the rules and regulations of the Navy that I have seen." [56]

A third case involved a peccadillo, but illustrated a problem that Forrestal took very seriously. This was the "old school tie" attitude that has been known to condone strange actions in more than one "poor John" or "good old Joe," in apparent memory of Annapolis days. Forrestal called this affair "the proper use of a legislative committee in aiding an executive department to carry out its duties." [57] It all began when a reserve Marine lieutenant colonel, making a routine inspection of a branch ammunition depot at Pearl Harbor, found and reported a ton of meat and butter from government stores, labeled the property of the regular naval commander in charge. Receiving the report, the latter's superior, also a regular, had the offending commander absolved and the Marine officer quickly transferred with an unsatisfactory fitness report. The Marine took the matter to Forrestal and a member of Congress; and the butter so to speak was "in the fire." The flames were fed when a general court-martial acquitted the commander, which Nimitz termed "a miscarriage of justice." A Deputy Inspector General sent to Pearl by Forrestal unearthed several other irregularities.

The Truman Committee, investigating the case in October 1945 and again in March 1946, was most concerned that it had not been discovered earlier and that such obvious favoritism existed toward regulars and against reserves.[58]

The Truman and Vinson committees usually avoided going over the same grounds. The latter made several studies of general subjects, notably a survey of civilian personnel matters and the related problems of congested areas, by a subcommittee under Lyndon Johnson. Thus, unlike the Senate committee, it did not always handle specific cases. For all its closeness to Forrestal through Vinson, it was not as someone jokingly called it, "a special laundry for the Navy's dirty linen." Its investigations were searching, and its criticism severe when due. The targets, occasionally, were naval officers, but the particular objects of suspicion, especially in the early period, were civilians who seemed to be making undue profits at the Navy's expense. Its counsel said that the Truman Committee expected "the Navy to produce sore spots voluntarily"; [59] but, not surprisingly, the Navy was more inclined to take their troubles to the Vinson group, where naval concerns were a full-time interest.

Congress also eventually investigated the Pearl Harbor attack after several other groups had examined the question of responsibility. Forrestal was involved only incidentally in these hearings, although he participated in some of the earlier executive investigations. The first of those, headed by Justice Owen Roberts put the blame solely on the local commanders, Admiral Kimmel and General Short. Further public statements, however, were postponed until late in the war, partly because so much hinged on the fact that the Japanese secret code had been broken and Japanese messages intercepted.

A month after Forrestal became Secretary in 1944, Congress grew restless and specifically directed the Secretaries of War and Navy "to proceed forthwith with an investigation into the facts surrounding the catastrophe." [60] On July 13, Forrestal established a Court of Inquiry composed of three retired four-star admirals. Their findings were not announced until after the November Presidential election, and then, for security reasons, only in part. They reversed the findings of the Roberts Commission. Aside from questioning Admiral Stark's judgment, they cleared the Navy. The Army board came to similar conclusions.

Neither Forrestal nor King was satisfied with that verdict. In his endorsement of the naval findings, King wrote in part that Stark and Kimmel had shown "lack of the superior judgment necessary for exercising command commensurate with their rank, rather than culpable inefficiency." Forrestal accordingly directed that they should "not hold any position in the United States Navy which required the exercise of superior judgment." [61] This involved some embarrassment in Stark's case, for he had been nominal commander of the naval forces in Europe during the interim.[62] The British were greatly surprised, Churchill himself attending the farewell dinner given him.

Forrestal did not stop with this. He assigned Admiral Hewitt to make a further investigation. As he told President Truman in April 1945, he felt that he "had an obligation to Congress to continue" the investigation, not being "completely satisfied with the report my own Court had made." [63]

Once the shooting stopped and the excuse for secrecy was gone, nothing could keep the Pearl Harbor question any longer under wraps. Senator Walsh called upon Forrestal on August 17 for "the complete file of investigation made by the Navy Department," and the Army and Navy reports were made public in full, three days before the Japanese surrender. Congress set up a joint committee which had an element of partisanship, not evident in the Truman and Vinson groups. Its hearings, with which Forrestal personally had little to do, lasted from November 15, 1945 to May 31, 1946. The results were inconclusive.

Forrestal had read enough history to know what had always happened to American armed forces after a war and realized that many in high places were blind to the politico-military perils ahead. Although never one to risk wrecking the economy for guns instead of butter, he felt that the White House and the Hill would look out for the balance between them. To him, his own responsibility was to urge adequate armed forces and do what he could to get the Navy in good shape before the usual peacetime retrenchment. As he wrote a former assistant when his fears began to materialize:

"God knows I am fully aware of the terrific task which this country faces if it is to keep a free economy and a free society. But the next eighteen months look to me to be about the most critical that this country has ever faced, and to deny Marshall the cards to play, when the stakes are as high as they are, would be a grave decision." [64]

As peace drew nearer and the Naval Affairs Committees were reviving their authorization and general legislation functions, Forrestal saw a chance to get something done in the latter sphere before the clamor to "bring the boys home" broke out or the questioning "Why do we need a Navy any more?" arose. Just after the German surrender, he began to direct thinking along the lines of the Navy's postwar organization. He drafted a letter informing Vinson that the Department was studying matters of education, manning the postwar Navy, promotion and selection, Navy organization, public education and news of the Navy, the laying up of ships, research, and a continuing program for the construction of new types of naval vessels embodying the war experience.[65]

With the Japanese surrender in September 1945, Forrestal and Vinson knew they could not wait; with the enemy fleets gone, many already saw no further need of a large Navy.[66] Forrestal gave his answer to that in the hearings on "House Concurrent Resolution No. 80," introduced by Vinson, in pointing out that the two World Wars had demonstrated that "no enemy could reach this country nor could American forces reach the enemy without crossing the sea." [67] This Resolution was primarily psychological, as time had been lacking for an adequate analysis of postwar requirements. It stated that it was the "sense of Congress" that the Navy should consist of 27 carriers, 18 battleships, and other types in very generous quantity.[68]

Truman was not pleased that the Navy with Vinson's aid was taking the offensive. Forrestal told him, "we had our case very thoroughly in hand and the Army did not, but we were being blamed for being forehanded." [69] That forehandedness was to "pay off," in some very useful legislation during the next few months.[70]

In addition, Forrestal had to carry on a strenuous defensive in the field of budgets and appropriations. The days were gone when nothing was too good for the one hundred billion dollar Navy. The wartime cooperativeness of Congress had meant an almost complete abdication of the control of the purse strings with a virtual blank check for the Navy. On combat needs, Congress did not pit its judgment against the professional officers. While swallowing camels, however, it did strain at gnats, such as in the case when the House Committee gave the Navy most of the four billion asked, but it specifically voted to eliminate one laborer, one pipefitter, and one electrician's helper at the Naval Academy! [71]

Several considerations complicated Forrestal's struggle over appropriations. Truman and his advisers set a fixed and rather low ceiling upon military expenditures, determined purely from the fiscal standpoint. The Bureau of the Budget had grown more influential than the Appropriations Committee and thoroughly worked over the annual estimate before the President submitted the figures to Congress. Forrestal and the Navy could see no justification, moreover, for Congress and the Budget Bureau to determine the exact categories of ships, planes, shore stations, or other items where the Navy must make cuts. They recognized, albeit reluctantly, the necessity for economy, but how and where reductions were to be made seemed to them the legitimate sphere for professional naval judgment.

It normally took the Navy twelve months to obtain an appropriation which it was to spend in the following twelve. The yearly ritual began around the end of June, when Naval Operations presented its operation plan for the fiscal year beginning July 1 of the following year. The various bureaus and offices drew up their estimates of what they needed—or at least wanted—to carry out their share of that over-all plan. These were then correlated by the Navy's Fiscal Director and Budget Officer; next, early in September, they were submitted by the Secretary to the Budget Bureau, which held informal hearings and generally made some heavy slashes in the figures presented. Here Forrestal had some complaints. Late in 1946, he recorded that "people down the line in the Budget not much above the status of clerks made allocations within Departments and between various bureaus and offices." He told President Truman "that a young man recently a seaman second class . . . who had been a student of administration at the University of Colorado" had been making up the naval figures.[72]

Next, the Budget Bureau recommendations were embodied in the over-all budget submitted by the President to Congress early in January. After that, the subcommittee of House Appropriations held detailed hearings, calling for "justification" of each item, followed by briefer hearings by the Senate subcommittee. Late in the spring or early summer, the appropriations bill would receive the President's signature, but not much before the fiscal year it covered was about to begin. The Navy could sometimes get extra amounts through supplementary or deficiency acts.

When the gunfire died away in the Pacific in August 1945, "Fiscal 1945"—the largest in the Navy's history—had expired. The Navy was just beginning to spend its Fiscal 1946 appropriations, and was preparing its estimates for Fiscal 1947, both of which would concern Forrestal. The Executive branch began to shut down on spending, even before Congress began to exercise its traditional power of the purse, still straining at gnats, but no longer swallowing camels. Fiscal 1946, drawn up in anticipation of a huge invasion of Japan, quickly began to be whittled away before it could be spent. Altogether, more than $20 billion of Navy funds were cut back.

At the same time, a bitter battle was being waged over Fiscal 1947, for the Navy knew that its future peacetime strength was at stake. The Budget Bureau, without consulting Forrestal, cut the Navy's estimates from $6.3 billion to $3.9; what was more, every one of the 97 appropriation items had been slashed. Forrestal rushed to the White House to register his strenuous protest. He persuaded Truman to raise the amounts for personnel and some other items, bringing the total to $4.2 billion. Congress simply cut off another $100 million, and further cuts were made during the year. That $4.1 billion for Fiscal 1947 would be a precedent for the $3.6 in 1948 and $3.7 for 1949.

With Fiscal 1948, it looked as though the Hill rather than the Budget Bureau and the President might take the offensive against the Navy. The epithet "meat axe" was being applied to John Taber of New York, chairman of the full House Appropriations Committee, who had strong, and in some eyes ruthless, ideas about economy. Furthermore, Truman issued a "muzzling order" on November 15, 1946, forbidding criticism of the estimates.[73]

But for Forrestal's constant skillful pressure, the reductions might well have had serious consequences for the fighting power of the Fleet. No "gag rule" could keep him from discussing the situation freely with Senators and Representatives, particularly with the Republican leaders currently in power. He also had much to say in connection with the proposed unification of the armed forces which was coming to a head. His formal and informal Congressional contacts during the first four months of 1947 were eloquent evidence of his very active campaign on two fronts.[74] These were the sort of very small affairs, at which Forrestal was always at his best. Early in March, however, he invited the entire House Appropriations Committee to lunch at the Navy Department, where he and several admirals spoke as strongly as they could about Fiscal 1948. Afterward, Forrestal wrote, "The attitude of the committee was one of keen interest, although I do not believe that the presentation very much affected Mr. Taber's determination for cuts" (See Appendix J).[75]

That pessimistic estimate was borne out when Forrestal appeared formally before that committee in April. Taber wanted Forrestal to make the cuts himself, but he told Taber "that if there was any reduction in Naval funds, it would have to come from Mr. Taber as a decision by him; that I could not act in the position of accepting or approving such a cut." [76] In the end, the Taber committee made a 10 percent cut in the already perilously low naval budget, reducing it to $3.1 billion. There had been fears that it might go still lower. But Senator Saltonstall, chairman of the Senate Appropriations subcommittee, managed to relieve the situation somewhat by an "astute compromise." By increasing new funds to be voted along with a "cutback in old funds, already appropriated, mainly for shore establishments and construction," he achieved more immediate money for the operating forces. The Senate voted $200 million more, making it $3.3 billion. The final compromise in mid-July split the difference between House and Senate at $3.2 billion.

This was not a clear-cut victory for Forrestal by any means; neither was the National Security Act providing unification of the armed services, that became law ten days later. In both cases, however, had it not been for his tireless work the Navy would not have been as well off, even though it did not get all that it desired. The last word in that appropriations battle reaffirmed Forrestal's "strong belief that intelligent cooperation between committees of the Congress and the Executive Departments of the government is best secured by free and continuous exchange of pertinent information between them." [77] He wrote that on July 17 to Taber in a letter of appreciation for

the hard work that you and your staff put in with us on the task. We did not always see eye to eye—it has been my experience that the seeker after funds and the provider of them usually do not—but in our differences we always had courteous and considerate treatment from you.[78]

8

"Those Who Hate War"

"THOSE WHO hate war must have the power to prevent it"—that thought lay behind Forrestal's urgency to have the nation ready for the world leadership that he was sure lay ahead.[1] His advancement to the Secretaryship had intensified his old interest in foreign affairs, as the new duties brought him into close contact with the international situation. His awareness of the realities of the changing position of the United States was particularly evident in the vital borderline between international diplomacy and armed force which was beginning to be called "politico-military affairs." Increasingly, with President Roosevelt's illness and death, he felt a personal responsibility, since at one of the most crucial turning points in history, foreign policy was in the hands of President Truman and two successive Secretaries of State, who had scant background in that intricate field.

The world picture in that final year of the war revealed tremendous changes in the international power setup. Germany and Japan were obviously heading for defeat and at least temporary eclipse. Britain, no longer "workshop of the world" and seriously exhausted, was going to be unable to continue as "mistress of the seas" or "policeman of the world." France and Italy would not carry weight for a good while. The United States was the logical heir to the responsibilities inherent in Britain's former role. Forrestal also saw that the United States must act with despatch or Russia would move into the vacuum among the powers.

He had already begun to fear that the nation's foreign policies would outrun its military might. This caused him to believe that close and continuous cooperation was vital between the State Department and the armed services.[2] Gradually, he came to a further conclusion that within the Navy Department, politico-military affairs ought to be a particular concern of the Secretary, and were, moreover, another field wherein civilian skills combined with military experience might bring excellent results. In the first instance, the need led to the creation of the National Security Council in 1947 [3] and, in the second, to Forrestal's establishing within the Department a new organization to feed him information about politico-military concerns.

In his customary way, Forrestal went after the facts—discussions on foreign developments on any and all occasions, a rush of assignments to his staff, and much reading on his own. His background in this area had not hitherto been extensive, although in the 1920s his interest had been keen, when as a Dillon, Read official, he had been abroad a number of times and had participated in some of the frenzied financing of German industry. But as to the immediate situation, his mind and time had been too centered on procurement aspects for much reading in this area; and even during his trip to England in 1941, all his attention had been drawn to the industrial aspects of the British experience.

He considered that for some purposes foreign and military policy were intertwined as parts of national security:

Both the Army and the Navy are aware that they are not makers of policy, but they have a responsibility to define to the makers of policy what they believe are the military necessities of the United States, both for its own defense and for the implementation of its responsibility for the maintenance of world power.[4]

The record of Forrestal's activities in this area—considered by some to be far removed from a Navy Secretary's business—seemed to indicate that the difficulty in determining politico-military policy stemmed from the weakness, indecision, and poor organization of the Department of State rather than from the overemphasized strength of the military. This was not unlike the situation within the Navy Department, where concern about the professional military strength sometimes concealed the traditional weakness of the office of civilian Secretary. If State were well organized and intelligently led, the role of War and Navy tended to become secondary; but otherwise the reverse inclined to be true.[5]

Forrestal sometimes seemed to share the popular belief that "we lose our shirts" at the conference table, where the homespun American is outwitted by the wily foreign diplomat. He probably did not go that far, but he showed his doubts. For example, at a State-War-Navy meeting, the State Department proposed to send negotiators who could trade on a *quid pro quo* basis regarding Switzerland's trade with Germany. Forrestal commented in his diary:

I injected that the military were in accord with that, with the qualification that we would like to be sure of getting the *quid* before we gave the *quo*. I said it came down to who did the negotiating, and Mr. Stimson supported me in this, saying that the State Department normally did not produce the type of negotiator who dealt in the vulgar language of being sure of what he got before he signed a document.[6]

Forrestal's immediate objective was toward closer working relations of the military departments and State. The American record had been, and still was, a very sloppy one in respect to such liaison. Even when the Secretaries had come together to discuss a situation, there was no mechanism for a continuous joint planning group to brief them on the background nor to see that their decisions were implemented.

From early days down to fairly recent times, the Navy and the State Departments had far closer and more constant relations with each other than either had with the Army. Until 1898, the Army, having been primarily concerned with Indians, had only spasmodic peacetime contacts with Navy. Even in the Civil War, when the Army and Navy were continually staging joint military operations, Secretary of the Navy Gideon Welles wrote: "The Navy Department has, necessarily, greater intimacy or connection with the State Department than any other."[7] More often than not, when cruisers were sent to prowl through lonely seas, when marines were landed on troubled shores, or when the battle fleet held special maneuvers for moral effect upon some potential enemy, the Secretary of State usually had had a hand in the matter. Such relationships between State and Navy not only involved high policy, as in sending Commodore Perry to open up Japan, but also routine business of naval visits to foreign ports, a matter on which State claimed the controlling voice. At times, it might veto a projected visit for no better reason than that the liquor supply of the local legation had already been depleted by thirsty sea dogs. On the other hand, the departmental discussions over sending the battleship *Maine* to Havana in 1898 led to an incident far from routine.

Unlike any other department in earlier days, State and Navy also supplemented their high-level Washington contacts with others far distant from the capital. As Secretary Gideon Welles further pointed out, "our squadrons and commanders abroad come in contact with our ministers, consuls, and commercial agents, and each has intercourse with the governments and representatives of other nations. Mutual understanding and cooperation are therefore essential and indispensable." [8] In the days before fast communications made "damned errand boys at the end of a telegraph wire" of State and Navy officials and officers on distant stations, these often had to take action on their own in emergencies, with no chance for consultation with their superiors in Washington.[9] But even with rapid communications, the contact between Washington and outlying posts is not always dependable, as at Pearl Harbor in 1941. Admiral Kimmel had undue faith that radio was bringing him all pertinent information for him to adjust his plans to the changing Japanese situation. Some of the most significant information was not forwarded, but he did not know that: "This failure not only deprived me of essential facts. It misled me." [10]

There were occasions, too, when unilateral State action without thinking through the military aspects of a situation could be dangerous. In 1881, for example, the Navy was called upon to support the futile efforts of the State Department to tone down Chile's demands after its victorious war with Peru. No one in Washington seemed to realize that Chile's modern steel ships could have made short work of the obsolete wooden vessels of the American Pacific Squadron; it apparently took a blunt and indignant Chilean admiral to point that out to the American naval commander.[11] On the other hand, in 1898, the State Department had no part in the determination of Assistant Navy Secretary Theodore Roosevelt, temporarily Acting Secretary, to extend the Caribbean quarrel with Spain to include the Philippines. This led, to be sure, to an easy, spectacular victory at Manila, but the ultimate consequences had not been considered. Later, "Teddy" himself termed the Philippines the "Achilles heel" of American naval strategy.[12]

In Washington, there was a long tradition of aloofness on the part of the Department of State toward the service departments. Its attitude often indicated that it felt it enjoyed a special relation-

ship with the White House and a primacy among executive departments. State showed no enthusiasm for the efforts of the Navy
Department over the years to bring about closer relations, in the
hope of having a voice in policies while they were still in the
formative stage. Navy's advances were regularly rebuffed; State
was prone to operate in a carefully cultivated atmosphere of splendid isolation. Even a petty dispute over fresh air and partitions in
1882 illustrated this. In the partially completed State-War-Navy
building, just west of the White House, State had partitions erected
in the corridors to close off its offices, despite protests by War
and Navy. The dispute reached Congress. In a committee hearing,
the Secretary of State voiced his Department's characteristic aloofness:

the quiet and privacy which are essential to the proper conduct of
business in the Department of State, which is the confidential office of
the President, would be interfered with and endangered, if a free
communication was made, inviting visits from the clerks of the other
departments at any and all hours of the day.[13]

The Navy Secretary stressed the view that such open communication with State would be of value. The War Secretary supported
this but with emphasis upon the circulation of air rather than of
ideas—the Army on the western plains having scant contact with
foreign affairs. Congress decreed that the partitions come down.[14]

For years thereafter, writes Ernest May, "consultation among
the State, War, and Navy Departments took the antique form of
correspondence among the three secretaries," which "failed to
bring about effective coordination of policies. As a rule, in fact,
diplomatic and military recommendations reached the White
House separately." [15] There were a few scattered efforts at coordination. In 1919, Franklin D. Roosevelt, then Assistant Secretary
of the Navy, drew up elaborate proposals for a Joint Plan Making
Body, for "defining American objectives for each possible war
and assessing the force needed for success." The letter went astray
in the State Department and was never even acknowledged.[16] In
December 1921, during the Washington Conference, the Secretaries
of War and Navy proposed collaboration between the State Department and the Joint Board; this time there was a reply, but a
brusquely negative one.[17]

When Forrestal was first appointed to the Department, the same complaints at the lack of day-to-day contacts with State were current according to Stark, then CNO:

In view of the actual situation in the Far East and elsewhere, we might well say that we need "Tension Plans" as well as "War Plans." But to prepare well considered "Tension Plans" we need a planning machinery that includes the State Department and possibly the Treasury Department as well as the War and Navy Departments. Of course, we have planning machinery for the Army and Navy which now provides for a better coordination of planning effort than has existed in the past. We do not, however, have regularly set planning machinery that brings in the State Department. It is true that we have frequent consultation with the State Department, but things are not planned in advance, and often we do not receive advance information of State Department action which might well have affected our own activities.[18]

Those frequent discussions referred to the Standing Liaison Committee set up in 1938, "the first American agency for regular political-military consultation on foreign policy." [19] The three departments were represented by Under Secretary Sumner Welles as chairman, General Marshall, and Admiral Stark. Though it dealt largely with Western Hemisphere matters, it gave its members some insight into what the others were planning and thinking.[20] Likewise inadequate were the wholly unofficial weekly meetings of the full Secretaries of State, War, and Navy, started in 1940 through the influence of Stimson, who called them useful "in keeping the three Secretaries informed on one another's major problems," but having "no connection with Mr. Roosevelt's final determination of policy." [21]

Valuable as such devices might be as "clearing houses," they failed to produce a thorough integration of foreign with military policy during those critical months. Formal cohesion and collective responsibility were lacking. There was, moreover, no adequate secretariat to collate intelligence, prepare agenda, or assure an orderly "follow through" in the matters discussed. Knox would never dictate a memorandum on his return to his office, although his assistants urged him to do so; he preferred to rely on his "newspaperman's memory." [22] After Pearl Harbor the meetings dwindled away, with Hull wasting time with his recurrent complaints of being sidetracked by his Under Secretary Welles's direct access to the President. Eventually, they stopped altogether. Forrestal blamed this situation on that lack of sound organization and adequate communication between departments, mentioned by Stark, rather than on "empire building" and jealousy of its prerogatives on the part of State or on attempts to seize power by moving into a "civilian" area by the "military."

During the two critical years before Pearl Harbor, Hull, who was ever conscious of the primacy of his department, had often gone his own way without coordinating policy decisions with Stimson and Knox. However proper or necessary his "ultimatum" to Japan on November 26, 1941 may have been, he had issued it without finally consulting the Army or the Navy, which were seeking to stall for time, until their Pacific preparations were more complete. The next day, he said to Stimson: "I have washed my hand of it and it is now in the hands of you and Knox—the Army and the Navy." [23]

Hull probably did not realize how thoroughly he was "signing off" for the duration. Thereafter, he was quite completely out of the high policy picture as far as major war planning went. So, too, to a considerable degree were the civilian War and Navy Secretaries. This stemmed from the way Roosevelt took most of the high policy into his own hands and, even for consultation, preferred to turn to Harry Hopkins and the professional officers of the Joint Chiefs of Staff.

This was not the first time that a President had taken over foreign policy during a war; what was unusual was to have a Secretary of State so completely ignored. Hull found himself in a condition of isolation that was anything but splendid; he was excluded from nearly all the major Roosevelt-Churchill conferences. Roosevelt went so far as to ask Churchill to omit Foreign Secretary Anthony Eden from the British delegation at the first Quebec Conference lest his presence be an argument for Hull's inclusion. Hull resented being on the sidelines: "I feel it is a serious mistake for a Secretary of State not to be present at important military meetings." [24]

The Department was left the area of postwar planning, but the significance of that lay in the future; otherwise, its current sphere of action was cut down to little more than relations with the neutrals —Latin American, some smaller European nations, and for a while, Vichy France. One writer described its wartime role, as "the status of a querulous maiden aunt whose sole function is to do all the worrying for the prosperous family over the endless importunities of the numerous poor relations on the other side of the tracks." [25]

The Department was also in a bad way administratively. Hull and his Under Secretary, Welles, were constantly at loggerheads; and Assistant Secretaries came and went by the squad. When on occasion Roosevelt did turn to the Department, it was more often to talk with the experienced career diplomat, Welles, than with Hull. To further the unhappy confusion, the Department was rumored to be "full of leaks as well as creaks." [26] Even its codes were believed to be compromised; and so, Roosevelt preferred the more rigidly guarded Army or Navy communication system for his critical messages. In the spring of 1942, for example, when plans were being perfected with the British for the seizure of Madagascar, to prevent its falling to the Japanese, who were sweeping out into the Indian Ocean, secrecy and surprise were vitally essential. The communications went out over the Navy system and came back by the Army's, so that only Roosevelt's naval aide, Captain John L. McCrea, knew the whole story. Late one evening, just as the news was about to break, McCrea was called to the telephone to hear an irritated voice: "This is the Secretary of State. What in hell goes on around here anyway?" [27]

Ill health forced Hull's resignation in the fall of 1944, but he stayed until after the election at Roosevelt's request. Edward R. Stettinius, Jr., who had already replaced Welles as Under Secretary, succeeded to the Secretaryship. His background in international relations was slight. He had inherited a position as head of United States Steel and came to the Department from directing Lend-Lease. "There is much less than meets the eye" was one of the jibes at his being at the helm of State in wartime. One newspaper referred to him and his associates as "bush league diplomats." Such sneers provoked Forrestal to the retort, "it was clear that Mr. Stettinius was not a Disraeli, a Metternich, or a Machiavelli, but I remarked neither had I seen anyone else on the horizon who had such abilities." [28]

That virtual vacuum in the administration of foreign affairs was to continue. Stettinius was in office only seven months. After presiding at the founding of the United Nations, he was succeeded in July 1945 by James F. Byrnes. The latter had had ample governmental experience as Senator and Director of War Mobilization, but not in foreign affairs. He and Forrestal seemed to have gotten along very well together, although Forrestal worried because Byrnes did not understand the basic ideological patterns of other countries and, in particular, of the Soviet Union. As Truman was now President, there were two novices in the international field.

Back in 1942, when the war was passing from defense to offense, came the first step toward better coordination between State and the military, because of an emergency situation. With the occupation of North Africa by the Allied armies, some form of civil government had to be established, and this involved a host of political problems. Consequently, a Civil Affairs Committee was created, consisting of the Assistant Secretaries: James C. Dunn of State, John T. McCloy of War, and Gates for the Navy. Forrestal had no hand in this operation, naturally, being still fully occupied with the industrial mobilization.

One of the difficulties faced by this Committee—and for that matter by most civilian politico-military policy-making bodies—was that civilian Secretaries in the service departments did not usually have access to top military planning information. In this case, to be sure, Marshall was so eager for civilian advice, that sometimes he even "bootlegged" important Joint Chiefs of Staff papers to McCloy, in order that the Civil Affairs Committee might give him their views. King, on the other hand, told his civilian superiors very little. McCloy recalls that several times, talking with Forrestal about the Committee, he found the latter knew nothing of military plans that had come to him from Marshall; and even Gates, a Committee member, was kept in ignorance, also.[29]

McCloy was definitely instrumental in bringing home to Forrestal the Navy's stake in foreign affairs. The two men lived around the corner from each other in Georgetown; both played tennis; and they were often together after hours. McCloy went out of his way to lead their talks into the international area, especially the administration of occupied territories.[30]

Particularly annoying to the service Secretaries was the habit of other departments by-passing them to deal directly with the Joint Chiefs of Staff. A new approach to State-War-Navy cooperation came out of one such instance, which caused Stimson, in November 1944, to write Hull strongly urging that the State Department receive military advice only through the Secretaries of War and Navy.[31] McCloy talked to Forrestal about it the next day at lunch, and then they both saw Stettinius. Apparently, from that came the plan to revive the Secretaries' meetings, and also to add a "pick and shovel," or working-level, committee to provide continuous staff work.

When Stettinius succeeded Hull ten days later, the State-War-Navy Secretaries Committee was quickly reconstituted, holding its first meeting on December 19. It was better organized than before. It now had an agenda and minutes were kept, with Assistant Secretary McCloy brought in as recorder.[32] Its weekly meetings were the clearing house for matters of top importance. This senior committee was not a part of the formal structure that was to develop from the creation of a junior committee.

The latter, the State-War-Navy Coordinating Committee (SWNCC, or SWINC as it was dubbed), was like the Joint Chiefs in being the capstone of an organization that included a secretariat and other full time "working" groups. Though not formally established until later, it was initiated in November 1944, when Stettinius had pretty well spelled out its composition in writing Forrestal and Stimson:

As I visualize the proposed Committee (i.e. the working level or junior committee) it should have a secretariat composed of at least one competent and experienced representative of each department, and it should be authorized to call upon the three departments for such technical advice and assistance as may from time to time be required. The secretariat would be charged with the proper disposition of communications requesting the views of the War Department and Navy Department on politico-military questions and arranging with the Committee members for references of such inquiries, for the contents of the Joint Chiefs of Staff.[33]

Stimson and Forrestal jointly replied that they were "in hearty agreement with the proposal and believed it should be carried into effect promptly." [34] In the secretariat and the smaller "working" groups, the departments were represented by men of fairly equivalent grades and responsibilities. The military members were usually colonels or naval captains. In the secretariat, in addition to a secretary, there were two deputy secretaries, and other assistants as seemed necessary, with at least one from the Army Air Forces. At the next lower level, the working committees were of two sorts:

permanent standing committees for problems that required continuing attention and temporary *ad hoc* committees for immediate special tasks.

SWINC was the first device to provide competent, effective participation of those three departments. The initial members of the senior committee were Dunn, McCloy, and Gates, the same trio already working together on the Civil Affairs Committee. They were empowered to make positive commitments for their departments. SWINC's original purpose, "formulating recommendations to the Secretary of State on questions having both military and political aspects," was later restated to place the three departments on a more equal basis. Its formal charter designated it as the

agency to reconcile and coordinate the action to be taken by the State, War, and Navy Departments on matters of common interest and, under the guidance of the Secretaries of State, War, and Navy, establish policies on politico-military questions referred to it. . . . Action taken by the Coordinating Committee will be construed as action taken in the names of the Secretaries of State, War, and Navy.

Its scope, six months later in a joint announcement of the three Secretaries, was further extended to include the work of the Civil Affairs Committee. This made SWINC "responsible for the coordination of United States policy" in the administration of the occupied areas and "for its communication through appropriate channels to the United States representatives in the field." [35] Although the Committee was capable of rapid staff work, it had certain limitations. Some policy-making decisions, lying beyond the powers of its Assistant Secretaries, were made by the President and the full Secretaries—sometimes with little or no preliminary staff study. The Committee, moreover,

went to work only when a question was referred to it by one of the departments. As a result, it failed to handle some questions well within its purview. The four-power arrangements for occupation of Berlin were worked out hastily by soldiers and diplomats in the European Theater and approved by a nod from President Truman. . . . [SWINC] never had a chance to examine these arrangements, and no provision was made for guaranteeing access to the city.[36]

The principal standing subcommittees, established in January 1945, included Europe, the Far East, Latin America, and the Near and Middle East. In many cases, in which strictly military oper-

ations would be a factor of prime importance in a politico-military
situation, SWINC papers were referred to the Joint Chiefs. On
the whole, the SWINC and JCS systems worked well together.
The most distinctive achievement was made by the Far Eastern
subcommittee, which fully justified the important responsibilities
entrusted to it in regard to the Japanese surrender terms and the
subsequent occupation. After V–J Day, this subcommittee became
the main channel for coordinating Washington staff work on occupation policy. Eventually, the subcommittee on Europe did the
same with Germany's occupation. Between April and August 1945,
a very important independent committee of high officials, the Informal Policy Committee on Germany (IPCOG), formed on the
President's initiative, determined the policy immediately following
the surrender. This included representatives from the Treasury
Department and, in effect, superseded SWINC in that period.
SWINC also had *ad hoc* subcommittees to handle immediate situations, arising in various parts of the world.[37]

Forrestal's diaries show how month after month such problems
ranged from Central Europe to the Far East, with Russia involved
in many of them.[38] His share in those discussions and decisions
indicated his strong convictions that careful consideration should
be given to the nation's capabilities, before any commitments were
made. Early in 1946, he called a one hundred-page State Department document a substantial step forward in setting forth American objectives and policies in regard to other countries. It had
been prepared in answer to the question "What is American
Policy? ", posed by the Secretaries Committee. He criticized the
too free use of such terms as "culture," "democracy," and "peace-
loving nations," although admitting they underlined American
aspirations and differences from the Russian.[39] Thus, in this area
as well as others, Forrestal's thinking was along the line of whether
the United States had the power to obtain her goals as well as to
determine what these should be.

He became increasingly aware of a loophole in the coordinating
machinery of the two committees. Useful as they were, their new
arrangement worked properly only in cases of unanimous consent.
It was still possible to by-pass the Secretaries Committee and
SWINC by an end-run to the President. This led Forrestal to
advocate more effective controls toward the end of the war.

His first and what proved to be his longest contact in the politico-military field, lasting throughout his three years as Secretary, concerned the postwar status of the "Mandated Islands" in the Central Pacific. The Carolines, Marshalls, and part of the Marianas had been taken from Germany at the close of World War I and given to Japan as League of Nations mandates, the obligations of which she had flagrantly disregarded. American forces had captured many of them in bloody encounters as they moved across the Pacific. There was talk, by 1944, of converting them, like the other League mandates, into further international status as trusteeships of the proposed United Nations. The United States Navy, however, felt strongly that, in view of their strategic importance, they should be under more definite American control.

Within a few weeks of becoming Secretary, Forrestal was disturbed by a State Department memorandum and told Stettinius, then Under Secretary, that he thought "a *sine qua non* of any postwar arrangements" should be that "who ran the Mandated Islands" was not a subject for debate.[40] When "position papers" were being prepared for the Yalta Conference of 1945, Stimson argued in a thoughtful memorandum to Stettinius that the Pacific Islands were not colonies but rather defense posts, necessary to big-power responsibility for the area's security.[41]

It turned out that little attention was given the matter at Yalta. But in what discussion there was, Roosevelt and Stettinius took a very different stand; they followed along the lines of the proposal of Hull and his postwar planning group for international control of the islands under the United Nations.[42] The State Department feared that if the United States claimed a special right to them, the Soviet Union would advance similar claims elsewhere.[43] At a Cabinet meeting after his return, Roosevelt said—according to Forrestal—that he suggested to Churchill and Stalin that sovereignty be invested in all the United Nations, which would then request the United States "to exercise complete trusteeship for purposes of world security." Thereupon, Stimson quickly expressed the hope that the basis of American power under such a plan be stated very clearly to avoid any future misunderstanding.[44]

None of this allayed Stimson's and Forrestal's anxiety. The issue was brought up at the next meeting of SWINC, but no agreement was reached. Stettinius next asked Roosevelt to discuss the question personally with Stimson and Forrestal; and on April 10, the President wired, from Warm Springs, Georgia, that he would do so immediately upon his return. But two days later, he died.

As another international conference was scheduled soon at San Francisco to draw up the charter for the United Nations, Stettinius briefed President Truman immediately on the trusteeship problem.[45] Senator Vandenberg, a senior member of the Senate Foreign Relations Committee, reporting a discussion within the American delegation, said:

Our government has itself been sharply divided on the subject. The Army and Navy are insistent that we must keep full control of most of the Pacific bases taken from the Japs. The State Department is afraid this will set a bad example to the other great powers. Secretary of War Stimson made a particularly moving speech—told of the mistake we made after the last war in letting Japan get the mandated islands. . . . He said he didn't care so much about the title of these islands if we have absolute, undisputed control over our base needs. Navy Secretary Forrestal backed him up 100%.[46]

It was decided that only the machinery for trusteeships would be taken up at the conference, leaving to another time the question of which territories would be included. Stimson and Forrestal regarded this as putting the cart before the horse, but they had to accept it.[47] Admiral Nimitz summarized the Navy's stand in a memorandum to Forrestal, who promptly sent it on to Secretary Byrnes:

. . . that the ultimate security of the United States depends in major part on our ability to control the Pacific Ocean, that these lands are part of the complex essential to that control, and that the concept of trusteeship is inapplicable here because these islands do not represent any colonial problem nor is there economic advantage accruing to the United States through their ownership.[48]

The handling of this issue, the following December, when Byrnes was in London for the first meeting of the United Nations, emphasized sharply the loophole that weakened State-War-Navy coordination. He suddenly cabled to ask whether he might state that the United States would agree to place the islands "either under ordinary trusteeship arrangement or as strategic areas." [49] Dean Acheson, Acting Secretary during Byrnes's absence, without consulting either War or Navy, went straight to the White House; Truman approved the statement. Forrestal was incensed at this violation of the spirit of the interdepartmental understanding to consult before final decisions were made. Accompanied by Under Secretary of War Royall, he protested to Truman:

I told the President that I think Acheson's method of securing his approval to Mr. Byrnes' request was not consistent with our general ideas of cooperation between War, State, and Navy and rather in my opinion was a desertion of the general idea of cooperation by getting hasty decisions out of him on behalf of a particular view.[50]

A year later, before the meeting of the Council of Foreign Ministers, in November 1946, Byrnes, more seasoned in his job, had several long telephone talks with Forrestal over the perennial trusteeship program. Apparently, these talks were to their mutual satisfaction. Also, the President called a meeting of the three Secretaries, about which Byrnes wrote:

The Secretary of the Navy was very reasonable. He did not want us to do anything that could show lack of confidence in the United Nations, but, because he felt keenly the loss of life these islands had cost us, he wanted to make certain that the terms of the arrangements would permit the Navy to maintain adequate bases.[51]

At the Council meeting, when Soviet Foreign Minister Molotov demanded that all trusteeship proposals for Pacific islands must be approved by the five great powers, Byrnes quickly pointed out that this would, of course, include the Russian-occupied Kurile Islands of northern Japan. Molotov retorted that a trustee arrangement was not contemplated for those islands, since that matter had been settled at Yalta. But Byrnes, prepared for that too, stated that Roosevelt, while promising American support for that Soviet claim at Yalta, had repeatedly said that territory could be legally ceded only at the peace conference. Byrnes added that by that time the United States would want to know the Russian attitude toward having the mandated islands under American trusteeship. Thereupon, according to Byrnes, "Mr. Molotov quickly grasped the implications of this remark."[52]

Eventually, in April 1947, the Security Council of the new United Nations approved an American proposal to make mandated islands a "Strategic Trust Territory" under the administration of the United States. The Soviet went along with the other members in this vote. Three months later, approval by Congress and the President crowned Forrestal's persistent and often frustrating efforts with success. For many years as a result of his vigilance, the Stars and Stripes would fly alone over those islands and atolls of the Marianas, Carolines, and Marshalls, which had cost so heavily to wrest from the enemy.

Forrestal participated in several shorter but very vital policy negotiations, particularly during the four months between the collapse of Germany and of Japan in 1945. The way in which these matters were handled further impressed him with the need for more effective coordination. He realized with mounting dismay that the Americans, thanks to their lack of advance planning and their inept negotiations, were not holding their own in decisions that might well determine the shape of things to come for many years. It was during this critical time that he had Eberstadt undertake the unification study that led, among other things, to the National Security Council and other devices for politico-military coordination.[53]

Forrestal was probably most disturbed by the four different policies under debate for bringing about the surrender of Japan. The one being followed—a continuation and acceleration of land, sea, and air attacks, culminating if necessary in an invasion of the Japanese islands proper—was predicted to entail a half million or more American casualties. That grim prospect gave urgency to a quest for other means. On this situation, Herbert Feis wrote that each of the proposed alternatives "could lead to the end of the war, or two or three of them could do so, in combination or succession. Within the American government each had its own group of activators who nursed their plans and evolved their policies more or less separately from the others." The various plans "were conjoined only in fitful and irregular consultation between the men in the small circle of ultimate decision-makers and with the President." [54]

In the application of armed force, the Navy did not agree with the Army on the need for that final assault upon Japan. All through that spring and early summer, the bombers of the Air Forces and Navy were inflicting terrific punishment on Japanese cities and bases, while other naval forces were ever tightening their strangling blockade. Admiral King believed that "the defeat of Japan could be accomplished by sea and air power alone, without the necessity of actual invasion of the Japanese mainland"; while Admiral Leahy was "unable to see any justification for the invasion of an already defeated Japan" and feared "the cost would be enormous in both lives and treasure." [55] But General Marshall prevailed here as in other stages of the discussion—to President Truman, he was an infallible oracle. A top strategy meeting was held on June 18, when the Joint Chiefs, Stimson, Forrestal, and McCloy, met with the President; no one from the State Department was invited.[56] There was general concurrence in Marshall's presentation of the necessity to invade the southernmost island of Japan, Kyushu, in November, and later to make an assault on the Tokyo region.

For some time, the Army had also stressed another possibility —the desirability of having Russia enter the war in the Far East to pin down Japan on the mainland. At Yalta in February, Stalin indicated that he would move his forces eastward against Japan three months after Germany surrendered. Consequently, the United States made many generous concessions to the Russians, particularly there at Yalta.

That February Forrestal discussed this matter with MacArthur in the Philippines, when returning from Iwo Jima and his wide swing around the Pacific. According to Forrestal:

He felt that we should secure the commitment of the Russians to active and vigorous prosecution of a campaign against the Japanese in Manchukuo of such proportions as to pin down a very large part of the Japanese army; that once this campaign was engaged we should then launch an attack on the home islands. . . . He expressed doubt that the use of anything less than sixty divisions by the Russians would be sufficient.[57]

Later, when the Forrestal diaries appeared, MacArthur's friends tried to discredit that embarrassing passage. Gradually, some, including Forrestal, began to question the wisdom of bringing in Russia. On May 11, for instance, Forrestal called in two of the top admirals to discuss this with Harriman, who was about to return to Moscow. The latter "thought that it was time to come to a conclusion about the necessity for the early entrance of Russia into the Japanese war. He said he was satisfied that they were determined to come in it because of their requirements in the Far East." King's chief of staff said "he thought the necessity for Russia's early participation was very much lessened as a result of recent

events, although the Army he didn't think shared that view." [58]
That same June 18 strategy meeting, which approved the Kyushu
invasion, also reaffirmed this Army view that the "Russian entry
will have a profound military effect in that almost certainly it
will materially shorten the war and thus save American lives."
King, however, thought that the Russians were not indispensable
and the United States should not "go as far as to beg them to come
in." [59]

A third plan came to the fore with the approaching completion
of the atomic bomb. The decision to drop the first bomb on Japan
without warning found the Navy leaders unable to stop an act
they strongly felt was both unnecessary and wrong. The Navy
had not formally been in the A-bomb picture until that spring, more
than three years after the possibilities of utilizing nuclear fission had
been mentioned to Stimson, who had continued in close touch with
the two billion dollar Manhattan Project, called "the best kept
secret of the entire war." [60] However much Forrestal may have
known about it, the only entry in his secret diary concerning the
bomb, before it was dropped, was not until May.

On that date, he recorded that at the close of a State-War-Navy
meeting, Stimson told him and Under Secretary of State, Joseph
C. Grew—Ambassador to Japan for ten years—about the civilian
committee he was forming at Truman's direction "on manhattan
to be headed by Jimmy Byrnes and including Conant, Compton,
and Bush. He asked whether Bard would be satisfactory as a Navy
representative and Grew whether Clayton would serve for State." [61]

This "Interim Committee's" function was to discuss the use of
the bomb. On June 1, it decided that it should be dropped without
previous warning on a Japanese industrial center, despite the inevitable huge civilian casualties. The Army saw in this, as in the
Russian intervention, a "shock" device that might induce an early
surrender and thus prevent the American casualties anticipated in
a Kyushu invasion.

Strong dissent quickly came from those in the secret. Scientists
by the score who had been working on the project voiced their
opposition. So, too, did some of the Air Forces and Navy leaders,
as part of their belief that the Kyushu invasion was unnecessary.
Lewis L. Strauss, investment banker-reserve officer, in close contact
with Forrestal, suggested that "the weapon be used in Japan over

either an uninhabited area, or, after a warning, over a sparsely inhabited area . . . without leaving the aftermath of resentment and grief that the employment of so dreadful a weapon would entail." [62] The argument against such advance warning to Japan was the fact that there were too few bombs ready to risk the consequences of having a "dud" follow a warning.

Bard brought his four years as Assistant and as Under Secretary to a very honorable climax on June 27, when he became the sole member of the Interim Committee to register formal dissent:

> Ever since I have been in touch with this program, I have had a feeling that before the bomb is actually used against Japan that Japan should have some preliminary warning. . . . The position of the United States as a great humanitarian nation and the fair play attitude of our people generally is responsible in the main for this feeling.
>
> During recent weeks I have also had the feeling very definitely that the Japanese government may be searching for some opportunity which they could use as a medium for surrender. . . . It seems quite possible to me that this presents the opportunity which the Japanese are looking for. I don't see that we have anything in particular to lose in following such a program. . . .[63]

This made no headway, however, against the Truman-Marshall decision to use the bomb. As for Forrestal's feelings about this, what indirect evidence there is, seems to indicate he shared the views of Bard and Strauss. As Bard indicated later, he knew he would certainly remember if Forrestal had had any objection to the position he took.[64]

In the fourth proposal, however, Forrestal's part was anything but passive. This was that terms less harsh than "unconditional surrender" were the key to achieving Japan's surrender. This approach might undermine the will of Japanese to keep fighting, as Wilson's Fourteen Points had done in Germany in 1918. Such a "political" civilian proposal might very easily, it was felt by its proponents, obviate the need for Kyushu, Russian intervention, and the use of the atomic bomb. Forrestal, in his outspoken support of this, called it "one of the most serious questions before the country." [65] With the appointment of a new liberal prime minister at Tokyo in April, there seemed hope that a modification of the "unconditional surrender" terms to let Japan retain the Emperor, might bring an end to the fighting. In successive meetings of the State, War, and Navy Secretaries in May and June, Forrestal, Stimson, and McCloy all took an active part in the discussions, but the immediate initiative came from Grew, with a seasoned diplomat's intimate knowledge from ten years at the Tokyo embassy. Time and again, he urged Truman to include in a message to Japan the assurance that the Emperorship would be continued in case of surrender. The President appeared to be fairly receptive, but postponed action. Then Stimson exerted what pressure he could on Truman and the new Secretary of State, Byrnes, as they left for the Potsdam conference and gave them the draft of a proposed proclamation. Drawn up under McCloy's direction, this made allowance for "a constitutional monarchy under the present dynasty." Grew, aware the State Department was divided on this, told Forrestal he feared the draft "would be ditched on the way over." [66]

The "summit" conference at Potsdam between July 17 and August 2 was to take the final action on all four of those propositions to expedite the surrender. But for the tremendous grist of intricate and controversial problems the two top American negotiators had scant preparation to come up against the Stalin-Molotov and Churchill-Eden combinations. Truman had been in office less than three months, and Byrnes less than four days, when they set out in the cruiser *Augusta*. Not until aboard ship did they begin to study the "Briefing Book papers" prepared by the State Department. Byrnes apparently "did his conscientious best to prepare himself" during the eight-day crossing, but Truman's "great and grave chore did not prevent him from spending much time in informal talk with his friends . . . or interfere with his enjoyment of dinner concerts and movies and card games." [67] With Russia and Japan not at war, the Japanese problems were not on the agenda for the "Big Three," and consequently were dealt with only informally, while European problems received the main attention.[68]

Forrestal had not been invited; Stimson had, because of the pending trial of the atomic bomb. Concerned anyway about the way matters would probably be handled, Forrestal had become really disturbed by July 13, when he learned that "The first real evidence of a Japanese desire to get out of the war came today through intercepted messages" from the Japanese foreign minister to his Ambassador in Moscow.[69] The Navy continued to intercept more of these, which Forrestal kept forwarding to Stimson. He became increasingly convinced that Japan might be more ready for peace than ever, if assured about the Emperor. On July 25, still more urgent Tokyo messages were picked up; and he decided to fly to Potsdam with these himself and "crash" the conference. He left the next day—officially to inspect naval operations in Europe. In Paris, the evening of July 27, he discussed matters with some prominent Americans—primarily Admiral King, returning from Potsdam, who passed on "all available information as it appeared to him." [70] Reaching Potsdam the following day, Forrestal personally told Truman and Byrnes of the latest developments.[71] But he was too late.

All three Japanese questions had already been settled in the way that Marshall wanted. Just as the conference began, the news of the first successful A-bomb test in New Mexico had reached Stimson. General Eisenhower, then Supreme Commander of the Allied Forces in Europe, told Stimson that he hoped that the United States would not be the first to use the bomb in warfare, particularly because the Japanese were so nearly beaten anyway. But he was not among the advisers consulted by the President. Agreeing that the bomb should be used, Truman on July 25—the day before Forrestal left Washington—gave final approval to dropping it without warning. In consequence, some 135,000 Japanese died at Hiroshima on August 6, and some 64,000 at Nagasaki three days afterward. In a later analysis of the fateful decision, it was argued that "it would have been possible to employ the bomb in such a way as to produce surrender at a smaller cost in lives" by using it "against a purely military target, followed by a warning" as Bard and Strauss had urged.[72]

As for the Russian intervention, the efforts of Forrestal and its other opponents were equally fruitless. Truman later recorded: "There were many reasons for going to Potsdam, but the most urgent, to my mind, was to get from Stalin a personal reaffirmation of Russia's entry into the war against Japan, a matter which our military chiefs were most anxious to clinch." [73] In this also, Eisenhower differed from the Marshall doctrine; he begged Truman, according to Forrestal, "not to assume that he had to give anything away to do this, that the Russians were desperately anxious to get into the Eastern war." Byrnes, moreover, told Forrestal, upon his arrival at Potsdam, that he was "most anxious to get the Japanese affair over with before the Russians got in." [74] On July 24, however, Truman and Churchill had approved the recommendations of the American and British Chiefs of Staff, including the provision that, "The Soviet Union was to be encouraged to enter the war; and such aid to its war-making capacity as might be needed and practicable was to be provided." [75] By the time Forrestal reached Potsdam, on July 28, staff conferences had been held with the Russians to work out details. As it was, Russia declared war on Japan on August 8, two days before the Japanese decision to surrender. They received rich compensation for their brief and unnecessary intervention; as someone expressed it in American football language, Stalin had "sent his army in at the last minute to make its letter."

In the third failure to influence the course of events, the principal stumbling block seems to have been Byrnes. This rejection of the Grew-Forrestal-*et al.* struggle to have Japan told the Emperor might be kept was perhaps the most frustrating "might-have-been" of all. Consulting Hull before leaving for Potsdam, Byrnes had apparently been persuaded by the latter's arguments that the proposal smacked of appeasement, that it might preserve the feudal privileges of Japan's ruling caste, and that a rejection of the offer might bring "terrible political repercussions in the United States." [76] The Combined Chiefs of Staff thought otherwise, and Stimson pleaded hard with the President "up to the last minute to make the stipulation about the Emperor." [77] But the allied ultimatum, or Potsdam Declaration, delivered to the press on July 26 just as Forrestal was leaving Washington, did not specifically state that the Emperor might continue in office.

Grew, in his memoirs, later declared that he and others still felt that "if such a categorical statement about the dynasty had been issued in May, 1945, the surrender-minded elements . . . might well have . . . come to an early clear-cut decision." [78] Herbert Feis, speculating in "this misty and alluring land of what might have happened" declared that a search of the Japanese records indicates "that the Japanese government would not have surrendered before July" but that the inclusion of the provision in the Potsdam Declaration might possibly have brought results. "The curious mind," he adds, "lingers over the reasons why the American government waited so long before offering the Japanese those assurances which it did extend later." [79] The irony was that when, on August

10, after the bombs on Hiroshima and Nagasaki and the Russian intervention, the Japanese finally decided to surrender, but held out on that one point, it was quickly conceded at Washington, at a conference in which Forrestal participated.

That piecemeal and uncoordinated story, which represented Forrestal's first important contact with policy-making at the top level, stands in contrast to the quiet but highly effective way that SWINC's Far Eastern subcommittee, headed by Eugene H. Dooman of the State Department, went to work with amazing thoroughness. Their findings were important in Grew's recommendations concerning the Emperor and in the drawing up of the occupation terms. The findings were embodied in a paper entitled "The United States Initial Post-Surrender Policy for Japan," released by the White House on September 22.[80] In contrast to the friction producing four-power occupation of Germany, this provided a very satisfactory American control under one man—MacArthur. Originally, he had wanted the help of some contingents from the other Allies, but Stalin refused to have his troops serve under American command and tried to have the occupation under Allied control, although already that was not working out well in Germany.

Ultimately, on his trip around the world the following year, Forrestal commended MacArthur highly for his accomplishments in Japan, but the letter he drafted to the President, on August 9 indicated that he then had reservations, although he did not mention MacArthur's name. As Forrestal felt the over-all command of the projected attack on Kyushu should be under the Navy, which had had the major share of the Pacific war, he tactfully suggested to Truman that Nimitz be appointed to that post. In lieu of that, he put forward the names of Marshall or Eisenhower. His implication was clear:

. . . it is far too important a matter and bears too heavily on the loss of American lives for pride of Service to enter. . . . I think that the constitution of the Joint Chiefs of Staff as well as the matter of personalities in the Pacific Theater makes this a difficult problem for that body to deal with. It is my opinion that it will have to be dealt with by you.[81]

The letter was never sent—the Japanese surrendered at once.

Likewise, because of the Navy's contribution to the Pacific victory, Forrestal utilized his best persuasive powers to have Nimitz participate in the surrender ceremonies in Tokyo Bay. The Allies had agreed that MacArthur should accept the surrender, but Forrestal argued to Byrnes that while MacArthur might sign for the victorious Allies as a whole, Nimitz ought to sign for the United States. Byrnes was sympathetic and recorded in his memoirs how Forrestal's tactical skill took advantage of the fact that Truman came from Missouri to make that arrangement:

When Secretary Forrestal is really interested in a course of action, he doesn't sleep and he doesn't let others sleep. That night the telephone awakened me. It was Secretary Forrestal suggesting that the surrender ceremonies take place on board the battleship *Missouri.* I was sufficiently awake to recognize what the Army would call a "Navy trick." Had he said simply "a battleship," it would have remained a debatable question, but when he mentioned the *Missouri,* I knew the case was closed. The President, upon receiving the suggestion, of course thought it an excellent idea. Thus was averted a great crisis in Army-Navy relations.[82]

Forrestal moved quickly into the center of matters concerning the new atomic power. Just eleven days after the first A-bomb was dropped, Lewis L. Strauss, soon to be a reserve rear admiral, sent him a memorandum, significant in view of subsequent developments:

During the interval between World Wars I and II, there was inadequate testing of large charges (torpedo warheads) against ship structures due to a penurious policy for research and development.

This leads me to the suggestion that we should at once test the ability of ships of present design to withstand the forces generated by the atomic bomb. If such a test is not made there will be loose talk to the effect that the fleet is obsolete in the face of this new weapon and this will militate against appropriations to preserve a postwar Navy of the size now planned. If, on the other hand, the tests should substantiate so radical a contention, the Navy itself would certainly wish to be the first in the field with a revision of its program.

What I have in mind is the selection of a number of the older ships of each type and their assignment to a task force for the purpose of such a test. These ships could be equipped with automatic controls, and could be, without personnel aboard, subjected to both air and *an underwater* explosion of the new type bombs. Suitable instruments on the ships if they survived could indicate the possible effect on personnel. By proper spacing of the ships the effect upon them at varying distances from the center of the disturbance could be approximated.

If this suggestion has merit, it would have to be inaugurated before the ships in question are laid up or scrapped—that is to say, promptly. I assume that because of the controls established around the new weapon this program would require the approval of the President.[83]

That suggestion eventually made Bikini a household word. Forrestal pushed the idea; in November, Admiral William H. P. Blandy, former Chief of Ordnance, was appointed Deputy Chief of Naval Operations for Special Devices and was given command of a Joint Army-Navy Task Force which carried out the proposed tests at Bikini Atoll in the far Pacific in July 1946. Forrestal was present at the first of the tests and then continued on around the world. At a time when the unification negotiations were gaining momentum, the Navy was glad to take this prominent role in what had been originally under the direction of the Army Engineers.

In the meantime, Forrestal had taken a strong stand against sharing the secret of atomic bomb construction, particularly with the Russians. The matter had been suggested first at Potsdam; Marshall and Byrnes both had strongly opposed telling the Russians how the bomb was made, until an adequate agreement for international inspection and control was reached. Stimson was less positive, feeling that "the way to win trust was to give it." [84] He returned to the subject in September; on the twelfth, he took a strong memorandum to the White House, where President Truman read it through in his presence. Stimson argued that the question of just when the Russians learned the secrets of production was "not nearly as important to the world and civilization as to make sure that when they do get it they are willing and co-operative partners among the peace-loving nations of the world." [85]

The President brought the matter up September 21 before the full Cabinet—the ensuing discussion "made this the longest session of the Truman Cabinet." [86] It was Stimson's last day in office, and he argued strongly for the principles of his memorandum. He had staunch support from the Secretary of Commerce, Henry Wallace, who, according to Forrestal, was "completely, everlastingly and wholeheartedly in favor of giving it to the Russians. . . . Failure to give them our knowledge would make an embittered and sour people." Forrestal was one of the most outspoken of the opponents of that view, who included Secretary of State Dean Acheson. Forrestal insisted that the bomb and the knowledge of its production were "the property of the American people" and the administration had no right to give it away unless very certain that they approved. He pointed out that the Russians, like the Japanese, were essentially Oriental in their thinking, "and until we have a longer record of experience with them in the validity of engagements . . . it seems doubtful that we should endeavor to buy their understanding and sympathy. . . . There are no returns on appeasement." Trust, he continued, had to be more than a one-way street.[87] Those arguments impressed Truman, who received similar opinions upon consulting Vannevar Bush, head of the Office of Scientific Research and Development, and the Joint Chiefs of Staff. On October 3, the President asked Congress to establish a domestic Atomic Energy Commission and announced that he would consult the British and the Canadians on the question of international policy.

In the discussion over the makeup and powers of the proposed Atomic Energy Commission in late 1945 and early 1946, Forrestal seems to have taken a compromise stand midway between extreme proposals for military or civilian control. The military proposition was embodied in a bill, sponsored by the chairman of the House Military Affairs Committee, while the civilian side was put forward by Senator Brian McMahon, chairman of the Senate's Special Committee on Atomic Energy.[88] Secretary of War Patterson strongly supported the former. Forrestal had his own proposal—he would give the armed services a voice in the matter, but through their civilian Secretaries. He recommended to the McMahon Committee that the Atomic Energy Commission consist of the Vice-President; the Secretaries of State, War, and Navy; and four full-time additional members. In his testimony, he argued:

We believe that the prestige of the Commission would be insured by the fact that members of the Government were included in it, men who are also responsible for the national security and for our international relationships. The full time members would provide continuous surveillance of actual administration. . . .

What we are trying to do is be sure this Commission does not get set up on an academic and remote basis where it is operating without relation to the other parts of the Government. . . .

He readily agreed with Senator Byrd that one of the vital questions involved in the legislation was the extent to which the military would be subordinated to a civilian commission in the manufacture and use of atomic bombs. He admitted that the proposal would give only minority representation to the military but said:

I am counting on the fact that the authority and prestige of the people who speak for those responsible departments of government [State, War, and Navy] could not be ignored.[89]

President Truman, however, wrote a strong, joint letter to Patterson and Forrestal upholding the McMahon civilian control viewpoint; and that was to prevail in the resultant Atomic Energy Act.[90] The Commission was established in 1946, with Strauss, Forrestal's close friend, one of its initial five members, and later to be its head.

In such a developing world situation, Forrestal's suspicions of Soviet aims and ideas multiplied rapidly. Earlier in the war, to be sure, he had been more sympathetic than Knox regarding material aid to Russia. He had gone along with Roosevelt that the psychological factor in encouraging an ally was worth more than the consequent delay at home. According to McCloy, Forrestal had, in fact, worked well with the Russians in the few contacts he had had as Under Secretary.[91]

But long before Washington as a whole came around to distrusting that ally, Forrestal was one of a number, including George Kennan and Herbert Feis, who had been drawing attention to the dangers from that source. In the summer of 1944, while many policy makers were still confident of Russian good will, he wrote Palmer Hoyt, publisher of the Denver *Post:*

Whenever an American suggests that we act in accordance with the needs of our own security, he is apt to be called a god-damned fascist or imperialist, while if Uncle Joe suggests that he needs the Baltic Provinces, half of Poland, all of Bessarabia and access to the Mediterranean, all hands agree that he is a fine, frank, candid and generally delightful fellow who is very easy to deal with because he is so explicit in what he wants.[92]

The opinion of his friend, Averell Harriman, Ambassador at Moscow, did nothing to abate his growing apprehension. By early 1945, the way that Stalin took advantage of the dying Roosevelt at the Yalta conference apparently convinced Forrestal conclusively, the rosy accounts brought home by Roosevelt and Stettinius notwithstanding. The latter went so far as to say that the Russians desired to cooperate! [93] Forrestal may not have voiced his doubts as openly as Stimson and some others were doing but his diaries indicate the turning point in his thinking, as in this statement by Harriman that he quoted:

we now have ample proof that the Soviet government views all matters from the standpoint of their own selfish interest. . . . we must clearly realize that the Soviet program is the establishment of totalitarianism, ending personal liberty and democracy as we know and respect it. . . . the only hope of stopping Soviet penetration is the development of sound economic conditions.[94]

Roosevelt's death and Truman's accession to the Presidency did nothing to allay Forrestal's uneasiness. In May, he wrote to Senator Homer Ferguson of Michigan, enclosing some articles from *The Economist* which Eberstadt had brought to his attention:

As *The Economist* writer points out, the Bolsheviks have the advantage over us of having a clear-cut line of economic philosophy, amounting almost to a religion, in which they believe is the only solution to the government of men. It is the Marxian dialectic. . . .
There is no use fooling ourselves about the depth and extent of this problem. I have no answers—I have been concentrating on something else, just as you have. But we had better try to get an answer.[95]

Some months after his frustrating experience at Potsdam, he turned to his research assistant Edward F. Willett, in his continuing quest for that answer. What Forrestal wanted to know was whether Marx or Stalin had ever outlined a program of conquest such as Hitler had done in *Mein Kampf*. He appreciated the value of the old motto "Know thy enemy"; and he was determined that the error of not taking Hitler's assertions seriously should not be repeated. Willett, naturally familiar with the Marxist thesis, focused his study on its interpretation by Communist leaders, and among others, consulted frequently with the well-known Jesuit scholar, Wilfred Parsons. In his report, "Dialectical Materialism," Willett found the answer to Forrestal's query was "No," as far as an exact table for world conquest was concerned. There was no doubt, however, that that was the eventual goal, with the movement varying to suit the needs of the moment and with war not necessarily the method. Much pleased with the report, Forrestal, as was his habit, had copies distributed fairly widely—to the President, fellow members of the Cabinet, and a number of others in government and industry. Myron Taylor, Special Representative of the President to the Vatican, later requested a copy to present to the Pope. Parsons and Willett had a quiet chuckle about this as it looked to them like carrying coals to Newcastle; though a chief leader in the fight against Communism might well have a special interest in such an analysis.[96]

During this period since the end of hostilities, Forrestal kept urging Truman to take the story of deteriorating relations with the Soviet to the public.[97] Much of Russia's wartime popularity remained, and the new developments were not generally known. It would be some time, however, before the President did so.

Forrestal himself, in his capacity as head of the mightiest navy in the world, succeeded in establishing effective and continuing resistance to Soviet aggression in the highly sensitive waters of the eastern Mediterranean. His appreciation of what Mahan termed the "influence of sea power" was demonstrated time and again in his speeches, letters, diaries, and private discussions. Among his notes for a book he planned to write was the passage:

Sea power—what it means. Seventy-one per cent of the earth's surface is water. . . . Sea power has still the same meaning it had when the Romans had to get a fleet to conquer the Mediterranean. The same as when Britain, one by one, cut off the tentacles of Napoleon's octopus. The same as in 1917, when Anglo-American control of the Atlantic spelled defeat for Germany. . . . The Army's failure to understand and appreciate sea power—their fundamental attitude that this is a simple matter of transportation. The Air Force much nearer to common understanding because they too operate in fluid element. Three dimensions of power: the surface of the seas, the air above it, and the sub surface. . . . The Army's views are usually mortgaged to land masses. Seamen have always had to be flexible of thought because with natural elements and natural forces which man cannot yet fully master and control. You cannot argue with a rip-tide or a typhoon.[98]

In fighting off the threat of a drastic postwar slashing of the Fleet, Forrestal used a Congressional committee as a sounding board on the subject, saying that there were two fundamental reasons for not making such cuts:

First, the outstanding lesson of the past quarter century is that the means to wage war must be in the hands of those who hate war. The United States should always remain strong.

Second, the Navy is a major component of that strength. In each of the past two wars, our enemies failed to control the seas—and they were defeated. . . . Attacks upon us or by us must cross on, over, or under the sea. . . . No enemy can reach us without crossing the sea. We cannot reach an aggressor without crossing the sea.[99]

Forrestal's conception of sea power and global strategy was no better illustrated than in his advocacy of the reestablishment of American naval forces in the Mediterranean. Here was an example of the practical application of sea power in support of foreign policy and also a demonstration of the skill with which he developed ideas and convinced his colleagues that they should be adopted.

Britain's straitened finances after the war forced a drastic reduction of the powerful naval forces she had been maintaining in those waters for two centuries. Yet the need for a deterrent there to Russian expansion was essential. During the war, when the Russians were overrunning the Balkans, Churchill had rushed British troops to Greece, foreseeing that if they gained air and sea bases on the long fingers stretching down into the Mediterranean, the Allied hold on that strategic area would be threatened. Now, Russia was putting pressure on Turkey, hoping to realize her centuries-old ambition to control the Dardanelles, and Communist Yugoslavia had designs on the key Adriatic city of Trieste. Forrestal realized that a strong naval force in the Mediterranean could reach all those disputed points, could demonstrate American striking force, and might encourage the free nations by discouraging aggression against them in that area.

Five months after the Japanese surrender aboard the *Missouri* in Tokyo Bay, the State Department hit upon an ingenious flag-showing by that great battleship. On February 28, 1946, after a State-War-Navy meeting, recorded Byrnes:

Secretary Forrestal asked if it would be agreeable to me if the Navy sent a task force to the Mediterranean. I promptly told him I hoped it would and suggested that the force accompany the battleship *Missouri*, which we planned to have take to Turkey the body of the Turkish Ambassador who had just died in Washington. Forrestal's proposal was timely. He and I thought it would give encouragement to Turkey and Greece. When I told the President the plan he approved it and Jim Forrestal was delighted.[100]

Unfortunately, the *Missouri* had to sail without the task force, because of the rapid demobilization in the United States and the demand for naval forces in the Far East. Churchill, discussing the situation with Forrestal shortly afterward, expressed regret that the entire task force could not have sailed into the Sea of Marmara— "a gesture of power not fully implemented was almost less effective than no gesture at all." [101]

Though temporarily defeated in his project, Forrestal persisted. Byrnes agreed with his suggestion that "casual cruisers unannounced—not as a fleet or task force, but in small units—be sent to the Mediterranean to establish the custom of the American flag being flown in those waters." [102] Naval Operations, however, continued to raise objections; Forrestal's suggestion that the Eighth Fleet hold its maneuvers in the Mediterranean was rejected—it went to the Caribbean instead. Forrestal became more concerned when the State Department began to send stiff notes to Yugoslavia in the Trieste dispute, where dangerous tension was increasing. He urged State to ask the Joint Chiefs, "What we had to back up the notes with." [103] Later he commented: "The State Department loves to run the ball until it gets too hot to carry. Then, without calling signals, it is swiftly passed to the military, who are expected to make a touchdown." [104]

Finally, at the end of September 1946, Forrestal obtained the formal reestablishment of a Mediterranean force, soon to be known as the Sixth Fleet. He prepared a public announcement, which he first cleared with the State Department and the White House. He called this "typical, in my opinion, of the kind of statement which we should make from time to time to the American public so that there will be no misapprehension." He outlined the fleet's mission as, "First, to support the Allied Forces and Allied Military Government in the discharge of their responsibilities in the occupied areas of Europe. Second, to protect the United States interests and support United States policies in the area. . . ." He pointed out that this was not a new departure, for the United States had periodically kept vessels in those waters.[105] He referred specifically only to the time immediately following World War I, when ships had been sent there for temporary duty, but he might have traced the history of the old Mediterranean Squadron from the days of the Barbary pirates in 1801 until 1904.[106] He made it clear that the new force would be more or less permanent, and that it was to be the bulwark of American foreign policy in that part of the world.[107] His statement was welcomed by the press generally: called, by the New York *Times*, "a firm and clear statement of naval policy" and, by the *Herald Tribune*, "a formal expression of politico-military policy. Its mission is avowedly the support of American rights and interests in those vital matters." [108]

The new policy quickly bore fruit. Byrnes, in a long drawn-out conference of foreign ministers at Paris, was finally able to block Russian insistence on a base in Libya. Walter Lippmann commenting on this attributed Byrnes's success

in the last analysis to the decision to reinforce the United States Mediterranean fleet. That decision made plain in language the Kremlin fully understands that the United States has a vital interest of her own in the Mediterranean. This American act spoke louder than all the long speeches.[109]

Forrestal in his testimony before the Senate Foreign Relations Committee in March 1947 mentioned another satisfactory incident. As he recorded it:

I also reminded the committee of the fact that last summer when the Russians began making their representations to Turkey on the Dardanelles, the appearance of American war vessels in the Mediterranean was followed by the first amiable utterances of Premier Stalin in late September.[110]

Usually based around a large carrier or two, the Sixth Fleet went on, month after month and year after year, as one of the most stabilizing forces for peace in the world. It was, in fact, sometimes called the "fire department" because it managed to turn up at one smoldering trouble spot after another in time to prevent the start of a real conflagration. Unlike the Seventh Fleet in Korean waters, it did not have to engage in actual shooting. Yet, with its carrier planes capable of ranging far inland, it must have exercised a powerful deterrent effect, ever ready, as it boasted, "for a fight or a frolic."

Early in 1947, Forrestal's concern with the eastern Mediterranean involved him in a still broader policy problem in that area. In his diary for February 24, he wrote:

Lunch today with the President. Just before it Marshall showed me a memorandum . . . saying that the British Ambassador had called this morning at the State Department for the purpose of informing the

United States government that Britain could no longer be the reservoir of the financial-military support for Turkey and Greece. Such support, he said, would involve expenditures of about $250 million in the current year and Britain simply could not afford it. Marshall said that this dumped in our lap another most serious problem—that it was tantamount to British abdication from the Middle East with obvious implications as to their successor.[111]

SWINC and the Joint Chiefs started to work immediately on the planning, and so too did various others. "Secretary of the Navy Forrestal, in particular," wrote President Truman later, "participated actively and had several conversations with Dean Acheson. It was the latter, however, as Under Secretary of State, who coordinated the planning being done." [112] On March 12, Truman not only urged a joint session of Congress to provide $400 million for the immediate Greek and Turkish crisis but went on to declare "it must be the policy of the United States to support free peoples who are resisting attempted subjugation by armed minorities or by outside pressure." [113] Just as John Quincy Adams had been the "ghost" in drawing up the Monroe Doctrine in 1823, so Acheson, with possible help from Forrestal, may have had a similar role with the Truman Doctrine in 1947. On that point, it has been remarked that "How much Forrestal's thought and counsel may have contributed to it there is, obviously, no way of knowing; but at least the new course ran parallel to the moral, strategic and tactical ideas which Forrestal had long been developing." [114]

Once the doctrine was enunciated, however, conjecture regarding Forrestal's connection with it ends. There are no doubts about the prominent and energetic part he took in developing popular and Congressional support for the new principle and in implementing it with naval strength. Truman appointed him to a Cabinet committee, headed by Secretary of the Treasury Snyder "to lay out a program of communication with leaders throughout the country." Forrestal stated that he felt "a gathering of big shots was not what we wanted—we had to reach men who were active in business and who would have to do the job." [115] On the day following the President's enunciation of the doctrine, Forrestal had a long telephone conversation with James Reston of the New York *Times* on ways and means of marshaling support for it:

I told Dean and Snyder that I thought we should move on three fronts: one, get the people like yourself, who are pretty well in-

formed now, get the publishers like Arthur Sulzberger and Ep Hoyt
and Paul Smith and Luce, not to educate them but to make them
aware of the fact that this is going to be difficult and will need sus-
tained educational effort. The next thing is the radio people; and
finally the debate; and see to it that people like Vandenberg get the
powerful and most potent stuff that we can give them for the defense
on the floor of the House. That I think has to be done all over the
country and it has to be followed up, not on too big a machine basis,
but selection of people in different parts of the country.[116]

That skill in the tactics of persuasion was a factor without doubt
in bringing a favorable decision in Congress; and the measure became law on May 22.

During those busy weeks of spring and early summer of 1947
when Forrestal was working overtime on the final stages of unification and budget problems, he saw to it that strong naval support
was applied in the eastern Mediterranean. On July 16, when the
Greek situation became serious with guerrilla raids, Truman asked
Forrestal:

. . . how large a part of our Mediterranean fleet he might be able to
move to Greek ports. Secretary Forrestal informed me that it would
be entirely practicable to have a large part of the Mediterranean
squadron shifted in short order. He expressed a belief that such a visit
would have some deterrent effect on the activities of the Communist
guerrillas but was unwilling to estimate how the American public
might react.[117]

One scholar who has been making a special study of the Truman
Doctrine and its application writes:

I am fairly positive that the Navy, with Forrestal leading the way,
proved the major source of service support for the Doctrine. The Army
and Judge Patterson appear to have had doubts about the strategic
feasibility of a land commitment in Greece; but these doubts were
never allowed to predominate over the determination to proceed
demonstrated by Navy and State.[118] [It might be pointed out that the
Navy would have naturally more freedom of action in withdrawing
from a deteriorating situation than a landbased force.]

The pressing need for better coordination, that had been so
urgently brought home to Forrestal during the war years, was to
bring about some significant organizational developments. Through
his initiative, the movement began shaping up during the final weeks
of fighting. A further incentive to explore better methods arose

when the Navy felt the need to make some tangible counter-proposals to the Army's drive for merger of the armed forces.

Through all the discussion of SWINC and other interdepartmental agencies ran the problem of the lack of proper channels within the Department itself for determining a position in politico-military matters. It was not enough to establish a regular system of contacts between departments. And this naturally involved the perennial question of civilian authority. At a meeting of Forrestal's Top Policy group in September 1945, he said that he wanted "to identify those places in the Navy that have contact with the determination of national foreign policy, military governments, terms on Japan, and all the things that come up in SWNCC." [119] Gates replied that there was need of "a single office . . . responsible for obtaining coordination among the interested bureaus and agencies within the Department. . . . The Secretary's Office is handling some matters, and Cominch is handling some matters." [120] He cited a recent paper about the disposition of the Italian fleet which came before SWINC. Several naval officers were consulted but through an oversight, "it was not sent to Cominch. Later it was discovered that this matter had been treated at Potsdam and that Admirals King and Cooke knew more about what had been agreed . . . than did the State Department." In London, Byrnes, having been at Potsdam, knew this and took a position in line with the Navy view, which was contrary to that of State. Gates said his understanding was that instructions had been sent to Byrnes's naval adviser at London, Admiral Hewitt, Commander in Europe, "as to the Navy's point of view, but as far as I know they were not cleared with . . . the office I represent." [121]

This was but one of a series of politico-military matters involving the relationship between the Secretary's Office and Naval Operations. Another instance concerned the international conference called at Dumbarton Oaks, near Washington, in July 1944 as preparatory for the United Nations Conference at San Francisco the next year. Forrestal first learned of this from the newspapers, though arrangements had been well in hand for some time through the regular liaison channel that had been operating in the area of postwar planning since 1942 between Naval Operations and the State Department. Forrestal did not know about this liaison arrangement and asked his staff to find out the general purpose of the conference, who the Navy's representatives were, and "how thoroughly are we prepared." [122]

It was the same astonishing story, whether in top strategy or postwar planning. Naval Operations was the point of contact, but the civilian Secretaries knew nothing about it! This was the same situation that had faced Forrestal as Under Secretary, when for ten months he had not known that an obscure section in CNO was working on industrial mobilization planning.[123] In these instances, the civilian Secretaries, coming in with little if any prior knowledge of the Department, were not properly briefed and so were by-passed in the development of Navy policy.

Admiral King at the Top Policy group meeting urged that Naval Operations through its Central Division was the proper clearing-house. Forrestal objected; to him this meant the Navy had two points of view: the civilian in SWINC and the military in Naval Operations. He found, moreover, that such willingness to supply integrating machinery was usual on the part of naval officers, and that it meant that the Secretary's Office became walled off from the main current of happenings. King argued that he did not see why Naval Operations' Central Division should not do all the co-ordinating for the Department, but Forrestal answered: "because it doesn't get through unless somebody in my office or Gates's office is seeing to it that we are briefed. The result is that I do not know what McCrea [Chief of the Central Division] is doing because I don't ever get to talk to him." [124]

In relation to the State Department, where postwar planning had been just about the only function left in Hull's hands by Roosevelt, there had been in 1942 a short-lived interdepartmental committee. Admiral Arthur Hepburn, with Rear Admiral Harold C. Train as alternate, had been appointed to this to advise Hull about a post-war organization, international security, and trusteeships. Hull, who was ill most of the time, had a sizable staff under a special assistant, Leo Pasvolsky of the Brookings Institute. Apparently, the Navy Department paid little attention to what was being done beyond having the head of the Central Division on a special subcommittee.

But it was the Central Division, itself, that for years was the contact with State not only on postwar planning but on all sort of routine matters, including reports of naval attachés and missions, visits of warships to foreign ports, and the administration of naval island governments. During the war, it had charge of the leased bases in the British islands and furnished the naval representatives for some interdepartmental groups.

With the increased interest in politico-military matters under the Forrestal stimulus, a new unit was set up in Naval Operations to furnish the naval portion of the working staff for SWINC. This had been expanded by the end of 1945 into the Political-Military Affairs Division under Captain Robert L. Dennison as Assistant Chief of Naval Operations (Political-Military Affairs). It was something of a coincidence that this same Dennison, later a White House naval aide, who had been the pioneer in the Department in carrying out the idea of closer working liaison between strategy and diplomacy, would be eventually Commander-in-Chief of the Atlantic Fleet and Supreme Allied Commander, Atlantic, of the North Atlantic Treaty Organization (NATO).

But above that new Naval Operations group, Forrestal insisted that there be a civilian—Assistant Secretary Gates—the Navy's representative on SWINC. Forrestal was thus the first Secretary to appoint one of his immediate staff to this politico-military area, where the Navy's only representation had hitherto been through certain military units in Naval Operations. Thus, in effect, he was insisting that the civilian Secretary had the right to be informed of, and to participate in, whatever the Navy Department was doing in any capacity.

Another innovation that Forrestal felt would improve coordination in policy matters was a secretariat for the President's Cabinet. The idea, of course, was not new having been discussed for years in academic circles and learned journals. But Forrestal was apparently the first department head to advocate such procedure for the Cabinet.

While Under Secretary, Forrestal first became interested in this device from talks in London with General Sir Hastings Ismay, Churchill's military secretary, and Sir Maurice Hankey, former secretary of the British Cabinet. He next had the feasibility of an American Cabinet secretariat examined by his staff.[125] The indications are that he was at first somewhat confused as to how it would operate. He was not quite clear in distinguishing between a secretariat and what later was to become the National Security Council. Like many other Americans, moreover, he did not fully recognize the fundamental difference between parliamentary and Presidential systems. In the former, the Cabinet members—in theory at least —are equals, simply being headed by a first minister and they have joint responsibility. The American President, however, has no equals, only subordinates, hence he alone is responsible. Thus, policy is often made in the British Cabinet, but rarely in the American. Nevertheless, Forrestal still believed that an advance agenda would make for more intelligent understanding and records for better follow-up, whether a President chose to use his Cabinet for discussions from which policy might be made or simply as a device for communicating his instructions.

One instance in particular in which he had a major part as full Secretary concerned the confusion surrounding the sale of surplus tankers to Western European nations so that they could supply their own oil needs.[126] The State Department was anxious to sell a "considerable number," but by the Merchant Marine Act of 1946 such vessels could only be sold abroad after the Secretary of the Navy certified they were not needed for American defense. Forrestal was worried lest they find their way into Russian hands. The whole question probably should have been settled by the President, but instead he had General Marshall, now Secretary of State, present it to the Cabinet.[127] Marshall and Forrestal, however, came away from two Cabinet meetings with very different ideas about what had been decided. At the meeting on May 16, 1947, Marshall presented State's request for a "considerable number" of tankers to be sold, but whether this meant the thirty-five proposed by the Navy or the whole available one hundred as desired by the buyers was apparently left in the air. "Whether there actually was a cabinet 'decision' or a flat ruling by the President or whether the Navy reserved its right is unknown and probably unknowable," since there were "no minutes and no written decision." [128] Marshall, nevertheless, informed Forrestal of his desire for the prompt execution of the decision of the Cabinet. No action was taken, for Forrestal felt that the Navy's statutory responsibility and authority had in no way been altered. The consensus of a second meeting a month later was that the whole total of one hundred tankers be sold; and, in the course of time, that was done.[129]

To Forrestal, this dispute with its discussions, telephone calls, and passing of letters without any procedural pattern, was further tangible proof of the need of a secretariat. He did not raise the broader issue of the authority of the Cabinet, or whether this was the agency to make this kind of decision. The President, of course, could remove a Secretary who refused to act—as State thought Forrestal had—but the Cabinet itself had no power to insist on a decision being carried out.

Eventually, Forrestal made his formal recommendation for a secretariat, but Truman proved to be cool to the idea. It was introduced in 1954, however, by President Eisenhower. There seems little doubt that it was Forrestal's espousal of the plan which focused attention on it and had a bearing on its later adoption.

Probably the most significant result of his experiences and thinking in politico-military affairs was the creation of the National Security Council. In the fateful summer of 1945, he asked Eberstadt to consider this aspect in the study he was making on unification of the armed services.[130] In Eberstadt's Report, made public in October, Forrestal's half-formed ideas on what might be done to bring about better coordination of foreign and military policies were developed into definite plans, which led to the establishment of that Council.

In all the discussions and, at times, acrimonious debates, on the ensuing unification bills, there was no dispute between the Army and Navy over the National Security Council. The really amazing aspect was the slight interest shown by the Department of State in the extended Congressional hearings. When invited to testify, General Marshall, now Secretary of State, refused on the ground that he did not "under existing circumstances in my present position think it advisable for me to participate in this discussion." [131]

It has been charged that the National Security Council was

based on a misconception about the Executive Branch in the American Government. Whether the NSC "germinated" out of the British Committee of Imperial Defense, as Forrestal told Churchill, and as the Eberstadt Report indicates, or was derived from long standing Navy views about a Council of National Defense, makes little difference because both were inappropriate. Cabinet solidarity may be the cement of the British government, and interdepartmental committees may have certain uses, but the American Executive Branch is held together, if at all, by the authority of the President. The Eberstadt Report treated the powers of the President as something which could be embodied in a committee.[132]

It would seem more reasonable to assume that Forrestal's advocacy of the National Security Council was not a plot to usurp Presidential power but rather a method of providing preliminary pick and shovel staff work. His experience during the war and immediate postwar years clearly indicated the need for just such careful evaluation and planning so that military resources might match foreign commitments.

Like many another administrative device, the new Council could be misused and on occasion, especially in its early years, it did not function exactly as its creators had hoped. Thus, it did not always prevent hasty policy making. The familiar hurly-burly of *ad hoc* conferences was still in evidence when the Berlin crisis broke in June 1948. Nor did the NSC always function as Forrestal had expected in providing guidance for the military budget during the Truman regime. On the other hand, it did furnish a staff of planners, accustomed to working together, who, if called upon, could draft plans rapidly. Even though the Council might not be forehanded enough to have a special plan on tap for situations that might arise, its staff, experienced in sorting out issues and stating alternatives, helped make its decisions better in a crisis. It had become clear in the preparation of strategic war plans in World War II that experienced planners were much more important than a ready plan of action. The latter usually had to be changed again and again to meet a particular emergency, and for that the prime essential was a quick-working staff, which was just what the Council provided for politico-military problems.

In the 1950s, Eisenhower, as President, made fairly constant use of the National Security Council. He later wrote: "In my experience, satisfactory decisions in foreign and defense matters can best be made with the invaluable assistance of the National Security Council and its supporting working groups." In case of strong differences of opinion among advisers, in his opinion, a President gets "a better comprehension of all the complexities of any problem" by having them "discussed, debated and argued . . . before him in person, while he listens and makes occasional comment." [133] Although the next administration in 1961 tended at first to handle grave problems informally, it before long resumed recourse to the Council's advice.[134]

On Forrestal's initiative, as Secretary of Defense, a unit was established in that Department to link politico-military contacts more closely. This was along the lines of the one already set up in the Navy Department. Forrestal originally assigned a special assistant to this, but in the Fifties after his death, an Assistant Secretary of Defense headed such an organization. The unit reached down into each of the three military departments. Its staff specialized in foreign affairs, with an emphasis upon civilian participation in policy making. The vast military assistance programs to American allies, the North Atlantic Treaty Organization, and similar arrangements in Southeast Asia, as well as the Korean War, all intensified the operating relations between the three military services and the Department of State. It would seem that a good portion of the credit for this development belonged to Forrestal; it was built upon foundations laid by him in 1945–48, particularly the National Security Council.

9

Ability and Experience

DURING A controversial discussion of a nomination, Forrestal wrote in his diary that he had told President Truman:

I am most anxious to preserve the principle upon which Colonel Knox and I had run the Navy Department since we came into the Department in the midsummer of 1940, namely that the posts in the Department should go to men who had been at work in the Department —for two reasons: First we didn't have time during the heat of the war to train new people, and, second, because it was a great benefit to the morale of the many very capable men we had brought in from civil life to see such recognition given for good work.[1]

Those "very capable men brought in from civil life" represented an achievement that would leave its lasting mark on the administration of the armed services.

Forrestal was one of those, moreover, who had come to realize that the United States needed to abandon the old practice of filling policy-making posts with appointees whose chief qualifications were that they were Deserving Whigs, Deserving Democrats, or Deserving Republicans. War and Navy Secretaryships, like other Cabinet portfolios and diplomatic posts, tended to be used by the party in power in that fashion. For every statesman that this habit produced, several "stuffed shirts" might be cited. Forrestal thoroughly recognized the importance of a policy-maker's party allegiance, as it definitely helped his success as an administrator to have the confidence of his party leadership in the White House and on the Hill. He personally had no objection to "Deserving Democrats" as such, but he wanted them to be more than that.

In earlier days, when national stakes had been much smaller, the consequences of wrong decisions by officials of that sort were not necessarily too serious. The continuation of that custom might well be calamitous with the new responsibilities of the nation. What the situation demanded, in his view, was able men with experience. That experience, he felt, was better if it included some time in private business, but that alone was not enough. The necessity for government experience was probably his main point. He believed that top policy positions in the Department should be filled by "promotion from within"; no one should be appointed until he had served for a time in some lesser Secretarial post. He tried to make this a rule in his Department. In doing so, he had to challenge long-established political traditions.

The two main factors in the appointment problem, as he saw it, were the individual's basic ability and his experience in office. The first was obviously indispensable, and the longer he was in Washington, the more vital the second seemed to him, especially for an enterprise of the Navy's size. Sometimes, of course, an able, inexperienced new appointee did a good job from the start; but he was fully aware from his own case that he had become more useful in naval administration by 1947 than he had been in 1940 or even in 1944.

The only civilian group in the top structure of the prewar Navy Department that stayed long enough to accumulate such experience were the chief clerk and his subordinates; and they were only infrequently possessed of executive ability. It has been said that Secretaries might come and go, but the chief clerk stayed on forever. Often those who occupied that post entered the Department at an early age, and by careful attention to Navy Regulations and the accounting manual had won promotion. Forrestal strongly opposed the chief clerk system, though a prime example of "promotion from within," because to him seniority alone was not the proper criterion. As Frederick the Great is said to have put it to some of his senior officers in explaining why bright young men were being promoted over their heads: "See that mule over there! He has been through forty campaigns, but he is still just an army mule."

The pitfalls of overemphasis upon seniority in the retention and even promotion of the mediocre were pointed out in a speech by Forrestal: "One of the great dangers of a civil service system is that it can become clogged at its lower levels by a group of mediocre people unfit for further advancement but not quite bad enough to be discharged." He referred to the possible "corroding effect of continuous government service, that ultimately might affect the most dynamic individual with that atrophy of thinking which we have come to associate with bureaucracy." He suggested that the ranks of the civil service be filled by "competitive selection on basis of character and ability," with emphasis upon "breadth of knowledge as well as technical aptitude"; that a periodic review be made of the administrative staff, similar to the Army-Navy system; and, that for the higher positions at least, a prerequisite for eligibility be two years employment in some non-governmental activity.[2]

In regard to the last suggestion, he felt that perhaps business offered the most desirable experience, "the inexorable logic of the profit and loss statement and its corollary, the ability to merchandise" constituting a "sound background." [3] To be sure, a successful business career was often given as the justification for Cabinet appointments. But at times, the degree of "success" was questionable and all too often was far outweighed by the extent of party contributions.

The most striking aspect of the "spoils system" was the lack of pertinent governmental experience. Obviously, relatively few appointees would be likely to have an intimate knowledge of a highly specialized mystery like the Navy, but it was surprising that so few had had any contact with any form of high-level administration in Washington or even in state capitals. A naval officer upon his appointment as Chief of Naval Operations might well murmur, "Thank God, at last!" for that represented the ultimate goal of decades of professional effort; but the usual recipient of the Navy Secretaryship might more correctly exclaim, "But, this is so sudden!"

Forrestal said, in commenting upon the creation of the still more exacting post of Secretary of Defense:

It took me several years to grasp the details involved in administration of an organization as large and complex as the Navy Department; and while it may be said that a good administrator should not concern himself with details, I hold that there are some details that he must understand. For the balance, he has to know the instruments and the machinery through which they are administered. I mean by that, that he has to know the places to go, he must know the people who have the knowledge, and he must have the swift intuition, so to speak, that will enable him to get at the sources of information on how things are done.[4]

The tragic wastefulness of the system was that top level posts —and the Navy portfolio was not unique in this—might be said to have customarily floated in a vacuum, utterly unrelated to the past or the future. Not only Forrestal but a good many other Secretaries and Assistant Secretaries estimated that it took at least two years to learn the intricacies of the Naval Establishment; yet the average tenure was scarcely three years. Thus, the professional officers were often able to resist much civilian control; admirals were not apt to take too seriously a man on the way out. What was more, the painfully acquired experience was usually wasted, for the government seldom made further use of a former Secretary's services; Forrestal's promotion to the Defense Department was a rare exception. Usually the spirit of the spoils system argued that a Secretary had already had his reward, and it was time to make some other deserving partisan happy.

That the American system differed radically from British traditions in this respect is indicated in the accompanying comparison of the First Lords of Admiralty and the Secretaries of the Navy in the half century before World War I. In Britain, at least until the days of the Labor ministries, very few achieved a major Cabinet post without having served in at least one and generally several junior posts. There had been available, to be sure, in those days, a leisure class, of which many members were able to afford to serve in a succession of government posts, while their party was in power. While only four of those eighteen First Lords had had direct Admiralty experience, all had had an opportunity to learn what was involved in a ministerial post. Ten of them had already held major Cabinet positions, in contrast to only two American Secretaries of the Navy. Legislative experience has been omitted from the table since all First Lords had to be members of Parliament and few Navy Secretaries had been in Congress. Judgeships and Ambassadorships are not listed, not being properly executive experience.

Previous Pertinent Experience of First Lords of the Admiralty and Secretaries of the Navy, 1861–1915

FIRST LORDS OF THE ADMIRALTY

(1859) Duke of Somerset, Lord of the Treasury, 1835–39; Secretary of the Board of Control, 1839; Secretary of State for Home Department, 1841; First Commissioner of Works, 1851–52.

1866 Sir John Parkington (II), Secretary of State for Colonies, 1852; First Lord of the Admiralty (I), 1858–59.

1867 Henry T. L. Corry, Junior Lord of the Admiralty, 1841–45; Secretary of the Admiralty, 1858–59.

1868 Hugh C. E. Childers, Junior Lord of the Admiralty, 1864–65; Financial Secretary to the Treasury, 1865–66.

1871 George J. Goschen, Vice President, Board of Trade, 1865–66; President, Poor Law Board, 1868–71.

1874 George W. Hunt, Financial Secretary to the Treasury, 1866–68; Chancellor of the Exchequer, 1868.

1877 William H. Smith, Financial Secretary to the Treasury, 1874–77.

1880 Lord Northbrook, Junior Lord of the Admiralty, 1857–59; Under Secretary of State for India, 1859–61; Under Secretary of State for War, 1861–66, 1868–72; Governor General of India, 1872–80.

1885 Lord George Hamilton, Under Secretary of State for India, 1874–78; Vice President of the Council, 1878–80.

1886 Earle de Grey and Ripon, Under Secretary of State for War, 1859–61; Secretary of State for War, 1863–66; Secretary of State for India, 1866; Lord President of the Council, 1873; Governor General of India, 1880–84.

1886 Lord George Hamilton (II).

1892 Earl Spencer, Lord Lieutenant of Ireland, 1868–74, 1882–85; Lord President of the Council, 1880–83, 1886.

1895 George J. Goschen (II), since first term, Chancellor of the Exchequer, 1887–92.

1900 Earl of Selborne, Under Secretary of State for the Colonies, 1895–1900.

1905 Lord Tweedmouth, Parliamentary Secretary to the Treasury, 1892–94; Chancellor of the Duchy of Lancaster, 1894–95.

1908 Reginald McKenna, Financial Secretary to the Treasury, 1905; President, Board of Education, 1907.

1911 Winston S. Churchill, Under Secretary of State for Colonies, 1905–08; President, Board of Trade, 1908–10; Secretary of State for Home Department, 1910–11.

1915 Arthur J. Balfour, Private Secretary to the Foreign Secretary, 1878–80; President, Local Government Board, 1885; Secretary for Scotland, 1886; Chief Secretary for Ireland, 1887–91; First Lord of the Treasury, 1891–92, 1895–1905; Prime Minister, 1902–05.

SECRETARIES OF THE NAVY

1861 Gideon Welles, Bureau Chief, Navy Department, 1846–48.
1869 Adolph Borie
1869 George M. Robeson

1877 Richard W. Thompson
1881 Nathan Goff, Jr.
1881 William H. Hunt
1882 William E. Chandler, Solicitor, Navy Department, 1865; Assistant Secretary of the Treasury, 1865–67.
1885 William C. Whitney
1889 Benjamin F. Tracy
1893 Hilary A. Herbert, Chairman, House Naval Affairs Committee, 1885–89, 1891–93.
1897 John D. Long, Governor of Massachusetts, 1880–82.
1902 William H. Moody
1904 Paul Morton
1905 Charles Bonaparte
1906 Victor H. Metcalf, Secretary of Commerce & Labor, 1904–06.
1908 Truman H. Newberry, Assistant Secretary of the Navy, 1905–08.
1909 George von L. Meyer, Postmaster General, 1907–09.
1913 Josephus Daniels, Chief Clerk, Department of the Interior, 1893–95.

Sources: First Lords of the Admiralty from *Statesman's Year Book, Dictionary of National Biography, Who Was Who;* Secretaries of the Navy from *Dictionary of American Biography, Who Was Who in America;* W. H. Smith, *History of the Cabinet of the United States.*

The type of civilian selected obviously had a marked bearing upon the amount of civilian authority exercised at a given time; and the British method resulted on the whole in maintaining it at a consistently high level. Moderate differences in the caliber of the First Lords naturally existed, but were not enough to produce the violent fluctuations in civilian control that took place in the Navy Department with its far greater variations in Secretarial qualifications.

Real authority on the part of civilian officials was a tender plant in the environment of a military department and could wither quickly from neglect. Those inexperienced men in the high civilian posts of the Department meant not only poor administration but also caused the office itself to be disregarded for long periods as of little account. The result was a weakening of civilian control, while a succession of able professional officers shed luster upon their posts, with consequent increase of military authority. Previous pertinent experience was not, of course, the whole story in either system. A few excellent Secretaries of the Navy, such as William H. Hunt, "Father of the New Navy," lacked that background completely, while the earlier Paulding, with the longest previous naval experience of any incumbent, was unduly conservative in appreciating the importance of introducing steam and begrudged the time demanded by his routine tasks.[5] But some of the worst Secretaries would probably never have been appointed, if junior posts had demonstrated their worthlessness.

Forrestal, with his strong personnel theories had to combat that long-standing history of years of weak Secretaries and brief scattered intervals of strong leadership that had preceded this period. That pattern began to develop before the federal government had been in existence thirty years. Before that, at the very outset, however, Washington and John Adams had picked men whom they personally knew had special qualifications for the posts. When a separate Navy Department came into existence in 1798, it was decided for many reasons that merchant shipowners would be most likely to make the best Secretaries. The happy first choice, Benjamin Stoddert, not only had that maritime background but also had served during the Revolution as Secretary of the Continental Board of War. Three of his immediate successors also had merchant shipping experience.

A new factor came into Cabinetmaking in 1818. President Monroe began what was to become a long-standing pattern of basing selection largely on geographical considerations rather than upon proper qualifications. Until 1885, not more than one Cabinet member was chosen from any state. There continued usually to be a "New England seat," a "Southern seat," a "Western seat," and so on.[6]

The most extreme fluctuations in Secretarial caliber appeared in three distinct periods, between 1861 and 1893. It was extraordinary luck that crusty, bewhiskered Gideon Welles of Connecticut came to Lincoln's Cabinet in 1861. Aside from his good sense and stubborn courage, he had learned the wartime working of the Navy as civilian chief of Provisions and Clothing in the Mexican War. He had, moreover, an invaluable deputy in his Assistant Secretary Gustavus V. Fox, who had been a regular naval officer before turning to industry.[7]

Immediately after Welles's eight years, civilian authority almost disappeared for twelve years during the "dark ages" of the Navy. Professional "line" influence became unusually strong in the person of Admiral David Dixon Porter, a superlative fighter afloat and a dangerous intriguer ashore. Grant was his friend and saw to it that he had the real power during the Secretaryship of a wealthy and highly respected Philadelphia merchant, Adolph Borie. For a hundred days, Porter "went the limit" in "turning off the light" to produce the "dark ages." [8] When Borie resigned in disgust at his figurehead role, his successor was George M. Robeson, described as "a first-rate judge of wine, a second-rate trout fisherman, and a third-rate Jersey lawyer." [9] He was a lax administrator, whose impeachment was demanded by the Democratic minority in the committee investigating his administration.[10] In 1877, Hayes picked the first Secretary from beyond the mountains, Richard W. Thompson, a Terre Haute lawyer, who proved to be the one weak member of his Cabinet. It was alleged that on his initial visit to a navy yard, his first glimpse of a warship brought forth: "Why, the durned thing's hollow!" Civilian authority sank even lower in his term, which ended with his abrupt dismissal by Hayes for accepting what was virtually a $25,000-a-year bribe from the French company seeking to build a Panama canal.[11]

Then, in 1881, began twelve years in which the post was held in turn by four men whose success was more a matter of innate caliber than previous executive experience. Between them, they brought the "New Navy" into existence and guided its formative years. Before William H. Hunt, an erstwhile federal judge, had been four months in office, he appointed the first advisory board for the new steel navy and enlisted Congressional support for it.[12] William E. Chandler, one of the sharpest "operators" in the Republican party, who had served briefly in a legal capacity in the Navy Department, translated the new movement into actual ships. This was continued by William C. Whitney, a wealthy financier, and Benjamin F. Tracy, a New York lawyer and judge who backed Alfred Thayer Mahan's arguments for the need of battleships rather than simply cruisers.

That variegated pattern was to remain much the same while the Navy grew. In 1897–98, although only Assistant Secretary, Theodore Roosevelt exercised very real civilian authority; his driving initiative did much to prepare the Navy for the Spanish-American War and also promoted, for better or for worse, the acquisition of the Philippines. Then, as President, he was able to act pretty much as his own Secretary because of the rapid turnover of six different Secretaries in less than eight years.[13] He constantly promoted the Navy toward its second place among the world's fleets.

In the next decade, George von L. Meyer and then Josephus Daniels had both had previous experience in Washington administration and proved strong Secretaries, although the latter was a controversial figure, the wisdom of whose actions was often questioned by the naval officers.

Harding, whose Cabinetmaking was almost as bizarre as Grant's, selected Edwin M. Denby, a prosperous Detroit industrialist, who had been a former Navy enlisted man and then a reserve captain of Marines. He was a virtual cipher during the Washington Naval Conference of 1921–22, while his Assistant Secretary abetted the Secretary of State in inflicting more physical damage upon the Fleet than any hostile admiral had ever done. When Denby stumbled into the booby trap of the Teapot Dome naval oil reserves scandal, which sent another Cabinet member to prison, the Senate asked Coolidge—by then Harding's successor—to dismiss him. Coolidge refused, but Denby resigned anyway. "Stupidity is the high crime and misdemeanor of which the Senate accuses Mr. Denby and the only one," declared one newspaper.[14] Some journalistic memoirs elaborated this point:

His "I don't know's" and "I don't remember" . . . were the simple directness of the dumb. . . . His tragedy was that nature after giving him the features that would have fitted a Bismarck, had neglected to fill in the space behind the features with Bismarck material.[15]

The selection of his successor is said to have come about from Coolidge's casual inquiry at a press conference, as to where he might find a new Secretary. "Wilbur of California" was the name suggested. Whether or not Ray Lyman Wilbur, President of Stanford and eventually Hoover's Secretary of the Interior, was meant, the bid went to his brother, an Annapolis graduate who was a state judge. He proved a weak administrator; his main achievement while Secretary appeared to be his syndication of a series of children's bedtime stories.[16]

The best of the "between-the-wars" Secretaries was Charles Francis Adams, Boston financier, crack yachtsman, and descendant of two Presidents. He was prevented, however, from exercising a strong direction of events because of Hoover's ultra-negative policy toward the Navy.

The next Secretary, Claude A. Swanson also faced a Presidential handicap, but in his case Franklin D. Roosevelt, never forgetting his Assistant Secretary days, liked the Navy too well and tended "to be his own Secretary." Swanson had had twenty-two years on the Senate Naval Affairs Committee and was briefly its chairman, but he came to office a very sick man. By retaining him until his death six years later, Franklin D. thus achieved the same goal that Theodore Roosevelt had with his rapid turnover of six Secretaries.[17] This was the climax of almost twenty years, prior to the coming of Knox and Forrestal in 1940, of weak Secretarial leadership and domination by the admirals or the President.

There was one source of experienced men, the professional naval officers, which has not been utilized by the United States for naval administration nor by the British since 1806. The latter had had ten professional First Lords before that, but only two since had the remotest connection with naval service. In the Admiralty, the naval point of view was represented by the professional First Sea Lord as the "number two" man. The Germans, on the other hand, used admirals exclusively before World War I. The Japanese decreed in 1900 that their ministers and vice-ministers of marine must be admirals or vice admirals on active service.[18] Between 1871 and 1914, the Italians had a civilian minister in only one year, while the French seem to have divided just about evenly between civilians and admirals.[19]

No professional naval officer has, as yet, been Secretary of the American Navy, though several seem to have declined the opportunity. The closest approach was in the Assistant Secretaryship on two occasions. The feeling that the appointment of professional officers to such posts was a negation of the basic idea of civilian authority led Forrestal and the other framers of the unification act of 1947 to insert the proviso that a "person who has within ten years been on active duty as a commissioned officer in a Regular component of the armed services shall not be eligible for appointment as Secretary of Defense." [20] Congress, however, obligingly and speedily made a special exception to that in 1950, when President Truman wanted to name General George C. Marshall to the post.[21]

As full Secretary, Forrestal, himself an outstanding example of promotion from within the Department, had his hands full trying to keep that principle from continually running afoul of the time-honored Presidential policy of using appointments as rewards for political service. His insistence upon nominees who had qualifications other than having been a party worker or donor to the party's war chest naturally did not endear him to the professional politicians. But this had much to do with making his office an effective instrument of civilian control. Even for some of the lower posts, he fought for proved executive ability in merit appointments, as well as for departmental experience.

Roosevelt kept a promise to Knox that he would have the right to pick his own deputies or at least might veto outside suggestions.[22] There is no indication that Roosevelt gave the same assurance to Forrestal. Possibly, Forrestal thought he was not in a position to request this, being well aware he lacked political influence. He could have been mistaken, as Roosevelt forced no candidates upon him. At the same time, Roosevelt did disregard, month after month, Forrestal's pleas to fill vacancies. Under Truman, Forrestal faced not only similar delays but also months of dogged Presidential persistence for a political candidate, as well as a major appointment made without his knowledge.

Both Knox and Forrestal were generally successful in obtaining experienced candidates. More men were promoted within the Department at the Secretarial level between Swanson's death in 1939 and Forrestal's transfer to the Pentagon in 1947 than in all its previous history. A good share of the credit belongs to Forrestal, as most of these appointments came in his term. Until Edison's promotion in 1940, only one of the forty-six Secretaries had been advanced from Assistant to full Secretary;[23] and only three others, years before, had had previous departmental experience.[24] Now, between 1939 and 1947, three of the four Secretaries and four of the five men in the new Under Secretary post were promoted directly from deputy roles, while four of the six Assistant Secretaries rose from lower positions in the Department. On the other hand, all three in the revived post of Assistant Secretary for Air came from outside. After the war, two departmental veterans successively held the new semi-Secretarial position of Administrative Assistant to the Secretary (see Appendix I). Letters in Forrestal's file give many clues to the usually elusive circumstances leading up to such appointments.

Following Knox's death and Forrestal's elevation to his post, Presidential procrastination in filling vacancies left the Department with only three instead of four Secretaries during more than nineteen months. This was almost two-thirds of the time between April 1944 and November 1946. First, Forrestal's former berth, the Under Secretaryship, was left vacant for almost two months until Bard's appointment to it. Thereupon, nine months elapsed before Bard's former post, the Assistant Secretaryship, was filled. Forrestal, Bard, and Gates had thus to struggle through nine of the busiest months of the war with the task that had overworked them in a team of four. The Under Secretaryship again became vacant for the first five and one-half months of 1946 and the Assistant Secretaryship for Air for almost five months in the second half of that year.

These delays were not Forrestal's fault; he tried to apply pressure on the White House from the start. The day before he was sworn in as Secretary, he sent Roosevelt a brief note and followed it in more detail in early June by outlining his "promotion-from-within" program:

My dear Mr. President:

You have far bigger things to think about, but—I think a further delay in filling the vacant position here may have some undesirable results. I want to suggest therefore:

1. That you name Ralph Bard as Under Secretary.
2. That Charles Thomas be made Assistant Secretary in Ralph's place.

I believe these appointments will be well received by the country. If my own is any criterion, whether it was merited or not, the public likes the idea of someone who is familiar with the work.

From a practical standpoint, as you know, we are responsible for appropriation of around 115 billions. The honeymoon which we enjoyed while we were building posthaste and while the country was scared I think is almost over. The dustpan phase, as I call it, will be more onerous and difficult than the original letting of contracts and I will need people who are intelligent, will work hard, and whom I don't have to educate.

Thomas would reflect credit on the Administration on the Coast. He is not a "name" but he will work and that is what I need. In addition, he has an equable temperament and gets along with Navy people instead of fighting them. The other man of high ability who knows the Navy is H. Struve Hensel. He was a partner in Harrison Tweed's firm in New York before he came down here in 1941. He is strong, vigorous, and I think you will find he stands exceedingly well on the Hill.

The last alternative suggestion is Major General William H. Harrison. He knows the Navy through his work at W.P.B. They like him, and he also is a worker.[25]

Although Roosevelt within three weeks elevated Bard, a Republican—even though it was an election year—political interests were to dominate the situation from then on. The President procrastinated month after month in filling the Assistant Secretaryship vacated by Bard. This resulted not only in a stupendous load for the three Secretaries but a sort of catch-as-catch-can arrangement in the interim during which the new appointment was momentarily expected. Bard retained the same functions he had had as Assistant Secretary arguing that it would be a waste of valuable Navy time were he to throw away his three years of experience. This proved to be a permanent shift in cognizance, as the assignments of the new Under Secretaryship had not yet been crystallized; but for the time being it left material procurement rather in the air.

Forrestal had at once begun his persistent urging for that appointment:

Nineteen out of the twenty-three members of the California Congressional delegation have signed an endorsement of Charles Thomas for Assistant Secretary of the Navy and have sent it to the White House.

After combing over the field, Thomas and Hensel are the best candidates I have from the standpoint of the business of the Department. It is my understanding that the Congress will recess on Friday: I should like very much to get the post filled so that we can plan the administrative division of responsibility.[26]

Thomas, as well as Hensel, was already in the Department.[27] Head of the large West Coast clothing firm of Foreman and Clark, and a World War I aviator, he had come as special assistant to Gates; and then was utilized by Forrestal in establishing the inventory and stock control system. Incidentally, both men in the next ten years were to give further distinguished service in several administrative posts in the armed services: Thomas, as Under Secretary of the Navy, Assistant Secretary of Defense for Supply and Logistics, and Secretary of the Navy; and Hensel as Assistant Secretary of the

Admiral Chester W. Nimitz (left) greeting the Secretary of the Navy upon arrival at Izzley Field, Saipan

"If you walk into the Navy Department whistling 'Old Nassau,' the doors just fly open." Three Princeton alumni (left to right): Under Secretary Bard '06, Secretary Forrestal '15, and Assistant Secretary Hensel '23

Navy, General Counsel of the Department of Defense, and Assistant Secretary of Defense for National Security.

During that pre-election summer of 1944, when the war was in full course, Roosevelt refused to budge in favor of either of them, despite Forrestal's insistence on the need of a fourth Secretary. After his safe re-election for a fourth term, the President was apparently ready to approve Hensel, but tied that in with his desire to bring two "Deserving Democrats," John L. Sullivan and Edwin W. Pauley, into the Department—the post remained vacant through half the winter of 1944–45.

Although long and prominent party activity in their own states of New Hampshire and California was the prime reason for Roosevelt's endorsement of them, Sullivan had plenty of other justification from his past career. A Dartmouth graduate and a lawyer in his home town of Manchester, he had been Assistant Secretary of the Treasury since 1940. Later, he would be an able Secretary of the Navy himself. He made brilliant appearances before Congressional committees, when properly briefed, but was less ready than Forrestal to do much administrative spadework.

Pauley lacked such pertinent experience; oil had been his main business since his graduation from Berkeley. He had achieved marked success as the head of several companies, along with some activity in construction and real estate. He had been secretary and then, at Roosevelt's request, treasurer of the Democratic National Committee. His raising of more than a half million to meet the party's deficit had placed him in the ultra-deserving "pass the hat" category that later produced Louis Johnson as Forrestal's successor at the Pentagon. He had, moreover, directed the party's 1944 National Convention, aggressively backing Truman for vice-president. He became coordinator of oil supplies for Britain and Russia and now was United States representative, with Ambassadorial rank, on the Allied Reparations Commission.

The immediate Secretarial vacancy was filled in late January, 1945, when Roosevelt nominated Hensel as Assistant Secretary. This rounded out the Secretarial foursome for the first time since Knox's death. Nothing was done about Sullivan or Pauley for the moment, but they were not forgotten. Bard talked of resigning—partly for health reasons—and that left the door open for them.

It was Pauley's interest in tideland oil that was to stir up the

strong opposition to a naval appointment for him. Ever since the
Teapot Dome scandal of the 1920s, oil had been a sensitive point
with the Navy. At the beginning, Forrestal took a mild attitude
toward Pauley; he damned him with faint praise or praised him
with faint damns, as one chooses. Thus, on the day before Hensel's
nomination:

I saw President Roosevelt today on general Navy Department business and talked, among other things, about the vacancy in the Assistant
Secretaryship. He suggested the name of Edwin W. Pauley. I said
that I knew Mr. Pauley only slightly and asked Mr. Roosevelt if he
knew him well enough to say to me that he was the proper man for
the post. He did not answer directly but made the comment that Mr.
Pauley had been the most energetic and successful fund-raiser of the
party.[27]

He wrote President Roosevelt on March 10, 1945, about a month
before the President's death:

1. Ralph Bard went to the hospital Friday . . . I am enclosing a
note I thought you might want to send to him.
2. As I told you, my arrangement in general with him was that he
would stay until some time in the late spring. . . .
3. This raises the question of his successor. You mentioned Ed
Pauley at our meeting in January. I have nothing against him—in fact
what I have seen of him I like. On the other hand, I think that both
of us have more or less of a commitment to John Sullivan if he still
wants the place, which I know to be the case. Also, John has the advantage of experience with the Treasury, of I believe reasonably good
acceptance on the Hill, and of known loyalty. There is only one reservation—I should want him to sever any outstanding business connections
which he may have. If he does not want to do this and you still want
Pauley I will find a way to work that out.[28]

Another letter he wrote to the President ten days later amplified
his lack of enthusiasm:

I believe your memo of the 12th re Edwin Pauley crossed mine on
the same subject.
It is entirely agreeable to me to have him come in as an Assistant
but I would like to suggest that we make his appointment to the
secretariat contingent on whether he likes us and we like him and,
second, I would like him to start as an Assistant Secretary. I know
you will agree with me that it is easier if we can follow seniority of
service in bringing in new people.
Would you be willing to consider letting War and Navy have one

or two additional Assistant Secretaries with a time limit, say of a year or a year and a half on their incumbency. . . .

I would like good men available for these jobs and it is increasingly difficult if not almost impossible to get the right combination of energy and judgment to come to Washington now.[29]

Perhaps Robert E. Hannegan, chairman of the Democratic National Committee, best summed up the situation when briefing President Truman a few months later.

Shortly after the election on November 7, President Roosevelt talked with me about appointing Struve Hensel as Assistant Secretary of the Navy. His appointment was agreed upon on condition that Secretary Forrestal would appoint Mr. John L. Sullivan or Edwin W. Pauley as a special assistant, and that after a rather brief time Mr. Ralph Bard, Under Secretary of the Navy, would be leaving the service and that Mr. Sullivan or Mr. Pauley might move forward to Mr. Bard's place.

Mr. Pauley is now unavailable for this appointment and I should like to suggest that the prior agreement with Secretary Forrestal to appoint John Sullivan be put into effect at once, and I should suggest that this be taken up with Secretary Forrestal at the earliest convenience.[30]

With Pauley not available at this juncture, that departmental headache was put off for another eight months and the way cleared for Sullivan.

By the end of June 1945, Bard resigned; he was later president of the Navy League and a member of a United Nations committee. Gates was promoted to Under Secretary. The full quota of Secretaries was retained when, on July 1, Sullivan replaced Gates as Assistant Secretary for Air. He was sworn in under conditions unique in naval annals—aboard a carrier not far off the coast of Japan. Both appointments met Forrestal's policies: Gates was a promotion-from-within the Department, and Sullivan had pertinent executive experience.

Another angle in the temporarily quiescent picture was the recurrent rumor of Forrestal's own imminent resignation, which began circulating almost as soon as the shooting stopped. Asked in September how long he was remaining in office, he was quoted as replying "You can say as long as the President wishes me to stay, up to a limit of six months." [31] Shortly after, a newspaper commented: "Navy scuttlebutt is confidentially naming Secretary James

Forrestal as the next Ambassador to Great Britain." [32] But Forrestal felt that Ambassadorships were generally pay-offs to get rid of Cabinet officers no longer wanted, and that anyway there was not much usefulness in such posts with the instantaneous communications of the day. It was also his view that no man should take one unless he were close to the President and the Secretary of State—and he was not. [33] Early in 1946, he told the press, "The President knows that I want to get out this year. I am no believer in the indispensability of any man." [34]

His diary at this time indicated that he would turn his back on other governmental opportunities:

> Justice Douglas dined with me this evening and proposed that I have a definite stand on either the New York State governor or Senate nomination next autumn. He said he felt confident I could get either. I told him that I had concluded to get out of public life and stay out when I had quit as Secretary of the Navy. He strongly urged that I reconsider, which I said I would but that I felt that my conclusion would be the same. [35]

The extent to which the top party leaders would have backed him is not clear but there were occasional letters among his papers from lesser figures, to whom his answer was invariably noncommittal. [36]

Those hints of Forrestal's retirement added to the political implications when two vacancies loomed among his deputies. Gates resigned in December, and Hensel, the following March. The latter had ably filled the Assistant Secretaryship for only a year, but he decided he could not afford to stay away longer from his private law practice. The Pauley boom began rolling again. It appeared likely that Pauley would get Gates's post, but only as a brief stop on his way to the Secretaryship itself. Forrestal apparently shared this view with his phrase "top change" in a letter to Truman in January:

> Program for Navy:
> 1. Submit Ed Pauley's name on reconvening of Senate.
> 2. W. John Kenney to succeed Struve Hensel when latter leaves.
> 3. Inform John Sullivan of his advancement to Under Secretary when the top change is made effective. I think this is most important. I think we should face the fact that we may run into real difficulty in the Senate on Ed. So far as the Naval Affairs Committee is concerned I think that will be all right—I have talked with Dave Walsh and he

said he believed they would follow without question the recommendation of the President backed up by the Secretary of the Navy.[37]

That prediction was unduly optimistic. Pauley was openly opposed the day after Truman sent his nomination as Under Secretary to the Senate. One Senator charged that this was a case of Truman's paying off his political debts; there happened to be three other nominations up at the time that were likewise suspect.[38] The fireworks blazed from the Cabinet itself two weeks later when the hearing on Pauley started in the Senate Naval Affairs Committee under Walsh. Harold L. Ickes, Interior Secretary and Petroleum Administrator for War, launched a violent attack against Pauley for attempting to obtain large funds from California oilmen for the party war chest in return for a pledge that the government would withhold projected action on the disputed tideland oil reserves. He further charged that Pauley had even tried to approach him in the matter on the train returning from President Roosevelt's funeral.[39] Ickes resigned from the Cabinet in disgust on February 13.

Forrestal was dragged in by Truman's statement that the initiative in proposing Pauley had come from Forrestal. Flatly contradicting the President, Forrestal explained that he had merely acquiesced with Truman's idea, while discussing the matter with him at the Potsdam Conference in August 1945.[40] A few days later, in direct testimony before the Senate Committee, Forrestal conceded that Pauley had done a good job in reparations and that he was willing to give him the "benefit of the doubt" on his oil record.[41] In continuing his testimony, Forrestal declared himself to be "jealous in the highest degree of the good name and integrity" of the Navy and of the fact that during the war, ninety billion had been spent with the single aim of spending it economically, honestly, and efficiently. He said that he had told Pauley, when the appointment first came up, that he expected him to surrender any directorships and to avoid all business activities while with the Department, "not only because of ethical considerations but also because I did not want the energy and thought of anyone in the Navy Secretariat distracted by outside interests." He concluded with:

I can assure you that while I regard my own personal fortunes in terms of reputation as quite secondary to the considerations I have named above, I do not propose lightly to expose myself or the splendid associates who have helped me in this tremendous task to the risk of blotting the copy book at the end of the record.[42]

Ickes had taken a similar stand: "This is the rawest proposition that has been made me. I don't intend to smear my record at this stage of the game." [43]

For some weeks the President and Pauley stuck by their guns. Then, conferences with Senators Walsh and Tydings eventually brought Pauley to the decision to request the withdrawal of his nomination, which Truman did on March 13.[44] Pauley continued in his work in reparations until 1947.

For a short while, Colgate Darden, governor of Virginia and former member of House Naval Affairs Committee, was seriously mentioned for Under Secretary. He had powerful backing from Chairman Vinson of that committee.[45] Nothing was to come of it. In the meantime, the latest word on Forrestal's pending resignation indicated that he had consented to stay until after the Bikini atom bomb tests, scheduled for the summer.[46] He seemed still to be turning thumbs down on other government posts, but just what his plans were cannot be determined exactly; in June he sold his Beekman Place home in New York to Irving Berlin, the composer. One close associate felt that he was "so proud that he'll never let anyone know his real ambitions, so that no one will know that he failed to get something he really wanted." [47]

The Pauley situation was the most acute case of political pressure to which Forrestal was subjected while in the Navy Department. At lower levels, however, he received a good many requests to review rejected applications for commissions and to intervene in disciplinary cases.[48] Many came from party sources through Postmaster General James A. Farley, at the time, national Democratic chairman; but he apparently accepted without further pressure the usual Forrestal reply, "I cannot interfere." Such was not the case with some persistent politicians, of whom Ickes was one. Forrestal would feel the aftereffects of some wartime refusals in the Pentagon.

In sharp contrast, at the same time as the Pauley commotion, the Senate quickly confirmed as Assistant Secretary, W. John Kenney —Hensel's successor as General Counsel, who now followed him in this higher post, too. This choice, like that of Hensel, might be called departmental-promotion-from-within at its best. Kenney was, moreover, a Californian, which was most fortunate coming close on the heels of Pauley's rejection. A graduate of Stanford and Harvard Law School, he was a division chief in the Securities Exchange Commission before coming to Washington in 1941 as a Forrestal importation for Hensel's legal setup. As the story goes, he was arguing a Securities Exchange case before the Supreme Court, when Justice Douglas told of Forrestal's quest for good lawyers. Kenney saw Forrestal and was signed up on the spot. Asking "Aren't you going to check up on me?" he was told, "No, Bill Douglas's word is ample." [49] After two years as Assistant Secretary, he moved up to Under Secretary, where he remained until 1949—the last of the wartime "first string." Credited with unusual administrative ability, his eight years of service did much to provide continuity in the Secretary's office.

In June, the Under Secretaryship, vacant for six months since Bard resigned, was at last filled by the advancement of Sullivan from the Assistant Secretaryship for Air. The latter in its turn was now to go unfilled for five months, although in August Forrestal recommended Edwin Mark Andrews—a Texas oil operator who was ultimately to be Assistant Secretary. This was another effort to promote within the Department, for Andrews had been active in the organization of the procurement setup. Forrestal pointed out that he would make the Secretaryships geographically well distributed; but Truman did not approve him.[50]

Up to this point, Truman had at least notified Forrestal of his intentions before acting upon appointments, but in November he filled the Assistant Secretaryship for Air in an amazingly informal manner. Not only was Forrestal unaware that the appointment was made, but the nominee, John Nicholas Brown, was given the impression by the casual White House handling of it, that he was slated for the regular Assistant Secretaryship itself instead of the Assistant Secretaryship for Air!

Brown had not sought the appointment in any way, nor could it be called political on his part. He had not been politically active and had not made "any significant contribution since 1931." [51] The appointment seems to have stemmed from Rhode Island's Senators. Scion of that state's outstanding family, he had served as an apprentice seaman in the Naval Reserve in World War I, and was a Harvard graduate. Subsequently, he participated in several of his family's far-flung economic interests. During World War II, he served abroad and was General Eisenhower's cultural adviser on the recovery and restoration of art treasures taken by the Germans.

Forrestal's first intimation that the White House had selected his new Air Assistant Secretary was Brown's arrival at his office one afternoon. When, in the course of the call, Forrestal suggested that Nash, his special assistant, take Brown next door to meet Assistant Secretary Kenney, Brown was surprised, too. He suddenly realized that the historic post of Theodore and Franklin D. Roosevelt was already occupied, and he was being offered a quite different post.[52] Forrestal, thoroughly angered at Truman's highhandedness, rushed off to play two sets of the most vicious tennis his opponent had ever encountered from him.[53] Although lacking in aviation background, Brown also had cognizance over much else in the fields of personnel and research, with which he was familiar. His enthusiastic devotion to his new duties quickly won him Forrestal's respect.

Brown's was the last of the Secretarial appointments in the independent Navy Department, but Forrestal, before moving to the Pentagon, developed a new civilian executive post within the Department. Since the first, he had been disturbed by the lack of continuity in the occupants of its top positions. Neither naval officers under the strict rotation policy nor top civilians as a rule remained in one job more than four years; and beneath them were no administrative personnel of the junior executive type. During turnovers in the higher echelons, there was, in fact, no one capable of carrying on the business. In the Navy's early days, some naval commissioners and bureau chiefs ran totals of twenty years or so in continuous service, not to mention the more than forty years of Charles W. Goldsborough, an outstanding civilian official. Now, except for the chief clerks, who were not likely to be of executive caliber, the Navy had no counterparts of the Permanent Secretary of the Admiralty and similar British officials, who might remain in office for fifteen or twenty years, becoming thoroughly acquainted with the running of the ministry.

Forrestal, determined to do something about such a position, gathered information on the British system, including a report on "The Career Service in Departmental Administration, Domestic and Foreign Experience." That was one of the particular objects of research, when a group went over to London with Assistant Secretary Hensel to study the workings of the Admiralty.[54] More than once, Forrestal sounded forth on this subject; at the Herald-Tribune Forum in New York in 1943, he said in part:

Many of us in government for the first time during the war have come to have a good deal of respect for the work of our British colleagues—mind you, I said "respect" and not "inferiority." They come to joint conferences thoroughly informed and briefed in the most complex situations. Their basic information is sound and they speak for an established policy which has stood the test of time. These advantages, I believe, grow out of the fact that they have available to them the long experience of able civil servants. . . .

Failure to secure continuity of service, which the British have in their government departments, is a waste. During the three and a half years of our preparation for war and our fighting in one, our own government has used the talents of men from many fields. . . . the Navy, where opportunities for the abilities of civil servants were limited, was forced to recruit from industry managerial capacity which industry could ill afford to give up when it was, itself, called upon to multiply a hundred-fold. The burden of administration fell upon commissioned officers, themselves in demand afloat in their professional capacities, or upon civilians or civilians-in-uniform hastily recruited from business, the professions, and industry. The war's end will mean the return of these men to their normal pursuits. . . .

Actions which these men have taken, the solutions that they have worked out for complicated problems, and the wisdom which they accumulated during this period should not be allowed to rust, if only for the reason that it is essential from the standpoint of national preparedness that it be kept alive and useable.

It is my experience that in the Navy Department some kind of permanent civil servant, whether you call him a permanent under secretary or not, would be of great value . . . in affording continuity of knowledge which would be readily available to succeeding Secretaries of the Navy.

This permanent under secretary would have charge of the Department's fiscal estimates, keeping its accounts, recruiting and keeping alert its civil personnel, revising its organization to meet new needs and—most important of all—storing up in his skull each day's lessons on how to make the vast mechanism of government responsive to the Navy's requirements.[55]

He developed this favorite theme further in 1946, when he presided at a session of Princeton University's bicentennial celebration, devoted to "The Universities and Public Service." [56]

Returning from that conference, Forrestal took immediate steps to establish something of the sort. The functions of the proposed office were fairly obvious, but not its status and title. It was pointed

out by some that if such a title as "Assistant Secretary for Administration" were used, the post would be another object for the political spoils system.[57] The incumbent, therefore, was called "Administrative Assistant to the Secretary of the Navy," a status that did
not carry with it the honors and dignities that helped make the
Secretarial posts attractive. On the other hand, the duties, semi-
Secretarial, included taking over a share, along with the four Secretaries, in the allocation of specific administrative responsibilities
wherein continuity was most important.

The first appointee in the post—established in February 1947—
Wilfred J. McNeil turned out to be one of Forrestal's most important personal discoveries. He had a variegated background: bank
cashier, bank president, automobile dealer, and newspaper agency
manager in Iowa before coming East as assistant circulation manager
of the Washington *Post*. During the war a Supply Corps reserve
officer, he eventually became Disbursing Officer for the Washington area. His uncanny knack of thinking straight in the intricacies
of financial matters caught the attention of the organization experts,
and in 1945 Forrestal made him the Department's first Fiscal
Director.

His career in the long run was a shining example of the value
of continuity of service as well as pertinent experience and ability;
but as "Administrative Assistant to the Secretary," he was far from
that "permanent" element for which the post was created. Within
seven months, McNeil went to the Pentagon with Forrestal as one
of his three assistants. Two years later, he had moved up to Assistant Secretary of Defense and Comptroller. Years afterward, an
article in a leading weekly, "Mystery Man of the Pentagon,"
queried: "Is this the official who makes U.S. military policy? Critics
say so. This much seems sure: he's one of the most powerful, most
capable, most criticized and least known men in the Defense Department." [58] A few weeks earlier, the military expert of the New
York *Times* summed up an analysis of the fiscal problems of the
armed services: "The gospel of dollar efficiency still has a long way
to go in the Pentagon, but the word is spreading. And the men who
deserve major credit for the results so far achieved and those still
to come are Ferdinand Eberstadt, Wilfred J. McNeil, Assistant
Secretary of Defense and Comptroller, and the late Secretary of
Defense, James Forrestal." [59]

The second "Administrative Assistant," John H. Dillon, had an extremely unconventional background, coupled with long experience in the Department. Prevented by family reverses in 1929 from entering engineering school, he enlisted in the Marines and remained in the Corps most of the years since, but he had little of the usual enlisted Marine's pattern of service. Detailed almost at once as orderly to an admiral, he soon caught the eye of an Assistant Secretary, who needed an orderly. He remained in the Department in an unequaled position for "watching the wheels go around." Keen, observing, discreet, firm, and with good judgment, he had the intimate confidence of the succession of men whom he served. Knox had him commissioned a reserve major and made him his Marine aide and confidential secretary. He was then a Special Assistant in Public Relations and later Assistant Administrative Officer of the Department, until he succeeded McNeil. In that new office, he was to give, through the years, the intelligent administrative continuity that the Department had lacked, and to confirm Forrestal's judgment that the Navy needed such a post.

Not only in the top places but all the way down the line, Forrestal brought into the Department many first-rate men. He had been building this noteworthy reservoir of experience from the first; it was, of course, an essential foundation of his personnel policies. Of these scores of able men, some came in temporarily to perform specific *ad hoc* tasks. Of the remainder, on a more permanent basis, some came through Forrestal's direct efforts and some were brought in by others; a part of them remained civilians, the rest became reserve officers.

A loose-leaf notebook bound in black leather, entitled "Business Executives" but popularly known as the "Good Men Book," was an important piece of equipment in Forrestal's office. Each sheet contained comprehensive data on men whom he felt might at some future time be useful to the Department. This included not only the details of business or professional achievement but also the source of that information and sometimes suggestions as to the best channels of approach. Data on those already in the Department were there also. He lost no opportunities to add to his collection in his social or business contacts; sometimes a friend would send in a whole list of names. Occasionally, an officer's name appeared.

A note from Gates, for example, contained the comment on a commander: "He enjoys one of the finest reputations of any officer in the Supply Corps . . . if you want to get something done, see Boundy." [60]

Of the *ad hoc* specialists, Eberstadt stands unquestionably at the top—it is doubtful if anyone but Forrestal could have persuaded him to come to Washington.[61] To mention but a very few of the others, who contributed so much to the success of the Forrestal regime, C. Douglas Dillon, former Forrestal partner and future Ambassador to France, Deputy Secretary of State, and Secretary of the Treasury, made a survey of production statistics early in the war; John M. Stevenson, president of Penn Mutual, headed the comprehensive naval manpower survey; Paul Grady put the cost accounting system on its feet; and Arthur A. Ballantine's studies had a valuable influence on the court-martial and penal systems.

Of those in the less temporary group, there was a difference, more obvious than fundamental, as to whether they were serving in a reserve officer or civilian capacity. Age was the main determining factor, since it was in the Navy's interest to place well-qualified men, liable under Selective Service, in uniform to keep them in the Department. Except for the able-bodied under thirty, the Navy was relatively generous with reserve commissions through the grade of lieutenant commander for duties as specialized as cost accounting, management and production engineering, or records administration. But it was adamant against higher initial reserve rank. Eventually some of those reserve officer-specialists—sometimes dubbed "civilians in ship's clothing"—rose to captain, and a few to rear admiral. Forrestal had to push the promotion of some of the latter against the stubborn resistance of Admiral King and others; on the whole, however, most of those older men remained civilians. It was doubtless the natural reaction to the Army's lavish bestowing of high rank on inexperienced men that led the Navy to adhere to this policy since Civil War days. There is Lincoln's much quoted regret over the drowning of some mules, because they cost fifty dollars apiece, whereas he could create "a brigadier general with the scratch of a pen."

A British liaison officer, studying the whole American Naval Establishment, enthusiastically commended the use of these reserve specialists, calling it the most important opportunity that the Royal

Navy had missed.[62] Their uniforms, of course, had certain disadvantages, with the liability to disciplinary action, though that was almost never realized. Now and then, a young officer with relatively low rank but an important administrative post would arouse an admiral to declare that "no so-and-so j.g. is going to tell me how to run my office!"

The civilian assistants had problems of "status" also. But with no insignia to indicate how "close to God" they might be, it was anyone's guess whether they were on a first-name basis with the Secretaries or were being left to wither on the vine. Many regular officers acquired an uncanny psychic accuracy in gauging such relative prestige. That group, as civilians, of course, were in a position to exercise freedom of speech and action in contrast to the circumspect attitude which some regular officers felt the better part of wisdom for their chances of an admiral's flag. Despite that civilian independence, Forrestal knew how to bring out the loyalty and cooperation of those who worked with him.[63]

Of the many outstanding men, who gave, as Forrestal expressed it, "substantial periods of service," some like Hensel, Kenney, Thomas, and McNeil went on to higher things. Among them was Lewis L. Strauss, onetime senior partner of the financial house of Kuhn, Loeb & Company, who came into the Bureau of Ordnance as a reserve lieutenant commander, and was soon drawn into the Forrestal orbit through his suggestions for consolidating the material inspection services. Thereafter, Forrestal turned to him for many varied and difficult tasks, including service on the board studying the ticklish problem of the status of reserve officers. His own promotion to reserve rear admiral was among those most strenuously opposed by the "old school tie" group. Succeeding Bard on the Interdepartmental Committee on Atomic Energy, he suggested the Bikini tests. Later he became head of the Atomic Energy Commission and then Secretary of Commerce.[64]

The continuation in government service of such men was in line with Forrestal's hope that "these links with civilian life be maintained in so far as possible." He instructed his naval aide during the war to keep a list "for future reference" of the civilians who were coming and going in the Department. He added that failure to keep in touch "between the last war and this one was a mistake which I hope will not be repeated." [65]

The Department continued to profit from Forrestal's appointment policies for some time after he left Navy to become the first Secretary of Defense in the fall of 1947. In fact, in all but three of the next 13 years, the top post was held by men promoted from within the Navy or Defense Departments. The Navy Secretaryship in those years no longer rated Cabinet membership nor did it function in the realm of high policy, but it was still an important administrative post, wherein the effectiveness of its civilian control depended, to a considerable degree, on the quality of the men appointed. As the record of the past had shown: "Experience does not indicate, nor study disclose, any organizational substitute for alert and competent men in positions of authority and responsibility." [66]

Forrestal's immediate successor was Under Secretary Sullivan, whose post went to Assistant Secretary Kenney. Andrews came in as Assistant Secretary, while Brown remained as Assistant Secretary for Air. But by mid-1949, all four had resigned—one after another. It looked then as though Forrestal's build-up of civilian control was going to lose momentum completely with Truman's selection for Secretary of an Omaha lawyer, quite unversed in the ways of Washington and the Navy. Civilian direction almost disappeared under his uninspired group of Secretarial mediocrities. Within two years, however, he was made Ambassador at Dublin; and the next Secretary, Dan Kimball, had already served as Assistant Secretary for Air before being jumped to Under Secretary. The advent of the Eisenhower administration in 1953 brought the revival of civilian leadership to a high point. The first appointee, Robert B. Anderson, to be sure, like Forrestal in 1940, lacked Washington experience; but he, too, was very able. Likewise, in his case, promotion from within came afterward. At the end of a year, he moved up to Deputy Secretary of Defense. Later, he became Secretary of the Treasury.

Two of the most striking examples of the Forrestal concept followed in the Secretaryship. Charles S. Thomas, one of Forrestal's original nominees for promotion to Assistant Secretary, when serving in the procurement setup, became Under Secretary of the Navy briefly in 1953. That summer, however, he was shifted to the Department of Defense as Assistant Secretary for Supplies and Logistics; then, returned to the Navy Department as Secretary the following year. After an excellent three-year record, he suddenly announced his resignation, "purposely so as to give recognition" to his deputies and "give them a chance to advance." [67] By this time, there was a whole group of Assistant Secretaries in the Navy Department and other services to continue the Forrestal legacy of a reservoir of experienced talent. Before the war, a Secretary and one Assistant Secretary in each service was customary. When Forrestal was appointed Under Secretary in mid-1940, there were only four others at that executive level in the armed services. By 1960, between Defense, Army, Navy, and Air Force, there were four full Secretaries, one deputy Secretary, three Under Secretaries, and seventeen Assistant Secretaries, and some ten other civilians around that executive level—a grand total of thirty-five in contrast to the four of twenty years before. When Thomas resigned, his successor was Thomas S. Gates, who had been Under Secretary for three years, and as one Senator remarked had "proved an enormous competence." [68] One of the Assistant Secretaries moved up to the "No. 2" post, while Gates ultimately reached the highest pinnacle as Secretary of Defense, after serving as Defense Under Secretary.

10

". . . Unto the Civilians"

IN ONE sense the problems that confronted Forrestal as Secretary were ones which confront every Cabinet officer—relations with the President, with Congress, and with other executive departments. Even organizational struggles within a department frequently give any Secretary acute headaches. But the Navy was a unique institution and its professional naval officer caste posed problems in the area of departmental organization much more critical than in an ordinary civilian department. Forrestal faced all those problems, moreover, in time of war and in a period of crisis in his Department's development.

One of Forrestal's most durable contributions to the Navy was his ability to blend various rival elements into a fairly well-integrated whole. He never lost sight of the importance of the personal element in organization; as he told a Senate committee: "Good will can make any organization work. Conversely, the best organization chart in the world is unsound if the men who have to make it work do not believe in it." [1] After World War I, a bitter and public discussion had arisen between Secretary Daniels and Admiral Sims over the exercise of civilian authority during the war. All the explosive makings of an equally acrimonious public encounter were present toward the close of World War II, but Forrestal forestalled it by bringing the rival contenders together to work out an adjustment even before the war was over.

The reorganization that resulted was successful, as someone rather impiously put it, in "rendering unto the civilians the things that were civilian, and unto the brass the things that were brass."

("Brass," incidentally, has been formally banned by the Navy as "an improper term.") Forrestal would never have agreed that the solution was that simple, nor that the dispute turned solely on the issue of "civilian control." Few terms, as he was well aware, have been more abused than "military" and "civilian," which are apt to mean different things to different people. Part of the confusion comes, of course, from the difficulty in defining such terms. At this time, they were, as usual, being bandied about so indiscriminately that they lost much of their real meaning. When Donald Nelson was quarreling with Forrestal, Patterson, and Eberstadt, he called them "the military," but the Navy regulars dubbed them "interfering civilians." Unless one goes behind the façade to find out who makes decisions and how they are made, the words "civilian" and "military" have little valid meaning. Also, the emotional connotations of such terms have added heat, if not light, to many a bitter debate.

Although Forrestal was able to rise above the temptation to view all differences of opinion as "civil-military" struggles, he appreciated thoroughly that on some matters, there was bound to be a professional naval point of view and a civilian non-military position. He felt that his task was to create an organization, in which both views could be freely developed and upon which a decision could be made, blending the best of both positions. Forrestal did not believe that civilian supremacy should be maintained by reducing the power of the military. Rather, he sought to make civilian influence greater, especially in areas where civilians had skills which the military lacked. He had staffed his procurement organization and legal offices with civilians and reserve officers. Now he faced a larger problem of a similar kind—the creation of a departmental organization to bridge the gap between the professional military group in Cominch and CNO, under King, to the offices with strong civilian overtones, concerned with management, procurement, science, education, and foreign affairs. His goal organizationally was to establish a balance between these various groups in which a well-informed Secretary could supply the deciding weight. This is what every Cabinet officer at the head of an executive department, or for that matter any effective administrator in a large organization, must attempt to do. Forrestal's task was made more difficult, however, because the professional experts were more caste conscious, and few past Secretaries had succeeded in becoming decisive factors in the management of the Navy Department.

Forrestal's attitude was indicative of the role he thought a civilian Secretary ought to take. He did not carry a chip on his shoulder for the admirals to knock off, nor did he indulge in what journalists call "pushing the brass around." At the same time, he was fully conscious of the great power that was his, and, on occasion, he left no one in doubt of it. He resisted encroachments by the professional naval high command upon what he regarded as the prerogatives of his post, but made it clear that he respected their opinions as military experts; as a consequence, he held the loyalty of the regular officers to an unusual degree. An admiral, who had been very close to Forrestal during the war, wrote:

Forrestal had great loyalty and respect from the Navy top brass because he picked good men for the important jobs. . . . He then listened and comprehended what they told him and was in turn loyal to them in helping them with other government agencies, and on Capitol Hill. He was, however, meticulous in not posing as an expert on naval operations; all he required was results. They also admired his intellect and his insistence on precise facts. Both Forrestal and the naval commanders knew that the less that was left to chance, the more probable the success of the endeavor. It was for the above reasons that the Navy instinctively looked to him as their leader and as a great Secretary of the Navy.[2]

He was referring particularly to those closest to Forrestal in the Department, but there was warm regard for him out in the fighting forces as well. One of the top officers of the Pacific Fleet wrote: "One look at James Forrestal would convince anyone that the naval end of our war would be carried through on schedule and that men on the fighting fronts would be supported with every power at his command."[3]

There were others, to be sure, who took exception to his Secretarial authority, whatever else they might have thought about him. Four admirals were standing outside the door of his office a few days after he became full Secretary. Suddenly, one of them drove his clenched fist into his left hand, and in a voice that carried up and down the long corridor of the Department's "second deck," declared "Gentlemen, it's high time that someone showed these civilians that they can't run the Army and the Navy." The other three nodded solemnly.[4] Any one of them probably gave lip service to the idea of ultimate civilian authority but his conception of it would doubtless have resembled that of the Briton toward his monarch, whom he expects to reign but not to rule. Naval officers as a whole were ready to give a Secretary the proper ceremonial sideboys, ruffles, and nineteen guns when he visited a warship. Yet they would probably have felt that Victor Metcalf, one of President Theodore Roosevelt's short-termed Secretaries, had no justifiable cause of complaining because, as he said, his duties consisted "of waiting for the Chief of the Bureau of Navigation to come in with a paper, put it down before me with his finger on a dotted line, and say to me 'Sign your name here.' It is all any Secretary of the Navy ever does." [5] As late as 1953, an article on the Navy opened with the words "To the Navy's top brass, the ideal Secretary of the Navy is a civilian who soaks up briefings, cuts an impressive figure before Congressional committees, signs his name legibly, and relies for all his decisions on the Navy's top brass." [6]

Five years after Metcalf's lament, a very different attitude was expressed. The outgoing Secretary, George von L. Meyer, on March 4, 1913, tapping the huge Secretarial desk in the old State-War-Navy building, told his successor, Josephus Daniels, "Keep the power to direct the Navy *here*." [7] That advice had its effect. The Navy is still undecided whether Daniels was an asset or liability; but no one could call him a rubber stamp.

Secretaries have discovered, sometimes to their sorrow, that the public generally holds them responsible for what happens in the Navy. This same Daniels was barely in office, when he was blamed for issuing orders changing port and starboard to left and right; he had merely approved the order already drafted when he took over, on a recommendation of the General Board. Actually, it was signed by "that lover of naval traditions, of white water and stiff breeze," his Assistant Secretary, Franklin D. Roosevelt. [8]

Civilian leaders in military departments have often been charged with being simply the spokesmen for the military and sometimes, "more military than the military themselves." Stimson seemed to give some support to this view in saying, "The pearl of highest price for a democracy at war is well-placed confidence in its military leadership. It thus becomes the duty of the Secretary of War to support, protect, and defend his generals." [9] It has been pointed out that an executive's functions include keeping his organization strong by giving "opportunity and scope" for the "zeal and abilities of his personnel," and at the same time establishing "bounds for and restraint upon" them.[10]

Forrestal was fortunate during his first five years in that the country's needs and the professional naval officers' natural desire for an expanded Navy coincided. He could thus be spokesman for his Department's huge program with a clear conscience. It was another matter when he had to preside, against his better judgment, over its postwar diminution. In neither case could he have operated as successfully as he did without the confidence and respect of his professional subordinates. Fortunately, Forrestal was able to identify himself with them through common goals, yet as a good administrator he held himself sufficiently aloof to provide an objective control and to be a restraint against waste and inefficiency. This was only possible with a sound departmental organization balancing military and civilian units which gave Forrestal independent sources of information and centered decision making in his hands. This in essence was his system.

Admiral Mahan, in 1903, set forth some principles of civilian control so far as they concerned the Navy Department.

We find . . . two fundamental yet opposite elements, neither of which can be eliminated. Nor can they be reconciled, in the sense of being sympathetic. In its proper manifestations the jealousy between the civil and military spirits is a healthy symptom. They can be made to work together harmoniously and efficiently; to complement, not to antagonize each other; provided means are taken to insure to each its due relative precedence and weight in the determination of practical questions.

He went on to say, "The Secretary of the Navy has no associates, but he has subordinates. In them he has capable advisers, so far as he chooses to use them." Officers assigned to coordinate bureau operations should be "advisers only." The Secretary alone should have the power of decision, but principal officers should still have direct access to him and should be allowed to express their views.[11]

Quite different was the Army's system. Secretary of War Elihu Root, who was chiefly responsible for the creation of the General Staff in 1902, said:

We are providing for civilian control over the military arm, but for civilian control to be exercised through a single military expert of high rank . . . who is bound to use all his professional skill and knowledge in giving effect to the purposes and general directions of his civilian superior or make way for another expert to do so.[12]

Instead of being simply an adviser to the Secretary, this Army Chief of Staff was the operating head of the Army, who had the duty of carrying out policies determined by the Secretary and the President. In its day, "Chief of Staff" was regarded as emphasizing civilian authority and much to be preferred to "Commanding General," the former title, which seemed to imply supreme authority.

During the war, Stimson insisted that Marshall's authority as Chief of Staff "must unconditionally be recognized by every other officer in the Army"; [13] he himself retained direct control only over Public Relations. He did not establish independent agencies to report to him directly but, as he put it, "I did intend to do what Theodore Roosevelt did, which was to feel perfectly free to dip down into the lower echelons, so to speak, and interest myself keenly and directly with what was going on in exceptional cases." [14] He explained that his "dipping down" was of the kind that would suggest itself to a senior officer on inspection. Otherwise, he left Marshall free to run the Army.[15] Such was the gist of the rival Root "single chief-of-staff" system.

Under Secretary of War Patterson ultimately became a staunch convert to that system. As he told Forrestal in one of their frequent discussions, he "did not see much use for civilians in the organization except on essentially civilian matters such as public relations." In recording that, Forrestal added, "it is astonishing to see the extent to which his mind has been perverted by Army thinking." [16]

Despite his high regard for the opinions of his close friends, Lovett and McCloy, as well as Patterson, Forrestal thought they did not have the right machinery for sufficient civilian authority. In his view, since it did not provide enough information to control day-to-day operations, they were isolated from the normal flow of work and were in touch only in whatever special situations they might happen to be investigating. He based this conclusion on the fact that the Secretary's information came regularly from the Chief of Staff only, who furnished such reports as he felt necessary. No matter how much "dipping down," the Secretary or his deputies might do, their normal channel of information still was the Chief of Staff. Stoutly denying this, the War Secretaries in their turn insisted it was Forrestal who did not know what was going on in his Department.[17]

As a matter of fact, both sides could cite instances in which the Secretary was unfamiliar with some plan or current operation of his service. This might well have been true no matter what system was used in the enormous and complex wartime military establishment. The example cited by McCloy that Forrestal was ignorant of the plans of the Joint Chiefs was not the system's fault. Roosevelt and King excluded Forrestal, whereas Marshall conscientiously briefed Stimson.[18]

Civilian management specialists would be more inclined to the Forrestal thesis. According to the wartime Assistant Director of the Budget Bureau, Paul Appleby, it was not enough to provide a civilian Secretary to sit on top of a military pyramid. He could only serve an ornamental purpose with no real control without a civilian secretarial staff and internal structural balance in his department. The key to the whole situation was "the matter of secretarial management of a department." [19] And that, of course, was what Forrestal worked to attain. According to Appleby, no civilian Secretary could manage a military department solely through professional officers; experts are needed in areas of civilian management skills, either civilians or reservists. Internal balance—a sort of "divide and rule" principle—involved having subordinates assigned different functions to avoid anyone acquiring a concentration of power comparable to that of a Chief of Staff. Only with a good civilian staff combined with a balanced structure would a Secretary have a broad perspective of his organization, a knowledge of available alternatives, and thus the ability to make sound decisions.

Appleby further warned that the military "tended to make their own staffs cover the field of the secretarial staffs, thus doing violence to the reality of the staff idea." [20] Naval Operations, for example, was always ready to provide a professional staff. Some Secretaries, lacking appropriations for large enough staffs, used the military, but this, in effect, made them captives.

King's reorganization proposals, which both Knox and Forrestal resisted,[21] would in effect have given the Navy a powerful general staff similar to the Army's. In its place, Forrestal developed his own personal staff and a balanced administrative structure, hoping thereby to ensure that problems would reach his desk for decision and that an adequate staff would furnish him the essential background facts. He fully realized that,

Power over the Navy guaranteed by the Constitution and the law, lies in the Secretary's desk, but knowledge of the Navy cannot be guaranteed by the Constitution and the law. Without knowledge of the organization over which he presides, it has been feared that the authority of the Secretary would, as a practical matter, be transferred to the agency . . . where knowledge would reside.[22]

It was a major gain that all the offices, which Forrestal grouped around him, performed coordinating functions above the bureau level. From the standpoint of civilian authority, they gave him information about the Navy never before available to a Secretary. Reaching down through the bureau level, they provided another channel of information that checked to some degree at least the information given him by CNO and the bureau chiefs, and so were a means by which he could be sure his orders were followed. Contacts, for example, were not cleared by his Procurement Legal Division until its bureau representative certified the Secrtary's directives had been carried out.[23] Problems could be and often were taken to him, when the bureau and the legal or fiscal chiefs disagreed; and as an arbitrator, he seems to have been very successful.

The plans to divide King's functions by transferring control of logistics to Horne were left in the air by Knox's death.[24] Forrestal decided otherwise. Although he had vigorously opposed King's designs since the attack on his Office of Procurement and Material two years before, he had been relatively quiet while Knox "carried the ball." His decision was doubtless influenced by his innate aversion to allowing friction to build up when it might do more harm than the objective warranted. Also, the Navy's activity was at a feverish pitch with the great attacks on Normandy and the Marianas just ahead; and tampering with King's dual role might seriously jeopardize vital cooperation. That was probably the decisive factor in Forrestal's abandonment of the proposed change.

He instructed Horne to terminate the planning, previously directed.[25] When the latter asked what had happened, Forrestal is said to have replied that as King was being unusually cooperative,

he did not want to "spoil the honeymoon." Not only did King retain his dual status for the duration, but the functions remained
combined in the postwar organization.

Instead of a frontal attack, Forrestal tried a new approach. The
next eighteen months witnessed remarkable efforts to blend the
civilian and military spheres of influence more satisfactorily. Since
a major area of dispute concerned the management of logistics in
its broader sense, that included distribution of material as well as
procurement, he turned again to the business world for help—
even before Knox died. In fact, Knox's last act was to sign a letter
asking the presidents of General Motors and United States Steel
to undertake a management study, concentrated upon general
principles rather than detailed suggestions, of the whole logistics
structure. T. P. Archer, vice-president of General Motors, and
G. W. Wolf, president of United States Steel Export headed the
team of experts.[26] Horne later stated that, as far as logistical methods
proper went, the Archer-Wolf recommendations all "came out of
our people and the things they were doing." [27] The report's value,
as Forrestal was quick to see, lay rather in

. . . three major suggestions. First was the need for what they call
a "top board" or "board of directors" for the Navy Department.
Second was the lack of any continuous organizational and procedural
planning. And third was the need for a fiscal control agency in the
sense of a corporation comptroller's department.[28]

Within a few weeks, he had them all in effect with far-reaching
results.

The most enduring, the creation of a Fiscal Director, which
gradually developed into the post of Comptroller—a prominent
element of civilian authority in the Navy Department and later in
the Department of Defense. Forrestal had asked the Archer-Wolf
group to look into something of this sort; it had been on his mind
ever since his embarrassing experience on the Hill from lack of
adequate fiscal coordination.[29] He lost no time in appointing
Wilfred J. McNeil, whose work as disbursing officer for the Washington area in Supplies and Accounts had already attracted his
attention. In the new system, accounting records were simplified so
that the Navy would know its fiscal position at the close of any
period, a knowledge not previously accessible.[30]

The other two proposals were of more immediate concern in

civilian-military developments. While a logistics organization was not suggested, logistic problems were analyzed. The report indicated, moreover, that both Knox, in his plan to split CNO and Cominch, and King, in his desire to keep them united, had grounds for their positions. To solve what seem insolvable, the report recommended that an "Organization Policy Group" or "Top Policy Group," composed of the top military officers and the civilian executives, be established as a sort of board of directors with authority to approve all policy matters relating to organization. This replaced a Secretary's Advisory Council, set up thirty years before by Secretary Daniels for policy discussions. Consisting of the Secretaries, the Chief of Naval Operations, and the bureau chiefs and their equivalents, it still held weekly meetings, but they had lapsed into routine occasions.

In less than six weeks, November 13, 1944, the new group met.[31] Its real value was that it not only brought together the divergent viewpoints of the military and the civilian top policy makers but it also had the definite goal of discussing basic organizational problems. The group thus served as a possible vent for the explosive emotions that had been developing between the Secretarial "second deck" and the Fleet "third deck" of the Navy Department building. Forrestal presided and King, who had boycotted the Secretarial Advisory Council during the Knox regime, attended regularly. Others included were Bard, Gates, and Hensel; Admirals Edwards, Horne, Snyder (Naval Inspector General), and Jacobs (Chief of Naval Personnel); also Captain George L. Russell, King's planning expert; and Commander Richard M. Paget, the "management engineer," who was made recording secretary.[32]

At that first meeting of the Top Policy Group, Forrestal announced that the "Organization Planning and Procedure Unit," which was to be the working body to implement their proposals, had been established in accordance with the third major Archer-Wolf recommendation.[33] In order to make this unit acceptable to King and his associates, Admiral Snyder was made its head, with Paget, who was close to Forrestal, as his assistant. Snyder was thoroughly "regular" and also a very understanding officer. He did much in reconciling the military and civilian views; so, too, did Edwards and Horne in bridging that gap. "We have Admiral Snyder the blocking back and Paget does the work" was the way

Forrestal explained it.[34] Russell, the future Judge Advocate General, and like these others a member of both bodies, was called back from sea command to resume his work as King's organization expert. His knowledge was invaluable in those aspects of reorganization which were primarily military in character. Now and then, Forrestal himself took an active part in the discussions; and there was always his constant pressure for results. Actually, Paget and his staff in the Office of Management Engineering did most of the work. This at first dealt simply with immediate problems, but then went on to postwar reorganization.

"Management Engineering" was a new term in the Navy's vocabulary, that had slipped in around mid-1940 with the coming of Knox to the Secretaryship. He suspected that the Department fell far short of modern standards of business efficiency. He called in Edwin G. Booz of the Chicago firm of Booz, Fry, Allen, and Hamilton, a leader in the new field of business diagnosticians, to have his firm examine departmental workings from the same standpoint as it would a business concern. Knox later told a Congressional committee: "I do not think I ever spent $200,000 of the Government's money more effectively than I did there." [35] The Booz firm made a series of surveys of the various bureaus and offices: and several of its efficient young Chicagoans, including Paget, a junior partner, stayed on to continue the Booz type of analysis and were to perform valuable services during the war years.

Paget, only twenty-eight, was made Management Engineer early in 1942 and commissioned as a reserve officer, eventually rising to captain. He gathered a staff of reserve officers "carefully selected for outstanding work in the field of management, most of whom were commissioned directly from civilian life." [36] The major original job was personnel control, which involved examining existing and proposed positions to determine whether they were really needed, but management officers also served a highly useful role as the "eyes and ears" of the Secretaries since their tasks carried them into offices all around the Department. Bard told a committee on the Hill that that Office was his "right arm in investigating. It is what I use to find out, to check on all things in the Navy Department that seem out of order or off kilter, or concerning which there are criticisms." [37] Such an intelligence service proved a useful adjunct to civilian authority. This enthusiasm of Bard, Paget's immediate chief, soon spread to Forrestal, Hensel, and others of the civilian group, and then to some top admirals. Paget was asked to "sit in" on an increasing number of important conferences, and often helped prepare material for the agenda. It was not surprising that he became the guiding spirit of the Organization Planning and Procedures Unit.

In that first investigation by the Snyder-Paget task force of the Office of Procurement and Material, at King's suggestion, and of the Office of Chief of Naval Operations, included at Forrestal's insistence,[38] it was found impractical to survey in detail the latter labyrinthine office. Efforts were concentrated on determining whether the functions of those two offices duplicated each other and whether any necessary logistic functions were not performed by either of them. The initial report in January 1945 found "no evidence of outright duplication," but it urged: "Since OP&M had been a constant object of attack by CNO and to some extent by the bureaus it is important that adequate steps be taken, not only to assure understanding . . . but also to enlist positive support." [39]

A major result of these studies and the discussions of the role of OP&M was that King, for the first time, recognized there was a liaison function that had to be performed by OP&M between the Navy and the outside industrial mobilization. With little direct connection with procurement, he had been much less impressed than Forrestal with the need of close day-to-day relations with the civilian agencies. While still holding to his earlier reorganization plans, he gave way somewhat in this area. A second important result was that the sudden end of hostilities found the Navy with a head start on postwar organization plans at all levels.

Early in April 1945, Paget suggested a public announcement of their efforts, but Forrestal objected because everybody would "talk reorganization again and then we travel around the barn with all kinds of scuttlebutt and rumors; it gets to the White House; you spend a lot of time explaining what you haven't done." [40] But Roosevelt died; and Forrestal and King had to go to the White House nine days later to seek the new President's opinion on several policy matters, of which reorganization was the first. He approved continuing it "on a staff basis." [41]

In August, four days after the Japanese surrender, Forrestal appointed the so-called "Gates Board" to study the whole "organization of the Navy Department and related matters." Gates, now Under Secretary, was chairman. The other principal members— Hensel, Snyder, Horne, Edwards, and Robinson—as members of the Organization Policy Group had the advantage of months of study of the problem. As a result, decisions came thick and fast. On September 23, General Order No. 223 made drastic changes in the Shore Establishment. The time-honored term "navy yard" was dropped from the naval vocabulary and renamed the over-all "naval base." Its subordinate parts became the specialized "naval shipyard" and other units, which for the first time were commanded by "Engineering Duty Only" or staff corps specialists. Four days later, the Snyder-Paget group presented "Recommendations Concerning the Top-Management Organization of the United States Navy" to the Gates Board as a basis for its discussions. Two days after that, Truman approved an Executive Order establishing a new Chief and Deputy Chiefs of Naval Operations arrangement. On November 7, the Gates Board issued its "Recommendations Concerning the Executive Administration of the Naval Establishment," which followed closer the earlier Snyder-Paget report. On January 12, 1946, the proposals were embodied in General Order No. 230.

This reorganization settlement represented a series of compromises between the extreme positions of King and the civilian executives in the stormy episodes of 1942 and 1943.[42] In the perennial question of the control of material policy, the clear thinking and forthright argumentative tactics of Hensel were particularly useful. The flexible phrase "logistics" was split into two parts, with terms borrowed from the business world. "Consumer logistics," involving the determination and distribution of requirements, was recognized as a proper military function and was lodged in Naval Operations. The more hotly debated area of procurement, or "Producer logistics," remained in civilian hands. Its immediate policy-making controls, under the Assistant Secretary, were continued in the Office of Procurement and Material, which by General Order No. 221 on August 20 was renamed the Material Division. Ultimately, it would receive statutory recognition as the Office of Naval Material.[43] Its head would normally be a former bureau chief with the rank of vice admiral. Thus did the procurement agency improvised by Forrestal after Pearl Harbor, to fill a vacuum in the Department, become a permanent part of its organization.

At the same time, King salvaged a portion of his objectives. Provision was made for five Deputy Chiefs of Naval Operations (DCNO), which on the surface looked like an approach to the Army's General Staff system. Their functions and even their numbers resembled the Army's. The Navy's Op-01 Personnel, Op-03 Operations, and Op-04 Logistics—all rejected in 1943—were identical with the Army's G-1, G-2, and G-4. The Army with its separate Air Force did not have a counterpart of Op-05, which the Navy had had since 1943, nor of Op-02 Administration (the Army's G-2 was Intelligence). The Op-02 billet was the novelty; according to King it was to be a "dust bin," a catchall for miscellaneous units that did not fit elsewhere.[44] Ultimately it included even Naval History. These posts, however, had had their teeth drawn, for they were assigned no special powers. In particular, the DCNOs did not receive the direct control over the bureaus that King had earlier proposed.[45] They did relieve the Chief of Naval Operations of a mass of minor details, that had, for example, immersed Stark as CNO to the exclusion of vital matters.[46]

Another new angle was that all the Deputy Chiefs were in line for the highest top posts—and it was a rare DCNO who forgot that fact for a moment. Heretofore, only three of the bureau chiefs—Ordnance, Aeronautics, and Naval Personnel—had been of the eligible seagoing line. Until the appointment of Admiral Arleigh Burke in 1955, all the post-Nimitz Chiefs of Naval Operations were former Deputy Chiefs: Denfeld and Fechteler had held the Personnel post; Sherman, Operations; and Carney, Logistics. Radford, in the still higher post of Chairman of the Joint Chiefs of Staff, had been Deputy Chief for Air. Virtually all the four-star Fleet commands, likewise, went to former Deputy or Vice Chiefs of Naval Operations. The Executive Order of September 29 creating the Deputy Chiefs also provided for a number of Assistant Chiefs of Naval Operations. Altogether, this new arrangement gave a considerable number of promising officers a chance to watch how things worked at high levels; and it also created some desirable new shore billets at a time when opportunities afloat were going to be scarce. In this diluted postwar status, these new posts could not be regarded as a serious threat to civilian authority.

The settlement of the top military policies, however, involved King and Forrestal in one of their liveliest disputes. The full powers of King's combined roles of Commander-in-Chief and Chief of Naval Operations were retained to his satisfaction, though now under the single traditional title of Chief of Naval Operations, who would have the powers of over-all Commander-in-Chief without the name. Though he was about to retire, the relation of the post to the Secretary meant much to him—and that was a different story.

Forrestal was determined to have that changed, for ever since the Executive Order of March 1942, the Secretary had been side-tracked by the phrase that the Commander-in-Chief was "directly responsible, under the general direction of the Secretary of the Navy, to the President." [47] King had used this vague phrasing to bypass Knox and then Forrestal in matters relating to the Fleet command and had dealt directly with the President. Forrestal "won his point" to have this relationship redefined, as the King biography affirms, but only "after several weeks of argument . . ." [48] The new Executive Order redefined this relationship to read: "responsible to the President *and to* the Secretary of the Navy." [49]

Forrestal took no chances that the fruits of his victory should slip away. When he agreed to Admiral Nimitz as King's successor, he discussed with him the new concept of the organization for the Navy Department as outlined in the Executive Order of September 29, 1945, and the desirability of having the appointments of the immediate deputies and assistants of the Chief of Naval Operations mutually agreeable to both Forrestal and Nimitz. Full agreement was reached on these points.[50]

Finally, in that General Order of January 12, 1946, that included the Gates Board recommendations, compact definitions of the over-all administrative system were listed: (a) the three major parts of the Naval Establishment—the Operating Forces, the Navy Department, and the Shore Establishment; (b) the four principal adminis-trative tasks—policy control, naval command, logistics administra-tion, and business administration; and (c) the four major adminis-trative agents—the Secretary of the Navy; his civilian executive assistants (Under and Assistant Secretaries); his Naval Command Assistant (the Chief of Naval Operations); and his Naval Technical Assistants (the bureau chiefs, Judge Advocate General, and Com-mandant of the Marine Corps). The crux of that settlement lay in the division of the four tasks among the four agents. Behind that formal verbiage lay a real achievement in dividing the powers and responsibilities among those best fitted to administer them.

Useful as that comprehensive analysis by the Gates Board was in itself, Forrestal did not stop at that high level. Special boards or groups probed into varied segments of the Navy's problems: personnel, Shore Establishment organization, relations with science, procurement procedure, and much else. As reports came in steadily during the postwar months, changes were effected in various areas, followed gradually by much permanent "legitimization" in statutory legislation by Congress.

Two fields, science and personnel, came within Forrestal's particular interests—though they seem very far apart to be in one man's sphere. As in the earlier procurement problems, the Navy had to depend to a considerable degree upon outside civilians for what it wanted in the scientific research situation. Here, too, the separate bureaus had their technical responsibilities and vested interests. Also, as in procurement when research began to look important under Secretarial stimulus, Naval Operations, which had long neglected it, sought to grasp control.

Scientific research had long been an administrative stepchild. The Bureau of Navigation, established to handle scientific matters in 1862, was quickly sidetracked to personnel cognizance. The Naval Research Laboratory, founded in 1925, had alternated between Secretarial and bureau control. Some bureaus also had their own research units.

By 1941, Secretary Knox had set up a Naval Research and Development Board primarily concerned with linking the Navy with outside scientific groups. The post of Coordinator of Research and Development was held briefly by a distinguished civilian scientist but then passed to a naval constructor, Rear Admiral Julius A. Furer. This wartime setup had little authority; Forrestal and many others did not agree with Furer's verdict that it was "highly successful." [51]

The next step, which ended that situation in May 1945, has been called "an outstanding Forrestal contribution." He established in his own office an Office of Research and Invention under dynamic leadership. Admiral Harold G. Bowen, a pioneer in the introduction of high-pressure, high temperature steam, was the brilliant and peppery former Chief of Engineering and Director of the Naval Research Laboratory. His deputy, Luis de Florez, a prolific inventor, eventually promoted to reserve rear admiral, had developed some unique devices for aviation training. Their strong belief in the encouraging rather than the authoritative directing of work, along with the more definite scope and authority of the office, brought excellent results.

"Legitimized" on a permanent basis with virtual bureau status on August 1, 1946, by Congress, it remained under the civilian Secretary with, in time, its own Assistant Secretary (Research and Development). According to the act, as passed, it was "to plan, foster, and encourage scientific research . . . to provide . . . a single office, which by contract and otherwise, shall . . . obtain, coordinate, and make available to . . . the Navy, world-wide scientific information and the necessary services for conducting specialized and imaginative research." The bill went unchanged through House Naval Affairs, with Vinson strongly criticizing the Navy for its delay in taking the step. In Senate Naval Affairs, its scope was cut down as a result of bureau opposition. Some wanted to retain control as much as possible of their own research; more strenuous protests came from Naval Operations, which wanted to bring research under military control with a special DCNO. Thanks to Assistant Secretary Kenney, who was "stagemanaging" the bill for Forrestal, civilian control was successfully retained.[52]

As events developed during the postwar years, Forrestal's role in establishing the Office of Naval Research was one of the most important of his innovations. With atomic power, long-range missile development, space exploration, and much else, the coordination and encouragement of research, and the dissemination of results throughout the service has become one of the most important branches of naval endeavor. Remaining under the over-all supervision of an "Assistant Secretary (Research and Development)" with a rear admiral as director, it has been a joint military-civilian activity. The blending of research with strategy and operations produced the Polaris submarine, made possible in particular by Admiral Hyman Rickover's achievement in atomic propulsion, Admiral William F. Raborn, Jr.'s development of the solid fuel missile, and Admiral Arleigh Burke's strategic concept of the deterrent influence of such a weapon.

Forrestal paid increasing attention to personnel matters as the war ended. Little of this met with King's approval. One episode concerning recommendations of a Selection Board for promotion from captain to rear admiral left him still resentful some years later. His memoirs, in their severest criticism of any individual, imply that Forrestal committed a sort of sacrilege in tampering with the selection system so long in force without such interference. Under the laws covering the process, the Secretary transmitted the Board's list with recommendations to the President, who had the right to strike out any names he disapproved. That power of review had become a "rubber stamp" during the previous thirty years, but Forrestal, having had some earlier contacts with wartime selection and with his own sources of information, decided that certain names were not the most deserving of promotion. This time he called in the senior member of the Board, Admiral Marc Mitscher, for whom he had a warm regard, and strongly criticized several of the choices. Thereupon King, according to his memoirs, informed Forrestal:

> . . . that the report was entirely proper . . . and that it was distinctly inappropriate for him to reproach Mitscher. . . .
> Forrestal asked King to accompany him to the White House to discuss the recommendations, and while driving there from the Navy Department, King tried once more to get Mr. Forrestal to accept them, assuring him that it would be a serious mistake to interfere with the selection board. In reply, Mr. Forrestal simply stared at him. King believed that the Secretary thought he would be supported by Mr. Truman, or that King would back down before the President. As it turned out the matter was not discussed with the President in King's presence, and the list, as changed by Mr. Forrestal, was subsequently approved by Mr. Truman without asking King's views.
> Mr. Forrestal's action in tampering with the established processes of selection seemed to King of gravest impropriety. King himself had always been careful to refrain from participation in the details of the selection process, which seemed to him eminently fair.[53]

In view of the way many senior officers were selected during the war, that pious indignation seems somewhat forced. With many of the leading naval leaders on active duty in distant waters, a sort of selection by mail was often resorted to; instead of the give-and-take of the usual round table discussions, the list of eligible officers was simply sent out to the absent admirals for them to indicate their choice. This left considerable power in the hands of those who counted the votes. An inspection of an early mail selection shows that one captain, who stood high in King's regard, was promoted to rear admiral though he had not received half the minimum number of votes received by the other successful candidates. There was another occasion, it is reported on good authority, when Forrestal asked to see the actual mail ballots upon which a list was based, only to be told that they had been destroyed. Much later, it was learned that they were still in a safe at Naval Personnel.[54]

Even if King did not personally intervene in such matters, he had a unique opportunity to predetermine who would be in line for promotion. With his very close associate, Randall Jacobs, Chief of Navy Personnel, he had probably the determining voice in the assignment of officers. Everyone knew that a captain given a new battleship or big carrier was pretty sure to get a flag shortly unless he fouled things badly, while one receiving an old battleship or the post of chief of staff of a naval district was probably nearing the end of the road.

Incidentally, the findings of Selection Boards would be reversed later in connection with the promotion from captain to rear admiral of two of the most distinguished postwar officers. Late in 1949, the selection of Arleigh Burke was temporarily withdrawn by Secretarial action; he had been very active in the Navy's "revolt" against Secretary of Defense Louis Johnson's unification policies. Widespread pressure from naval and Congressional circles quickly produced a reversal of that action, and Burke later became the first officer to serve three terms as Chief of Naval Operations. In contrast, Selection Boards passed over Hyman Rickover, "father" of the atomic submarine. He was facing compulsory retirement in mid-1953, with his pioneer Nautilus half completed, when, largely through the intervention of the Senate Armed Services Committee, a new Selection Board was directed by the Secretary to recommend for promotion one engineering officer "experienced and qualified in the field of atomic propulsive machinery for ships." Rickover was promoted and later went on to vice admiral.[55]

There were other causes of discontent with the handling of personnel affairs. Although it was known that Jacobs's actions many times followed King's views, he was the target of the criticism. The attitude toward reserve officers drew adverse comment; the "old school tie" was reflected in the low proportion of decorations bestowed upon them and in the reluctance to promote them above the rank of commander. After eventually appointing a board to study this, Forrestal was able to secure top promotions for a few of them to rear admiral, including Lewis L. Strauss, the later head of the Atomic Energy Commission. By the end of the war, Forrestal had replaced Jacobs with Admiral Louis Denfeld, who had served as Assistant Chief of Naval Personnel and was more open-minded in the areas of dispute.

The old line doctrine of versatility also came under attack.[56] As naval matters grew more intricate, it was becoming more and more difficult to maintain this. An agreement was eventually reached that nominal line officers might specialize in certain subjects such as research, law, communications, and public information among others, without jeopardizing their chances for promotion.

To meet the immediate need for more regular officers, some of the reserves and some enlisted men were given the opportunity to "go USN" as regular officers. Several hundred had done that after World War I, but had fared very poorly at the hands of Selection Boards. To protect this new group against that hazard, it was "declared to be the policy of Congress that in all matters relating to commissions in the Regular Navy there shall be no discrimination whatsoever against officers because of the source from which they entered the Regular Navy."[57] Late in 1943, *Time* remarked "In the Navy an officer fit for top command must be well weathered and a graduate of Annapolis." It pointed out that of the Army's 1,114 general officers, only 45 percent were West Pointers and of the remainder, 143, not quite 13 percent, were noncareer reservists.[58]

Forrestal while interested in broadening the base from which officers were selected also realized that the Naval Academy could not produce the number needed for the postwar Navy. He named a board headed by Rear Admiral James L. Holloway, which considered enlarging Annapolis, establishing a second academy on the West Coast, or utilizing the Naval Reserve Officers Training Corps in the colleges. The Board decided upon the last plan, with a very generous provision that the Navy would pay students' expenses for four years at one of the fifty-two approved colleges. If they completed this R.O.T.C. course satisfactorily and if after a period afloat it was mutually agreeable to themselves and to the Navy, they might become regular officers. An act of August 13, 1946 put this "Holloway Plan" into effect.[59] The Army and the Air Force were disgruntled at the Navy's forehandedness in getting these favorable terms; their R.O.T.C. students had to pay their own way. Annapolis students, envying the relative freedom from discipline and in choice of courses of the college groups, were said to have done much muttering. "They're going through the Holloway and we're going through the hard way." Although the Navy's general postwar reserve organization turned out to be more effective than those of the other two services, the Holloway plan was not an unqualified success. In particular, the number of its officers remaining in service was disappointingly small for a while.

As for that often overlooked personnel problem of courts-martial and penal conditions, Forrestal had not lost his earlier concern for the men involved; after the fighting stopped, there were more than 15,000 serving sentences. In 1945, he initiated a new study under Justice Matthew F. McGuire of the Federal District Court for the District of Columbia, who recommended a thorough revision of the Articles for the Government of the Navy. His report was turned over to a committee, chaired by Arthur Ballantine, for further study. Forrestal now brought in Arthur Keeffe of Cornell Law School to examine the record of every man under sentence and recommend whether the sentence should stand or be mitigated since the war was over. At the same time, a professional naval board was reviewing these cases also to determine whether the original sentences had been justified. Fully half were found to have been too severe; rectifying this was particularly essential where dishonorable discharge was involved. These various studies formed the basis of the Navy's position in the negotiations leading up to the adoption of the Uniform Code of Military Justice.

Forrestal authorized another survey in 1946 from the viewpoint of the prisoners themselves. Father Robert White, top ranking chaplain, Harvard Law graduate, and dean of the Law School of the Catholic University of America, interviewed a cross section of 500 men. Among his extensive findings was that about two-thirds of the 64,121 general court-martial convictions were for unauthorized absences (AWOL). Although 12 percent of the total personnel had been brought to trial, "only 1.1 percent were tried by general courts-martial, in which 97 percent were convicted." [60] Forrestal had long before become aware of the strong case for severer penalties for this too-common offense from a report of the captain of the cruiser *Salt Lake City*.[61] He blamed the light fines imposed and the frequent probation and stateside duty for those "AWOLs," when forty-eight of his crew jumped ship when it was ordered back to the war zone from San Francisco. He cited the serious harm to his crew's morale. In endorsing his report, both Nimitz and King had urged harsher penalties. Father White noted, among his other findings, that the lack of home discipline was responsible for much conflict with Navy regulations. Sex offenses amounted to less than one-third of one percent of the total, but not included were the 4,000 known homosexuals "discharged without prejudice." [62]

Little that was accomplished in this area came up to Forrestal's expectations, from the new Code of Military Justice to prisoner rehabilitation. The lack of men trained in prison administration, for instance, hampered the postwar efforts to introduce programs for training personnel and for proper rehabilitation of the men under sentence. Yet it was perhaps surprising that as much was achieved in a wartime Navy with infinitely more vital issues at stake. One may only speculate as to how much would have been accomplished in all these personnel aspects without civilian prodding.

There has been occasional grumbling in military circles about the numerous postwar Assistant Secretaries with their special functions confusing the chain of command. Less objective have been the complaints that they, and other civilians were keeping officers out of good Washington billets. These attitudes are voiced vigorously in Admiral Furer's official account of the wartime administration. Complaining that Knox and Forrestal brought in many such civilians, he says:

It is human for the ambitious, competent, and industrious civilians who were attracted to these positions as permanent careers during and after World War II to strive for the authority and the prestige they consider essential to the performance of their work. In many places naval officers had necessarily to be subordinated to civilians in order to give effect to the new policy. Thus, the policy of broadening the base of civilian participation in the administration of the Navy Department opened up areas of friction and conflict between career naval officers and civilians that had not existed before.

Against the gains that may be expected from high level civilian participation in the administration of the Navy Department, there must be expected also the delays that result from reviews, additional justification studies, re-appraisal of objectives and programs, and increased refinement in fiscal controls. These have inevitably slowed down administrative procedures by increasing paperwork and adding to red tape. . . .

It would be even more serious if, as a result of this change in policy, the talents and experience of the men in uniform were not fully utilized. . . . Shore duty at regular intervals must in any case be provided for the seagoing elements of the Navy because it is a social and psychological necessity.[63]

Within the Navy Department, however, the valuable impact of Forrestal's civilian-role setup was very definitely recognized in 1954. Secretary of the Navy Robert Anderson had designated eight distinguished senior officers and civilians as a committee to "review the organizational structure of the Department . . . to ascertain any organizational problems or difficulties which adversely influenced the efficient performance of assigned tasks and missions." After twenty full sessions and discussions with dozens of military and civilian executives, the committee in reporting said:

The committee has reviewed the historical development of this organization and has observed the application of these concepts to the current problems.

The organization essentially is that which evolved out of the experience of World War II. The Secretary of the Navy has full authority over the department. This authority is commensurate with his responsibility to the Secretary of Defense for the supervision of the Department.

The organization utilizes the specialized abilities of both civilian and military executives for the particular tasks for which they are best fitted by experience and training. It affords effective civilian control and participation in the management of its daily affairs. . . . The Committee concludes that the basic characteristics of the existing organization of the department are sound and require no change. The organization has proved its ability to respond to changing demands of great magnitude.[64]

Most civilians who have been connected with the Department —and Forrestal was no exception—have been impressed by the high caliber of the usual officer, despite the occasional exception even in high place. He put this very strongly in a talk just before becoming Defense Secretary. Taking issue with some current columnist attacks on the nation's military leaders, he said that he found that Americans in "uniform are just about the same as those out of uniform. It is simply that a pompous man is more conspicuous in a military suit . . . and an egotist has more opportunity to display his basic qualities if he has some military authority behind him." Forrestal said there was "no group more devoted to the principles upon which our society and government are founded, nor men who understand more thoroughly that power and authority come from the people." He quoted Admiral King's definition: "True discipline is intelligent obedience of each for the consequent effectiveness of all," and added that despite the talk "about the military mind" and "the tendency of officers to arrogance . . . the record of this war does not bear out any such charge." [65]

II

The Road to the Pentagon

BECAUSE KNOX lay dying that day in April 1944, it fell to Forrestal to fire the first gun of the Navy's counterattack on the plan of the Army and the Air Forces to "merge" the armed services into a single entity. He was not the first to speak at those Congressional hearings, for already the supporters of the proposal had launched a full-fledged offensive with Secretary of War Stimson, Under Secretary Patterson, General Marshall, and other leaders.

Forrestal was not enthusiastic over the idea; what Knox's reaction would have been is not definitely known. There is reason to believe that he might have gone along with the movement, regarding it as inevitable.[1] Forrestal saw certain possible advantages in the proposals, but he also realized the danger of a "monolithic" setup, placing everything under the control of a single chief of staff.[2] The Navy as a whole shared a general suspicion and antipathy toward the plan, fearing that it would be "not merged, but submerged."

The unification movement marked the climax of Forrestal's career with the Navy, but the fundamental problems in balancing civilian versus military control were to be found far back in Army-Navy relations. At the outset of the federal government in 1789, the last ship of the Revolutionary Navy had already been sold and the whole regular Army had only a few hundred men. Consequently, the two services started off in a close administrative embrace, with the Secretary of War having cognizance over any naval affairs that might arise. But in 1798, with hostilities imminent and new ships being built, the inadequacy of the Secretary of War in handling the emerging naval complexities caused the establishment of a separate Navy Department. For the next hundred years, there was almost no common denominator between the scattered army posts on the edge of the Indian country and the remote squadrons on distant seas. Only in coast defenses, where the two services met at the water's edge; in their mutual utilization of the same type of heavy guns; and in their rare wartime joint operations did they share any major problems.[3] The first Army-Navy football game was played in 1890, but it might be argued that the emotional stresses involved did little to bring the two services together.[4]

Then suddenly, in the very year of the last real Indian fight, 1898, the acquisition of the Philippines, Hawaii, and other outlying possessions gave the Army and the Navy common defense problems. Formal joint strategic planning began in 1903 with parallel directives from the respective Secretaries establishing the Joint Army and Navy Board to advise on matters involving interservice cooperation. The Board was a part-time affair, composed of the leading officers and planners, and continued until 1942 except for an amazing interlude, when President Wilson suspended it in 1916 for three years. As he explained later, he had feared that the "officers might be encouraged to turn their minds actively toward preparation for war."[5]

That same year 1898, five years before the Wright brothers' successful plane flight at Kitty Hawk, saw a request for service funds to assist the preparation of the Langley plane. This led to the creation of a "Joint Army-Navy Board to Examine the Langley Flying Machine." Its report was, surprisingly, not only open-minded toward aviation possibilities but was a harmonious interservice decision.[6] Aviation, however, was soon to become the apple of discord between the services that would gradually overshadow all the other factors affecting their relations. Since neither fliers nor aircraft fitted the traditional mold of either Army or Navy, the adjustment was a grave problem. In the internal question of how far aviation should be integrated with the conventional surface or ground forces, the Navy decided to integrate them extensively; the Army did not. Then, a potentially more troublesome problem concerned the adjustment of Naval Aviation to "Army Air" (a title that was to have several variations). This produced a thriving crop of jurisdictional disputes where the rival air forces overlapped. The rapid growth of aviation led eventually to proposals for a separate air force and for an integrated organization comprising all the armed forces.

Barely out of the experimental stage at the start of World War I in Europe, American military and naval air forces had suddenly achieved a respectable size and an aggressive consciousness by the end of the war in 1918. There had been some friction already when the head of Army Air declared that the Navy might bomb submarines but not submarine pens along the coast, as the latter were land targets. This went right to the heart of the "roles and missions" problem of which service had jurisdiction at the high water mark; a problem that would still plague Forrestal thirty years later.

Early in 1919, Brigadier General William Mitchell, returning from a successful wartime air command, launched the movement that led straight to the National Defense Act of 1947. As the principal spokesman of a promising group of Army aviators, dissatisfied with their status, he persisted in his determination to do everything possible for Army Air, which has seldom been called a "silent service." He immediately attacked both within the Army itself and against the Navy in general and naval aviation in particular. Inside the Army, neither then nor later were the aviators fully "part of the family," but the tight control of the General Staff system kept them from getting very far in their grievance against the "ground mentality" of the senior officers, particularly in the all important matter of appropriations for the growth of "air." That was why they were working for an independent air force so they could negotiate directly with Congress on budgetary questions.

The same matter of appropriations also lay behind the vicious Mitchell attacks upon the Navy. An immediate objective was the absorption of naval aviation into a single air service. He publicly blamed its rather hazy status in the Navy's organization for its occasional air accidents. He shortly extended those belittling tactics to the Navy as a whole, and to battleships in particular. If they could be discredited, a larger share of the defense budget might be available for aviation. As it was, the Navy—still favored in the popular mind as the nation's "first line of defense"—was producing in 1919 the most expensive and extensive building program in its history. By taking part in bombing tests on old battleships, Mitchell arranged that the headlines made the most of the "doom" of the dreadnought.[7] He supplemented this with speeches, writings, and Congressional testimony.

The Mitchell stimulus gave Capitol Hill a heavy grist of business throughout the early 1920s. The more one reads in the hearings, debates, and public recriminations of those years, the more they stand out as dress rehearsals for the later unification discussions of the Forrestal period. In both instances, Army Air took the initiative while the Navy stood firm in opposition. The main difference was that the Army ground forces and the War Department opposed their airmen in the 1920s but supported them in the 1940s. Also, in both periods, the projects "sounded reasonable" to the man in the street, and his views were bound to be reflected in Congress. An increasing proportion of the public were persuaded that the airmen were battling for progress against the hidebound forces of reaction.

The first victory for the Mitchell group came in the spring of 1920, when they managed to slip into the Army Appropriation Act for Fiscal 1922 a rider providing: "That hereafter the Army Air Service shall control all aerial operations from land bases." Those words became the law of the land and would serve as powerful ammunition for Army Air in its perennial efforts to restrict the Navy's use of land-based planes.[8]

Meanwhile, bills were being introduced to create a separate Department of the Air Service. Many did not get beyond the committee stage, but in 1925 the matter broke into the open to provide one of the most dramatic years in aviation policy discussion. As usual, the Secretaries of War and Navy, together with most of the generals and admirals, testified against the separate air force. General Mitchell made some of his most sensational charges against both the Army and the Navy. A court-martial convicted him of making utterances detrimental to discipline. In February 1926, he dramatically resigned from the Army and became a martyr. His agitation brought one immediate advantage to Army Air; on July 2, 1926, the Army Air Service was renamed the Army Air Corps and, more important, a definite five-year expansion program was authorized.[9]

In the meantime, the drive for a separate air force had been accompanied by the broader question of "merger" or "unification" of the armed forces. Early in 1925, when the Mitchell agitation was at its height, Representative Hill of Maryland offered a resolution authorizing the investigation of the advisability of creating a Department of Defense, with Under Secretaries of the Army, the Navy, and the Air.[10] A proposal for "the consolidation of the War and Navy Department under one head" had been made as early as 1869, but nothing had come of it.[11] The Hill resolution, on the other hand, was to be followed by a steady stream of bills, some originating from Army Air initiative and others directly from the Congressional desire for economy. Most of them died in committee.

In 1932, however, at the depth of the depression, unification came within a few votes of being approved by the House. This was an out-and-out economy measure, predicted to save $100 million. In words prophetic of Forrestal's opening comments in 1944, Secretary of the Navy Adams declared that a single department would "create a job too big for any man to handle." [12] The Secretary of War spoke likewise, as did the Chief of Naval Operations, and even the head of Army Air. The strongest words, however, came in a letter from the Army's Chief of Staff, General Douglas MacArthur:

> No other measure proposed in recent years seems to me to be fraught with such potential possibilities of disaster for the United States as this one. . . . Each must be free to perform its mission unhindered by any centralized and ponderous bureaucratic control. To those who have practical experience in the conduct of war, this principle is so basic that it seems almost impossible that serious thought should be given to any other arrangement.
>
> Pass this bill and every potential enemy of the United States will rejoice.[13]

On April 30, the House defeated the proposal by the very narrow margin of 153 to 135. After that, the movement dwindled away to occasional bills for the next twelve years. By that time, General MacArthur and most of the rest of the Army would have changed their views.

An Army officer who made an exhaustive study of the unification movement writes:

> Concretely, all that resulted from the postwar wave of agitation for reform was the Air Corps Act of 1926. However, the three years preceding its passage had been years of education for Congress, the public, and the War and Navy Departments. Probably the most important single lesson learned was that the airplane had broken many traditions and had come to stay as an element of national strength. . . .
> For a century and a quarter, the Army and Navy had each been

building a set of customs, traditions and usages which added up to a complete way of life. The result was an unconscious, *a priori* manner of behaving and thinking, as though the existing organizational system of cooperating, independent Departments was innately excellent.[14]

Two of the new developments early in World War II affecting Army-Navy relations received full Navy support. One was the integrated over-all planning of strategy through the creation of the Joint Staffs. The other was the system of wartime over-all theater commands set up by the Americans and British just after Pearl Harbor. Some of these were "joint," involving the several services of one nation, but several important ones were "combined," involving both nations. Thus the Pacific Ocean Area was commanded by an American admiral (Nimitz); the Southwest Pacific, by an American general (MacArthur); the Southeast Asia Command, by a British admiral (Mountbatten); and the Mediterranean, by an American general (Eisenhower) who was succeeded by a British general (Wilson) when Eisenhower was given command of the European Theater of Operations. During the postwar unification discussions, the Navy spokesmen kept stressing that they did not question that wartime unified command aspect. Yet some confusion remained on that point, especially in the public mind. Answers to a Gallup Poll question, late in 1945, "Do you approve or disapprove of unified command for the armed forces of this country?" were interpreted as opinions on the merits of unification.[15] Even the most die-hard naval aviator or Marine fighting unification might well have been confused by that question and have answered that, of course, he approved unified command, under the impression that wartime theater command was meant.

In a third of these wartime adjustments, soon after the creation of the Joint Chiefs early in 1942, Army Air received a considerable share of the separate status it sought in unification. It was set up as a virtually autonomous element, on a level with the Ground Forces and the Services Forces of the Army.

The coming discussions of unification, from an evolutionary standpoint, were the culmination of the movement twenty-odd years before under General "Billy" Mitchell, but there were new factors in the situation. Aviation, already expanded to a status rivaling the traditional ground forces of the Army and the surface forces of the Navy, was threatening to outstrip them. The Army's strategic bombers, acting independently, had blasted distant targets, both in Europe and in the far Pacific. The Navy's fast carrier task forces had supplanted the conventional battle line of superdreadnoughts as the prime element of naval strength.

This rapid growth was reflected in the enhanced status of the aviators in both services. The Commanding General of the Army Air Forces sat on the Joint Chiefs of Staff. No corresponding separation had taken place in naval aviation in the Department or the Fleet. The aviator was a naval officer first and a flier second, though one of the top posts in every major command now went to an aviator.

Friction naturally developed between two such rapidly expanding forces. If any single spark may be said to have touched off this fresh campaign for "merger," it was the Navy's renewed insistence upon land-based planes for reconnaissance and antisubmarine work. The British had already evolved an apparently workable solution with their integrated Coastal Command. Altogether, it was not surprising that four of the most prominent officers in the disputations and negotiations were aviators: General Joseph McNarney, General Lauris Norstad, Admiral Arthur Radford, and Admiral Forrest Sherman. Their stake was obviously far higher than that of field artillerymen or destroyer men, who were not treading on each others' toes.

A second influential factor was the new international status of the United States. Her power and responsibilities now tended to make any wrong decisions regarding weapons, organization, or employment of force of incalculable consequences to the whole free world.

Third, there were huge sums being devoted to national defense, along with the widespread urge to have the crushing wartime financial burdens eased as fast as possible. The promises of economy in unification, however illusory some of them might be, made the idea particularly attractive.

The two widely divergent schools of thought about the proper solution had strong partisans among distinguished outsiders as well as in the officers and officials of the services. On one side, Army Air sought a fairly complete "merger" or integration of all the armed forces. Significantly, the Army as a whole, which had joined the Navy opposition to the earlier measures, now supported this principle. A "monolithic" pattern of a single over-all department and a single authoritative chief of staff was proposed, with a corresponding diminution of the traditional separatism of the different forces. The unquestioned plausibility of such a project "sounded good" to the man in the street and to many in high places. The story of Pearl Harbor, revived afresh in the lengthy postwar investigation, seemed at first glance to call for such integrated control. So, too, did the accounts of apparently wasteful duplication of effort in airfields, hospitals, procurement, and much else. The proponents of unification could and did serve up those points again and again with telling effect.

The Navy, provided anything had to be done at all, preferred a looser, "federal" coordination, which would leave each service a fair degree of autonomy. Its proponents stressed the inconsistency of scrapping the very system that had just carried the United States to a smashing victory over the Germans and Japanese, both of whom had practiced a more unified control by a single service. An administrative merger, they contended, was a basically different problem from unity of theater command, where the clear-cut authority of one man in wartime operations was granted to be essential. In policy making, on the other hand, the Navy believed that the best results could be obtained from a free, vigorous interchange of views untrammeled by the rigid imposition of command authority. The chief of staff setup, it was felt, would permit one man to exercise a too powerful "Yes" or "No" while matters, upon which varying views might exist, were still in the formative stage. The Navy would also stress the fact that such a chief of staff would tend to nullify the authority of the civilian Secretary. Finally, the Navy was firmly convinced that naval matters were a specialized mystery, "too damned complicated," as one admiral put it, "for any outsider to understand."

As the debates waxed hotter, the Navy was pictured as a reactionary group, struggling to retain its relative importance of an earlier day. The tireless publicity of Army Air, following the pattern set by Mitchell, reiterated that its own bombers and fighters had now become the nation's first line of defense, while the naval forces were becoming as obsolete as the defunct cavalry. The Navy, for its part, regarded the merger tactics as a "power push" on the part of Army Air, backed by the Army, designed primarily to achieve a commanding two-to-one majority in the allocation of appropriations, with the absorption of naval aviation and the Marine Corps as important by-products. Attention was also called to the apparent anomaly that at the very moment Army Air was seeking to include the Navy in an integrated over-all control, it was also working to set up its own separate third service. There would be occasions, during the bitter interchange of views, when the public reaction was one of "a plague on both your houses." Yet many officers and officials believed that national security was at stake to such an extent that they were ready to sacrifice personal career prospects or high position to protest against what seemed a dangerous situation.

The final passage of the National Security Act on July 26, 1947, was preceded by four years of intermittent activity. Begun by the War Department in 1943, the matter came into the open in the spring of 1944 with hearings before a special committee of Congress, the occasion of Forrestal's first connection with the situation. There was intense debate again toward the end of 1945 and during the spring of 1946. Then came the negotiations to find an acceptable compromise, to which Forrestal contributed a great deal. These in turn resulted in the "unification" proposals submitted by President Truman to Congress early in 1947, and which became law that summer.

The Navy's sole advocacy of unification was in a letter from its General Board in June, 1941, which went the rounds from the Secretary of the Navy to the Secretary of War to the Joint Planning Committee. There, Brigadier General Eisenhower favored it and Rear Admiral Richmond Kelly Turner opposed it. But the real opening of the pro-merger campaign came in 1943 from the War Department, when two groups of Army planners each proposed an over-all general staff and a chief of staff. Then, a special division was set up by General Marshall to study demobilization problems and this recommended a single department with a Secretary, four Under Secretaries, and a Chief of Staff. These proposals were all studied by the Joint Chiefs, who recommended in March 1944 that a new special committee of two officers each from the Army and Navy thoroughly examine the whole question.[16]

By that time, the subject was out in the open with a full dress investigation underway on Capitol Hill. Late in March, the House set up a special "Committee on Post-War Military Policy," under the chairmanship of Representative Clifton A. Woodrum of Virginia. The "Woodrum Committee" held hearings from April 24 to May 10.

The fruits of these months of Pentagon planning were presented strongly at the outset by General McNarney—sometimes called "General Marshall's hatchet man." He showed a simple plan for merger: a single Secretary of the Armed Forces, with three Under Secretaries for Army, Navy, and Air; a common supply service; and the Joint Chiefs of Staff as a permanent organization, headed by a Chief of Staff, who would not report to the Secretary but directly to the President. Secretary Stimson, General Marshall, and other War Department spokesmen heartily supported this plan. McNarney tried to push the plan through Congress immediately, with the details left to be worked out later. This further aroused apprehension in naval circles, for those were the tactics by which he had rushed the Army's reorganization of 1942 through, giving no previous warning. "If this plan is submitted to staff divisions and other interested parties," he had told General Marshall, "the result will be numerous non-concurrencies and interminable delay." [17]

This time, after getting off to a rousing start, the McNarney tactics were slowed down by naval gunfire. Forrestal set the pattern of the Navy's opposition to being stampeded into signing a blank check for so fundamental a step while the war was still going full blast. He told the committee:

Whether you increase efficiency by throwing it all into one lump or keeping it somewhat separate, I have a question. The business of the Navy in this year is $28,000,000,000. The business of the Army is in the order of $70,000,000,000.

Then he continued with the words, grimly prophetic of his own future:

There is no human being capable, in my judgment, of sitting on top of all that and assuring that you have the fine integration and efficiency which it is presumed would result from that consolidation.[18]

Admiral King, General Vandegrift of the Marine Corps, and many others joined in those delaying tactics and left no doubt of their disapproval. Only two witnesses on the Navy side spoke for the measure: a distinguished retired four-star admiral, Harry E. Yarnell, and Josephus Daniels, former Secretary of the Navy. Assistant Secretary Artemus L. Gates enlivened the hearing with the clever observation that the Navy itself could serve as a framework for merger, "it can operate on the sea, under the sea, in the air, in amphibious operations, on land. This force by itself can police the world." [19] That naval opposition destroyed the Army's hopes for an immediate victory. The Woodrum Committee formally reported in mid-June against "any comprehensive or revolutionary changes at this critical period." [20]

Forrestal had no illusions that this was more than a temporary truce. "I have been telling King, Nimitz and Company it is my judgment that as of today the Navy has lost its cause," he wrote a friend that summer, "and that either in Congress or in a public poll, the Army's point of view would prevail." [21]

For almost a year, while the Allied forces swept forward to victory in Europe and the Pacific, the public heard little more on the subject. The four-man committee of the Joint Chiefs of Staff was still continuing its study, and at the end of 1944, they visited the theaters of active operations and interviewed the various commanders. They reported that nearly all the army officers and half the naval, including Nimitz and Halsey, favored consolidation. The committee itself divided three to one, with its chairman, Admiral Richardson—one-time commander of the United States Fleet— alone opposing merger.

By the next spring, however, Nimitz, Halsey, and most of the other naval officers had reversed their attitudes. Admiral John S. McCain, an outstanding task force commander wrote to Forrestal:

General LeMay's statement that B-29's have rendered carriers obsolescent is the first overt act in the coming battle for funds. . . .

The Army banks on controlling the individual who will head this single unit, and, historically they will be correct in that assumption. . . .

It is beginning to look to me that the war after the war will be more bitter than the actual war. Which, of course, is a shame.[22]

That statement reflected the increasing disillusionment of naval officers about unification, as a result of certain developments in the Pacific. They had been assured that the Navy would retain its own aviation and Marine Corps intact; now there was evidence of Army designs upon them. Even in the principle of unity of theater command, in which the Navy had cooperated thoroughly under Army command in Europe and the Southwest Pacific, strange exceptions were being made. For the projected attack upon Japan, command was to be split three ways. A separate strategic air force was set up, while most of the Army forces previously under Nimitz's Pacific Ocean Areas command were being transferred to MacArthur. The Army had stated, moreover, that its troops would never again serve under Marine command.[23]

In that same spring, President Roosevelt's death had a fundamental effect upon the whole situation. What his attitude toward postwar unification would have been seems to be unknown. A member of the White House staff told of discussing this in a group of those who had been closest to him, including Leahy, and none of them recalled having heard Roosevelt express a definite opinion about it.[24] His persistent opposition to a general staff for the Navy Department as a threat to civilian control, however, would imply that he would not have favored an over-all chief of staff.

His successor, however, left no doubts as to how he stood. While a candidate for vice-president in August 1944, Truman had come out flat-footedly for unification. In a magazine article entitled "Our Armed Forces *Must* be United," he drew heavily upon the Pearl Harbor findings of the Roberts Commission and upon costly duplication unearthed by his own investigating committee.[25] Before the year was out, he directly urged the Army's unification plan upon Congress. His ebullient military aide announced in an informal talk to a group of Washington suburbanites, "During the Roosevelt administration, the White House was a Navy wardroom; we're going to fix all that!" [26]

The Navy reacted immediately to the new threat. On April 18, six days after Truman became President, Forrestal and King went to the White House to discuss several important matters. As the final point, Forrestal suggested that Truman reread the report of the board on aviation policy headed by Dwight Morrow in the 1920s, "with the thought that this form might be followed in the study of the desirability of consolidating the two services." [27]

At the end of April, Forrestal began another series of conversations that would ultimately bear valuable fruit. He discussed possibilities of Army-Navy cooperation with his friend Assistant Secretary of War McCloy, the most approachable of the excellent

War Department Secretarial quartet on this subject.[28] Secretary Stimson and Under Secretary Patterson, later Secretary, would remain fairly stubborn in support of the Army program while Assistant Secretary for Air Lovett would ultimately back McCloy in attempting to reach a mutually acceptable compromise.[29] Stimson, however, felt that some of the Army-Navy troubles came from the "peculiar psychology of the Navy Department, which frequently seemed to retire from the realm of logic into the dim religious world in which Neptune was God, Mahan his prophet, and the United States Navy the only true Church." [30] Conversely one of King's staff officers characterized Stimson as living "in an ivory tower on the slopes of Olympus, as befitted an elder statesman and his voice was as the murmur of distant thunder." [31]

In May, the Navy's Organization Policy Group took up unification. Unable to be present, Forrestal gave his ideas beforehand to King, Hensel, and Gates. The latter reported:

Having gone before the Woodrum Committee last year and been a party to their postponing consideration at that time, I feel that we have got to be very positive this time in some kind of plan which is a Navy plan. I don't think we can be negative any further as far as Congress is concerned. I don't think the reaction of the public last year was too favorable to our position. I don't think we can again say "Let's postpone this, let's postpone that." [32]

By coincidence, or through Secretarial suggestion, the same idea reached Forrestal a week later from the Senate. Walsh, the Naval Affairs chairman, wrote him suggesting that instead of "merely objecting" to unification plans, the Navy Department might make a thorough study of the subject and perhaps formulate a more effective plan, possibly proposing the establishment of a Council on National Defense.[33] Forrestal agreed on the need for positive and constructive action, and suggested the inclusion of industrial mobilization in the study.[34]

This paved the way for what might be called the most important single step in the whole unification negotiations—the so-called Eberstadt Report. Not content with simply criticizing negatively the Army plan as "hasty," "superficial," and "dangerous," the Navy now came forward with its own positive, constructive suggestions. Extending the scope of unification beyond the purely military field emphasized by the Army, these recommendations would have a lasting effect in integrating the functions of the armed forces with the determination of politico-military policy and with the nation's industrial system.

Forrestal's part in this lay particularly in selecting the right man to undertake the task—Ferdinand Eberstadt, who had already done such invaluable work with the Army and Navy Munitions Board and with the War Production Board.[35] On June 19, Forrestal wrote him:

I would appreciate your making a study of and preparing a report to me with recommendations on the following matters:
1. Would unification of the War and Navy Departments under a single head improve our national security?
2. If not, what changes in the present relationships of the military services and departments has our war experience indicated as desirable to improve our national security?
3. What form of postwar organization should be established and maintained to enable the military services and other Government departments and agencies most effectively to provide for and protect our national security? [36]

Before starting, Eberstadt decided to make sure that he would be acceptable to the interested Congressional leaders. Vinson, the veteran chairman of House Naval Affairs asked him "What do you know about this subject?" "Nothing at all," replied Eberstadt. "Why did Forrestal pick you?" "That's just what I've been wondering." "You'll do," said Vinson, "you don't know all the answers beforehand." [37]

Eberstadt assembled a small staff of able assistants with pertinent background experience. The last weeks of the war were hot in Washington, but he impressed everyone with his constant tireless energy. In a loose seersucker suit, he purposefully strode around the Department at all hours, or sat pumping one person after another for reactions in his cubbyhole across the hall from Forrestal's office. The "log" of his daily reading and interviews is eloquent testimony to his "indefatigable personal energy" and that of his staff. He was in almost constant contact with Forrestal.[38] In the 250-page final report which he submitted on September 28 to Forrestal, the tremendous mass of material had been thoroughly analyzed and integrated.

Only in answer to Forrestal's first question was the report negative. The idea of a single unified department was rejected; instead, "federal" coordination was preferred to unification. Eberstadt did not believe that "under present conditions" unification would improve national security. He admitted that in theory unification ". . . looks good on paper. It sounds good in words." He believed, however, that its very plausibility challenged analysis; it seemed to be "such a simple and easy panacea for solving difficult and complicated problems." The experience neither of unification in foreign countries nor of business mergers here had realized the promised benefits, partly because they had proved unduly cumbersome. Eberstadt questioned whether one civilian Secretary, with limited tenure of office, could successfully administer such a structure. He and his staff were convinced that most of the present ills could be "remedied within the existing framework." Their preferred solution would be "a coordinate one having three departments—War, Navy, and Air—each headed by a civilian secretary and tied together by strong ligaments of coordination expressed by formal inter-organizational links." That form would foster civilian and Congressional influence and control over the military departments.[39]

The principle inherent in an over-all chief of staff was vigorously opposed. The report pointed out that while the principle of unified command was highly desirable for military operations in the field, it was positively dangerous for strategic planning, because

collective responsibility for long-range planning allows full weight to the capabilities of each of the military branches in the planning stage, while at the same time it permits the assignment of the actual conduct of operations to a single commander.[40]

In the radical broadening of the horizons of unification thinking lay its most distinctive and far-reaching influence. Those opinions on a single department and strategic planning were pretty much in accord with the prevailing Navy thought and emotion, but a new and quickly appreciated element was injected into the discussions by the tangible suggestions for new agencies beyond the field of purely military organization. The present situation, Eberstadt said,

calls for action far more drastic and far-reaching than simply unification of the military services. It calls for a complete realignment of our governmental organizations to serve our national security in the light of our new world power and position, our new international commitments and risks and the epochal new scientific discoveries.[41]

The wartime experience, the report continued, had revealed serious defects of coordination in many spheres. On the purely military side, on the other hand, the performance had been good—in the strategic planning, the operational execution, and the cooperation between the services.[42] In view of that, Eberstadt felt that the pre-occupation of the Army planners with a single department and single chief of staff did not really go to the heart of the matter.

Virtually all of the new agencies he recommended for special purposes found their way into the National Security Act of 1947, very much in the form advocated in the report. Of all these, the National Security Council proved, as one scholar has put it, "the most remarkable and enduring element in the Eberstadt Report." [43] Representing as it did the Navy's long standing—and often re-buffed—desire for closer liaison with the State Department in policy making, it was later called by Forrestal "perhaps the most important feature" of the unification bill.[44] At the same level, the recommended National Security Resources Board would be always "ready and able to implement military plans in the industrial and civilian fields." [45] Forrestal also had a hand in the Central Intelligence Agency, designed to coordinate and evaluate intelligence information.[46] It would have a longer useful career than the National Security Resources Board. Also proposed were a Central Research and Development Agency and a Military Education and Training Board.[47] For the first time, the Joint Chiefs of Staff were recommended for a permanent basis.[48]

In regard to the questions of organizational structure so strongly emphasized in the discussions, Eberstadt stressed that the real essential for successful operation lay not in a perfected structure but in "alert and competent men" in the key positions.[49]

This report had a pronounced effect upon the ultimate settlement. During the Senate Armed Services Committee's hearing, when the National Security bill was in almost its final form, Senator Salton-stall asked Eberstadt: "How nearly does this compromise plan come to your plan? From my memory it seems reasonably close, does it not?" Eberstadt replied, "Well, with the exception of the single Secretary and the War Council, I think it is practically identical." [50]

Some ten days before Eberstadt's proposals were first made public in October 1945, the Army launched another offensive that ushered in two months of extremely heated hearings before the Senate

Military Affairs Committee. The Army's plan, identified by the name of General Collins, had much in common with the original proposals eighteen months before of General McNarney, now in Europe. At best, the Eberstadt report was to the Army simply a supplement to its own, not a substitute. General Somervell, head of the Army Service Forces, at the ensuing hearings sarcastically announced "We are not up here trying to reorganize the United States Government; the Navy has a plan for that." [51] The "Collins Plan" proposed to extend the familiar War Department organization to all the armed forces, with a single over-all Secretary and Under Secretary, together with subordinate Chiefs of Staff for Army, Navy, and Air. The Chiefs of Staff could make recommendations on military policy, strategy, and budget requirements. They would have a more decisive voice than the Secretary himself for though their budget recommendations had to be "submitted through" him, he was "required to transmit them, without modification, to the President." [52]

Understandably, the Navy fought back strenuously, but it took a while to achieve the excellent stage management of the Pentagon planners. Not only did the Army again get its message in first but this time fortified it by making public the three-to-one verdict of the Joint Chiefs of Staff Committee in favor of unification. Eventually the naval counteroffensive was skillfully managed by a newly created committee including two of its outstanding aviators—Rear Admirals Arthur W. Radford and Forrest P. Sherman. The headlines followed the story day by day throughout the two months: "Forrestal Hits Doolittle Slur on Navy Role"; "King Foresees Dictator Threat in Unification"; "Leahy Assails Army-Navy Merger"; "Halsey Blasts Idea of Merging Forces"; "Vandegrift Sees End of Marines in Unification"; "Hensel Tells Senators 'Realm of Fancy' was Entered in Picturing Merger Savings." Those were, on the whole, livelier than the Army's "Patterson Backs Doolittle Opinion"; " 'Merger Vital for Defense,' Ike Says"; "Arnold Urges Single Command"; and so on.

By the time the hearings were halfway through, it was obvious that President Truman might throw his weight on the Army side. On November 21, Forrestal went to the White House with Walsh and Vinson, both of whom told Truman that they hoped he would not try to introduce a bill for unification. Vinson predicted that such a bill "would not pass either this winter or the winter after." Truman said his proposed message would not impair the Navy as an entity and that, in the meantime, the Navy was entirely free to continue the presentation of its case. Forrestal replied that he "held no brief in behalf of the Navy," that what he wanted was "the best answer for the country," and that he felt the President had "not yet had an opportunity to consider the real merits of the case and . . . hoped he would give it such consideration." [53]

At a Cabinet meeting on December 18, the day after the hearings ended, an effort was made to hold up that proposed Presidential message to Congress. Robert E. Hannegan, Postmaster General and leading Democratic tactician, said he thought Truman was making a mistake and was "inviting an unnecessary fight which he might lose." Truman answered that he felt it was his duty to send the message because it represented his convictions. Forrestal, referring to the hearings, charged that the "committee before which it was presented was a highly prejudiced body which had reached a conclusion in advance." [54]

Nevertheless, Truman the next day sent that special message to Congress, starting it with the flat statement, "I recommend that the Congress adopt legislation combining the War and Navy Departments"; he gave particular support for a single chief of staff. Following the Army blueprint, he indicated definitely subordinate roles for the separate services. He did, however, reflect some points with which Forrestal had tried to indoctrinate him. He recognized the responsibilities that went with the nation's new commanding position in world affairs and spoke favorably of some Eberstadt proposals. [55]

The fact remained, however, that the civilian Commander-in-Chief had inflicted a severe setback to the views held by Forrestal and the Navy. This left them with the embarrassing question of how far they were free to continue their opposition. For months to come, the word "muzzling" would keep cropping up in charges and denials. It seemed as if the Navy's hands were tied; moreover, the presentation of its case became a steadily heavier burden. How far an individual officer was free to express his own convictions without danger of reprisals was not a new question. The matter had arisen in dramatic fashion after World War I, not only with General "Billy" Mitchell but also when Admiral William S. Sims had sharply criticized Secretary Daniels's administrative methods. Also, it depended in some degree whether remarks were made informally, in published articles, in official speeches, or before Congressional committees. There was also the difference between backing one's own service against higher political authority and, on the other hand, departing from its views or those of superior officers.

On that matter of service "party line," Forrestal called attention to the remarkable unanimity of views, which seemed more than a coincidence, expressed by Army witnesses in the "Collins Plan" hearings. He suggested that both the Chief of Staff and the Chief of Naval Operations assure their officers that anything said in the hearings would not be made a part of their official record or held against them. "I am confident," he said, "that there are many officers in both the Army and the Navy who do not share the unanimity of opinion which has been expressed in testimony before this committee." [56]

Now, the immediate issue—the situation of officers who wanted to uphold the Navy's views, even though they ran counter to the President's—was another aspect of free speech; even though, at that December 18 Cabinet meeting, Truman had declared that he "did not intend now to cut off discussions or to muzzle anyone." That afternoon, Forrestal, in talking over the ticklish situation with Nimitz, who had just succeeded King as CNO, indicated he felt it was not appropriate, once the Presidential message reached Congress, to make public appearances in opposition. But he suggested that "we consider ourselves free to present our untrammelled point of view to the committees of Congress." The next day, when Truman rushed in his message, Forrestal promptly embodied those views in a directive to all ships and stations.[57]

Twelve days later, he relaxed that self-imposed muzzling by another directive which quoted Truman's remarks at a press conference, on December 20, to the effect that he did not intend to muzzle anyone. "I want everybody to express his honest opinion on the subject and I want to get the best results that are possible. In order to do that, I want the opinions of everybody. And nobody has been muzzled." Forrestal's directive closed with the statement that all officers and others in the naval service "shall be guided accordingly." [58]

Within four months, Truman had given up those good intentions.

Rear Admiral A. Stanton Merrill, Commandant of the Eighth Naval District, in an interview at Dallas, said: "When the next war comes, we will need the finest army and air force in the world, because with a greatly weakened navy, submerged under army control, the fighting will be on our own shores." [59] Merrill escaped the fate of "Billy" Mitchell, but an angry outburst came from Truman at his press conference on April 11, 1946:

President Truman yesterday accused the Navy of lobbying and using propaganda to block his plan for a merger of the armed forces. . . .

He said it was true that he had authorized Navy officers to express an honest opinion when called to testify. But, he added, when the President as Commander in Chief sets out a policy, it should be supported by the heads of the Army and Navy. That, he said, did not mean that individuals were muzzled.

"Do you plan to take any steps to punish the admirals if they continue their fight?" he was asked. Mr. Truman said that he would attend to that a little later.[60]

A week later, Forrestal visited the White House with Assistant Secretary Sullivan and Admiral Nimitz. Forrestal called it "a most satisfactory interview," but he added, "I share the President's wishes that discussion of unification be confined henceforth, to appearances before Congressional committees." [61]

A double standard, so far as freedom of speech went, was in effect from that time on. The Navy "gag" did not extend to the Army or to Army Air. This situation brought some angry reactions from Congress. Senator Willis Robertson of Senate Naval Affairs declared, "I feel it necessary for national harmony and the future national defense that the President either rescind his order to the Navy or extend it to every other branch of the armed services." [62]

Army Air took full advantage of the situation. Its publicity was aggressive, persuasive, and in naval eyes sometimes inaccurate. Even individual officers appeared to be able to speak with relative impunity. At a dinner in Norfolk early in 1947, for instance, when a group of businessmen were entertaining Army, Navy, and Air officers, an aviation brigadier announced in an "off-the-record" talk:

You gentlemen had better understand that the Army Air Force is tired of being a subordinate outfit. . . . It was a predominant force during the war. It is going to be a predominant force during the peace,

and . . . we do not care whether you like it or not. The Army Air
Force is going to run the show. You, the Navy, are not going to have
anything but a couple of carriers which are ineffective anyway, and
they will probably be sunk in the first battle.

Now, as for the Marines, you know what the Marines are. They are
a small, fouled-up army talking navy lingo. We are going to put those
Marines in the Regular Army and make efficient soldiers out of them.
The Navy is going to end up by only supplying the requirements of
the Army—Air and Ground Forces, too.[63]

A columnist picked up that vigorous declaration of policy, which
had not been disavowed by the senior Air Forces officer present.

The Senate Armed Services Committee expressed a desire to hear
the brigadier on the subject, but received official word from the Pentagon that the remarks "were intended to be entirely humorous." [64]

Forrestal, in the meantime, had had far more fundamental things
to concern him in the unification dispute. The first quarter of 1946
had been relatively tranquil, but on April 9, 1946, Congress resumed
action with a new bill, "S.2044," drawn up by three members of the
Senate Military Affairs Committee, Chairman Elbert D. Thomas
of Utah, Lister Hill of Alabama, and Warren Austin of Vermont.
Like the earlier Army measures, this "Thomas Plan" retained a
single department and single chief of staff but, unlike its predecessors it made certain compromises with the Navy point of view.
Not only did the preamble indicate that a "merger" was not intended but that the three separate services would each have its own
civilian Under Secretary. The senators had consulted with Eberstadt in preparing the plan, which embodied some of his proposals.[65]

The Navy continued to resist the principles of a single department and a single chief of staff in a stormy set of hearings before
Senate Military Affairs, but, on May 13, the bill was reported out
favorably by a 13-to-2 vote. That, however, did not get it onto the
floor, because the Naval Affairs Committee hearings on it—begun
three weeks after those of Military Affairs—were not completed.
Forrestal had suggested that referral to Naval Affairs to Senator
Ernest W. McFarland of Arizona.[66]

It was soon obvious that an impasse had been reached. The President might throw all the influence of his high office behind the
Pentagon plans, but the ultimate decision rested with Congress—
and Congress was not ready to force the Navy into a "shotgun
marriage." On May 15, Walsh and Vinson told Forrestal it was

doubtful Congress would approve a single department. The Senate Naval Affairs hearings lasted until mid-August, but the bill was never reported out and was eventually withdrawn.

During the months following, Forrestal took probably the most decisive role of any individual in the quest for an agreement. In never-ending discussions and cogitations, he gradually approached a position midway between the oversimplified "monolithic" stand of the Army and Air and the thoroughly negative attitude of the Navy. Week after week and month after month, as his diaries indicate, he talked with everyone conceivable—admirals, civilian executives, and generals of Army and Air, senators, representatives, and numberless others, some of whom were closely related to the problem and others, like Winston Churchill, more objectively distant.[67]

The major conflict centered on the triple recommendations of the successive Army-Air plans: an over-all Department of Defense, an over-all Secretary of Defense, and an over-all chief of staff. The Navy wanted none of the three, but Forrestal was to arrive at the compromise position that found its way into the 1947 settlement. The Eberstadt recommendations were to be gradually accepted by the Army and Air without too much difficulty. The fears of naval aviation and of the Marine Corps continued to be an active problem.

Forrestal and the Navy remained adamantly opposed to the single chief of staff, because of the latent negative and positive power therein. Admiral Robinson told Forrestal: "The very worst thing that could happen to the country would be to have the military going directly over the civilian heads of such a department to the President. There is no telling what that might lead to. In short, I am agin [sic] it." [68] The Army argued that the comprehensive authority of the chief of staff, with which it had forty years experience, was essential to effective control. Forrestal replied that until the Army chief of staff was able to control the Army Engineers and General MacArthur, he was not impressed.[69]

Gradually, Forrestal became ready to concede the idea of an over-all Secretary of Defense but not a comprehensive Department of Defense. His first major victory came on May 13, 1946, when Truman assembled the principal civilian and military leaders at the White House "to identify their points of agreement and disagreement." Admiral Leahy forcefully attacked the idea of an over-all chief of staff, saying that his experience during the war convinced him that the idea was too dangerous. Thereupon, Truman, declaring that the idea was "too much along the lines of the 'man on horseback' philosophy," said that he had finally made up his mind against it. Secretary of War Patterson said that he still felt that the single chief of staff would provide the greatest efficiency but that he was not prepared to "jump into the ditch and die for the idea." [70]

On that victory, in killing the single chief-of-staff concept, the editor of the Forrestal diaries has admirably summed up the essence of his unification tactics:

The battle was very far from over, yet this meeting represented a decisive victory for Forrestal, largely reversing the effects of the defeat he had suffered in December with the President's initial message on unification. Later, Forrestal was to be criticized on the ground that there was a certain lack of iron in his methods. Yet here his chosen tactics of patient pressure, persuasion, and, above all, a thorough grounding in the essentials of the problem and a complete understanding of all the factors in it, had paid off. . . .

If in the end Forrestal was largely the winner in the unification fight, it was because he had thought more deeply, because he had enlisted Eberstadt and others to think for him, because he had looked at the real and central problems involved rather than accepted quick solutions which under the test of time and events could not stand.[71]

At that same meeting, Truman asked Patterson and Forrestal to report by the end of the month on the still-disputed points. The next day, while lunching with Eberstadt and Nimitz, they found a fairly wide field of agreement. Though unconvinced, Patterson was not fighting further for a single chief of staff, and accepted most of the Eberstadt proposals except on the relationship of the over-all Department to the three services. He stubbornly held out "for a single Department with what he calls a straight line of command," as Forrestal recorded that meeting, "he did not see much use for civilians in this organization except on essentially civilian matters such as public relations (it was rather astonishing to see the extent to which his mind had been pervaded by Army thinking)." Forrestal countered that he

could not agree to anything which would involve the destruction of the integrity of the Navy. By that I meant its ceasing to have the status of a separate entity rather than merely a branch, its own Secretary having a seat in the Cabinet and access to the President.[72]

Patterson and Forrestal, in a joint letter to Truman on May 31 indicated only four major fields of disagreement still remaining. Each clearly set forth his views on them: the idea of a single department; the status of the three coordinate branches; the scope of naval aviation; and the future of the Marine Corps.[73]

Truman on June 15, in letters to the two Secretaries and to the chairmen of the Military and Naval Affairs Committees, once again supported the War Department point of view on all four points. In connection with the scope of aviation, he went so far as to state that "land-based planes for naval reconnaissance, antisubmarine warfare, and the protection of shipping can and should be manned by Air Force personnel." [74]

Four days later, Forrestal was at the White House and made quite clear his dissatisfaction with that latest Presidential statement. He and his Navy Department colleagues were preparing an answer; in the meantime, he openly hinted that he might resign.[75] Just before he left on his world tour on June 24, that reply went to Truman. When Forrestal reached Pearl Harbor, there was word to call the Department—it seemed that the tone of the letter was not satisfactory to the President. Without enthusiasm, Forrestal consented to a slight modification. Later, after his Pentagon disillusionment had set in, he said that perhaps it would have been better if he had not done so.

Obviously the Navy would not willingly agree to the White House views, and Congress would not pass a measure too distasteful to the Navy. The doubtful future of naval aviation and the Marine Corps was something for the professionals to work on later; for the moment, the civilian negotiators were primarily concerned with the single department and the status of the three separate services. During the summer and early autumn, they managed to bring matters to a point where the Army and Navy would at last talk final terms.

The first of three important conferences came on August 27, when Forrestal was host at dinner aboard his yacht—Patterson, Eberstadt, General Thomas T. Handy, and Assistant Secretary of the Navy Kenney were all present. The discussion centered on the suggestion that the points already agreed upon be embodied in an executive order of the President, with the disputed issues to be settled later by Congress. "Throughout the evening," wrote

Forrestal, "it was quite clear the Army had not surrendered any of its objectives." [76]

Nor was much more progress made two weeks later when the President brought Patterson, Forrestal, Eisenhower, Leahy, Nimitz, and his assistant Clark Clifford together at the White House "to consider plans for the introduction of merger legislation at the next Congress." Patterson and Forrestal still clung to their respective points of view about the Secretary of Defense. Forrestal felt that his authority should be "limited to providing a source of decisions on these fundamentals: (1) Missions and means; (2) Cognizance of weapons; (3) Composition of forces; (4) Finances; (5) Resolution of command disputes; (6) Personnel (training, education and recruiting)." Eisenhower "repeated what he had said at earlier meetings that the broad principle of a Secretary of Common Defense should be accepted with the details left to be worked out afterwards." That was exactly what the Navy had been worrying about from the beginning. "I was again constrained to say," wrote Forrestal, "that the Navy *did have* deep apprehensions as to what would happen to it under such a plan as the War Department has proposed." [77]

The next two conferences were more fruitful because the Army's civilian representatives were now of a more elastic nature than Patterson. Great progress was made on September 27 when Eberstadt and former Assistant Secretary of War McCloy met with Robert A. Lovett—who was just getting through as Assistant Secretary of War for Air—at the latter's office, in the investment house of Brown Brothers, Harriman. With their Wall Street backgrounds, all three "spoke the same language." McCloy and Lovett pretty much came around to agreement with Forrestal on the disputed status of the over-all Secretary and the three services. Eberstadt wrote McCloy:

Dear John:

I do not think there can be any misunderstanding between us, but to guard against even the most remote possibility, I take the liberty of stating below the kind of set-up that I understand us to have discussed.

1. There are to be three autonomous departments: Army, Navy, Air, each to be headed by a Secretary with its conventional staff of assistant secretaries, etc., nothing to be said as to whether the departmental secretaries should or should not be members of the Cabinet. This could be left entirely to Presidential discretion. . . . The depart-

mental secretaries shall be responsible for the administration of their respective departments.

2. There shall be organized a department of national security headed by a secretary of national security who in Presidential discretion might or might not be a member of the President's cabinet. The functions of this Department shall be to coordinate various matters of common or conflicting interest between the three military departments, and final decisions on these questions, subject to the President's presiding, in the Secretary of National Security. The Department of National Security shall, for example, have authority to integrate the budget, to coordinate and integrate logistic and procurement matters, research programs, military intelligence, education and training, personnel policies, etc., and the general power to determine conflict between the services; also to allocate respective fields of competence among the services and the use and development of weapons where they are in dispute; also generally to settle conflicts and disputes between the military departments. This Department and Secretary, however, shall have no general nor specific responsibility with respect to the administration of the three military departments nor any general control over them other than the authority specifically conferred upon them nor any right to interfere therein. If any of the Departmental Secretaries fail to carry out the orders of the Secretary of National Security, the latter's recourse is to the President, to whom the departmental secretaries shall also have the right of appeal.

Under the Department of National Security would also be the Joint Chiefs of Staff. . . .[78]

This agreement to the loose "federal" system with the three services retaining a great deal of autonomy was a victory for Forrestal and Eberstadt, whose combined persistent persuasiveness had done much to bring it about.

In Eberstadt's opinion, that afternoon at Brown Brothers, Harriman was the crucial turning point. Admiral Forrest Sherman, on the other hand, gave the credit for turning the tide to another meeting, held November 7 at Forrestal's home in Georgetown. It was natural that each should have such a point of view. The New York meeting of civilians had settled high-level civilian control; at Georgetown a meeting of the minds had been reached among the military, who were represented by aviators as the parties most directly concerned.

The latter meeting was a masterpiece of Forrestal management. It was small—only four beside himself. The only other civilian, Stuart Symington, had recently succeeded the able and cooperative

Lovett as Secretary of War for Air. The others were three of the most brilliant aviation officers available, two Deputy Chiefs of Naval Operations, Rear Admirals Arthur Radford for Air and Forrest Sherman for Operations, and the latter's "opposite number," Major General Lauris Norstad, Director of the War Department's Plans and Operations Division. Sherman, one of the ablest men the Navy has produced, combined the high intellectual capacity of King with Leahy's shrewd skill in personal negotiations. His staff work in the Pacific had been exceptional and he had become virtual factotum of Naval Operations—"Have you cleared with Forrest?" was a byword in every sort of matter. Forrestal now determined to use him to arrange the military details of unification just as he had been counting on Eberstadt for the high-level civilian aspects. Each side was thus represented by a rather immoderate extremist and a moderate. Radford had been one of the most outspoken opponents of the whole unification project; still fairly "unreconstructed," he could be counted upon to pull no punches in voicing the objections of the naval aviators. From Army Air, Forrestal might have picked General McNarney, who had fired the opening gun in the whole business; General Spaatz; or one of the other Air radicals as an offset to Radford. Instead, he chose Symington, who, despite his relatively brief connection, was showing signs of becoming an ardent disciple of the Mitchell tradition.

While Radford and Symington could be relied upon to leave no stone unturned in the matter of objections, Sherman and Norstad were the men to whom Forrestal looked for constructive results. Broad-minded enough to look beyond their service prejudices, they had the prestige as top planners to speak for their services. Though all these men were in important positions, they were still young, had relatively open minds, and the probability of many years ahead of them to implement a settlement; both Radford and Sherman were fifty years old, Symington was forty, and Norstad thirty-nine. As for Forrestal himself, one can picture him at the meeting, sitting silently smoking his pipe for perhaps a quarter or even a half hour at a time, and then, quietly breaking in to sum up in a few words the gist of an argument that might well be getting out of hand.

Sherman later called this meeting the "time when we agreed to make concessions, and make a compromise, and to get an organization in which we realized that each would have to make important concessions." [79] Before the evening was over, they had a seven-point program; the first part of which gave approval to the September 27 agreements:

First. Three separate administrative departments;

Second. A single Secretary of National Defense to coordinate the three military departments and to direct policy;

Third. A very small executive force for the single Secretary;

Fourth. The Joint Chiefs of Staff as at present;

Fifth. A joint staff, under the Joint Chiefs of Staff, of approximately the same size as at present but to be better organized for getting things done;

Sixth. A definition of the functions of the services which would provide for the continuance of the Marine Corps and the safeguarding of naval aviation including the antisubmarine warfare and naval reconnaissance components;

Seventh. Resolution of the overseas command problem by considering it on an overall or global basis.[80]

It was also decided that Sherman and Norstad would work out a plan along these lines agreeable to all the services.

For two months, they met two or three times a week, as well as daily over a private wire.[81] They found that their problem fell into three distinct categories, each requiring a separate agreement. The least controversial—unified overseas command—was settled in mid-December by a Joint Chiefs of Staff directive, after approval by the President. Another, the highly explosive matter of "roles and missions," involved the future status of naval aviation and the Marine Corps. These purely military considerations were defined, but by no means finally, in an executive order. The administrative setup, the third question, would be decided by Congress.[82]

Forrestal, in the meantime, was keeping constant track of developments, sounding out the ideas of others, implanting his own, and endeavoring to reduce the remaining field of disagreement. On Sunday, December 1, he went to work on Symington in a conversation concentrated upon land-based aviation. Forrestal told Symington that no sensible person in the Navy ever considered a naval strategic air force. But, the Navy had, he continued, "very strong fears of the Army's desire to roll up Navy Air and get control of all aviation under the Army Air Forces." Finally, Symington conceded that Army Air might possibly agree to a statutory assignment of certain land-based aviation to the Navy for antisubmarine and reconnaissance work.[83]

Four days later, Forrestal lunched with Symington, Radford, Sherman, and Norstad and was left with a feeling that they were "farther away than ever from reaching an agreement." Radford brought out clearly and sharply the fears of the naval aviators that separate departmental status for Army Air would simply be the first step in "much larger and ambitious plans of the Air Force to take over the whole business of national defense." He aroused the ire of Symington and Norstad particularly by asking what foundation there was to believe "that there was a place in the war of the future for a strategic air force." [84]

With the coming of 1947, things began to move rapidly. On January 3, Patterson, riding back with Forrestal from a Cabinet meeting, said that he was much disturbed by the growing evidence of bitterness between the services. Forrestal replied that "unless the two services were honestly and thoroughly back of a plan for integration and coordination it would not be successful. . . . The whole conversation," he recorded in his diary, "was in an entirely different key and tenor than any talk I've ever had before with Patterson." [85]

Within two weeks, success was in sight. On January 16, Sherman, Symington, and Norstad agreed on the final draft of a letter reconciling the Army and Navy views. Clark Clifford, at the White House, wanted to release the news immediately, but Forrestal insisted first on having "an opportunity to inform the principal Navy friends in the House and Senate—Senators Robertson, Byrd, Tydings, Brooks, Russell and Austin, ex-chairman Vinson of the Naval Affairs Committee, Cole, etc., in the House." He wanted to do that "not merely from the standpoint of the Navy's obligations to these men, but also by way of enlisting their sympathetic cooperation in the future." [86]

The documents were released to the newspapers that evening at six. That same day, the joint letter of Forrestal and Patterson received a reply from the President, the tone of which was quite different from his earlier one-sided pronouncements:

Gentlemen:

I am exceedingly pleased to receive your joint letter of January 16 in which you advise that you have reached full and complete agreement on a plan for unification of the armed services.

I recognize that each of the services has made concessions . . .

and I feel that it constitutes an admirable compromise between the various views that were originally held.

The agreement provides a thoroughly practical and workable plan of unification and I heartily approve of it.

You have both worked ably and effectively, with your respective staffs. . . . I appreciate your fine efforts and I congratulate you upon the accomplishment. . . .[87]

Before the week was out, Sherman and Norstad were instructed to draw up a bill. It was late February before their eighth and final draft was ready. White House representatives had sat in on some of their sessions and insisted on altering certain provisions "which would have taken powers of the President and lodged them in the National Security Council and the National Resources Board." That had been one of the chief adverse criticisms of the initial Eberstadt proposals.[88]

Truman submitted the bill to the new Eightieth Congress on February 26.[89] As it was under Republican control, a new Senate Armed Services Committee handled the bill ("S758"). The members showed a broad-minded reasonableness in the hearings between March 18 and May 9. In the House, the twin bill ("H.R.2319") did not go to House Armed Services, possibly because of Vinson's known pro-Navy influence, but went instead to the Committee on Expenditures in the Government Departments, which was far less experienced in defense matters.

This time Forrestal was the first to testify, in recognition of his active role. He limited his prepared statement "to the expression of general over-all approval of the proposed bill when taken in its entirety." [90] Representing as it does the views he had on the eve of the consummation of unification, it shows that his intensive study of the problem had brought him a considerable distance from his original negative stand before the Woodrum Committee in 1944. In his heart, he probably still wished the matter had never come up, but under the circumstances he gave the bill his earnest, if not enthusiastic, support:

I should be less than candid if I did not admit that this bill is a compromise. But it is a fair compromise and, as the President stated, a sound and workable solution. It is a compromise which would not have been possible without the unselfish and cooperative attitude with which the negotiators of both services attacked this problem. . . .

Because this bill is a compromise I should like to emphasize . . . that the bill should be considered in its entirety. Both sides made concessions. There are no doubt certain provisions which the War Department would have preferred to omit and there are probably some things which the War Department would like to have included. The same thing is true of the Navy, and I expect of the Air Force. It has been a case of give and take on both sides and the bill is the result of that attitude on the part of all participants. If any single item were withdrawn or modified to the advantage of any one service, the mutual accommodation would be thrown out of balance.

Any step of this sweeping character for the unification of the services must rest fundamentally on the belief of all concerned that it is for the good of the country and that it will work. Military services are accustomed to discipline but even military men cannot be stuffed into strait-jackets through a charter or blueprint. The good will of the working organization is necessary whether it is a business organization or a military one. . . . Conversely, the best organization chart in the world is unsound if the men who have to make it work do not believe in it. . . .

This bill provides an organization which will allow us to apply the full punitive power of the United States against any future enemy. It provides for the coordination of the three armed services, but what is even more important to me than that, it provides for the integration of foreign policy with national policy, of our civilian economy with military requirements; it provides continuing review of our raw material needs and for continued advance in the field of research and applied science.

Neither this bill nor any other can legislate a spirit of unity among the branches of our armed forces, but this bill is the result of a spirit of accommodation which is a better augury of unity than any legislative fiat. Therefore our defense potential will be increased without endangering the corps spirit of any branch of the service and without weakening the democratic concept of civilian control over the Military Establishment.

I hope this bill becomes law.[91]

On one point, Forrestal virtually repeated the scepticism he had voiced earlier—whether any one man could adequately administer a more concentrated over-all defense setup:

It is my belief that in any field of human activity, whether it is business or government, there is a definite limit to the size of an administrative unit which can be successfully directed by any one man. . . . There is a point, in other words, beyond which human beings cannot successfully direct an organization with the hope of having even casual knowledge of the operation of its component parts.[92]

In the course of questioning, by Senators Bridges, Tydings, Byrd, and Hill, Forrestal gave more of his ideas on administration, constantly emphasizing the subjective and personal aspects. He told Bridges: "I think the success of this undertaking is going to depend upon the kind of men that man all these posts, not only the Secretary of National Defense, but also the Secretary of the Army, the Secretary of the Navy and the Secretary of Air." [93] In that same vein, he told Tydings: "I do not think you can take out insurance against human nature." To Byrd, he remarked, "after all, you run things through men," and "the only point of disagreement between us, Senator, is that I do not believe you can, by law, direct the way organizations run." [94] A remark to Tydings was prophetic of what took place shortly after Forrestal became head of the new organization:

Of course, as I visualize the practical application of this new organization, it is the one in which the man who takes the job, this top job, would, I hope, have the right to select the men who work with him. Because while some of my associates in the War Department have wanted to insist upon the right to fire, I maintain that in Government the right to hire is the important thing.

If you hire men of good will, that is the important thing. I do not care what your right to fire is.

You know as well as I do, that once a man is in Government for some length of time, it takes quite a lot of blasting to get him out. [95]

Four months later, he was to indicate his reluctance to "hire" Symington as Secretary of the Air Force, and later still, despite strong provocation, he would refrain from trying to "fire" him. [96]

Forrestal's energy in discussing those questions with members of Congress had kept him in close communication with them for many weeks before he made that formal appearance (see Appendix J). The published edition of his diaries gives such an adequate picture of his active role that there is no need to repeat the story here. [97]

The bills were reported favorably out of both committees, and for the first time unification actually reached the floors of the two houses. The Senate passed its bill on July 9, and the House passed its bill ten days later, after introducing some amendments. A conference committee finally ironed out the differences by July 23. The compromise agreement went through both houses quickly, and on July 26 the "National Security Act of 1947" received the President's signature.[98]

Its principal underlying provision, the setting up of an over-all Secretary on a loose "federal" basis over the autonomous departments, was very much along the line of the Eberstadt proposal to McCloy of the previous September. The final text of this section, with italics indicating the passages inserted in the progress of the bill through Congress, ran:

Sec. 202. (a) There shall be a Secretary of Defense, who shall be appointed from civilian life by the President, by and with the advice and consent of the Senate: *Provided, That a person who has within ten years been on active duty as a commissioned officer in a Regular component of the armed services shall not be eligible for appointment as Secretary of Defense.* Under the direction of the President and subject to the provisions of this Act he shall perform the following duties:

(1) Establish general policies and programs for the National Military Establishment and for all of the departments and agencies therein;

(2) Exercise general direction, authority, and control over such departments and agencies;

(3) *Take appropriate steps to eliminate unnecessary duplication or overlapping in the fields of procurement, supply, transportation, storage, health, and research;*

(4) Supervise and coordinate the preparation of the budget estimates of the departments and agencies comprising the National Military Establishment; formulate and determine the budget estimates for submittal to the Bureau of the Budget; and supervise the budget programs of such departments and agencies under the applicable Appropriation Act; Provided, that nothing herein contained shall prevent the Secretary of the Army, the Secretary of the Navy, or the Secretary of the Air Force from presenting to the President or to the Director of the Budget, after first so informing the Secretary of Defense, any report or recommendation relating to his department which he may deem necessary; *And provided further, That the Department of the Army, the Department of the Navy, and the Department of the Air Force shall be administered as individual executive departments by their respective Secretaries and all powers and duties related to such departments not specifically conferred upon the Secretary of Defense shall be retained by each of their respective Secretaries.*

There was to be no formal Department of Defense. That would come two years later with the Tydings Act, which would strip the three military departments of their "executive" status. For the moment, the new Secretary was simply "authorized to appoint from civilian life not to exceed three special assistants to advise and assist him," in addition to "such other civilian personnel as may be necessary." It was further provided that "Officers of the armed services may be detailed to duty as assistants and personal aides to the Secretary of Defense, but he shall not establish a military staff."

Another provision, which had been pretty much a foregone conclusion and had been scarcely discussed during the long negotiations, completely divorced the Air Force from the rest of the Army, splitting the War Department into a Department of the Army and a Department of the Air Force.

The staff agencies recommended by Eberstadt came into being without major changes. Three of these—the National Security Council, the Central Intelligence Agency, and the National Security Resources Board—were to be outside the National Military Establishment proper. Five others were to be inside, under the supervision of the Secretary of Defense. Four of them had proven their worth in wartime—the Joint Chiefs of Staff, which for the first time received formal "legitimization"; the Joint Staff; the Munitions Board; and the Research and Development Board. The one new agency, not mentioned by Eberstadt, was the War Council. Altogether, these special agencies went through Congress virtually unchanged and would remain quite uncontroversial during the next two years when so many other unification provisions would come under fire.

If those were "safe" topics, the reverse was true of the question of "roles and missions," which involved the future status of naval aviation and the Marine Corps. It was originally intended in the Sherman-Norstad negotiations that this matter would simply be handled in a separate Executive Order. Such an order, in fact, was signed by President Truman the same day as the unification act.[99] Congressional friends of the Navy, however, wanted something more durable than such a document, which could be altered overnight. Consequently, passages were written into the act in connection with each of the services, with special safeguards for naval aviation and the Marine Corps carefully spelled out.

The public had expected some sort of unification, and here it was. In that form, however, it was satisfactory to very few of those immediately involved. The new system fell short of the glorified "monolithic" War Department pattern that McNarney and Collins had advocated; the Army and Air Force testimony during the recent hearings had at times hinted that this was only a beginning. They had lost out on the drive for a single over-all department and, above all, for a single over-all chief of staff, who could have put the Navy in its place. The Navy's action had been defensive, on the whole, except for the new Eberstadt agencies which Forrestal considered the most important part of the whole act. The naval aviators and the Marines still had misgivings about what might happen once the camel got its nose under the tent. From members of both those groups, around dinner tables or elsewhere "off the record," that summer, came bitter charges that Forrestal and Sherman had "sold us down the river."

President Truman had signed the National Security bill aboard his private plane at the Washington airport, before he rushed to the bedside of his dying mother, in Missouri. Earlier that day, he had had a talk with Forrestal at the White House—one of the most important talks in Forrestal's life. As he told it:

Talked with the President. The President told me he proposed to send my name up as Secretary of Defense. Bob Patterson wouldn't take it. He said he had talked to him about it, but Patterson was so hard put to it for money that he felt he was unable to stay longer in government. I told the President I would have been very happy to serve under Patterson as long as I could be useful to both of them. The President replied that Patterson could not be considered for the reason stated.

He said he would like me to have my offices in the Pentagon. He was critical of some of the people in the Navy and Air Force who, he said, had not gone along with him after the agreement of last January had been reached. . . .

I asked the President whether he intended that control of the military establishment should be in civilian hands, because I said that was the way I proposed to exercise the powers in this job. He repeated most emphatically that that was his concept and that I had his full approval in proceeding on that basis.

He asked me about the posts for Air and for the Navy. I said Mr. Sullivan was obviously the man to succeed me, and as regards Symington, I felt that he was an able man, the only reservation was whether two people who had known each other as long as he and I could work successfully together. I said one's friends were frequently more difficult as partners than strangers.

We talked for about forty-five minutes, the President then being in a position of awaiting receipt of the unification bill. . . .[100]

The offer could not have come as a complete surprise, for Patterson had resigned as Secretary of War nine days earlier. There was no boyish grin at this nomination—"he had no illusions about what he was getting into this time." [101] "This office will probably be the greatest cemetery for dead cats in history," Forrestal wrote to Robert Sherwood a month later.[102]

An officer who was closely associated with defense legislation said, some years later:

My views with respect to Forrestal's attitude concerning extreme unification proposals are still mixed. However, as a general conclusion, I feel that he was enough of a realist to see the forces which were arrayed against him and he tried, in his own way, to come out of that great conflict with as much protection as possible for those things in which he believed. In many ways his action in the struggle was comparable to a rear guard action. But, like a rear guard action, it served only to soften rather than avoid defeat. In fairness, though, I doubt if there was much more that he could have done. I still recall the dramatic moment of his testimony on the Unification Bill when committee members pressed him for *his own* views with respect to naval aviation, the Marine Corps, and the matter of protecting them by inclusion of roles and missions in the proposed legislation. His performance indicated the struggle he was making within himself to reconcile the official policy of his superiors with his own personal views.[103]

The date for Forrestal's induction as Secretary of Defense was selected with the military budgets somewhat in mind. These were traditionally submitted to the Bureau of the Budget in September; and if they were already in its hands before Forrestal took over his new office, his responsibility would be obviated for any but the Navy's. His induction was planned for the end of September after Truman's return from a trip to Brazil. But in the Adriatic the Yugoslavs were threatening to close in on Trieste and American troops were guarding that disputed port. Forrestal recorded on September 16:

Clark Clifford informed me that he had yesterday afternoon radioed the President the central facts of the situation in Trieste: . . . The President responded during the night with instructions that I should be sworn in immediately and take action to see that all available reinforcements were provided.[104]

Accordingly, on September 17, he was sworn in as the first Secretary of Defense in the same room at the Navy Department where he had become the first Under Secretary of the Navy in 1940 and the last full Secretary of the Navy in 1944. A few minutes later, for worse rather than for better, he was taking up his new duties across the Potomac at the Pentagon. But that is another story.

That ceremony might be regarded as the high-water mark of his career. He himself probably would have agreed that his major contributions were made in his seven years in the Navy Department. In Defense, the superstructure rose too slowly upon the foundations he laid for him to appreciate what he accomplished there. Torn between his desire to leave Washington and the feeling that his country was still facing very serious crises, he would stay on until the tremendous burdens that he had carried so long proved too much for him.

The Navy that he left that day in 1947 was far different from the one he found in 1940. Not only was it infinitely larger in terms of ships, planes, and men, but even more important it was much better organized to support the new responsibilities in the international scene. These were very real achievements for which the nation will long have cause to be grateful.

Appendixes

A

WARTIME GROWTH OF THE UNITED STATES NAVY

	July 1, 1940	June 30, 1945
VESSELS		
Total Tonnage, million tons	1.9	13.5
Total Number [a]	1,099	50,759
Total Combatant	383	1,171
Battleships	15	23
Carriers & Escort Carriers	6	98
Cruisers	37	72
Destroyers	225	373
Destroyer Escorts	—	365
Submarines	100	240
Other Vessels		
Patrol Craft	33	1,231
Mine Craft	35	611
Auxiliaries	134	1,693
District Craft	473	2,757
Landing Craft [a]	41	43,296
PLANES		
Total Number	1,741	40,912
Total Combat	1,194	29,125
Training	363	8,370
MILITARY PERSONNEL		
Grand Total Number	203,127	4,031,097
Navy Total	160,997	3,383,196
Marine Corps Total	28,364	476,709
Coast Guard Total	13,766	171,192
Officers, Total	16,341	367,066

A (continued)

WARTIME GROWTH OF THE UNITED STATES NAVY

	July 1, 1940	June 30, 1945
MILITARY PERSONNEL		
Navy	13,162	317,316
Marine Corps	1,819	37,067
Coast Guard	1,360	12,683
Officer Candidates, Total	2,714	65,948
Enlisted, Total	183,650	3,587,000
Navy	144,824	2,993,563
Marine Corps	26,565	435,439
Coast Guard	12,261	157,998
Women, Total (included in above)	442	100,423
CIVILIAN PERSONNEL		
Total Number	113,711	693,944
Navy Department	4,342	19,804
Field (Navy Yards, etc.)	109,369	674,140

ᵃ Landing craft figures for 1945 do not include the 17,193 rubber and plastic surf boats.

These figures, adapted from the *Annual Report of the Secretary of the Navy, Fiscal Year 1945,* Tables A-15, A-31, A-55 and A-129 should be regarded as relative, rather than absolute.

B

PRINCIPAL OFFICIALS OF NAVY DEPARTMENT, *1940–47*

Secretary of the Navy: January 1940, Charles Edison; July 1940, Frank Knox; May 1944, James Forrestal; September 1947 (non-cabinet) John L. Sullivan.

Under Secretary: August 1940, James Forrestal; June 1944, Ralph A. Bard; July 1945, Artemus L. Gates; June 1946, John L. Sullivan; September 1947, W. John Kenney.

Assistant Secretary: February 1940, Lewis Compton; February 1941, Ralph A. Bard; January 1945, H. Struve Hensel; March 1946, W. John Kenney; September 1947, Edwin M. Andrews.

Assistant Secretary for Air: September 1941, Artemus L. Gates; July 1945, John L. Sullivan; November 1946, John N. Brown.

Administrative Asst. to Secretary: February 1947, Wilfred J. McNeil; September 1947, John H. Dillon.

Director of Procurement & Material: January 1942, Samuel M. Robinson; November 1945 (Chief, Material Division) Ben Moreell; November 1946, Edward L. Cochrane; August 1947, Arthur C. Miles.

Chief of Naval Operations (CNO): August 1939, Harold R. Stark; March

1942 (also Commander-in-Chief, U.S. Fleet), Ernest J. King; December 1945, Chester W. Nimitz; December 1947, Louis E. Denfeld.

Vice Chief of Naval Operations: March 1942, Frederick J. Horne; October 1945, Richard S. Edwards; January 1946, Dewitt C. Ramsey; December 1947, Arthur W. Radford.

Sub Chief of Naval Operations: March 1942, John H. Newton; October 1943, William S. Farber.

Deputy Chiefs of Naval Operations:

Op-01, *Personnel:* October 1945, Louis E. Denfeld; February 1947, William M. Fechteler.

Op-02, *Administration:* October 1945, Bernard H. Bieri; January 1946, Richard H. Connolly; August 1946, John L. McCrea.

Op-03, *Operations:* October 1945, Charles M. Cooke, Jr.; December 1945, Forrest P. Sherman.

Op-04, *Logistics:* October 1945, William S. Farber; February 1946, Robert B. Carney.

Op-05, *Air:* August 1943, John S. McCain; August 1944, Aubrey Fitch; July 1945, Marc A. Mitscher; March 1946, Arthur W. Radford; March 1947, Donald B. Duncan.

Bureau Chiefs & Assistant or Deputy Chiefs:

Aeronautics, Chief: June 1939, John H. Towers; October 1942, John S. McCain; August 1943, DeWitt C. Ramsey; June 1945, Harold B. Sallada; May 1947, Alfred M. Pride. *Asst. or Deputy Chief:* June 1939, Marc A. Mitscher; July 1941, DeWitt C. Ramsey; May 1942, Ralph E. Davison; November 1943, Lawrence B. Richardson; August 1946, Thomas S. Combs.

Medicine & Surgery, Chief: December 1938, Ross T. McIntyre; December 1946, Clifford A. Swanson. *Asst.-Deputy Chief:* December 1936, Dallas G. Sutton; June 1940, Luther Sheldon, Jr.; November 1944, William J. C. Agnew; December 1946, Herbert L. Pugh.

Navigation-Naval Personnel, Chief: June 1939, Chester W. Nimitz; December 1941, Randall Jacobs; September 1945, Louis E. Denfeld; February 1947, Thomas L. Sprague. *Asst.-Deputy Chief:* September 1939, Randall Jacobs; December 1940, A. T. Bidwell; June 1941, John F. Shafroth; January 1942, Louis E. Denfeld; March 1945, William M. Fechtler; January 1946, Thomas L. Sprague; February 1947, John W. Roper.

Ordnance, Chief: August 1937, William R. Furlong; February 1941, William H. P. Blandy; December 1943, George F. Hussey, Jr.; September 1947, Albert G. Noble. *Asst.-Deputy Chief:* January 1940, Glenn B. Davis; July 1942, Theodore D. Ruddock; December 1943, George F. Hussey, Jr.; December 1943, Willard A. Kitts, III; April 1946, Malcolm F. Schoeffel.

Ships, Chief: June 1940, Samuel M. Robinson; February 1942, Alexander H. VanKeuren; November 1942, Edward L. Cochrane; November 1946, Earle W. Mills. *Asst.-Deputy Chief:* June 1940, Alexander H. VanKeuren; February 1942, Claude A. Jones; November 1942, Earle W. Mills; November 1946, Charles D. Wheelock.

Supplies & Accounts, Chief: April 1939, Ray Spear; June 1942, William B. Young; March 1945, William J. Carter; October 1946, Walter A. Buck. *Asst.-Deputy Chief:* June 1939, Ellsworth H. VanPatten; June 1942, William J. Carter; March 1945, Horace D. Nuber; February 1947, Edwin D. Foster.

Yards & Docks, Chief: December 1937, Ben Moreell; November 1945, John J. Manning. *Asst.-Deputy Chief:* January 1938, Lewis B. Combs; February 1946, Joseph F. Jelley.

Judge Advocate General: June 1938, Walter B. Woodson; September 1943, Thomas L. Gatch; November 1945, Oswald L. Colclough.

Commandant, Marine Corps: December 1936, Thomas Holcomb; January 1944, Alexander A. Vandegrift; November 1947, Clifton B. Cates.

Commandant, Coast Guard: June 1936, Russell R. Waesche.

Chief, Procurement Legal Division-General Counsel: July 1941, H. Struve Hensel; January 1945, W. John Kenney; January 1946, J. Henry Neale; August 1946, James T. Hill, Jr.; May 1947, Hudson B. Cox.

PRINCIPAL OFFICIALS OF WAR AND STATE DEPARTMENTS, 1940–47

WAR DEPARTMENT

Secretary: September 1936, Harry H. Woodring; June 1940, Henry L. Stimson; September 1945, Robert P. Patterson; September 1947 (Department of Army), Kenneth C. Royall.

Under Secretary: December 1940, Robert P. Patterson; November 1945, Kenneth C. Royall; September 1947, William H. Draper.

Assistant Secretary: June 1937, Louis A. Johnson; July 1940, Robert P. Patterson; April 1941, John J. McCloy; December 1945, Howard C. Petersen.

Assistant Secretary for Air: April 1941, Robert A. Lovett; February 1947, W. Stuart Symington.

STATE DEPARTMENT

Secretary: March 1933, Cordell Hull; November 1944, Edward R. Stettinius; July 1945, James F. Byrnes; June 1947, George C. Marshall.

Under Secretary: May 1937, Sumner Welles; October 1943, Edward R. Stettinius; December 1944, Joseph C. Grew; August 1945, Dean G. Acheson; July 1947, Robert A. Lovett.

C

FORRESTAL'S IMMEDIATE ASSISTANTS

Naval Aides: John E. Gingrich, John W. Roper, Edmund B. Taylor, William R. Smedberg, III, Charles A. Buchanan.

Legal Assistants: Charles F. Detmar, Jr., James D. Wise, William M. Dulles, Matthias F. Correa, John Sonnett, Frank C. Nash, John T. Connor, Marx Leva.

Public Relations Assistants: Eugene S. Duffield, John A. Kennedy, William G. Beecher, Robert Berry.

Personal Secretary: Katherine Starr Foley.

D

FORRESTAL'S SOCIAL ENGAGEMENTS, APRIL–MAY 1944

Compiled from Appointment Calendar, Personal Papers
(This period marked his transition from Under Secretary to Secretary)

April 1	6:00	Cocktail Buffet, Mme. Loudon, 2209 Wyoming
3	12:15	Bond Club Lunch, Address, Bankers Club, 120 Broadway, N.Y.C.
4	12:45	Lunch, Mr. Stevens, Charles Thomas
5	12:30	Lunch, Secretary Knox
6	12:30	Lunch, Congressman Thomas, Adm. Robinson
	7:30	Sen. & Mrs. Robertson, Newbolds
8	7:30	Dinner, *Sequoia*, Cdr. & Mrs. Thorne Donnelly, Major Lawson, Col. & Mrs. C. V. Whitney (4 regrets)
12	12:30	Lunch, Secretary Knox
	1:00	Lunch, Mr. Eberstadt
13	12:30	Lunch, Mr. Henderson
	6:15	Cocktails, Sir John & Lady Dill, 3023 Que St.
	7:15	Dinner, *Sequoia*, Greek Ambassador & Mme. Ambassador, Mr. and Mrs. Frederick Sterling, Adm. & Mrs. W. W. Smith (11 regrets)
14	12:30	Lunch, Metropolitan Club, F. Davis
	7:30	Dinner, *Sequoia*
15	1:15	Lunch, Sec. of State & Mrs. Hull, Carlton Room, Hotel Carlton
		Dinner, Grews, 2840 Woodland Road
16		Buffet Supper and movie, Navy Building. Asst. Sec. and Mrs. Bard. Adlai Stevenson and numerous admirals with wives
17	12:45	Lunch, Adms. Robinson, Horne, Farber
	7:15	Dinner, *Sequoia*, "Laurance Rockefellers, etc."
18	12:45	Lunch, Mr. Fraser
	6:00 –8:00	Cocktails (Oil Delegation) Mr. Wilkinson, 2728 36th Pl.
	7:45	Cocktails with Mr. Peters, Carlton Room, Hotel Carlton
		Dinner, *Sequoia*, Mrs. Warren Delano Robbins, Gen. Lindman
19	8:30A.M.	Breakfast, McGraw Hill editors, Statler
	12:30	Lunch, Secretary Knox

		8:00	Dinner, British Embassy, for Oil Delegation
	20	12:30	Lunch, Chester Bowles
	22	7:00	Dinner, Palmer Hoyt, Statler
	24	5:30	
		–7:30	Reception, Prime Minister & Mrs. Curtin, Australian Legation, 3120 Cleveland Ave.
	26	8:00	Dinner, Sen. & Mrs. Brewster, Sulgrave Club
	27	12:45	Lunch, Chester Bowles
	28	1:00	Lunch, Joseph Powell, 1925 F. St.
		6:30	
		–8:00	Commodore Carter, 2921 Cathedral Ave.
May	1	12:30	Lunch, Adm. King, Secys. McCloy, Bard, Gates
		(2:00	Funeral services for Secretary Knox)
	3	1:00	Lunch, Sec. Ickes
	4	7:30	Dinner, *Sequoia*, Judge Patterson, Wilson, Commodore Carter
	5	12:45	Sec. Bard
	6	6:30	"You told Capt. Miles you would go to dinner for Stu. Scott, Statler "
			"Drop in after dinner, Justice Douglas' home, for Mr. Grady"
	9		(White House, between 12:15 and 12:30, to confirm)
		7:30	Dinner, Mr. Stettinius, Shoreham
	10	12:45	Lunch, Mr. Folsom, Lindley, Kern
		6:30	Buffet Supper ("Re Single Dept. of Defense), Sec. Gates, Adm. Horne, Adm. Radford and 10 newspapermen
	11		Dinner, Mr. Bullitt
	12	12:30	Lunch, Press Club, for Capt. Lovette
		1:00	Lunch, Mr. Elliston, Adm. Radford
			Dartmouth Dinner, Mayflower, "to drop in between 8 and 9"
	15	12:45	Lunch, Col. Draper, Capt. Strauss
		7:45	Dinner, "Lippmanns and McCloys"
	18	6:30	Dinner, *Sequoia*, Ambassador and Mrs. Martins, daughter of Brazilian Ambassador, Mr. & Mrs. Jesse Jones, Mrs. Longworth, Stewart Symington, Mme. Soong, Gen. Lindemann (British Embassy), Cdr. Alan Brown (2 regrets)
	19	(9:00A.M.	Oath of Office as Secretary of the Navy)
		12:45	Lunch, Sen. LaFollette
		7:00	Dinner, Mayflower, "J. Russell Young School of Exp."
	22	12:30	AWVS Luncheon, Waldorf ("Mrs. Mills notified you will come at 1")
	23	7:30	"Dinner, Waldorf, The Churchman for Mr. Baruch"
	24	1:00	Lunch, "H. M., Jr." (Morgenthau), Treasury
		6:30	Telegraph Dinner, Statler
	25	1:00	Lunch, Mrs. Forrestal, 1642 29th St. (Cdr. Steichen)
	26	12:45	Lunch, Sen. LaFollette
		5:00	
		–6:30	Cocktails for Dr. Dodds, 1925 F St.

	7:00	Dinner, Princeton Club of Washington, Statler ("They expect you around 9.")
29	12:30	Lunch, Congressman Sheppard

Dinner, *Sequoia*, Gen. Marshall, Gen. Arnold, Gen. Somervell, Secs. Lovett, Bard, McCloy, Gates; Adms. King, Horne, Fitch; C. E. Wilson, Judge Patterson, Adm. Radford, Adm. Robinson (Sec. Stimson regrets)

E

FORRESTAL'S FORMAL SPEECHES, 1944

Compiled from Index of Speeches, Personal Papers

F

MEMBERSHIP OF PRINCIPAL INDUSTRIAL MOBILIZATION AGENCIES

War Resources Board: August 4, 1939

Edward R. Stettinius, Jr., chairman of the board of the United States Steel Corporation
Karl T. Compton, president of Massachusetts Institute of Technology
Walter S. Gifford, president of the American Telephone and Telegraph Company
Robert E. Wood, president of Sears, Roebuck Company
Harold G. Moulton, president of the Brookings Institution
John Hancock, a partner in Lehman Brothers
Colonel Harry K. Rutherford, Ordnance Department, U.S. Army (Secretary)

Army and Navy Munitions Board: February 21, 1942

Ferdinand Eberstadt (chairman)
Robert P. Patterson
James Forrestal

National Defense Advisory Commission: May 28, 1940

William S. Knudsen
Edward R. Stettinius, Jr.
Sidney Hillman
Chester C. Davis
Ralph Budd
Leon Henderson
Harriet W. Elliott   (no chairman)

Coordinator of Purchase: June 27, 1940

Donald M. Nelson (whom the NDAC agreed should sit with it and for all practical purposes be regarded as a member)

Office of Production Management: December 29, 1940

William S. Knudsen (director)
Sidney Hillman (associate director)
Frank Knox (Secretary of the Navy)
Henry L. Stimson (Secretary of War)

Office of Price Administration and Civilian Supply: April 11, 1941

Leon Henderson (administrator)

Supplies, Priorities, and Allocations Board: August 28, 1941

Henry A. Wallace (chairman)
Donald M. Nelson (executive director)
William S. Knudsen
Sidney Hillman
Frank Knox
Henry L. Stimson
Leon Henderson
Harry L. Hopkins

War Production Board: January 16, 1942

Donald M. Nelson (chairman)
Frank Knox
Henry L. Stimson
Jesse H. Jones
William S. Knudsen
Leon Henderson
Sidney Hillman
Henry A. Wallace
Harry L. Hopkins
(The chairman with the "advice and assistance of the Board" was to exercise general direction over war procurement and war production)

Office of Procurement and Material (Navy Department): January 30, 1942

Vice Admiral S. M. Robinson (chief)

Office of War Mobilization: May 27, 1943

James F. Byrnes (director)

G

PAPERS PREPARED FOR FORRESTAL BY HIS RESEARCH ASSISTANT, EDWARD F. WILLETT, OCTOBER 1945–June 1946

BATTLESHIPS, CRUISERS, AND CARRIERS
COMPLETED IN PRIVATE AND NAVY YARDS,
1886–1947

	Thousand Tons				Number of Vessels		
	Total	1886–1913	1914–1939	1939–1947	Battle-ships	Cruisers	Carriers
Private Yards							
Newport News	879	178	216	485	13	18	16
"N.Y. Ship"	717	110	195	412	9	26	12
Quincy	633	76	114	442	6	28	7
Cramp	286	211	35	40	9	14	
Other	216	147	33	36	5	32	
Total	2667	723	584	1396	42	118	35
Navy Yards							
New York	488	47	162	278	10	6	5
Philadelphia	298		19	198	3	4	3
Norfolk	125	9		116	2	1	3
Other	81		81		1	4	1
Total	994	56	273	593	16	15	12
Grand Total	3661	780	857	1989	58	133	47

PROMOTION IN NAVY DEPARTMENT TOP EXECUTIVE POSTS, 1939–1947

	Other Department Posts	Administrative Assistant	Assistant Secretary for Air	Assistant Secretary	Under Secretary	Secretary of the Navy
Charles Edison				1937–39		Jan., 1940
Lewis Compton	1937–40			Feb., 1940		
Frank Knox						July, 1940
James Forrestal						May, 1944
Ralph A. Bard				Feb., 1941	Aug., 1940	
Artemus L. Gates			Sept., 1941		June, 1944	
H. Struve Hensel	1940–44			Jan., 1945	July, 1945	
John L. Sullivan [a]	1941–46		July, 1945		June, 1946	Sept., 1947
W. John Kenney			Nov., 1946	Mar., 1946	Sept., 1947	
John N. Brown						
Wilfred J. McNeil	1941–47	Feb., 1947				
John H. Dillon	1931–47	Sept., 1947				

[a] Assistant Secretary of the Treasury.

J

FORREST AL'S CONTACTS WITH MEMBERS OF CONGRESS, JANUARY–JULY 1947

Compiled from Appointment Calendar, Personal Papers

January	8	Rep. R. J. Welch (R—Cal.)
	15	Buffet dinner (for "Freshman Senators")
	16	Rep. W. S. Cole (R—N.Y.)
	17	Sen. Chan Gurney (R—S.D.) Chairman Sen. Armed Services
	20	Sen. H. M. Kilgore (D—W. Va.)
	21	Hearing, House Appropriations, subcommittee
	22	Sen. B. B. Hickenlooper (R—Ia.) Chairman Joint Committee on Atomic Energy; with Sec. of War Patterson.
	23	Lunch, Senate Armed Services Committee
	28	Rep. D. A. Reed (R—N.Y.)
	30	7:30 P.M. Rep. & Mrs. John Taber (R—N.Y.), chairman, House Appropriations, *et al.*
	31	5:00-6:30 Sen. Styles Bridges (R—N.H.), Carlton
		7:30 Rep. W. G. Andrews (R—N.Y.) chairman, House Armed Services
		8:00 House Armed Services Committee, 1925 F St.
February	6	"Dined with the 76-77 Club, being a club of Republican members of those Congresses"
	7	Lunch, Rep. C. J. Brown (R—Ohio)
	10	6:30 Buffet Supper, Navy Dept., Naval air officers and Congressmen
	12	Lunch, Sen. H. F. Byrd (D—Va.) *et al.*
	13	Rep. A. L. Bulwinkle (D—N.C.)
	15	Rep. W. C. Ploesser (R—Mo.)
	17	Lunch, Sen. H. A. Smith (R—N.J.) *et al.*
	18	10:00 A.M. House Armed Services Committee; lunch with same
		9:00 P.M. White House, Congressional Reception
	19	Lunch, Rep. J. G. Fulton (R—Pa.), Speaker's Dining Room, Capitol
	20	Dinner, Sen. & Mrs. Hickenlooper
March	1	Testify, House Appropriations, naval subcommittee
	3	Testify, House Armed Services, subcommittee on facilities
	4	Sen. W. B. Umstead (D—N.C.) *et al.*
	5	12:15 Lunch, House Appropriations Committee
		1:30 Testify, same
	6	Lunch, Sen. H. A. Smith, Dr. Vannevar Bush
	7	House Internal and Foreign Commerce Committee, re national science foundation

8 At home of Sen. Homer Ferguson (R—Mich.), Sens. W. F. Knowland (R—Cal.), Leverett Saltonstall (R—Mass.) *et al.*

9 Sen. B. B. Hickenlooper "came to my house"

11 Senate Armed Services, re unification

12 12:45, meet President at south end of H.R. for his address to Congress
Lunch, Sen. Owen Brewster (R—Me.)

13 Senate Foreign Relations Committee, re needs of Greece and Turkey, with Sec. of War Patterson and Acheson

14 House Foreign Affairs Committee, executive session
Lunch, Leslie Biffle, Staff Director, Senate Minority Policy Committee

18 10:30 Senate Armed Services, hearings on unification open

19 At home, at Culbertsons for Sen. & Mrs. Edward Martin (R—Pa.)

20 10:30 Sen. D. I. Walsh (ex-D—Mass.)
11:30 Testify, Senate Armed Services, unification

23 Rep. E. O. McCowen (R—Ohio)

25 Sen. J. L. McClellan (D—Ark.)
7:30 Rep. W. G. Andrews, 1925 F St. Club

27 10:30 Rep. Taber
11:00 House Foreign Affairs Committee

April 2 House Appropriations Committee

9 Rep. Plumley (R—Vt.) chairman House Appropriations subcommittee

11 Breakfast, Rep. Plumley

16 Dined with Sen. Millard Tydings (D—Md.)

17 Sen. E. V. Robertson

18 Rep. L. M. Rivers, (D—S.C.)
Lunch, Sens. Gurney, Robertson, Tydings, Saltonstall *et al.*

21 House Appropriations Committee

24 House Committee on Expenditures in Executive Depts; unification

25 Ex-Sen. Mead (D—N.Y.)
House Expenditures Committee, hearing

26 Lunch, Sen. Ferguson *et al.*

29 Lunch, Sen. Robertson *et al.;* after lunch, to Sec. of War's office

May 2 House Expenditures Committee
Lunch, Sen. Brewster
Cocktails, Sen. & Mrs. Saltonstall

7 6:30, Buffet, Rep. Andrews, Old House Office Bldg.
8:30, At home, Sen. & Mrs. Vandenberg for Speaker J. W. Martin (R—Mass.), Congressional Club

8 Rep. Andrews

12 Rep. Taber

14 Dinner, Rep. & Mrs. C. A. Herter (R—Mass.)

15 Rep. J. J. Heffernan (D—N.Y.)

17 Cocktails, Buffet supper, Sen. R. A. Taft (R—Ohio), Metropolitan Club

24 Rep. Taber for lunch

26 Rep. Plumley
Dinner, N.Y., Democratic State Committee

28 Hearing, House Armed Services, subcommittee on pay and administration; testify
Justice Burton's reception for Rep. (Mrs.) F. P. Bolton (R—Ohio), Congressional Club

June 2 Hearing, House Armed Services, subcommittee on pay and admn.

4 Sen. William Langer (R—N.D.)

10 Hearing, House Expenditures Committee, unification

11 2:30 Senate Appropriations Committee
7:15 Dinner? Sen. & Mrs. Robertson, Rep. Robert Hale (R—Me.) *et al.*

23 House Foreign Affairs Committee

25 House Foreign Affairs, testify on Inter-American Military Cooperation Bill
5:30 Gave cocktail party at Georgetown home for numerous Senators, Representatives, Cabinet officers, naval officers, and wives
Supper on *Sequoia*, Sens. Saltonstall and W. F. George (D—Ga.)

26 Rep. Taber

27 Dinner on *Sequoia*, Sen. & Mrs. J. W. Fulbright (D—Ark.)

28 Sen. Fulbright at Burning Tree (golf)
Rep. J. D. Lodge (R—Conn.)

30 Rep. Taber (with Mr. McNeil, Fiscal Director, at Capitol)

July 2 Dinner on *Sequoia*, Rep. Taber *et al.*

7 "Capitol (Room 53)"

8 12:30, Sec. of War Patterson's office, with Sen. Hickenlooper and Mr. Strauss
Senate Armed Services Committee

16 Naval Appropriations Act signed
Lunch, Sec. Patterson, Under Sec. Royall, Sens. Gurney, Tydings, Robertson, Under Sec. Kenney; discussion of methods for disposition of surplus

17 Appear before Senate Armed Services

22 Lunch, Sen. Saltonstall, Clark Clifford (White House)

26 National Security Act signed; Forrestal nominated as Secretary of Defense.

Notes

1: The Road to the Cabinet

1. Justice William O. Douglas to Albion, January 14, 1954.
2. Thomas G. Corcoran to Albion, January 14, 1954.
3. Undated *aide-mémoire* to President Roosevelt, "pursuant to his orders to give him 'Forrestal on one page' " (Papers of T. G. Corcoran).
4. Bernard Baruch to Albion, January 12, 1954.
5. Undated note, Forrestal to T. G. Corcoran (Papers of T. G. Corcoran).
6. Arthur Krock in conversation with Albion.
7. President's Committee on Administrative Management, p. 938.
8. Lindsay Rogers to Connery, September 30, 1954.
9. Forrestal "White House" file (Private Papers).
10. House Naval Affairs, Special Subcommittee, *Hearings on Reorganization of the Navy Department, 1940;* the various views, as expressed in hearings and correspondence, are presented in Elting E. Morison, ed., *Naval Administration.*
11. See Chapter III.
12. Naval Reorganization Act, 54 *Stat.* 492 (June 20, 1940).
13. "Third Vinson Act," 54 *Stat.* 394 (June 13, 1940).
14. "Fourth Vinson Act," 54 *Stat.* 779 (July 19, 1940).
15. Knox memorandum on White House visit, December 1939 (Knox mss, Library of Congress).
16. Louis Brownlow in conversation with Albion and Connery; Stimson and Bundy, *On Active Service,* p. 323; E. E. Morison, *Turmoil and Tradition,* p. 482.
17. Justice William O. Douglas to Albion, January 15, 1962.
18. Ickes, *Secret Diary,* III, 391.
19. Director, Franklin D. Roosevelt Library, Hyde Park, N.Y. to Albion.
20. Knox to Annie R. Knox, July 14, 1940 (Knox mss, Library of

Congress) similar expression in *Secret Diary of Harold L. Ickes,* September 22, December 13, 1940, III, 334, 391.

21. Telegram, Bernard Baruch to Forrestal, August 5, 1940 (Private Papers); Baruch to Albion, January 12, 1954.

22. Knox to Annie R. Knox, August 28, 1940 (Knox mss).

23. See Chapter IX.

24. A. D. Turnbull and C. L. Lord, *History of United States Naval Aviation,* pp. 259, 312.

25. Adlai Stevenson in conversation with Albion.

26. Knox to Annie R. Knox, August 17, 1941 (Knox mss); also Paul R. Leach in Chicago *Daily News,* May 4, 1944.

27. T. G. Corcoran to Albion, February 19, April 12, 1962, enclosing letter, President Roosevelt to Corcoran, January 21, 1941.

28. *Secret Diary of Harold L. Ickes,* III, 390–91, 623.

29. Knox to Admiral W. R. Sexton, General Board, February 25, 1942; Admiral Sexton to Knox, March 20, 1942 (Navy Department).

30. Forrestal to President Roosevelt, December 8, 1944 (Personal Papers).

31. Forrestal to Annie R. Knox, April 27, 1944 (Knox mss).

32. Quoted in Granville Clark to Mrs. Knox, June 7, 1944 (Knox mss).

33. Forrestal to Mrs. Knox, April 27, 1944 (Knox mss).

34. "Major" was Knox's highest wartime rank; the "Colonel" by which he was known came with postwar reserve service.

35. Chicago *Daily News,* May 2, 1944.

36. See especially Washington *Times-Herald,* April 29; Chicago *Sun,* May 1; Cleveland *Plain Dealer,* May 10; Charleston *News and Courier,* May 11, 1944.

37. Bernard Baruch to Albion, January 12, 1954.

38. Justice William O. Douglas to Albion, January 14, 1954.

39. Confidential communication to Albion, September 8, 1954.

40. Director, Franklin D. Roosevelt Library, Hyde Park, N.Y. to Albion, October 3, 1955; Katherine S. Foley in conversation with Albion; Secretary's Appointment Book (Personal Papers).

41. Director, Franklin D. Roosevelt Library to Albion, October 3, 1955; Philip H. Willkie to Albion, August 1, 1956.

42. New York *Times,* May 12, 1944.

43. Rear Admiral R. A. Theobald in conversation with Albion.

44. Katherine S. Foley in conversation with Albion.

2: Executive in Action

1. Walter Millis in *The Forrestal Diaries,* pp. 7–8. Hereafter this volume will be cited as Diaries. There are no citations of material in the original manuscript diaries at Princeton.

2. See Chapters IV, V.

3. Forrestal to Arthur Krock, October 17, 1945 (Personal Papers).

4. Memoranda, Gingrich to Forrestal, September 23, 1940; January 11, February 6, 1941 (Personal Papers).

5. Forrestal to "W. P. B." *et al.*, March 13, 1941 (Personal Papers).

6. Forrestal to "T. R. C.," August 11, 1941 (Personal Papers).

7. Forrestal to Senator Walter F. George, August 14, 1941 (Personal Papers).

8. Forrestal to Senator Tom Connally, August 14, 1941 (Personal Papers).

9. Princeton University alumni files, under J. V. Forrestal '15.

10. John Connorton in conversation with Connery.

11. Vice Admiral George L. Russell to Albion, December 13, 1954.

12. Private communication to Albion.

13. John J. McCloy, Frank C. Nash, and Katherine S. Foley in conversations with Albion; see "Golf List," August 29, 1946 and "Tennis List," June 7, 1948 (Personal Papers), for typical lists of names of those with whom he played.

14. Representative Jack V. Anderson to Albion, June 12, 1955; Appointment Calendar (Personal Files), June 17, 1944; see also other early appointments June 24, 1942; June 19, 21, 23, July 4, 11, 12, August 20, December 8, 1944.

15. Appointment Calendar, March 15, 1942.

16. *Ibid.*, May 15, 1944; Albion was among those present.

17. Private communication to Albion.

18. Admiral Frederick J. Horne to Albion, February 2, 1955.

19. *Newsweek*, May 30, 1949.

20. Transcript of Secretary Knox's press conference, September 11, 1942, the day Forrestal reported back from his Pacific trip (Navy Department).

21. Forrestal to President Truman, April 30, 1945 (Personal Papers).

22. *Ibid.*, December 20, 1945.

23. See Chapter V.

24. *Diaries*, July 7–19, 1946, pp. 173–87.

25. *Newsweek*, March 13, 1944.

26. Washington *Post*, March 6, 1945.

27. Forrestal to Carl Vinson, August 30, 1944 (Personal Papers).

28. Washington *Post*, February 26, 1945.

29. Princeton University, Registrar's records.

30. Private communication to Albion.

31. Memorandum, Forrestal to Eugene O'Dunne, June 4, 1941 (Personal Papers).

32. Memorandum, Forrestal to Commander Overfelt, February 19, 1941 (Personal Papers).

33. Memorandum, Forrestal to E. S. Duffield, July 2, 1944 (Personal Papers).

34. Memorandum, Forrestal to Under Secretary Bard, December 16, 1944 (Personal Papers).

35. Memorandum, Forrestal to Admiral King, February 27, 1942 (Personal Papers).

36. R. G. Albion, memorandum on "Organization of the Navy Department, 1940–1945" (Personal Papers).

37. Elting E. Morison, ed., *Naval Administration*.

38. Rear Admiral Robert L. Dennison to Albion, January 3, 1955.

39. E. F. Willett to Albion, May 16, 1946, enclosing list of topics requested by Forrestal (reproduced in Appendix VII). Connery followed Willett for a brief period, beginning also a preliminary assembling of material for a projected book by Forrestal himself. After Connery left active service, the research job was shared for the next 18 months by John Connorton and Valentine Deale.

40. Dennison to Albion, January 3, 1955.

41. Forrestal to Arthur Krock, October 17, 1945 (Personal Papers), quoted in New York *Times Magazine*, December 9, 1945.

42. Forrestal to Admiral E. C. Kalbfus, November 26, 1941 (Personal Papers).

43. Charles F. Detmar in conversation with Connery; see also Chapter VII.

44. E. S. Duffield in conversation with Albion.

45. Forrestal to Arthur Krock, October 17, 1945 (Personal Papers).

46. Index of Speeches, October 27, 1941–June 16, 1946 (Personal Papers).

47. Successive drafts of Forrestal speeches; latter episode observed by Albion.

48. Forrestal to Justice William O. Douglas, March 25, 1945 (Personal Papers).

49. Washington *Post*, September 18, 1946; see also Truman, *Memoirs*, I, 553.

50. That chair was eventually established at Harvard as the Gardiner Professorship of Oceanic History and Affairs.

51. Forrestal to Secretary Knox, January 16, 1944.

52. The text prepared for this course was *Foundations of National Power: Readings on World Politics and American Security*, Harold and Margaret Sprout, eds., Princeton University Press, 1945.

53. R. G. Albion and S. H. P. Read, *The Navy at Sea and Ashore: An Informal Account of the Organization and Workings of the Naval Establishment of the United States Today, with some Historical Notes on its Development* (Navexos P-472), Navy Department, 1947.

54. *Secret Diary of Harold L. Ickes*, III, 356.

55. New York *Times*, August 15, 1944.

56. See Chapter V.

57. New York *Times*, September 12, 1944, December 18, 1945; W. B. Kohl, "The Jaycock Story," *U.S. Naval Institute Proceedings*,

LXXII (January, 1956), 71–82; "Naval Industrial Association" folder (Personal Papers).

58. Admiral John Gingrich in conversation with Connery.

59. Admiral John Gingrich and Vice Admiral Morton L. Deyo in conversations with Albion.

60. Admiral John Gingrich in conversation with Albion.

61. D. J. Garrison, "The Longest Ship in the Navy," *Ships and the Sea,* IV (Spring, 1955), 59.

62. Forrestal to President Truman, April 14, 1945 (Personal Papers).

63. F. D. Overfelt to Albion, October 16, 1955.

64. E. S. Duffield in conversation with Albion.

65. *Ibid.*

66. Private communication to Albion.

67. Rear Admiral W. R. Smedberg III, to Albion, December 13, 1954.

68. See Chapter IV.

3: Traditions and Precedents

1. The earlier period of American naval administration is best covered in the articles by C. O. Paullin and the chapters by L. D. White; a brief, more recent survey is R. G. Albion "The Administration of the Navy, 1798–1945" in *Public Administration Review,* V (Autumn, 1945), 293–302.

2. See Chapter V.

3. Admiral Frederick J. Horne in conversation with Albion.

4. The clearest over-all picture of the Naval Establishment on the eve of the American entrance into the war is Hanson W. Baldwin, *What the Citizen Should Know about the Navy.* Considerable information is scattered through J. A. Furer, *Administration of the Navy Department in World War II.* For detailed factual data consult Bureau of Navigation, *Navy Directory, June 30, 1940;* Bureau of Supplies and Accounts, *Naval Expenditures, 1940; Congressional Directory, July 1940;* and J. C. Fahey, *The Ships and Aircraft of the U.S. Fleet, 1939,* and subsequent editions.

5. Lloyd M. Short, *The Development of National Administrative Organization in the United States,* pp. 53–54.

6. R. G. Albion, "Boards, Offices, Divisions, and Committees under the Direct Supervision of the Secretaries of the Navy, 1940–1946," processed, Office of Naval History, 1946, *passim.*

7. Secretary of the Navy Directive, "Allocation of Duties, Office of the Secretary," August 23, 1940.

8. *Ibid.,* March 21, 1944; also February 6, July 16, September 6, 1945; House Appropriations Committee, Naval Subcommittee, *Hearings, Navy Department Appropriation Bill, 1945,* p. 1024.

9. R. E. Basler, "The Origins of Engineering Duty Only," *Journal of the American Society of Naval Engineers,* LXV (November, 1953),

771–90; R. B. Madden, "The Bureau of Ships and its ED Officers," *ibid.*, LXVI (February, 1954), 9–40.

10. Naval Appropriation Act, 13 *Stat.* 80 (May 21, 1864).

11. Naval Reorganization Act, 54 *Stat.* 494 (June 20, 1940).

12. 54 *Stat.* 527 (June 25, 1940); R. E. Basler, "The Origins of Engineering Duty Only."

13. H. G. Bowen, *Ships, Machinery and Mossbacks*, pp. 117–18.

14. E. A. Wright, "The Bureau of Ships: A Study in Organization," *Journal of the American Society of Naval Engineers*, LXXI (February, May 1959), 7–21, 315–27.

15. See Chapter V for a case study of the Destroyer Escort Program.

16. Bureau of Ships, *Administrative History*.

17. Rear Admiral W. A. Kitts, in conversation with Albion.

18. Buford Rowland and W. B. Boyd, *U.S. Navy Bureau of Ordnance in World War II*, *passim*. The performance in each of the varied fields is described and appraised. See Chapter IV for torpedo episode.

19. D. B. Duncan and H. M. Dater, "Administrative History of U.S. Naval Aviation," *Air Affairs*, I (Summer 1947), 526–39.

20. Bureau of Yards and Docks, *Building the Navy's Bases in World War II*, *passim*.

21. Secretary of the Navy, *Annual Report, 1945*, pp. A-72, A-77. The coffee consumption was reckoned at forty cups to the pound.

22. See Chapter IV.

23. Henry L. Beers, "History of the Bureau of Navigation 1862–1942," *American Archivist*, VI (October 1943), 212–52.

24. On the development of the General Staff, etc., see Otto L. Nelson, Jr., *National Security and the General Staff*; Paul Y. Hammond, "The Secretaryships of War and Navy: A Study in Civilian Control of the Military," unpublished Harvard Ph.D. thesis, 1953; H. L. Stimson and McG. Bundy, *On Active Service, passim*.

25. Henry L. Beers, "The Development of the Office of the Chief of Naval Operations," *Military Affairs*, 1946–47.

26. *Ibid.*

27. See Chapter IV.

28. Fahey, *The Ships and Aircraft of the U.S. Fleet, 1939*, pp. 26–27.

29. William Howard Gardiner in conversation with Albion.

30. Fahey, *The Ships and Aircraft of the U.S. Fleet, 1939*, pp. 5–6.

31. *Ibid.*, 1945 ed. pp. 4–5.

32. For the northern diversion in the Leyte Gulf action, see J. A. Field, *The Japanese at Leyte Gulf*; C. V. Woodward, *The Battle for Leyte Gulf*; Hanson W. Baldwin, *Great Sea Fights and Shipwrecks*, Chapter 10; S. E. Morison, *History of U.S. Naval Operations*, Vol. XIII.

33. Hanson W. Baldwin, *What Every Citizen Should Know about the Navy*, p. 23.

34. Society of Naval Architects and Marine Engineers, *Historical Transactions, 1893–1943*; brief histories of various yards.

35. See *Navy Directory, 1940* for list of individual activities and officers assigned to each.

36. *Army & Navy Gazette*, quoted in *Army & Navy Journal*, XIII (January 13, 1876), 283.

37. Table of annual expenditures of the United States Navy, United States Army, and British Navy, 1798–1947, in Albion's unpublished "Makers of Naval Policy," Chapter VI.

38. See especially the reports of the Naval Investigation of 1876, 44th Congress, 1st Session, *House Report 784*, p. 160 and *passim*.

39. Naval Appropriation Act, 22 *Stat.* 291 (August 5, 1882).

40. General Order No. 112, March 17, 1869.

41. Comparison of British *Navy List* and American *Navy Register*, 1875.

42. Bureau of Supplies and Accounts, *Naval Expenditures, 1940*, pp. 210, 222, 320–24.

43. Society of Naval Architects and Marine Engineers, *Historical Transactions*, Section 3.

44. Compiled principally from Bureau of Construction and Repair, *Ships' Data*, annual editions; also *Jane's Fighting Ships*, and J. C. Fahey, *Ship and Aircraft of the U.S. Fleet*.

45. See Chapter IV.

46. Secretary of the Navy, *Annual Report, 1945*.

47. Bowen, *Ships, Machinery and Mossbacks*, Chapter V, "Plant Seizure and Operation."

48. Details of individual officers in *Navy Directory, 1940, passim*.

49. Secretary of the Navy, *Annual Report, 1945*.

50. Samuel P. Huntington, "Civilian Control and the Constitution," *American Political Science Review*, L (September 1956), 681; see also his *The Soldier and the State*, especially Chapter XVI.

51. Elias Huzar, *The Purse and the Sword, passim*.

52. See Chapter VII.

53. Louis Smith, *American Democracy and Military Power*, p. 104.

54. See Chapter X.

4: Getting Under Way

1. For an account of industrial mobilization planning in the twenty years preceding 1940, see Robert H. Connery, *The Navy and the Industrial Mobilization in World War II*, pp. 31–53.

2. E. J. King and W. M. Whitehill, *Fleet Admiral King*, p. 293.

3. Frank Freidel, *Franklin D. Roosevelt*, I, 165.

4. Herbert Feis, *The Road to Pearl Harbor*, pp. 138–39.

5. Charles Edison in conversation with Albion.

6. *Diaries*, November 14, 1944, with details of Forrestal's endorsement.

7. Bureau of Yards and Docks, *Building the Navy's Bases in World War II, passim.*

8. Brief biographical data on these various chiefs, with portraits, will be found in J. A. Furer, *Administration of the Navy Department in World War II.*

9. House Appropriations Committee, *Hearing, Supplemental Appropriations, 1943,* p. 49. The remark was quoted by Quentin Reynolds in *Colliers* (July 15, 1944), p. 16, as "You're in charge of production, Jim. Congress has just passed the Two Ocean Navy Bill. And, Jim, it's up to you to build it."

10. Secretary of the Navy Directive, "Allocation of Duties in the Office of the Secretary, August 23, 1940."

11. Third Vinson Act, 54 *Stat.* 394; Fourth Vinson Act (Two Ocean Navy), 54 *Stat.* 799 (July 19, 1940).

12. 54 *Stat.* 872 (September 9, 1940).

13. Conversations of Connery with Duffield and various staff members, Under Secretary's office.

14. Memorandum, H. Struve Hensel to James Forrestal, "Preparation and Signing of Navy Department Contracts," March 25, 1941 (Navy Department Files).

15. *Ibid.*

16. Memorandum, Judge Advocate General to Secretary of the Navy, July 2, 1941 (Navy Department Files).

17. Memorandum, Hensel to Forrestal, April 28, 1941 (Navy Department Files).

18. House Naval Affairs Committee, *Hearings, Sundry Naval Legislation 1941,* p. 1476.

19. *Ibid.*

20. 55 *Stat.* 559 (July 3, 1941).

21. Vice Admiral John L. McCrea in conversation with Albion.

22. Buford Rowland and W. B. Boyd, *U.S. Navy Bureau of Ordnance in World War II,* p. 129. The whole wartime torpedo situation is discussed fully and frankly in Chapter VI.

23. S. E. Morison, *History of U.S. Naval Operations in World War II,* IV, 230–31.

24. *Ibid.,* p. 231.

25. Rowland and Boyd, p. 129.

26. C. A. Lockwood, *Sink 'Em All: Submarine Warfare in the Pacific,* p. 75.

27. Rowland and Boyd, U.S. Bureau of Ordnance, pp. 126–27.

28. 41 *Stat.* 764 (June 4, 1920).

29. Created on recommendation of the Joint Army and Navy Board, June 27, 1922; approved by Secretaries of War and Navy, June 29, 1922 (Navy Department Files).

30. Industrial Mobilization Plan, 1939, p. 10.

31. Louis Brownlow in conversation with Connery.

32. Samuel I. Rosenman, ed., *The Public Papers and Addresses of Franklin D. Roosevelt* (1940), IX, 24.

33. Herbert Emmerich in conversation with Connery.

34. Charles Edison in conversation with Albion; the whole episode is treated in greater detail in Albion's unpublished "Makers of Naval Policy," Chapter XVIII; also in Connery, "*The Navy and the Industrial Mobilization*," pp. 46–49.

35. War Resources Board, *Minutes*, August 30, 1939.

36. Charles Edison in conversation with Albion.

37. War Resources Board, *Report to Army and Navy Munitions Board*, p. 4.

38. James Fesler, *Industrial Mobilization for War, 1940–1945* (Civilian Production Administration). Washington, D.C., Government Printing Office.

39. Ethan P. Allen, *Policies Governing Private Financing of Emergency Facilities*, W.P.B. Historical Series, Washington, D.C., Government Printing Office, (1945), p. 10.

40. Herbert Emmerich in conversation with Connery.

41. Donald Nelson, *Arsenal of Democracy*, New York (1946), p. 116.

42. Rosenman, ed., *The Public Papers and Addresses of Franklin D. Roosevelt*, IX, 623.

43. Nelson, *Arsenal of Democracy*, p. 139.

44. Ferol D. Overfelt, Memorandum on Bureau Chiefs' Meeting, December, 16, 1941 (Navy Department Files). No stenographic records were kept of those meetings.

45. Herbert Emmerich in conversation with Connery.

46. See Chapter II.

47. Michael Forrestal in conversation with Connery.

48. Ferdinand Eberstadt, Report to Under Secretaries Patterson and Forrestal in Regard to the Army and Navy Munitions Board, November 26, 1941, p. 7 (Eberstadt Papers).

49. Myron Gilmore, History of Op-24, Office of Naval History, Navy Department.

50. Memorandum, Rear Admiral Ray Spear to Forrestal, February 11, 1941 (Navy Department Files).

5: Impact of Pearl Harbor

1. New York *Times*, December 7, 1941, p.1; also in most of the major Sunday newspapers that day.

2. William R. Castle in New York *Herald-Tribune*, December 7, 1941.

3. New York *Times*, December 7, 1941.

4. *Ibid.*, New York *Times Magazine*.

5. Joint Committee on the Investigation of the Pearl Harbor Attack, *Hearings* (hereafter, *Pearl Harbor Hearings*), pp. 3902–12.

6. *Ibid.;* Samuel E. Morison, "The Lesson of Pearl Harbor," *Saturday Evening Post,* CCXXIV (October 28, 1961), 19–27. Author consulted Roberta Wohlsetter, "Warning and Decision at Pearl Harbor" in manuscript.

7. *United States Naval Institute Proceedings,* LXXXII (August, 1956), 904–6, reproducing article from *Nippon Times.*

8. *Pearl Harbor Hearings,* p. 3829.

9. Morison, "The Lesson of Pearl Harbor," *Saturday Evening Post,* CCXXIV (October 28, 1961), 19–27.

10. Admiral John E. Gingrich in conversation with Connery; also, record of Forrestal's telephone calls and appointments (Personal Papers).

11. Third Naval District, unpublished First Narrative History.

12. See Chapter VI.

13. See Chapter IV.

14. Admiral Ben Moreell to Albion, February 26, 1957; Moreell to Connery, January 29, 1962.

15. *Ibid.*

16. Executive Order 8984, December 18, 1941.

17. Executive Order 9096, March 12, 1942.

18. Admiral J. O. Richardson in conversation with Albion. Emphasis added.

19. Executive Order 9082, February 28, 1942. The episode is related in detail in F. S. Hayden, "War Department Reorganization, August 1941–March 1942," *Military Affairs,* XVI (Fall, 1952), 97–114.

20. Franklin D. Roosevelt to Henry Stimson, February 26, 1942, paraphrased, Hayden, "War Department Reorganization," p. 113.

21. See Chapter VII.

22. Forrestal's testimony before Eberstadt's Task Force on National Security of the Hoover Commission, in Connery's presence, unpublished.

23. See Chapter X.

24. Admiral Frederick J. Horne in conversation with Albion.

25. E. J. King and W. M. Whitehill, *Fleet Admiral King,* Chapter XXIX, "Cominch and CNO"; Albion's unpublished "Makers of Naval Policy," Chapter XVII.

26. See also Maurice Matloff and E. M. Snell, *Strategic Planning for Coalition Warfare, 1941–1942,* U.S. Army in World War II series.

27. King and Whitehill, *Fleet Admiral King, passim.*

28. H. Struve Hensel in *Harvard Business Review,* XXXII (January–February 1954), 102.

29. Rear Admiral George L. Russell to Albion, December 13, 1954.

30. Michael Forrestal in conversation with Connery supported by various opinions expressed to authors by colleagues and personal friends.

31. William D. Leahy, *I Was There,* p. 104; see also *ibid.,* pp. 75, 224; and Lord Cunningham, *A Sailor's Odyssey,* p. 466.

32. King and Whitehill, *Fleet Admiral King*, pp. 629–37.

33. *Ibid.*, p. 631.

34. Vice Admiral John L. McCrea in conversation with Albion.

35. Confidential communication to Albion.

36. Admiral John E. Gingrich in conversation with Connery.

37. Elting E. Morison, *Turmoil and Tradition*, p. 499.

38. Executive Order 9024, January 16, 1942.

39. Donald Nelson, *Arsenal of Democracy*, pp. 198–201.

40. Memorandum, Hensel to Forrestal, February 6, 1942 (Navy Department Files).

41. House Appropriations Committee, Naval Subcommittee. *Hearings on Supplemental Navy Appropriation Bill*, 1943, pp. 47–48.

42. H. L. Stimson and McGeorge Bundy, *On Active Service*, p. 453.

43. Memorandum, Admiral King, March 17, 1942. This and seventeen of the next twenty-two citations come from the Navy Department files.

44. *Ibid.*, May 22, 1942.

45. Assistant Secretary Franklin D. Roosevelt to Senator Frederick Hale, June 4, 1920; President Franklin D. Roosevelt to Assistant Secretary Henry L. Roosevelt, March 2, 1934; reproduced in Office of the Chief of Naval Operations, *Naval Administration: Documents Relating to Navy Department Organization*, 1915–1940 (Lt. Elting E. Morison, ed.).

46. President Roosevelt to Knox, May 26, 1942.

47. Admiral King to Knox, May 27, 1942.

48. Memorandum, Forrestal to Knox, May 24, 1942.

49. For detailed account of inadequacies of CNO see Robert H. Connery, *The Navy and the Industrial Mobilization*, p. 133.

50. CNO Directive, May 28, 1942.

51. *Ibid.*, May 15, 1942.

52. Vice Admiral Horne to Rear Admiral Jacobs, June 3, 1942.

53. Vice Admiral McCrea in conversation with Albion.

54. President Roosevelt's comment on CNO directive of May 28, 1942.

55. Memorandum, Knox to Admiral King, June 10, 1942.

56. King's endorsement on June 10 memorandum.

57. President Roosevelt to Knox, June 12, 1942.

58. Memorandum, Admiral King to Knox, June 13, 1942.

59. Admiral King in conversation with Albion.

60. Draft of proposed General Order, May 1943.

61. *Ibid.*

62. King and Whitehill, *Fleet Admiral King*, p. 477.

63. Memorandum, Bard to Knox, August 10, 1943.

64. Memorandum, Rear Admiral Blandy to Knox, 1943.

65. President Roosevelt to Rear Admiral Young, September 28, 1943.

66. President Roosevelt to Knox, received August 16, 1943 (Knox mss), Library of Congress.

67. See Chapter IV.

68. Eberstadt in conversation with Connery.

69. Forrestal, Patterson, and Eberstadt to Nelson, May 7, 1942 (Eberstadt Papers).

70. Eberstadt to Nelson, May 5, 1942 (Eberstadt Papers).

71. Eberstadt to Lucius Clay, March 9, 1942 (Eberstadt Papers).

72. Admiral Gingrich in conversation with Connery; Gingrich, as naval aide, accompanied Forrestal on his South Pacific trip.

73. *Ibid.*

74. *Ibid.*

75. Eberstadt in conversation with Connery.

76. Eberstadt to W. L. Batt, March 31, 1942; Eberstadt to J. S. Knowlson, August 9, 1942 (Eberstadt Papers).

77. See, for example, Bureau of the Budget, *The United States at War*, pp. 108, 281.

6: Midpassage

1. *Congressional Record*, May 19, 1943, Vol. LXXXIX, Pt. 4, p. 4631.

2. Memorandum, Hensel to Forrestal, Explanation of Navy Contract Procedure, April 3, 1943, p. 3 (Navy Department Files).

3. Memorandum, Hensel, How the December 13 Directive Came to be Issued. The official title of the Directive was "Reorganization of Procurement and Coordination of Procurement Legal Services" (Navy Department Files).

4. W. Browne Baker, "Brief History of the Negotiation Section, OP&M," May 22, 1943 (Navy Department Files).

5. See Chapter V.

6. Robert H. Connery, *The Navy and the Industrial Mobilization in World War II*, pp. 217–218.

7. Forrestal to Albert Bradley, Executive Vice President, General Motors Corporation, August 26, 1943 (Personal Papers).

8. House Committee on Naval Affairs, *Hearings, Sundry Naval Legislation, 1942*, p. 2493, *Hearings on Profit Limitations*, March 20, 1942. For comprehensive treatment of the period up to World War II, see Richard McClung, "Profit Limitation Controls Prior to the Present War" in H. Struve Hensel, *Law and Contemporary Problems*, X (1943), 187–217.

9. Senate Banking and Currency Committee, *Hearings on Price Control*, April 17, 1944, p. 629.

10. Office of Procurement and Material, Price Analysis Section, "Pricing in Navy Procurement," January 18, 1945 (Navy Department Files).

11. Patterson and Forrestal to Senator Robert F. Wagner, Chairman,

Senate Banking and Currency Committee, December 10, 1941 (Navy Department Files).

12. Patterson and Forrestal to President Roosevelt, December 19, 1941 (Navy Department Files).

13. President Roosevelt to Patterson and Forrestal, December 20, 1941 (Navy Department Files).

14. Price Control Act, 56 *Stat.* 23 (January 30, 1942).

15. Patterson and Forrestal to Leon Henderson, July 23, 1942 (Navy Department Files).

16. Henderson to Patterson and Forrestal, September 17, 1942 (Navy Department Files).

17. O.P.A. Press Release, November 14, 1942.

18. Ferdinand Eberstadt, *Report to James Forrestal, Secretary of the Navy, on the Unification of the War and Navy Departments,* printed for Senate Committee on Naval Affairs, October 22, 1945. (Hereafter *Eberstadt Report.*)

19. *Administrative History of the Bureau of Ships,* processed "First Narrative," includes table of successive priority lists for the various types of ships.

20. Details in various editions of *Jane's Fighting Ships* and J. C. Fahey, *The Ships and Aircraft of the U.S. Fleet.*

21. King and Whitehill, *Fleet Admiral King,* p. 298.

22. This section on the Destroyer Escort program is based principally upon Eugene S. Duffield's "Memorandum to James Forrestal re DE Program," April 21, 1943 (Personal Papers).

23. Cablegram, Admiralty to British Admiralty Supply Representative, June 14, 1941 (Navy Department Files).

24. Memorandum, Forrestal to Admiral Stark, December 23, 1941 (Personal Papers).

25. House Committee on Naval Affairs, *Report of Investigations of the Progress of the War Effort,* 78th Congress, 2d Session, December 11, 1945, pp. 54–57.

26. Memorandum, Knox to President Roosevelt, September 1, 1942 (Navy Department Files).

27. See Donald Nelson request to Admiral Leahy for new priority list, November 18, 1942 (Navy Department Files).

28. Requirements Review Board, *Transcript of Proceedings* (Navy Department Files).

29. Nelson to Knox, October 25, 1942 (Navy Department Files).

30. Directive, Knox to Bureau Chiefs, regarding construction, November 26, 1942 (Navy Department Files).

31. Admiral Ben Moreell to Knox, November 29, 1942 (Navy Department Files).

32. Hensel to Albion, December 21, 1960.

33. Admiral John E. Gingrich in conversation with Connery. See also testimony of Randall Jacobs on this subject, House Appropria-

tions Committee, Naval Subcommittee, *Hearings on Navy Appropriations Bill, 1945,* April 13, 1945, p. 145.

34. Admiral Gingrich to Rear Admiral Denfeld, Assistant Chief of
Naval Personnel, January 3, 1943; Denfeld to Gingrich, January 12,
1943 (Navy Department Files).

35. *Ibid.,* June 30, 1943.

36. Forrestal, Directive Concerning General Court Martial Prisoners,
July 24, 1943.

37. Franklin D. Roosevelt, Acting Secretary of the Navy, *General
Courts Martial,* April 10, 1918 (Navy Records Center Files).

38. Forrestal to Mrs. Franklin D. Roosevelt, July 28, 1942 (Personal
Papers).

39. Harold A. Manderson in conversation with Albion.

40. King and Whitehill, *Fleet Admiral King,* p. 629.

41. William D. Leahy, *I Was There,* p. 322.

42. Admiral Horne to Albion, February 2, 1955.

43. Draft for Executive Order, January, 1944 (Navy Department
Files).

44. See Chapter VII.

45. Draft for Executive Order, January, 1944 (Navy Department
Files).

46. Leahy, *I Was There,* pp. 182, 222.

47. Confidential communication to Albion.

48. King and Whitehill, *Fleet Admiral King,* p. 630.

49. Knox to Admiral King, January 23, 1944 (Navy Department
Files).

7: *The White House and the Hill*

1. W. H. Standley, *Ambassador to Russia,* p. 29.

2. Marriner S. Eccles, *Beckoning Frontiers,* p. 336.

3. Confidential communication to Albion.

4. Rear Admiral Dallas G. Sutton (MC), former Assistant Chief of
Medicine and Surgery, in conversation with Albion.

5. George M. Elsey, former assistant naval aide at the White House,
in conversation with Albion.

6. Knox to Admiral King, January 23, 1944 (Navy Department
Files).

7. Military Order, July 5, 1939; see also Ernest R. May, ed., *The
Ultimate Decision,* Chapter 7.

8. William Leahy, *I Was There, passim.*

9. Vice Admiral John L. McCrea, to Albion, January 16, 1962;
George M. Elsey in conversation with Albion.

10. Admiral King in conversation with Albion.

11. For Churchill's tendency to interfere, see especially S. W. Roskill,
The War at Sea, 1939–1945, I, 202; Lord Cunningham, *A Sailor's*

Odyssey, pp. 250, 277, 374–75, 378; Arthur J. Marder, "Winston Churchill as First Lord of the Admiralty, 1911–1915," *U.S. Naval Institute Proceedings,* LXXIX (January 1953), 18–27.

12. Undated memorandum, "White House" file, c. 1943 (Private Papers).

13. Appointment Calendar, 1941, *passim.*

14. Memorandum, Forrestal to President Roosevelt, March 12, 1941 (Personal Papers).

15. *Ibid.,* January 2, 1945.

16. New York *Times,* November 23, 1954; see Chapter VIII.

17. Robert H. Sherwood, *Roosevelt and Hopkins,* p. 242.

18. Eliot Janeway, *Struggle for Survival,* p. 20. See also Sherwood, *Roosevelt and Hopkins,* p. 11 for claim that Roosevelt "converted his friend to war purposes."

19. See Chapter VIII.

20. Harry S. Truman, *Memoirs,* I, 324–28, 555; see also *ibid.,* pp. 327, 331.

21. *Diaries,* July 4, 1944, p. 3.

22. *Ibid.,* July 30, 1945, p. 89.

23. *Ibid.,* November 21, 1945, p. 116; see also Chapter XI.

24. Memorandum, Forrestal to White House Naval Aide, April 11, 1946 (Private Papers).

25. Theodore Taylor, *The Magnificent Mitscher,* p. 331.

26. See Chapter IX, X.

27. Eugene S. Duffield in conversation with Albion.

28. At Forrestal's request, Connery, as a political scientist, was instructed to prepare a memorandum on these points.

29. Undated memorandum, c.1942, with replies (Navy Department Files).

30. See Chapter II.

31. See Chapter I.

32. R. G. Albion, "The Naval Affairs Committees, 1816–1947," in *U.S. Naval Institute Proceedings,* LXXVIII (November 1952), 1227–37, reprinted in *Congressional Record,* Appendix, January 13, 1953. More extensive details on all aspects on the relations between the Navy and Congress are in Albion's unpublished "Makers of Naval Policy," Chapters V–VIII, XX–XXII.

33. See Chapter XI.

34. Forrestal to Representative Carl Vinson, May 18, 1944, quoted in House Naval Affairs, *Hearings on Sundry Naval Legislation, 1945,* p. 1161.

35. *Ibid., 1946* (November 18, 1946) p. 3770.

36. Vinson to Forrestal, May 18, 1944, enclosing resolution of May 15, 1944 (Personal Papers).

37. House Armed Services, Hearings, 1949; No. 32, pp. 550–51; Farewell Ceremonies for Secretary of Defense James Forrestal.

38. Congressional Record, May 23, 1949, pp. 6720–25 (Senate); pp. 6770–73 (House).

39. Representative Jack V. Anderson to Albion, June 12, 1955; Rear Admiral Ira H. Nunn in conversation with Albion.

40. House Joint Resolution, 82d Congress, 1st Session, Public Law 90, Chapter 252, July 30, 1951.

41. Biographical sketch in *Congressional Directory, 1946.*

42. Albion, "Naval Affairs Committees," p. 1236; see also *Diaries,* November 4, 1944, p. 13.

43. Senator Frederick Hale, former chairman of Senate Naval Affairs like his father, Eugene, in conversation with Albion.

44. Robert E. Kline, Jr., in conversation with Albion.

45. Bradley A. Fiske, *From Midshipman to Rear Admiral,* p. 81.

46. Truman Committee, *Hearings,* p. 7705.

47. Confidential communication to Albion.

48. Truman Committee, *Hearings,* p. 7709.

49. *Recollections of Yesteryear: The Diary of John D. Long,* L. S. Mayo, ed., pp. 156–57.

50. House Appropriations Committee, Naval Subcommittee, *Hearings, Naval Appropriation Bill, 1945* (March 14, 1944), p. 619.

51. Organization Policy Group, *Minutes,* January 29, 1945, p. 12.

52. Forrestal to Arthur Krock, October 17, 1945.

53. Confidential communication to Albion.

54. Senator Harry S. Truman in conversation with Albion.

55. 78th Congress, 2d Session, *Senate Report 10,* pp. 133–68; see also Chapter IV.

56. Truman Committee, *Hearings,* p. 10608; for the whole Corrigan episode, see pp. 10479–10618.

57. *Ibid.,* 17066; see also pp. 16081–16133.

58. 79th Congress, 1st Session, *Senate Hearings,* Part 33 (May 9, 1946), p. 17065.

59. Unpublished Gingrich Diary, April 8, 1941 (Personal Papers).

60. Joint Resolution, 58 *Stat.* 276 (June 13, 1944); the Pearl Harbor Investigating Committee *Hearings* include full data on all the preliminary investigations of the subject.

61. Pearl Harbor *Hearings,* pp. 383, 385; New York *Times,* August 30, 1945.

62. Memorandum, Forrestal to President Roosevelt, January 2, 1945.

63. *Diaries,* April 18, 1945, p. 46.

64. Forrestal to Charles S. Thomas, February 27, 1947, quoted in *Diaries,* p. 240.

65. Draft of letter, Forrestal to Vinson, May 18, 1945, in Organization Policy Group Minutes, May 21, 1945.

66. Forrestal to Sheldon Clark, September 24, 1945, in *Diaries,* p. 97.

67. House Naval Affairs, *Hearings, Sundry Naval Legislation, 1945* (September 19, 1945), p. 1164.

68. *Ibid.*, pp. 1159ff.

69. *Diaries*, November 21, 1945.

70. See Chapter VIII.

71. House Appropriations Committee, Naval Subcommittee, *Hearings, Naval Supplemental Appropriation Bill, 1943*, p. 343.

72. *Diaries*, December 20, 1946, p. 237.

73. President Truman to Director of the Budget, November 16, 1946.

74. See Appendix J. compiled from Appointment Calendar, Diaries, etc.

75. *Diaries*, March 5, 1947, p. 250.

76. *Ibid.*, April 2, 1947, p. 268.

77. *Ibid.*, editorial note, p. 291. The whole system of naval appropriations is treated in full detail in Albion's unpublished "Makers of Naval Policy," Chapter VI for the earlier periods and Chapter XXI for 1940–47.

78. Forrestal to Chairman Taber, July 17, 1947, quoted in *Diaries*, p. 292.

8: *"Those Who Hate War"*

1. The phrase "Those who hate war must have the power to prevent it" was uttered in a conference on April 17, 1945, *Diaries*, p. 45; the similar phrase "The means to wage war must be in the hands of those who hate war," occurred in Forrestal's testimony before the House Naval Affairs Committee on September 19, 1945 and is in its *Hearings, Sundry Naval Legislation, 1945*, p. 1164, quoted in *Diaries*, p. 97.

2. The International Studies Group, The Brookings Institution, prepared for the Bureau of the Budget *The Administration of Foreign Affairs and Overseas Operations*, June 1951. Connery participated in this study and was chiefly responsible for the section entitled "The Department of Defense and the Conduct of Foreign Affairs." It recognized three alternatives: (1) furnishing strictly military advice; (2) furnishing military advice but taking into account economic and political factors; (3) having an equal partnership with the State Department in the formulation of foreign policy.

3. See Chapter XI.

4. *Diaries*, April 17, 1945, p. 45.

5. Arthur Macmahon, *Administration in Foreign Affairs*, p. 164.

6. *Diaries*, January 16, 1945, p. 25.

7. *Diary of Gideon Welles*, H. K. Beale, ed., I, 133, September 16, 1862.

8. *Ibid.*

9. R. G. Albion, "Communications and Remote Control" in *U.S. Naval Institute Proceedings*, LXXXII (August 1956), 832–36, based on remarks by the late Rear Admiral Caspar F. Goodrich.

10. *Pearl Harbor Hearings*, p. 2540.

11. G. H. Davis, *A Navy Second to None*, p. 32.

12. These episodes are discussed, along with many other considerations of State-Navy relations, in Albion's unpublished "Makers of Naval Policy," Chapters XIII–XV.

13. 47th Congress, 1st Session, *House Report 586*, p. 2.

14. This episode was related in Albion's "State, War and Navy— Under One Roof, 1882" in *U.S. Naval Institute Proceedings*, LXXV (July 1949), 793–95.

15. Ernest R. May, "The Development of Political Military Consultation in the United States" in *Political Science Quarterly*, LXX (June 1955), 163–64.

16. *Ibid.*, p. 168.

17. *Ibid.*, pp. 168–69.

18. Admiral Stark to Admiral Hart, February 9, 1940, in *Pearl Harbor Hearings*, pp. 2115–16.

19. May, "Development of Political Military Consultation," p. 172.

20. Harley Notter, *Post War Foreign Policy Preparation, 1939–45*, pp. 16–17; Mark S. Watson, *Chief of Staff: Prewar Plans and Preparedness*, pp. 89–92.

21. H. L. Stimson and McGeorge Bundy, *On Active Service*, p. 563.

22. Captain W. D. Puleston, USN, in conversation with Albion; Captain Puleston, former Director of Naval Intelligence, used to brief Knox for the State-War-Navy Secretaries' meetings.

23. Stimson and Bundy, *On Active Service*, p. 389.

24. *Memoirs of Cordell Hull*, II, 1109.

25. Robert M. Sherwood, *Roosevelt and Hopkins*, p. 756.

26. *Ibid.*, p. 227.

27. Vice Admiral John L. McCrea in conversation with Albion.

28. *Diaries*, May 1, 1945, p. 54.

29. John J. McCloy in conversation with Connery.

30. *Ibid.*

31. Stimson and Bundy, *On Active Service*, p. 389.

32. *Diaries*, December 19, 1944.

33. Secretary of State to Secretaries of War and Navy, November 29, 1944 (Personal Papers). See also Notter, *Post War Foreign Policy Preparation*, p. 348.

34. Secretaries of War and Navy to Secretary of State, December 1, 1944.

35. Secretaries of State, War, and Navy, April 20, 1946.

36. May, "The Development of Political Military Consultation," p. 175; see also H. W. Moseley, *et. al.*, "The State-War-Navy Coordinating Committee," U.S. Department of State *Bulletin*, XIII (November 11, 1945), 745–47; and R. S. Cline, *Washington Command Post: The Operations Division*, pp. 326–30.

37. Cline, *Washington Command Post*, p. 327.

38. *Diaries*, especially January 16, 1945, p. 25; May 29, 1945, p. 66; June 19, 1945, p. 69; October 16, 1945, p. 101; November 20, 1945, p. 108.

39. *Ibid.*, January 2, 1946, p. 126.

40. *Ibid.*, July 7, 1944, p. 8.

41. Memorandum, Stimson to Stettinius on Trusteeships, January 1945, Stimson and Bundy, *On Active Service*, pp. 599–605; see also Elting E. Morison, *Turmoil and Tradition*, p. 611.

42. Edward R. Stettinius, Jr., *Roosevelt and the Russians: The Yalta Conference*, p. 44.

43. Leo Pasvolsky, Chief of State Department Post War Planning Group, in conversation with Connery.

44. *Diaries*, March 9, 1945, p. 33.

45. Notter, *Post War Foreign Policy Preparation*, p. 432.

46. Arthur H. Vandenburg, *The Private Papers of Senator Vandenburg*, p. 169.

47. Notter, *Post War Foreign Policy Preparation*, p. 433.

48. James F. Byrnes, *Speaking Frankly*, p. 92.

49. *Diaries*, p. 130.

50. *Ibid.*, January 21, 1946, pp. 130–31.

51. Byrnes, *Speaking Frankly*, p. 221.

52. *Ibid.*, p. 212.

53. See Chapter XI.

54. Herbert Feis, *Japan Subdued*, p. 4.

55. E. J. King and W. M. Whitehill, *Fleet Admiral King*, p. 598; W. D. Leahy, *I Was There*, pp. 384–85.

56. *Diaries*, March 8, 1947, pp. 70–71, indicates that Forrestal was not present, but Feis, *Japan Subdued*, pp. 9–12, states that he was.

57. *Diaries*, February 28, 1945, p. 31.

58. *Ibid.*, May 11, 1945, p. 55; see also *ibid* pp. 50–51, 57, 74.

59. Department of Defense, *The Entry of the Soviet Union into the War against Japan: Military Plans, 1941–1945*, p. 85.

60. The whole story of Stimson's relation to the atomic bomb is analyzed in Morison, *Turmoil and Tradition*, Chapter XXXII, which indicates the other principal studies, particularly Louis Morton, "The Decision to Use the Atomic Bomb" in *Foreign Affairs*, January 1957, reprinted in K. R. Greenfield, ed., *Command Decisions*, pp. 388–410. See also Robert C. Batchelder, *The Irreversible Decision, 1939–1960*, Part II.

61. *Diaries*, May 8, 1945, p. 54.

62. Interview with Strauss in "Was the A-Bomb Necessary." in *U.S. News and World Report*, August 15, 1960, p. 172.

63. Full text of Bard note, *ibid.*, p. 74.

64. Ralph A. Bard to Albion, July 5, 1961.

65. *Diaries*, May 14, 1945, p. 57.

66. *Ibid.*, pp. 73–74; Feis, *Japan Subdued*, pp. 15–27.

67. Herbert Feis, *Between War and Peace: The Potsdam Conference*, pp. 159–60; Harry S. Truman, *Memoirs*, I, 334–37; James F. Byrnes, *All in One Lifetime*, p. 289.

68. Feis, *Japan Subdued*, p. 52.

69. *Diaries*, July 13, 1945, p. 74.

70. King and Whitehill, *Fleet Admiral King*, p. 618.

71. *Diaries*, pp. 77–78; Feis, *Japan Subdued*, p. 85n.; Byrnes, *All in One Lifetime*, pp. 297–98.

72. Feis, *Japan Subdued*, p. 178.

73. *Ibid.*, p. 62, citing Truman *Memoirs*.

74. *Diaries*, pp. 78–79.

75. Feis, *Japan Subdued*, p. 81.

76. *Memoirs of Cordell Hull*, II, 1591–94; Byrnes, *Speaking Frankly*, pp. 205–7; J. C. Grew, *This Turbulent Era*, II, 1424–27; Louis Morton, in *Command Decisions*, pp. 404–5.

77. Feis, *Japan Subdued*, pp. 78–79; Morison, *Turmoil and Tradition*, p. 633.

78. Grew, *This Turbulent Era*, p. 1593.

79. Feis, *Japan Subdued*, pp. 167, 176–77.

80. 82d Congress, 1st Session, Senate Judiciary Committee, *Hearings on the Institute of Pacific Relations, 1951*, Testimony of Eugene A. Doorman, September 15, 1951, p. 704.

81. Draft of letter, Forrestal to President Truman, August 8, 1945, never sent (Personal Papers).

82. Byrnes, *Speaking Frankly*, p. 212.

83. Memorandum, Lewis L. Strauss to Forrestal, August 16, 1945, enclosed in Strauss to Albion, May 17, 1961. Admiral Strauss's memoirs, *Men and Decisions*, are scheduled for publication in 1962.

84. Feis, *Japan Subdued*, pp. 88–89.

85. *Ibid.*, p. 160.

86. *Ibid.*, p. 161.

87. *Ibid.*, pp. 161–62; *Diaries*, pp. 95–96.

88. The rival views were well summed up by Arthur Krock, New York *Times*, March 15, 1946; see also *ibid.*, January 24, March 8, March 12 issues; *Diaries*, December 4, 1945; Truman, *Memoirs*, II, 25.

89. Senate Special Committee on Atomic Energy, *Hearings on Atomic Energy Commission*, January 23, 1946, pp. 76–89.

90. Letter quoted in Truman, *Memoirs*, II, 3.

91. John J. McCloy in conversation with Connery.

92. Forrestal to Palmer Hoyt, September 2, 1944, quoted in *Diaries*, p. 14.

93. *Diaries*, January 16, 1945, p. 25; May 29, 1945, p. 66; June 19, 1945, p. 69; October 16, 1945, p. 101; November 20, 1945, p. 108.

94. Ambassador Harriman's dispatches to State Department, quoted in *Diaries*, April-May, 1945, p. 39.

95. Forrestal to Senator Homer Ferguson, quoted in *Diaries*, May 14, 1945, p. 57.

96. Edward F. Willett and Wilfred Parsons in conversations with Connery.

97. *Diaries*, November 6, 1946, p. 107.

98. Draft notes in Private Papers at Princeton; Connery was, for a while in 1946, assisting Forrestal in the preparation of this material.

99. House Naval Affairs Committee, *Hearings, Sundry Naval Legislation, 1945* (September 19, 1945) p. 1164.

100. Byrnes, *All in One Lifetime*, p. 351; similar entry in *Diaries*, February 28, 1946, p. 141.

101. *Diaries*, March 10, 1946, pp. 144–45.

102. *Ibid.*, June 6, 1946, p. 171.

103. *Ibid.*, August 22, 1946, p. 196.

104. Forrestal in conversation with Connery.

105. *Diaries*, September 30, 1946, p. 211.

106. R. G. Albion, "Distant Stations," in *U.S. Naval Institute Proceedings*, LXXX (March 1954), 265–73.

107. New York *Times*, New York *Herald Tribune, et al.*, October 1, 1946, partially quoted in *Diaries*, p. 211.

108. New York *Times* and New York *Herald Tribune*, editorial comment, October 1, 1946.

109. Byrnes, *All in One Lifetime*, p. 363.

110. *Diaries*, March 13, 1947, p. 258.

111. *Ibid.*, February 24, 1947, p. 245.

112. Truman, *Memoirs*, II, 104.

113. *Ibid.*, p. 105.

114. Walter Millis, in *Diaries*, p. 253.

115. *Ibid.*, March 7, p. 252.

116. Recorded telephone conversation, Forrestal and James Reston, March 13, 1947.

117. Truman, *Memoirs*, II, 109.

118. John J. Iselin, preparing a study of the Truman Doctrine, to Albion, June 29, 1961.

119. Organization Policy Group, Minutes, September 20, 1945 (Navy Department Files).

120. *Ibid.*

121. *Ibid.*

122. Memorandum, Forrestal to E. S. Duffield, July 2, 1944 (Personal Papers).

123. See Chapter IV.

124. Organization Policy Group, Minutes, September 20, 1945.

125. This examination was conducted by Connery in particular.

126. A good account of the tanker sales dispute is contained in Harold Stein, *Public Administration and Policy Development*, pp. 445–530.

127. *Ibid.*, p. 467.

128. *Ibid.*

129. *Ibid.*, p. 474.

130. See Chapter XI.

131. Senate Armed Services, *Hearings, 1947*, p. 713.

132. Paul Y. Hammond, "The National Security Council as a Device for Interdepartmental Coordination," *American Political Science Review*, LIV (December 1960), 901.

133. Dwight D. Eisenhower, "My Views on Berlin," *Saturday Evening Post*, CCXXXIV (December 9, 1961), p. 24.

134. E. W. Kenworthy in New York *Times*, September 10, 1961.

9: Ability and Experience

1. Forrestal to Truman, February 14, 1946 (Private Papers).

2. Navy Department Public Relations release, "Address at Herald Tribune Forum," November 16, 1943, New York. Also quoted in *Herald Tribune*, New York *Times*, and other papers, November 17, 1943.

3. *Ibid.*

4. Senate Armed Services Committee, *Hearings . . . National Defense Establishment, 1947*, p. 23.

5. W. K. Paulding, *Literary Life of James Kirke Paulding, passim*; C. O. Paullin, articles on naval administration in *United States Naval Institute Proceedings*, Vols. XXXII–XL (1906–14).

6. The general development of the Cabinet is well discussed, with numerous pertinent illustrations, in M. L. Hinsdale, *A History of the President's Cabinet*. The selection and performance of the Secretaries of the Navy is treated in detail in Albion's unpublished "Makers of Naval Policy," Chapter III entitled "Unnatural Selection."

7. Richard S. West, *Gideon Welles; The Diary of Gideon Welles*, revised edition by Howard K. Beale; Naval History Society, *Confidential Correspondence of Gustavus Vasa Fox*, R. M. Thompson and Richard Wainwright, eds., *passim*.

8. Richard S. West, *The Second Admiral, A Life of David Dixon Porter, passim*.

9. John Kean to Hamilton Fish, cited in Allan Nevins, *Hamilton Fish*, p. 281.

10. 44th Congress, 1st Session, *House Report 784*, p. 160.

11. H. J. Eckenrode, *Rutherford B. Hayes*, pp. 242, 303; Hinsdale, *President's Cabinet*, pp. 227–35.

12. Livingston Hunt, "The Founder of the New Navy," *United States Naval Institute Proceedings*, XXXI (March 1905), 173–77; Thomas Hunt, *Life of William H. Hunt, passim*.

13. See Chapter VII.

14. New York *Tribune*, February 12, 1924.

15. Mark Sullivan, *Our Times*, VI, 294–95.

16. H. F. Pringle, *Big Frogs*, pp. 220–21.

17. See Chapter VII.

18. Imperial Ordinance No. 195, of May 9, 1900 (Japan).

19. Compiled from *Statesman's Year Book;* as the French ministries at that time averaged only nine months in duration, a few may have been missed in those annual volumes.

20. National Security Act of 1947, 61 *Stat.* 495 (July 26, 1947), Sec. 202.

21. 64 *Stat.* 853 (September 8, 1950). The act stipulated that after Marshall, "no additional appointments of military men to that office shall be approved."

22. See Chapter I.

23. Truman H. Newbury in 1908.

24. James K. Paulding, Gideon Welles, and William E. Chandler.

25. Forrestal to President Roosevelt, June 5, 1944 (Personal Papers).

26. *Ibid.* June 15, 1944; also Los Angeles *Times* and Los Angeles *Examiner*, May 20, 1944.

27. *Diaries*, January 20, 1945, p. 27.

28. Forrestal to President Roosevelt, March 10, 1945.

29. *Ibid.*, March 20, 1945.

30. Robert H. Hannegan to President Truman, May 5, 1945, forwarded to Forrestal by Matthew W. Connelly, May 14, 1945, with note of the President's approval.

31. Memorandum, "Personal Publicity" folder (Personal Papers).

32. Washington *Times-Herald*, September 7, 1945.

33. Eugene S. Duffield in conversation with Connery.

34. Washington *Post*, January 3, 1946.

35. *Diaries*, January 21, 1946, p. 130.

36. Exchange of correspondence (Personal Papers).

37. Forrestal to President Truman, January 7, 1946.

38. New York *Times*, January 20, 1946.

39. *Ibid.*, February 2, 1946.

40. *Ibid.*, February 16, 1946.

41. *Ibid.*, February 21, 1946.

42. *Ibid.*

43. *Ibid.*, February 6, 1946; Harry S. Truman, *Memoirs*, I, 554.

44. On May 17, 1949, President Truman withdrew the nomination of Senator Mon C. Walgren as chairman of the National Security Resources Board after strong opposition had led the Senate Armed Services Committee to table the nomination, New York *Times*, March 16, May 18, May 22, 1949. The Senate later confirmed Walgren's nomination to a "safer" position.

45. Washington *Post*, March 15, 1946; *Times-Herald*, March 19, 1946.

46. *Times-Herald*, March 19, 1946.

47. Confidential communication to Albion.

48. See Chapter II.

49. W. John Kenney in conversation with Albion.

50. Forrestal to President Truman, August 14, 1946 (Personal Papers).

51. John N. Brown to Albion, June 29, 1956.
52. Frank C. Nash in conversation with Albion.
53. Confidential communication to Albion.
54. Albion accompanied the group.
55. Navy Department Public Relations "Address at Herald Tribune Forum, New York, November 16, 1943"; see also Chapter X.
56. Joseph E. McLean, ed., *The Public Service and University Education*, reproducing papers given at the Princeton event; see also Chapter X.
57. W. John Kenney in conversation with Albion.
58. Charlotte Knight in *Colliers*, January 22, 1954, pp. 30–36.
59. Hanson W. Baldwin in New York *Times*, November 6, 1953.
60. This book, with others of a similar nature, is preserved in the Private Papers at Princeton.
61. See Chapters IV, XI.
62. Captain C. N. Lentaigne, R.N., liaison officer at Pacific Fleet headquarters, in conversation with Albion.
63. Detailed table in House Appropriations Committee, Naval Subcommittee, *Hearings, Naval Appropriations Bill, 1944*, pp. 756–64, giving details of education, years of practice, previous affiliations, and past and present compensation.
64. See Chapter IX.
65. Memorandum, "J.V.F." to Captain Gingrich, August 8, 1943.
66. *Eberstadt Report*, p. 2.
67. New York *Times*, March 2, 1957.
68. *Ibid.*

10: ". . . Unto the Civilians"

1. Senate Armed Services, *Hearings on S. 758, a Bill to promote the National Security by providing for a National Defense Establishment March 18 . . . May 9, 1947*, p. 23.
2. Admiral John E. Gingrich to Connery, January 12, 1957.
3. Charles A. Lockwood, *Sink 'Em All*, p. 86.
4. Observed by Albion, May 1944.
5. *Public Administration Review*, V (Autumn 1945), 295.
6. *Time*, August 10, 1953, p. 18.
7. Josephus Daniels, *The Wilson Era*, I, 119.
8. Jonathan Daniels, *The Age of Innocence*, p. 9.
9. H. L. Stimson and McG. Bundy, *On Active Service*, p. 409.
10. Paul H. Appleby, "Civilian Control of a Department of National Defense," in Jerome Kerwin, ed., *Civil-Military Relationships in American Life*, p. 71.
11. Alfred Thayer Mahan, "Naval Administration," reprinted in Allen Westcott, ed., *Mahan on Naval Warfare*, p. 114.
12. *Annual Report of the Secretary of War, 1903*, p. 6. For this

subject in general see Paul Y. Hammond, "The Secretaries of War and Navy, a Study in Civilian Control," unpublished Harvard Ph.D. thesis.

13. Stimson and Bundy, *On Active Service*, p. 451.

14. *Ibid.*

15. *Ibid.*, p. 453.

16. *Diaries*, May 14, 1946, p. 164.

17. Elting E. Morison, *Turmoil and Tradition*, p. 508.

18. F. S. Hayden, "War Department Reorganization, August 1941-March 1942," *Military Affairs*, XVI (Fall 1952), 113.

19. Appleby, "Civilian Control," pp. 72–73.

20. *Ibid.*

21. See Chapter V.

22. Elting E. Morison, ed., *Naval Administration*, p. 3.

23. See Chapters IV and V.

24. See Chapter V.

25. Admiral Frederick J. Horne to Albion, February 2, 1955.

26. T. P. Archer and G. W. Wolf, *Report to the Secretary of the Navy on Logistics, October 3, 1944.*

27. Organization Policy Group Minutes, April 9, 1945, p. 16. A copy of these valuable transcripts was given to the authors.

28. *Ibid.*, November 13, 1944, p. 1.

29. See Chapter VII.

30. Organization Policy Group Minutes, December 4, 1944.

31. *Ibid.*

32. *Ibid.*

33. *Ibid.*

34. *Ibid.*, November 13, 1944, p. 16.

35. House Appropriations Committee, Naval Subcommittee, *Hearings on Naval Appropriation Bill, 1945*, p. 1143.

36. "An Outline of the Development, Organization and Principal Activities of the Office of Management Engineer," "First Narrative," Office of Naval History, January 1946, p. 5.

37. House Appropriations Committee, *Hearings . . . 1945*, p. 1037.

38. Organization Policy Group Minutes, November 13, 1944.

39. Organization Planning and Procedures Unit, *Analysis of Material Functions*, January 1945, p. 34.

40. Organization Policy Group Minutes, April 9, 1945, p. 16.

41. See Chapter XI.

42. See Chapter V.

43. Navy Reorganization Act of 1948, 62 *Stat.* 66 (March 5, 1948).

44. Admiral King in conversation with Albion.

45. See Chapter VI.

46. See Chapter IV.

47. Executive Order 9096, March 12, 1942.

48. E. J. King and W. M. Whitehill, *Fleet Admiral King*, p. 631.

49. Executive Order 9645, September 29, 1945. Emphasis added.

50. The time relation would seem to rule out the story in Theodore Taylor, *Magnificent Mitscher*, p. 5, to the effect that Forrestal offered the CNO post to Mitscher late in November as Nimitz had already been appointed.

51. J. A. Furer, *Administration of the Navy Department in World War II*, p. 804.

52. 60 *Stat.* 779 (August 1, 1946); H. G. Bowen, *Ships, Machinery and Mossbacks*, pp. 350–52. Furer, *Administration of the Navy Department in World War II*, p. 805, does not mention Bowen and his account lacks objectivity.

53. King and Whitehill, *Fleet Admiral King*, pp. 629–35.

54. Confidential communications to Albion from three different officers, each of whom had been in a position to observe closely what was happening.

55. New York *Times*, December 16, 24, 25, 1949; July 25, 31, 1953.

56. See Chapter III.

57. 60 *Stat.* 892 (August 13, 1946).

58. *Time*, December 6, 1943; see also memorandum, Capt. Paul Foster to Rear Admiral Louis E. Denfeld, Assistant Chief of Naval Personnel, January 29, 1945.

59. 60 *Stat.* 1057; see also 993.

60. Report of Commodore Robert White, Chaplains Corps, to Forrestal, September 1946 (Navy Department Files).

61. Commanding Officer, *Salt Lake City*, to Cominch, March 1944 (Navy Department Files).

62. Rear Admiral Ross T. McIntyre, Chief of Bureau of Medicine and Surgery, to Forrestal, February 14, 1947 (Navy Department Files).

63. Furer, *Administration of the Navy Department in World War II*, p. 33.

64. *Report of the Committee on the Organization of the Department of the Navy, 16 April 1954.*

65. Address before the National Encampment, Veterans of Foreign Wars, Cleveland, Ohio, September 4, 1947 (Personal Files).

11: The Road to the Pentagon

1. Memorandum, Major John H. Dillon to Forrestal, May 8, 1944 (Navy Department Files); H. L. Stimson and McG. Bundy, *On Active Service*, p. 519. Secretary Stimson indicates that he would not have let the movement get started if he had not understood that Knox was in agreement; also E. E. Morison, *Turmoil and Tradition*, p. 482.

2. Ferdinand Eberstadt in conversation with Albion.

3. Lawrence J. Legere, Jr., "Unification of the Armed Forces," unpublished Harvard Ph.D. thesis, 1951, a comprehensive study covering

the background as well as the 1943–49 events; Major Legere's research included classified War Department material.

4. M. A. Beale, *Gangway for Navy*, pp. 25–29, an account of the first Army-Navy football game.

5. Ernest R. May, "The Development of Political-Military Consultation in the United States," *Political Science Quarterly*, LXX (June 1955), 164–66.

6. Clifford L. Lord, *The History of Naval Aviation*, p. 4, citing Adjutant General's Office files. This processed study, prepared in the Naval Aviation History Unit, contains more detailed quotations from the original sources than does the published A. D. Turnbull and C. L. Lord, *History of United States Naval Aviation*, which was based in part on it.

7. See Mitchell's own writings, including *Our Air Force—Keystone of Defense* (1921); "Air Power vs. Sea Power," in *Review of Reviews*, LXIII (March 1921), 273–77; *Winged Defense* (1935); for the naval aspects of the Mitchell episode, see Turnbull and Lord, *History of United States Naval Aviation*, pp. 892–94.

8. W. F. Craven and J. L. Cate., eds., *The Army Air Forces in World War II*, I, 62.

9. Air Corps Act, 44 *Stat.* 780 (July 2, 1926).

10. For a concise summary of the various earlier unification attempts, see *Eberstadt Report*, pp. 241–51. The various early stages are analyzed in Legere, "Unification of the Armed Forces."

11. *Diary of Gideon Welles*, H. K. Beale, ed., III, p. 519, February 3, 1869; *Army & Navy Journal*, February 3, 1869.

12. *Army & Navy Journal*, January 23, 1932; for a further account of the service reactions, see also the January 30 issue.

13. New York *Times*, February 19, 1932.

14. Legere, "Unification of the Armed Forces," pp. 126–27.

15. Washington *Post*, December 26, 1945.

16. R. S. Cline and Maurice Matloff, "Development of War Department Views on Unification," *Military Affairs*, XIII (Summer 1949), 65–74.

17. Memorandum, McNarney to Marshall, January 31, 1942, quoted in F. S. Hayden, "War Department Reorganization, August 1941–March 1942," *Military Affairs*, XVI (Fall 1952), 107.

18. House Select Committee on Postwar Military Policy, *Hearings on Proposal to Establish a Single Department of the Armed Forces* (hereafter "Woodrum Committee," *Hearings*), 1944, p. 129.

19. *Ibid.*, p. 226.

20. 78th Congress, 2d Session, *House Report*.

21. Forrestal to Palmer Hoyt, September 2, 1944; quoted in *Diaries*, p. 60.

22. Vice Admiral J. S. McCain to Forrestal, April 28, 1945 (Navy Department Files).

23. Senate Military Affairs Committee, *Hearings on a Single Department of National Defense*, 1945, p. 507.

24. George M. Elsey, former assistant naval aide at the White House, later Administrative Assistant to the President, in conversation with Albion.

25. *Colliers*, August 26, 1944. For President Truman's later summary of his views and reactions, see his *Memoirs*, II, 46 ff.

26. Transcript of talk by Major General Harry Vaughan.

27. *Diaries*, April 18, 1945, p. 46.

28. *Ibid.*, April-May 1945, pp. 59–64; see Appendix D.

29. Organization Policy Group, Minutes, May 7, 1945, p. 5.

30. Stimson and Bundy, *On Active Service*, p. 506.

31. E. J. King and W. M. Whitehill, *Fleet Admiral King*, p. 469n.

32. Organization Policy Group, Minutes, May 7, 1945, pp. 1–2.

33. *Eberstadt Report*, pp. iii–iv.

34. *Ibid.*, p. v.

35. See Chapter IV.

36. *Eberstadt Report*, p. 1.

37. Ferdinand Eberstadt in conversation with Albion.

38. See, for instance, *Diaries*, July 18, 1945, p. 37.

39. *Eberstadt Report*, pp. 3–5.

40. *Ibid.*, pp. 5–6.

41. *Ibid.*, p. 4.

42. *Ibid.*, p. 5.

43. Paul Y. Hammond, "The National Security Council as a Device for Interdepartmental Control," in *American Political Science Review*, LV (December 1960), 90.

44. Senate Armed Services, *Hearings on S. 758, a Bill to promote the National Security by providing for a National Defense Establishment, March 18 . . . May 9, 1947* (hereafter, Senate Armed Services, *Hearings, 1947*). This valuable volume contains a useful summary of the various stages in the unification movement, 1944–47, pp. 5–12.

45. *Eberstadt Report*, pp. 10–11.

46. *Ibid.*, pp. 8–9.

47. *Ibid.*, pp. 11–12.

48. *Ibid.*, p. 8.

49. *Ibid.*, p. 2, and see Chapter VII.

50. Senate Armed Services *Hearings, 1947*, p. 683.

51. Senate Military Affairs Committee, *Hearings on the Armed Forces, 1945*, p. 704.

52. *Ibid.*

53. *Diaries*, November 21, 1945, pp. 115–16.

54. *Ibid.*, December 18, 1945, pp. 118–19.

55. Congressional Record, 79th Congress, 1st Session, pp. 12573–77.

56. Senate Military Affairs, *Hearings, 1945*, p. 575.

57. *Alnav 447*, December 19, 1945. An "Alnav" was a Secretary's

directive to "All Ships and Stations." They were gathered periodically into the *Navy Department Bulletin.*

58. *Alnav 461,* December 31, 1945.

59. Washington *Times-Herald,* April 18, 1946; for a later vigorous expression of the Navy's objections, see Rear Admiral Daniel V. Gallery's "If This be Treason," *Colliers,* January 21, 1950, pp. 15–17, 45.

60. Washington *Post,* April 12, 1946.

61. *Diaries,* April 17, 1945, p. 152.

62. Washington *Post,* April 16, 1946.

63. Senate Armed Services, *Hearings, 1947,* p. 177.

64. *Ibid.,* p. 641.

65. *Ibid.,* p. 10.

66. *Diaries,* December 22, 1945, p. 121.

67. *Ibid., passim,* and see Appendix J.

68. Admiral Robinson to Forrestal, May 10, 1945 (Private Papers).

69. *Ibid.*

70. *Diaries,* May 13, 1946, p. 164.

71. Walter Millis comments, *ibid.,* p. 162.

72. *Ibid.,* p. 164.

73. *Ibid.,* May 14, 1946, p. 164.

74. *Ibid.,* 183–85.

75. *Diaries,* June 19, 1946, pp. 169–70.

76. *Diaries,* August 27, 1946, pp. 201–2.

77. *Ibid.,* September 10, 1946, pp. 203–5.

78. Quoted in Senate Armed Services, *Hearings, 1947,* pp. 687–88.

79. *Ibid.,* p. 40.

80. *Ibid,* p. 170.

81. Senate Armed Services, *Hearings, 1947,* p. 155.

82. *Ibid.,* p. 164 and *passim.*

83. *Diaries,* December 2, 1946, pp. 223–24.

84. *Ibid.,* December 5, 1946, p. 226.

85. *Ibid.,* January 3, 1947, pp. 228–29.

86. *Ibid.,* January 16, 1947, pp. 229–30.

87. Senate Armed Services, *Hearings, 1947,* p. 2, together with the Patterson-Forrestal letter to the President, quoted pp. 2–3.

88. *Ibid.,* pp. 160–61; Hammond, "The National Security Council," pp. 899–901.

89. Senate Armed Services, *Hearings, 1947,* p. 11, with full text of bill, pp. 11–21.

90. *Ibid.,* p. 26.

91. *Ibid.,* pp. 22–23, 26.

92. *Ibid.,* p. 23.

93. *Ibid.,* p. 36.

94. *Ibid.,* pp. 40, 44, 46.

95. *Ibid.,* p. 37.

96. *Diaries*, July 26, 1947, p. 295; July 23, 1948, p. 465.
97. See *Diaries*, especially pp. 269–71, 274, 292–94.
98. National Security Act, 1947, 61 *Stat.* 495 (July 26, 1947).
99. Executive Order 9877, July 29, 1947, "Functions of the Armed Forces."
100. *Diaries*, July 26, 147, p. 295.
101. Katherine S. Foley in conversation with Albion; see Chapter I.
102. Quoted in *Diaries*, p. 299.
103. Colonel J. D. Hittle, USMC, to Albion, May 18, 1955.
104. *Diaries*, p. 313; see also New York *Times*, September 13, 1947.

Bibliography

Unpublished Source Material

A considerable part of the material for this book came to Albion and Connery in oral form, particularly during the years when they were in the Navy Department. This is indicated in the references as "in conversation with" one of the authors; in a few cases, the phrase "confidential communication" indicates that circumstances have made it inexpedient to reveal the name of the informant. The original conversations have in some cases been supplemented by later correspondence.

Another extensive category of unpublished sources is listed under the designation of "Navy Department Files." Much of this was consulted shortly after issuance in the offices of the interested parties, or in the files of the various bureaus and offices; in later days it has been necessary to consult such material in the Navy's record depository at Arlington.

It was especially fortunate that access was granted to two highly restricted collections of Forrestal material at Princeton. Very useful in giving an all-round picture of his activities and interests, beyond what would be found in the official files, was the collection of "Private Papers," filling many filing cases. These were presented to the Princeton University Library in 1952 by Mrs. James V. Forrestal and her sons. Access is restricted during the lifetime of the donors, but is available to qualified scholars under certain conditions with their permission. Application for the use of these papers should be made to the Librarian of Princeton University.

The other collection, popularly known as the "Forrestal Diaries," was purchased and presented to the Princeton University Library in 1953 by C. Douglas Dillon and Laurance S. Rockefeller under an agreement with the United States Government. The collection is subject to restricted access until 1978. Forrestal did not begin these "diaries" until mid-1944. A large part of the significant material was edited by Walter Millis and Eugene S. Duffield and published by the Viking Press in 1951. The unpublished portions give occasional useful background, but there has been no occasion to give direct citation to them.

Unpublished Studies

Albion, Robert G. "Makers of Naval Policy, 1798–1947," Washington, D.C., 1950. In addition to the original typescript, prepared and deposited in the Office of Naval History, partial microfilm copies are available at Harvard and elsewhere. This was the first volume of a four-volume project to analyze the Navy's whole administrative experience; the project was cancelled in 1950.

Hammond, Paul Y. "The Secretaryships of War and Navy: A Study in Civilian Control of the Navy," Cambridge, Harvard University, 1953. Typescript doctoral dissertation.

Legère, Lawrence J., Jr. "Unification of the Armed Forces." Cambridge, Harvard University, 1951. Typescript doctoral dissertation.

Lobdell, G. H. "A Biography of Frank Knox." University of Illinois, 1954. Typescript doctoral dissertation.

U.S. Navy Department, Office of Naval History, "First Narratives of Naval Administration in World War II," c. 200 typescript vols., Washington, 1944–46. These were the outgrowth of Assistant Secretary Bard's appointment of Albion early in 1943 to "record the administrative experience of the Navy Department." It was decided that this could be accomplished most effectively by promoting widespread detailed accounts of the problems encountered in the various units. Albion accordingly arranged with the different bureaus and offices to appoint historical officers; in this connection he assigned Connery to the office of Under Secretary Forrestal. In 1944, when the Office of Naval History was established under an admiral to coordinate the administrative and operational history programs, Albion became Historian of Naval Administration and one of the Assistant Directors. His program was extended to the shore stations, naval bases, and shore-based Fleet commands. Altogether, the program produced more than 200 of what Admiral E. C. Kalbfus, the first director, designated as "First Narratives." Two copies of each were bound, one being deposited in the Office of Naval History and the other in the unit which produced it. The unclassified volumes are available for reference. Formal publication was an incidental consideration from the outset, but several of these studies, as the following list indicates, became formal published works.

Published Material

Albion, Robert G. "The Administration of the Navy," *Public Administration Review*, V (Autumn 1945), 293–302.

—— *Boards, Offices, Divisions and Committees under the Supervision of the Secretaries of the Navy, 1940–1946.* Washington D.C., Office of Naval History, 1946. Processed.

—— "Communications and Remote Control," *U.S. Naval Institute Proceedings*, LXXXII (August 1956), 832–36.

—— *The Development of the Naval Districts, 1903–1945.* Washington, D.C., Office of Naval History, 1945. Processed.

—— "Distant Stations," *U.S. Naval Institute Proceedings*, LXXX (March 1954), 265–73.

—— "The First Days of the Navy Department," *Military Affairs*, XII (Spring 1948), 1–11.

—— "The Naval Affairs Committees, 1816–1947," *U.S. Naval Institute Proceedings*, LXXVIII (November 1952), 1227–37; reprinted in *Congressional Record*, Appendix, January 13, 1953.

—— "State, War and Navy—Under One Roof, 1882," *U.S. Naval Institute Proceedings*, LXXV (July 1949), 793–95.

—— and S. H. P. Read, Jr. *The Navy at Sea and Ashore: An Informal Account of the Organization and Workings of the Naval Establishment of the United States Today, with some Historical Notes on its Development*. Washington, D.C., Navy Department (Navexos, P-472), 1947. Prepared at Secretary Forrestal's request.

Allen, Ethan P. *Policies Governing Private Financing of Engineering Facilities* (War Production Board Historical Series). Washington, D.C., War Production Board, 1945.

Baldwin, Hanson W. *The Price of Power*. For Council on Foreign Relations. New York, Harper & Brothers, 1948.

—— *What the Citizen Should Know About the Navy*. New York, W. W. Norton & Co., 1941; revised ed., 1942.

Ballantine, Duncan S. *U.S. Naval Logistics in the Second World War*. Princeton, Princeton University Press, 1947. Emphasis on the administrative aspects.

Basler, R. E. "The Origins of Engineering Duty Only," *Journal of the American Society of Naval Engineers*, LXV (November 1953), 771–90.

Beers, Henry L. "The Development of the Office of the Chief of Naval Operations," *Military Affairs*, X (Spring 1946), 40–68; X (Fall 1946), 10–38; XI (Summer 1947) 88–89; XI (Winter 1947) 229–37.

—— "History of the Bureau of Navigation" 1862–1942, *American Archivist*, VI (October 1943), 212–52.

Bowen, Harold G. *Ships, Machinery and Mossbacks: The Autobiography of a Naval Engineer*. Princeton, Princeton University Press, 1954.

Byrnes, James F. *All in One Lifetime*. New York, Harper & Brothers, 1958.

—— *Speaking Frankly*. New York, Harper & Brothers, 1947. These two volumes of memoirs represent a considerable duplication in subject matter.

Carrison, D. J. "The Longest Ship in the Navy," *Ships and the Sea*, VI (Spring 1955), 12–13, 59–61.

Cline, Ray S. *Washington Command Post: The Operations Division* (The United States Army in World War II). Washington, D.C., Office of the Chief of Military History, 1951.

—— and Maurice Matloff. "Development of War Department Views on Unification," *Military Affairs*, XIII (Summer 1949), 65–75.

Connery, Robert H. "The Department of Defense and the Conduct of Foreign Affairs" in Brookings Institution, *The Administration of Foreign Affairs and Overseas Operations*. Washington, D.C., Brookings Institution, 1951.

—— *The Navy and the Industrial Mobilization in World War II*. Princeton, Princeton University Press, 1949.

—— "Organizing the Navy's Industrial Mobilization," *Public Administration Review*, V (Autumn 1945), 303–312.

—— ed. "Administrative Problems in Naval Procurement and Logistics," *Public Administration Review*, V (Autumn 1945), 289–350.

Craven, Wesley F., and James L. Cate. *The Army Air Forces In World War II.* 7 vols. Chicago, The University of Chicago Press, 1948–58.

Daniels, Jonathan. *The End of Innocence.* Philadelphia, J. B. Lippincott Co., 1954.

Daniels, Josephus. *The Wilson Era.* 2 vols. Chapel Hill, University of North Carolina Press, 1944–46.

Davis, George T. *A Navy Second to None: the Development of Modern American Naval Policy.* New York, Harcourt, Brace & Co., 1940.

Duncan, D. B. and H. M. Dater. "Administrative History of U.S. Naval Aviation," *Air Affairs,* I (Summer 1947), 526–39.

Duffield, Eugene S. "Organizing for Defense," *Harvard Business Review,* XXXI (September–October 1953), 29–42.

Eberstadt, Ferdinand. *Report to James Forrestal, Secretary of the Navy, on the Unification of the War and Navy Departments* ("Eberstadt Report"). Printed for Senate Committee on Naval Affairs, October 22, 1945.

Eccles, Marriner S. *Beckoning Frontiers.* New York, Alfred A. Knopf, Inc., 1951.

Emerson, William R. "F.D.R.," in Ernest R. May, ed., *The Ultimate Decision: The President as Commander-in-Chief.* New York, George Braziller, Inc., 1960.

Fahey, James C. *The Ships and Aircraft of the U.S. Fleet.* New York, Ships and Aircraft, 1942 and later editions.

Feis, Herbert. *Japan Subdued.* Princeton, Princeton University Press, 1961.

Fesler, James. *Industrial Mobilization for War, 1940–1945. Washington, D.C.,* Government Printing Office for Civilian Production Administration, 1947.

Fiske, Bradley A. *From Midshipman to Rear Admiral.* New York, The Century Co., 1919.

Freidel, Frank. *Franklin D. Roosevelt.* Vols. I and II. Boston, Little, Brown & Co., 1952–54. The best account of Roosevelt as Assistant Secretary of the Navy.

Furer, Julius A. *Administration of the Navy Department in World War II.* Washington D.C., Government Printing Office for Office of Naval History, 1959. This 1,042-page compilation by a retired naval constructor falls far short, in critical quality, of the administrative history volumes prepared by professional scholars in the Army's comprehensive program.

Gallery, Daniel V. "If this be Treason," *Colliers,* January 21, 1950, pp. 15–17, 45. Vigorous comments on unification by an outspoken aviator admiral.

Greenfield, Kent R., ed. *Command Decisions.* Washington D.C., Office of the Chief of Military History, 1960.

Grew, Jospeh C. *This Turbulent Era.* Boston, Houghton Mifflin Company, 1952.

Hammond, Paul Y. "The National Security Council as a Device for Interdepartmental Control," *American Political Science Review,* LIV (December 1960), 899–910.

Hayden, F. L. "War Department Reorganization, August 1941–March 1942," *Military Affairs,* XVI (Fall 1952), 97–114.

Hensel, H. Struve. "Changes Inside the Pentagon," *Harvard Business Review,* XXXII (January–February 1954), 98–108.

Hinsdale, Mary L. *A History of the President's Cabinet.* Ann Arbor, Wahr, 1911.

Hull, Cordell. *Memoirs of Cordell Hull.* 2 vols. New York, The Macmillan Co., 1948.

Hunt, Livingston. "The Founder of the New Navy," *U.S. Naval Institute Proceedings,* XXXI (1905), 173–77. Secretary William H. Hunt.

Huntington, Samuel P. "Civilian Control and the Constitution," *American Political Science Review,* L (September 1956), 676–99.

—— *The Soldier and the State.* Cambridge, Harvard University Press, 1957.

Huzar, Elias. *The Purse and the Sword.* Ithaca, Cornell University Press, 1950.

Ickes, Harold L. *Secret Diary,* 3 vols. New York, Simon and Schuster, Inc., 1953–54.

Janeway, Eliot. *Struggle for Survival.* New Haven, Yale University Press, 1951.

King, Ernest J., and Walter M. Whitehill. *Fleet Admiral King.* New York, W. W. Norton & Co., 1952. A semi-autobiography.

Knight, Charlotte. "Mystery Man of the Pentagon," *Colliers,* CXXXIII (January 22, 1954), 30–36. Wilfred J. McNeil.

Kohl, W. B. "The Jaycock Story," *U.S. Naval Institute Proceedings,* LXXXII (January 1956), 71–82. The successor to Forrestal's Naval Industrial Association.

Leahy, William D. *I Was There: The Personal Story of the Chief of Staff to Presidents Roosevelt and Truman, based on his Notes and Diaries made at the time.* New York, Whittlesey House, 1950.

Lockwood, Charles A. *Sink 'Em All! Submarine Warfare in the Pacific.* New York, E. P. Dutton & Co., Inc., 1951.

Lord, Clifford L. *The History of Naval Aviation.* Washington, D.C., Bureau of Aeronautics, 1948. Processed. See also Turnbull and Lord.

Macmahon, Arthur. *Administration in Foreign Affairs.* University, University of Alabama Press, 1953.

Madden, R. B. "The Bureau of Ships and its ED Officers," *Journal of the American Society of Naval Engineers,* LXVI (February 1954), 9–40.

Marder, Arthur J. "Winston Churchill as First Lord of the Admiralty, 1911–1915," *U.S. Naval Institute Proceedings,* LXXIX (January 1953), 18–27.

Matloff, Maurice, and E. M. Snell. *Strategic Planning for Coalition Warfare* (U.S. Army in World War II). Washington, D.C., Office of the Chief of Military History, 1953.

May, Ernest R. "The Development of Political-Military Consultation in the United States," *Political Science Quarterly,* LXX (June 1955), 161–80.

—— ed. *The Ultimate Decision: The President as Commander-in-Chief.* New York, George Braziller, Inc., 1960.

McClung, Richard G. "Profit Limitation Controls Prior to the Present War," in H. Struve Hensel, ed., "Law and Contemporary Problems," *Duke University Law Review,* X (1943), 187–217.

McLean, Joseph E., ed. *The Public Service and University Education.* Princeton, Princeton University Press, 1949.

Millis, Walter. *Arms and the State: Civil-Military Elements in National Policy.* New York, Twentieth Century Fund, 1958.

—— and Eugene S. Duffield, eds. *The Forrestal Diaries.* New York, The Viking Press, Inc., 1951.

Morison, Elting E. *Admiral Sims and the Modern Aamerican Navy.* Boston, Houghton Mifflin Company, 1942.

Morison, Elting E. *Turmoil and Tradition: A Study of the Life and Times of Henry L. Stimson.* Boston, Houghton Mifflin Company, 1960. See also Stimson and Bundy.

—— ed. *Naval Administration: Selected Documents on Navy Department Organization, 1915–1940.* Washington, D.C., Office of the Chief of Naval Operations, 1945. Processed. Prepared at the request of Secretary Forrestal.

Morison, Samuel E. *History of U.S. Naval Operations in World War II.* 15 vols. Boston, Little Brown & Co., 1947–62.

Morton, Louis. "The Decision to Use the Atomic Bomb," *Foreign Affairs,* XXXV (January 1957), 334–53; reprinted in K. R. Greenfield, ed. *Command Decisions,* 388–410.

Moseley, H. W., *et al.* "The State-War-Navy Coordinating Committee," U.S. Department of State *Bulletin,* XIII (November 11, 1945), 745–47.

Nelson, Donald M. *Arsenal of Democracy.* New York, Harcourt, Brace & Co., 1946.

Nelson, Otto L., Jr. *National Security and the General Staff.* Washington, D.C., Infantry Journal Press, 1946.

Notter, Harley. *Post War Foreign Policy Preparation, 1939–45.* (General Foreign Policy Series, 15.) Washington, D.C., Department of State (Publication 3580), 1949.

Paullin, Charles O. "Naval Administration," *U.S. Naval Institute Proceedings,* Vols. XXXII–XL (1906–14). A series of articles covering the period 1775–1911; the only systematic detailed coverage except for the chapters of Leonard D. White.

Rosenman, Samuel I. ed. *The Public Papers and Addresses of Franklin D. Roosevelt.* 13 vols. New York, Random House, 1938–50.

Rowland, Buford, and W. B. Boyd. *U.S. Navy Bureau of Ordnance in World War II.* Washington, D.C., Bureau of Ordnance, 1953.

Sherwood, Robert H. *Roosevelt and Hopkins.* Revised ed. New York, Harper & Brothers, 1950.

Smelser, Marshall T. *The Congress founds the Navy, 1787–1798.* Notre Dame University Press, 1959. Written on a Forrestal Fellowship, administered by the Naval Academy.

Smith, Louis. *American Democracy and Military Power.* Chicago, The University of Chicago Press, 1951. Copyright (1951) by the University of Chicago.

Smith, William H. *History of the Cabinet of the United States of America from President Washington to President Coolidge.* Baltimore, Industrial Printing Co., 1925. Includes biographical sketches of each Cabinet member.

Sprout, Harold, and Margaret Sprout. *History of American Naval Policy.* Princeton, Princeton University Press, 1939.

—— eds. *Foundations of National Power; Readings on World Politics and American Security.* Princeton, Princeton University Press, 1945. Prepared at the request of Secretary Forrestal.

Standley, William H., and A. A. Ageton. *Admiral Ambassador to Russia.* Chicago, Henry Regnery Co., 1955.

Stein, Harold, ed. *Public Administration and Policy Development.* New York, Harcourt, Brace & Co., 1952.

Stettinius, Edward R. *Roosevelt and the Russians: The Yalta Conference.* Garden City, Doubleday & Company, Inc., 1949.

Stimson, Henry L. and McGeorge Bundy. *On Active Service in Peace and*

War. New York, Harper & Brothers, 1948. A semi-autobiography; see also Elting E. Morison.

Strauss, Lewis L. *Men and Decisions.* Garden City, Doubleday & Company, Inc., 1962.

Truman, Harry S. *Memoirs.* 2 vols. Garden City, Doubleday & Company, Inc., 1955–56. Subtitles: Vol. I, *Year of Decision;* Vol. II, *Years of Trial and Hope.* Copyright 1956 Time Inc.

Turnbull, Archibald D., and Clifford L. Lord. *History of United States Naval Aviation.* New Haven, Yale University Press, 1949.

U.S. Bureau of the Budget. *The United States at War.* Washington, D.C., Government Printing Office, 1946.

U.S. Congress. House Appropriations Committee, Naval Subcommittee. *Hearings . . . on Navy Department Appropriation Bill for 1943.* 77th Congress, 2d Session, 1942.

Appropriation Bill for 1944. 78th Congress, 1st Session, 1943.

Supplemental Appropriation Bill for 1943. 78th Congress, 1st Session, 1943.

1st Supplemental National Defense Appropriation Bill, 1944. 78th Congress, 1st Session, 1943.

Appropriation Bill for 1945. 78th Congress, 2d Session, 1944.

Appropriation Bill for 1946. 79th Congress, 1st Session, 1945.

—— House Naval Affairs Committee. *Hearings . . . Reorganization of the Navy Department.* 76th Congress, 2d Session, 1940.

Hearings . . . Sundry Legislation Affecting the Naval Establishment, 1941. 77th Congress, 1st Session, 1941.

Hearings . . . Sundry Legislation Affecting the Naval Establishment, 1942. 77th Congress, 2d Session, 1942.

Hearings . . . Sundry Legislation Affecting the Naval Establishment, 1945. 79th Congress, 1st Session, 1945.

Hearings . . . Investigation of the Progress of the War Effort. 78th Congress, 2d Session, 1945.

—— Special Senate Committee for the Investigation of the National Defense ("Truman Committee"). *Report.* 78th Congress, 2d Session, 20 parts, 1944.

—— Senate Banking and Currency Committee. *Hearings . . . Extension of the Emergency Price Control Act of 1942.* 78th Congress, 2d Session, 1944.

—— House Select Committee on Postwar Military Policy ("Woodrum Committee"). *Hearings on a Proposal to Establish a Single Department of the Armed Forces.* 78th Congress, 2d Session, 1944.

—— Senate Military Affairs Committee. *Hearings on a Single Department of National Defense.* 79th Congress, 1st Session, 1945.

—— Joint Committee on the Investigation of the Pearl Harbor Attack. *Hearings.* 79th Congress, 1st Session, 30 parts, 1946.

—— Special Senate Committee on Atomic Energy. *Hearings.* 79th Congress, 1st Session, 1946.

—— Senate Armed Services Committee. *Hearings on the Unification of the Armed Services.* 80th Congress, 1st Session, 1947. This is one of the most useful of all the sources on the unification movement.

U.S. Department of Defense, *The Entry of the Soviet Union into the War against Japan (1941–1945),* Washington, D.C., 1955.

U.S. Navy Department. Bureau of Ordnance. See Buford and Rowland.

U.S. Navy Department. Bureau of Ships. *Administrative History, First Narrative.* 4 vols. Washington, D.C., Bureau of Ships, 1954. Processed.

—— Bureau of Supplies and Accounts. *Naval Expenditures, 1940.* Washington, D.C., Government Printing Office, 1941.

—— Bureau of Yards and Docks. *Building the Navy's Bases in World War II: History of the Bureau of Yards and Docks and the Civil Engineer Corps.* 2 vols. Washington, D.C., Government Printing Office, 1944.

—— Secretary of the Navy. *Annual Report, 1945.* Washington, D.C., 1945.

Watson, Mark S. *Chief of Staff: Prewar Plans and Preparedness.* (U.S. Army in World War II.) Washington, D.C., Office of the Chief of Military History, 1950.

Welles, Gideon. *The Diary of Gideon Welles.* Howard K. Beale, ed. 3 vols. New York, W. W. Norton & Company, Inc., 1960. Unlike the earlier Morse edition, this indicates changes from the Secretary's original draft. The pagination is the same in both editions.

West, Richard S. *The Second Admiral: A Life of David Dixon Porter.* New York, Coward-McCann, Inc., 1937.

White, Leonard D. *The Federalists, A Study in Administrative History.* New York, The Macmillan Co., 1948. Chapters on naval administration also in his subsequent volumes: *The Jeffersonians* (1951); *The Jacksonians* (1954); and *The Republican Era* (1958). See also Charles O. Paullin.

Wright, E. A. "The Bureau of Ships: A Study in Organization," *Journal of the American Society of Naval Engineers,* LXXI (February, May 1959), 7–21, 315–27.

Index

Acheson, Dean, 171, 181, 189, 290

Adams, Charles Francis, 60, 206, 254

Adams, John, 204

Adams, John Quincy, 189

Adams family, 129

Adriatic Sea, 285

Aeronautics, Bureau of, 9, 42, 43; expenditures (*1940-45*), 44, 46-47; Chiefs of, 61, 89; contract procedure, 65, 110; Office of Production Management and, 75-76; Naval Operations and, 100, 239

Africa, 109, 116, 133, 165

Agnew, William C., 289

Air Corps Act (*1926*), 254, 331*n*9

Air Force, 90, 166, 185, 239; aviation development and, 43, 251-52; unification of armed forces and, 250, 251-60, 264, 266, 269-71, 273-74, 276, 277, 280, 281, 282, 283-84

Airplanes, 75, 86-87, 120, 251; construction of, 54, 68, 72-73, 115; costs, 113

Albion, Robert G., cited, 308*n*36, 53; 309*n*6, 311*n*37, 313*n*34, 314*n*25, 319*n*32, 321*nn*77, 9; 322*nn*12, 14; 336

Aldrich, Winthrop, 19

Alexandria Naval Torpedo Station, 69

Algiers, 133

Allen, Ethan P., cited, 313*n*39

Allied Reparations Commission, 211, 216

ALNAVs, 332*n*57

Alsop, Joseph and Stewart, 27

American Can Company, 69

American Telephone and Telegraph Company, 56

Anderson, John V., 19, 142, 307*n*14, 320*n*39

Anderson, Robert B., 224, 248

Andrews, Edwin Mark, 217, 224, 288

Andrews, Walter G., 143

Annapolis, Naval Academy at, 35, 44, 46, 52, 91; stadium for, 147-48; commissions and, 245-46

Annual Report of the Secretary of the Navy, cited, 44, 287-88, 310*n*21, 311*nn*46, 49; 328*n*12

Appleby, Paul, cited, 232, 328*n*10, 329*nn*19, 20

Archer, T. P., 234, 235

Armed Forces Industrial Association, 30

Armor plate, 44, 45, 55, 72, 147

Army, 40, 70, 74-75, 111, 137, 250; unification of armed forces and, 30, 181, 191, 195, 250-86; Pearl Harbor and, 84-85, 86, 105; Chief of Staff, 89, 230-31; Joint Chiefs of Staff and, 90; war contracts, 94; sea power and, 185. *See also* Air Force; War Department

Army Industrial School, 79

Army-Navy football, 251, 331*n*4

Army and Navy Munitions Board, 70, 79, 95, 263; reorganization of, 77, 78, 82, 103-5, 107, 108; priorities, 106-7, 120-21; National Security Act and, 283; membership, 296

Arnold, Henry Harley, USA, 90, 266

Articles for the Government of the Navy, 246

Atomic energy: bombing of Japan, 9, 22, 174-79; ships and weapons, 180-81, 242, 244; Russia and, 181-85

Atomic Energy Commission, 95, 182-83, 223, 245

Augusta (USS), 176

Austin, Warren, 270, 278